People in Transition

REFLECTIONS ON BECOMING CANADIAN

Trudy Duivenvoorden Mitic

Fitzhenry & Whiteside
Markham, Ontario

ACKNOWLEDGEMENTS

I wish to extend thanks to my special circle of people, Wayne, Caroline, Aaron and Laura, for keeping me buoyed (and fed) during the lengthy research and writing stages of this book. Thanks also to my editors, Richard Dionne and Peter Taylor, who brought encouragement to this project.

Fitzhenry and Whiteside Limited
195 Allstate Parkway
Markham, Ontario L3R 4T8

In the United States:
121 Harvard Avenue, Suite 2
Allston, Massachusetts 02134

www.fitzhenry.ca godwit@fitzhenry.ca

Fitzhenry & Whiteside acknowledges with thanks the Canada Council for the Arts, the Government of Canada through its Book Publishing Industry Development Program,
and the Ontario Arts Council for their support of our publishing program.

The author wishes to acknowledge the support of the Government of Canada through the Secretary of State for Multiculturalism for assistance for this book. The author also acknowledges the support of the Nova Scotia Department of Tourism and Culture, Cultural Affairs Division.

CANADIAN CATALOGUING IN PUBLICATION DATA

Duivenvoorden Mitic, Trudy, 1954–
    People in transition

    ISBN 1-55041-612-X

    1. Immigrants – Canada – Biography. 2 Canada – Emigration and
    immigration – History – 20th century. I. Title.

    FC104.D85 2001   304.8'71'00922   C00-932562-X
    F1035.AID85 2001

Photo Credits:
Pg. 19 Bohdan Nebesio; pg. 33 CPI, Sears Portrait Studio; pg. 47 Lothar Bode; pg. 61 Carlos Cacola; pg. 73 Chocolaterie Bernard Callebaut; pg. 87 Randy Dawe; pg. 103 Claire McCaughey; pg. 117 Adrian Dwarka; pg. 131 Henri Tsai; pg. 145 John Chan; pg. 163 Ruth Kaplan; pg. 177 Yatish Kotecha; pg. 191 Thea Jensen; pg. 205 Clair Perry; pg. 219 Art Abesamis; pg. 233 Brian Townsend; pg. 247 Central Photo; pg. 261 Yvonne Duivenvoorden; pg. 275 RG Photography; pg. 289 Caisse centrale Desjardins; pg. 305 Jennifer Modigliani; pg. 319 Bridglal Pachai; pg. 335 PCA International; pg. 351 Reflections by Richard; pg. 363 Mark Mainguy; pg. 377 Cheryl Tom; pg. 389 Ned Pratt; pg. 401 William Hart MPA, Station House Studio.

Design by Val Speidel
Printed and bound in Canada

For Jane Duivenvoorden

and to the memory of
Gerard Duivenvoorden, Minna Mitic and Milutin (William) Mitic

Newcomers five decades ago,
they gave me Canada and my future.

CONTENTS

Contents

CONTENTS

INTRODUCTION

Imagine the impact immigrant voices and hands have had, and continue to have, on the landscape of Canada. Now consider that each of these untold numbers of newcomers once had a complex life and history elsewhere, long before they chose to alter their destiny and become immersed in the requisite self-guided metamorphosis of becoming Canadian. Navigating the span between the old world and new, they struggled to remain true to their souls while redefining personal identities and shaping new beginnings on Canadian soil. And in their determination to make sense of their adopted society's endless nuances, they inadvertently expedited the coming-of-age of a nation that was fledgling a mere half century ago.

This book explores the theme of transition into Canadian society through the eyes and voices of a compelling collection of accomplished and energetic Canadians who have had beginnings elsewhere. As members of the generation that have traded one homeland for another, they are the solitary link between the ancestors who preceded them in the old country and the Canadian-born descendants to follow. Their unique generation, with its lingering accents and richly diverse backgrounds, has contributed an untold wealth to the Canadian economic, societal and cultural tapestries. All experienced the disquietude of relinquishing one passport for another; many gambled their security for the futures of their children.

It would be simplistic to suggest that traversing the path of transition takes little more than time. The notion of time, in fact, has little to do with any evolution. Time by itself is static and open-ended, its outcome nothing more than the present slipping into the past. The mere passage of days and months and years does little to nurture the human condition. However, the passage of time used dynamically to effect growth and change readily becomes a reference point for the appraisal of both past and future.

For some newcomers, this period of redefinition is navigated without inordinate measures of pain; the notion of Canada as home merges quite readily into their self identity. Others, the majority perhaps, take longer to arrive at a comfortable realization that they can be at home in Canada without relinquishing all that was previously dear to the heart. But there are also those who find the burden of their immigration experience a perpetual millstone on their psyche. Unable to transcend the emotional no-man's-land that stretches between the old and new citizenships, they carry the flag of an uneasy truce in their hearts and live suspended in their longing for a life left behind.

I can't remember exactly when the idea for this book seeped into my consciousness, only that it had begun to percolate there well before my own migration from Canada's east to west coast in late 1991. I suspect that in some ways it has hibernated deep within me for most of my existence, spawned years ago by the images and observations of a childhood spent under the wing of parents also in transition. As did hundreds of thousands of newcomers to Canada, my parents sailed for the new world in the 1950's, eager to transplant themselves on Canadian land, yet not without some burden of regret over roots severed and left behind.

They were but two years into the business of settling in when I came along. They had come from cozy Dutch villages where the women swept the sidewalks in front of their homes and the men cycled their produce to market. Now they owned 200 acres of Maritime land just south of the tiny village of Jacquet River, along the windy cliffs that hemmed in the petulant Bay of Chaleur. Weekdays were for farming— for coaxing fallow soil back into production, for propping up a barn so fossilized its shingled siding had the constitution of burnt toast, for cajoling milk out of a Noah's-ark collection of bovines that Noah himself would have been tempted to reject.

Sundays were for farming too, albeit at a more genteel pace. Sundays were also for writing letters 'Home' on fragile, blue parchment that had AIR MAIL/NO ENCLOSURES stamped across the accompanying onion-skin envelopes. Sundays were for reminiscing, especially when an infrequent Dutch visitor from a neighbouring town dropped in. Although my parents had cast themselves solidly in the present and future, Sundays were for nostalgia.

Such was the world of my early childhood, defined by the waters of the bay to the north and a railway track to the south that hurried, without apology, to other realities well beyond the edge of my horizon. I was utterly content there, yet I came to understand at an early age that we were intricately connected to a home elsewhere, a home as big as my imagination could muster. My 'Dutchness' was for the reaping of benefits—language, stories, culture, relatives, birthday cards and Christmas parcels—and also for relinquishing to a shelf in my mind where it could sit for indefinite periods of time, comfortably independent of my emotional energy.

For my parents, the old world-new world connection was much more intricate, like lace with its every delicate strand radiating to another in all directions. Although they neither regretted nor second-guessed their decision to immigrate, the ephemeral moments of sadness were nonetheless there—for family celebrations missed, for the loss of friendships forged in childhood, for parents not there to lean on when children were ill and finances worrisome.

But they understood their transition, and in those early Canadian years they strained to hear the land whisper that they were indeed home. In cultivating the fields, they planted and nurtured their own roots. Clearing pastures of rocks and stumps fomented a re-arrangement and, ultimately, an expansion of their own personal landscape. They knew they were Canadian. And yet....

In some subtle way their experience of transition, of searching for home, stayed with me and as the years went by I felt a compelling need to further understand this most human of conditions. All peoples of the earth invariably need a nest to feather, a place of belonging that goes beyond the need for language to validate it. While 'home' can have an infinite number of definitions and settings, the common denominator is always the same: home is belonging. For some, it is belonging to one place for all time. Others see modern life as transition, the migrations from here to there necessitated more often than not by economics and opportunity. Migrating from one Canadian home to another is one thing; migrating from one country to another is something else altogether, especially when the two countries are poles apart in terms of culture, language and social landscape.

While a period of transition seems part of every newcomer's baggage in the years of settling in, can it at some point be given the ablution of closure? Does it have to taste of loneliness, loss, and loose ends, or is it instead a time to seize new opportunities and practise discerning the world through different eyes? Is it an endless longing for an old world glorified in the imagination, or does it hint at new destinies to be furrowed and niches to be uncovered? Does its end come in tiny, hard-earned steps or all at once, like the cleansing wash of a rogue wave? Does it come at all?

Although the questions rolled around in my head like errant casino dice, the answers remained stubbornly elusive. My parents had long since embraced Canada as the home of their heart, utterly content on their New Brunswick acreage, yet serenity remained elusive for other immigrants I knew. If there were answers and insights to be gleaned at all, I suspected that they lay with those Canadians who'd had their beginnings elsewhere.

From the hundreds of thousands of newcomers cultivating a future in this country, I set about compiling a select group interested in exploring their beginnings as Canadians and articulating their uniqueness as members of the transition generation. I use the word 'select' not to suggest that they are exclusive in terms of title, wealth or intellect, but rather, that their dynamism, vision and contribution to their community is without dispute. I went in search of people with the mental energy to delve into their own immigration experience and reflect on how these experiences, both positive and negative, eased or hampered their finding a place for themselves in Canada.

I was fortunate to receive funding for this project from both the federal and Nova Scotia governments, and to have friends, colleagues and a variety of unlikely sources from across the country ply the landscape for possible candidates. My heartfelt thanks to all who provided valuable leads and information.

CBC Radio introduced me to Ranjit Kumar Chandra of St. John's who has twice been nominated for the Nobel Peace Prize in medicine, and to Bernard Callebaut of Calgary who makes the finest chocolate in the world. *Maclean's* magazine steered me to Jim MacNeill of Charlottetown, a venerable Maritime publisher, and Gary Ho, a wealthy Vancouver businessman whose sense of compassion and Buddhist convictions have resulted in the founding of one of Western Canada's most significant charitable organizations.

Rev. Louis Vermeersch of Saint John, known for his compassion in an era when 'compassion' and 'church' were not often seen in the same sentence, has been a beloved family friend since I was in grade one. CBC Television's *Mr. Dressup* sent a handwritten letter suggesting that Judith Lawrence of Hornby Island, British Columbia, the creator of and puppeteer for Casey and Finnegan, Canada's best known children's puppets, might be amenable to an afternoon in front of a tape recorder. (When I later pleaded with Judith for the chance to fawn over her puppets as well, she patiently complied, hauled them out of an old trunk and sat them on her knee where they instantly came back to life.)

A *Globe and Mail* article directed me to Martina ter Beek, Prince Edward Island's official Cheese Lady. The Montreal Centre for Research and Advocacy in Race Relations suggested both Leung Tom, inventor and entrepreneur, and Nguyen Trung, Senior Vice President of Caisse centrale Desjardins. An eloquent essay on racism published in the Summer, 1995 issue of *Homemaker's* led me to its author, Dr. Roz Roach of Toronto.

My younger brother introduced me to Dusko and Svetlana Mitrovic, then of Fredericton, who were still recovering from their harrowing escape from Bosnia a year earlier. My first visit with them lasted well past midnight, and when I happened to ask when they'd made their final escape from Sarajevo, Svetlana looked at the calendar, paused a moment and said, "A year ago today."

Terry Marner, Regina artist and film maker, was speaking in Victoria when I approached him with an envelope containing a synopsis for this project. And after scouring Manitoba, home of one of Canada's largest Japanese communities, for a possible candidate, I found Hiroko Noro—ironically, on faculty at the University of Victoria, just across town from my own home.

The majority of my first interviews were conducted during a seven-week trip across the country in the summer of 1996. In the days preceding our departure, the fax machine motored from early morning, Pacific Daylight Time, to closing time in the Eastern zone. For the first time ever, my long-distance bill stretched onto a third page.

Our itinerary, once established, was promptly etched in stone. We would allow ourselves a few tourist stops and factor in extra time for car trouble (which we thankfully didn't experience), then impressed upon our troop of three youngsters the need to stay on schedule. "No problem," they told us, cheerful co-conspirators in our decision to leave in mid-June, two weeks before the last day of school. Caroline in grade seven was encouraged to keep a journal of her travels while Aaron's grade three teacher provided some math work sheets "just for fun." (These were promptly stuffed under the seat.) Laura recovered quickly from her initial dismay over having to miss her grade one sports day.

Pleas to bring along the family dog fell on our deaf ears.

Snow fell during our third night on the road, dusting the evergreens of Yoho National Park all the way up to the Rocky Mountain tree line, and higher still, etching delicate hoarfrost on the ancient, rock faces hundreds of metres above us. Rain followed us into Alberta, through the starkly magnificent Badlands and along the endless fields of young wheat, the sky a bulbous pendulum of steel hanging directly overhead.

Touring a Saskatchewan grain elevator on a Sunday morning was not on our schedule but proved impossible to resist. "I guess I could give you a tour if you want," said the operator with the lopsided ball cap who blinked back surprise when we stood hopeful in his office doorway. Several times he snuck incredulous glances at us and when he was finally convinced that we weren't feigning interest, he launched into an explanation of pricing and storing, and the logistics of moving untold tons of grain from the prairie bread basket to the Port of Vancouver. As if to add emphasis, a Canadian Pacific freight train snaked by just then, with more than 100 empty grain hoppers in tow.

In the village of Nokomis, Saskatchewan, surrounded by no-nonsense working farms and windy, abandoned homesteads, the Nokomis Museum offered a crash course on birth, life and death on the prairies. Amid the milk cans and christening gowns hummed the rhythms of an era so recently relegated to the past that it still forms the undercurrent of modern-day prairie life.

Nokomis is a village without pretensions, a retirement haven for grain growers who've padlocked the farm gate behind the last rumbling truckload of wheat or canola. Its tidy streets could have been cut out of the prairie landscape with an Exacto knife.

"Guess how much they're wanting for that bungalow over there?" a retired farmer asks. We shrug our shoulders. It's hard to shock Victoria residents with real estate.

"Fifteen thousand."

In Manitoba the mosquitos finally locate us and waste no time exacting bloody retribution for the bug-free years we've been enjoying on the west coast. They've staked us out and converge on us every evening, about the time the tents go up and the Coleman stove sparks to life. The anti-bug cream adds to the children's grime; they seem happily grungier every day.

In contrast, the Royal Canadian Mint, just east of Winnipeg, is not unkempt at all. In fact, the sleek, plate-glass pyramid—home to a clever federal scheme for generating revenue that involves charging us money to watch them make more money—is decidedly at the other end of the clean-o-meter. It's also air-conditioned, and thus a fine reprieve from the landlocked, prairie heat that has arrived to herald the news of summer.

The heat follows us into Northern Ontario, where pristine lakes bid come-hither with the promise of a cooling dip, then strangulate our capillaries with water so bracing as to suggest the ice fishers folded up their shacks just yesterday. The rainfall on the night we spend in a Thunder Bay motel is measured in *inches*, and the next morning the townsfolk are eager to talk it up.

"That was some storm," the teen gas jockey opines, flipping back a chronically annoying strand of loose hair. "Can you believe it, my boyfriend's pool flooded over."

I pull away from the pump suspecting the storm anecdote is her way of letting it be known that *she* has a boyfriend and *he* has a pool.

The endlessly beautiful Northern Ontario behind us now, we begin our descent into Toronto, the thermometer drawn upward as cooling evergreens give way to heat-absorbing asphalt. Toronto feels nicely familiar; we once lived there for a year, dividing our time between the inner city trappings, and the pastures and farmers' markets just beyond its borders. But a day or two back in town invariably has me running up and down the keyboard of my emotions: although I enjoy the festival atmosphere and the perpetual sense that something exciting is about to unfold, the smalltowner in me is easily exhausted and soon ready to go home. (And although I've been a westerner for five years, at this point my sense of home is now tugging from the east.)

Ottawa, in contrast, is much more serene and reserved. If Ottawa were a person s/he would be handsome, impeccably dressed, articulate and cultured. Ottawa *The Person* would be comfortably self-assured in the way that people of privilege so often are.

Montreal is something else again. Noisy, cluttered and gregarious, Montreal was my home once too, although I spent much of my time there surviving university and pining for the air and space of my childhood home in New Brunswick. Montreal is open-faced and friendly, its reckless edge evident in the ribbons of roadway that intersect the city in a wheel-gripping, helter-skelter manner. At one point we sit gridlocked in traffic and wonder why every vehicle in sight seems freshly birthed from a dealership showroom.

"There's an easy one to answer," says a local camper in the site next to ours that evening. "Here, leasing is cheaper than buying, so everyone leases. And while they're signing the forms they're thinking, 'What the heck. It might as well be the sports car.'"

Into the Maritimes now, where the land speaks to me so definitively that I know in an instant I've come home again. How does one begin to describe that which takes up space in the heart, yet remains elusive to the entire inventory of tools that language offers for description and self-expression? I'm beginning to understand the challenge I've foisted on this project's participants.

The interviews could have gone any which way. Not wanting the final product to read like a survey report, I came bearing few specific questions. Instead, I offered ideas from which participants could form their own beginnings. From coast to coast I was met with unhurried and invigorating conversation. Often there was laughter, occasionally tears. Conversation often stretched well beyond the hours I had asked for, and the departing handshake more than once expanded into a spontaneous hug. Always there was undying hospitality and graciousness.

Yatish Kotecha, a Winnipeg family physician, met with me one summer evening even though he was in the midst of moving his young family to a new home and had spent a long, tiring day in practise. Marge Nainaar of Prince Albert, Saskatchewan, insisted on brunch together after our interview, and later that day Betty Ramshaw, Nokomis writer and one-time war bride, declared that her home-made roast beef and Yorkshire pudding dinner would put us both in the right disposition for an evening of talk. (It did.)

Nathan Kaplan of Montreal ordered pastries from a nearby French bakery, and Veselina Tomova on the shores of St. John's figured a beer and conversation on a summer Saturday night would be the perfect prescription for getting acquainted. (It was.)

And so it went. My journey in the summer of 1996 was that of a forager, gathering micro-cassette tapes filled with musings and reflections, stories and observations. My tattered journal was crammed with my own late-night thoughts, at times wild and incoherent, on this personal evolution of transition. On how transition is often prolonged by poverty. On how it comes in the little, unremarkable steps of everyday community life: the new friends who generated opportunities for interaction, and the economic stability that brings a place to hang one's hat. On how it is exacerbated by one's limitations in English or French, in a society that tends to assess a person's acumen by their command of these languages. (Being without the words to express oneself is not the same as having nothing to say.) On how it is more easily navigated when the navigator feels in control of the journey. On how Canadian society itself is being redefined in the process.

Other thoughts also fall on my consciousness like spring snow, evanescent thoughts that melt away before I've scarcely the time to ponder their significance. I think of the eloquence of English spoken haltingly, of the unexpected impact a literal translation can have. Of how we tend to think of integration in terms of economic success and cultural conversion, forgetting that it frequently also signifies loss—of culture, language, and a way of life. I ponder my own heritage and wonder why I feel protective of my Canadian identity when I'm with Dutch relatives, and my Dutch heritage in my day-to-day Canadian setting. Similarly, the easterner and westerner in me also straddle a mental teeter-totter. That's not to suggest I endure an ongoing emotional struggle, but rather that I might feel my sense of place differently on any given day. Which leaves me wondering: can the notion of 'home' even begin to be resolved in one generation?

I think of young immigrant children who generally leap ahead of their parents in terms of their immersion into Canadianism, and who are then placed in the awkward position of watching their parents struggle through the same transition. It's not easy to bear witness to the vulnerability of those you hold up to be omnipotent. And how do these children, embarrassed by and for their families, cope as they get older? Do they go on to cast resentment at the society that has dictated such exacting burdens on their families?

I've come to realize that integration involves not just the newcomer but also the rest of the community. It's less about accepting diversity in language, culture and skin colour, and more about not noticing those differences in the first place, or, at the very least, rendering them unremarkable. It means revising the tenet that because Canadian society is predominantly white, white is the standard by which to measure everything else.

The lives and voices of twenty-nine remarkable Canadians are featured in the chapters that follow. Each chapter begins with a short vignette of the participant in his or her own setting, and is further presented as a combination of biography, which comprises the first part of the chapter, and essay. The essay, the participant's own voice, begins with a quotation lifted directly from the transcript or other referenced source provided. Although the text of the essay spans beyond the verbatim transcription of the taped interview which, by nature, is replete with the half-starts, digressions, tangents, and chatty stuff that give life to conversation, it is nonetheless completely true to the voice and intent of the people being profiled.

The last in the series of contacts and interviews with each participant was conducted in January, 2000. I have been privileged to meet these wonderful 'new' Canadians, these articulate, singularly capable and passionate people who have remained modest in the face of great accomplishment and who readily laugh at the humour and irony in their own lives. Together they highlight the extraordinary multifariousness of Canadian society; their voices and frank deliberation on contemporary Canadian life add to our better understanding of ourselves and the society we live in. Imagine a Canada without them.

Ania Andrusieczko

KOSZALIN, POLAND—EDMONTON, ALBERTA

Ania Andrusieczko could well be mistaken for an ordinary citizen in a typical Canadian setting: She's quietly articulate, methodical in her thinking, not prone to hyperbole; her bright, urban townhouse is graced with a lively toddler, a jumbo-sized dog, a salmagundi of plants and books. But this is no average citizen, this mechanical engineer in high-tech research management who defected from Poland in her early twenties and now relates the experience in an understated, almost detached, voice. Luck, she muses with a scant laugh, has seemingly been on her side. Luck as much as impetuosity saw her out of Poland and into Canada. From the beginning she knew she was here to thrive, to take ownership of a viable future that finally lay within her grasp. "Right away I said to myself, this is it, I'm not going back," Andrusieczko recalls, "And now there isn't another country I could call home."

Back in 1981 an American television crew encircled Ania Andrusieczko and her fellow Ukrainian-Polish refugees as they sat placidly eating sandwiches on a lawn in Vienna, Austria. "Tell us your story," they implored the group of 20 composed but tight-lipped youth.

"At that point," Andrusieczko recalls, "we didn't want to talk, didn't want to have our picture taken. We still couldn't believe we'd just defected. The last thing we wanted was a newspaper headline. We figured we'd be packed up and sent back home to Poland anyway, and returning as would-be defectors would put us in enough hot water; add to that the attention of the foreign media and we might as well consider our lives ruined.

"But the Americans were persistent. They found a translator and

fired one question after another at us, determined to get some response."

The story that lead to Andrusieczko's defection from Poland began long before her birth in 1960. Though her Ukrainian ancestors had been reluctant citizens of Poland since the boundaries of the Ukraine had been redrawn in 1918, they retained their Ukrainian nationalistic fervour and lived in hope that a united Ukraine might one day resurface on the European landscape. Over the next few decades they refused to become placid Poles, fought in several unsuccessful skirmishes in an attempt to achieve independence, and in general remained a chronic burr under the seat of Polish government.

After the Second World War Poland acquired a significant portion of East Germany as decreed by the post-war Potsdam Conference of 1945. Thousands of Germans fled or were expelled from their homes and relocated back within the new German border. Almost overnight the villages and cities of the newly defined northwestern Poland were transformed into ghost towns.

Meanwhile, to the southeast the Polish Ukrainians remained boldly defiant to Polish authority. But now, in the wake of the Potsdam Conference, Poland realized it finally had the means to rid itself of the Ukrainian problem once and for all: it would scatter the troublesome community and dissipate its ardent sense of nationalism by transplanting it far to the northwest, into the houses earlier vacated by the Germans.

And so, in 1947, on very short notice, more than 300,000 Polish Ukrainians were forcibly relocated to the other end of Poland, far from their ancestral home. They would not be allowed to resettle as a community; instead they would be dispersed here and there, no more than a few families to each village. "That's how I came to be born in Miastko, near Koszalin, on the Baltic coast, rather than in the Carpathian mountains of my ancestors."

Although Andrusieczko and her family kept the Ukrainian culture and language alive within the walls of their home, her father forbade any form of cultural expression in public. "It was a survival tactic. Ukrainians were not well treated in Poland. When I started kindergarten my parents warned me not to speak Ukrainian or tell anyone I was Ukrainian. I went to school convinced that everyone was hiding a secret identity. There was no such thing as a true Pole, I thought, only 'other people.'"

However, like most official attempts at cultural assimilation, this initiative was flawed in its thinking and hence dramatic in its failure. The younger generation roamed between the villages to seek each other out, and eventually migrated to the cities where they continued their social interaction and the preservation of their language and traditions. When Andrusieczko herself moved to Warsaw to attend university, she took a long, discriminating look at life in Poland and concluded she didn't like what she saw.

"There was no future for me in Poland as a Ukrainian, and even for Poles the chance of a prosperous, fulfilling life was dismal. The economy was depressed, the government heavy-handed. Droves of people were trying to leave. My parents had earlier visited my father's sister in her Ukrainian community in Australia and had returned with the message that a better life existed for Ukrainians outside of Poland. Although I wasn't aware of it at the time, they were a major influence on my decision to go."

In the summer of 1981 Andrusieczko had just completed her second year of university and was feeling restless and defiantly non-Polish. She learned of a bus trip to Rome that was being organized for Ukrainian youth by the heretofore banned Greek Catholic Church, and decided to sign up. "My brother and his wife were going and I was quite sure they were planning to defect. I hadn't made up my mind yet.

"On our way back from Rome we stopped in Vienna, and my brother and sister-in-law got off the bus and said they were going no further. Then I figured, if they're not going back, I'm not either, so I got off too. When the bus pulled out to leave, it broke down and in the time it took to be repaired, another 17 people had decided to defect. We made our way to a refugee camp outside the city, with no idea of what might happen next."

At the camp gate the group was denied admittance on the technicality of having come via Italy rather than directly from Poland. Undeterred, they located a grassy knoll across the street from the camp, settled there and ate their bagged lunch. "We were giddy and laughing; our common sense had evaporated. How naive and foolish we were to have been so carefree. We should have been worried sick; our bus had long since departed and we knew we'd be in serious trouble if they sent us back to Poland."

The resolute American television crew arrived half-way through lunch, their curiosity piqued by the uncharacteristic cohesiveness of the group on the grass. "From where we sat we could see long lines of people pouring into the camp. In that situation it's very often every person or family for themselves. You are desperate, you elbow your way in and no one else matters. But here we were, sticking together as a group, refusing to be pried off into smaller components. For us, it was all or none. That's why the Americans found us intriguing."

When the television crew discovered through a hastily recruited interpreter that Andrusieczko and her group were Ukrainians fleeing from Poland, their interest soared. What would it take to get their story? The youth, made more daring by this unexpected spotlight, named their price: access to the refugee camp.

"Within the hour we were inside the gate. A few calls here and there, and then we were officially admitted, a procedure that normally took two weeks to complete. But the television crew wanted to document our saga, and since they didn't have two weeks to hang around, they fast-tracked us through the paperwork. The media has incredible clout.

"After documenting our story they left. But the publicity and special concessions we'd been given made us so sure of ourselves that we began making bold, reckless demands. I think we were driven by group strength and also, for the first time in our lives, by our Ukrainian identity.

"The authorities, who were aware of the plight of the Ukrainians in Poland, treated us well once they figured out who we were. The local Ukrainian community soon took up our cause. Most refugees could expect to stay in the camp for 18 months, yet here we were with our Ukrainian support and the subject of much interest all around. Three months after we had stepped off that bus, we'd acquired sponsors and were being interviewed by the Canadian Embassy. That's how preferential our treatment was. And for whatever unexplainable reason, providence was with us along the way."

Due to chronic overcrowding at the camp, a portion of the

refugees, usually families with children, were routinely selected to be transferred to hotels all over the country. When a few of the Ukrainians were offered hotel accommodations, the offer was unanimously rejected by the group. They would go together or not at all. "They weren't trying to separate us for reasons other than the logistics of finding accommodations for an entire group, but we realized that we would be safer and less vulnerable if we stuck together. So they found a hotel near St. Georgen im Attergau, a small town 40 kilometres from Salzburg, that would take all 20 of us. We stayed there for the next six months."

The most pressing challenge facing Andrusieczko's group, not one that usually comes to mind when pondering the plight of refugees, was a surplus of idle time. "The first few weeks in this rural setting were idyllic. We could come and go freely and although we weren't allowed to work, the novelty of our situation kept us buoyed. After a while, however, our routine became tedious and our spirits began to sag. When we grew too bored and lethargic to bother even with breakfast, there went our last reason for getting out of bed in the morning. Staying motivated was tough when we didn't know where, or when, we might resume a normal life.

"Again, however, the Ukrainian community was a wonderful support. They came to visit us and brought us little luxuries such as chocolates and coffee. They showed us there was hope for a normal life somewhere in our future and gave us the resolve to continue biding our time."

Although Andrusieczko and her brother had originally applied to go to Australia where family already resided, in the end it was the Canadian Ukrainian community that came forward with sponsorship for the entire group. "In early 1982 we arrived into the hands of various Ukrainian organizations in Toronto who had committed themselves to sponsoring us for a year. They opened their homes to us and were a wonderful support when we needed it most. Of course, there were minor conflicts arising from the expectations each generation had of the other. We found them old-fashioned; they were disappointed to find we were not at all like the Ukrainians of the era in which they had emigrated, decades earlier. But mostly they were our life line, and we were grateful."

Arriving in Canada in the middle of winter, with no English and a broken leg—the result of an ill-fated venture on a skateboard borrowed from the Austrian hotel chef—didn't lessen Andrusieczko's determination to find work and go about the business of becoming established. She enrolled in an English course, netted a library job and mere months later, landed part-time employment with the Ontario government. "It was a challenge to stick with that job. But providence was still there for me because my work setting forced me to begin using my limited English. It's fine to study a language in the classroom from nine to five, but after a while that becomes boring and you're not really using it anyway. You arrive at the point where it's better to go and study, in English, something that interests you, or to find a job that requires you to use and develop language skills.

"It wasn't that the work was exceptional—I was processing documents, putting them on microfiche, and filing—but the atmosphere was very supportive and conducive to learning. Several of my friends had taken factory jobs where they learned to speak improper English. And also, my job paid well and thus enabled me eventually to return to university."

Although she became romantically involved with Bohdan Nebesio, a fellow refugee and University of Toronto student, Andrusieczko remembers the university years as being far from easy. "There were periods of isolation and loneliness, and a sad kind of stagnation that comes from 'being here' without really being here. Fortunately I was able to continue living with the woman who had originally sponsored me, which was a great support."

After completing her mechanical engineering degree and conducting an unsuccessful job search, Andrusieczko returned to Europe for a time, roaming near the Polish border, frustrated over not being able to cross it to visit and reconnect with her family. Restless and unfocused, she returned to Canada and then fortuitously found work with a high-tech manufacturing company near Ottawa, "my first real job." In the meantime Nebesio had switched from engineering to literature, completed his degree, and gone on to graduate studies at the University of Alberta.

"For a year and a half we commuted between Ottawa and Edmonton, which took considerable time, energy and money. Then I moved to Alberta. I knew it would be a challenge trying to find work in the precision industry in a province that had grown up on the oil industry, but love won out and I became an Edmontonian."

As Andrusieczko had correctly predicted, finding work in her field took persistency in a town that virtually enshrined heavy industry. But she refused to sit idle in the interim, instead volunteering and becoming involved in the co-op housing project where she lived. When an employment opportunity finally came in 1995, it was extended by Westaim Corporation, a newly established research firm eager to carve a niche for itself in the land of big machines and rugged, outdoor work. Currently Andrusieczko is manager of production of electronic material.

Nebesio obtained a doctorate degree in literature and film, and in early 1997 the couple gave birth to a son. The following year they took him to Poland to meet his extended family.

"I miss my family now more than ever. Nestor should have his grandparents, aunts, uncles and cousins around him as he grows up. And I would like to share my joys with them as well. But that's the cost of being in Canada."

And so the well-adjusted, Canadian Andrusieczko knows the exacting price of immigration, of being the generation to forge the link between the old country and the new. She and her husband, their families back in Poland, and now their Canadian-born child, live with that awareness every day.

The most important thing about Canada is this:
there is a place for differences.

In retrospect, I could say that much of my life has been about transition. My ancestors were the spoils of historical conflict, long ago given to a foreign country by a treaty written in an alien script. And even within the borders of that country we became displaced people. I grew up straddling a secret culture within the larger, more dominant and sometimes malevolent presence. In my home I was a Ukrainian, privately learning the heritage, language and customs of my ancestors.

On the street I was Polish, a member of the mainstream, an official citizen of the country. On the street I learned there was no such thing as Ukrainian. Even the spelling of my name was changed to accommodate the Polish alphabet and appease Polish phonetics.

And yet, despite Poland's attempts at assimilation, the Ukrainian people managed to prevent the watering down of their culture in the next generation. Officially we were not allowed to congregate together as Ukrainian, but we knew where to find each other, and as we grew up and migrated to city universities, we discovered that our collective sense of being Ukrainian was solidly intact.

So it happened that my last two years in Poland, as a university student in Warsaw, were quite wonderful. I discovered my independence, enjoyed my studies and had a great social life. But even then, I was ready to give these things up in order to leave Poland; in fact, when I did leave, it was as a foreigner ready to adopt a new home and embrace the future. I had never considered Poland my homeland, had never felt genuinely welcome there. My only bond was with my family. So the attitude I came to Canada with was that there was no turning back and nothing to be gained from dwelling on the past and pondering all the 'what ifs.' I knew I'd have to go through an adjustment process, which is universal to all who pull up roots to settle elsewhere, regardless of who you are or where you come from. And it's a painful and lonely process, but there's no way of getting around it and, for the most part, you do it by yourself.

My situation was unique in that I came as part of the 'Famous 20' with whom I'd been in isolation and had come to know very well. We were each other's insulation against the trauma of the new and unfamiliar. We leaned heavily on each other, especially throughout that first year. Looking back, the dynamics of our group were intriguing: aside from our Ukrainian background and current situation, we didn't have all that much in common; back in Poland we might not have given each other more than a second glance. But here, because of our circumstances, we were a strongly bonded entity. The commonality of our experience was the glue that kept us together. Implicitly we understood the challenges that each of us faced in our own way. There was no need to explain to each other what we were going through.

Having said that, it was also inevitable that we would gradually drift apart. The bond was strong for as long as we needed to derive strength from group solidarity, but as we began making inroads into our own futures as Canadians, the need for leaning on each other slowly diminished. For a while we had a reunion every year but now it's more sporadic and no longer involves the entire group. Perhaps we'll get together in 2001 to celebrate the twentieth anniversary of our defection. If that reunion happens, it won't be because we need each other, but because we want to come together socially to ruminate with some fellow Canadians on the year or two we shared with each other some two decades ago.

When I came to Canada I was assigned to the home of a woman only a few years older than I. Fortunately for me, we had much in common and she was fluent in Ukrainian. Through her I found it easy to make my way into the Ukrainian-Canadian community. Although my own small group was still very important to me at that time, I met many Ukrainian young people who had been born in Toronto and they helped me ease myself into the Canadian mainstream. In a way, being in their circle felt a bit like a reincarnation of the university climate I had so enjoyed and left behind in Warsaw.

Even with all that support, however, there was no getting around the challenges of those early years in Toronto. I hadn't come with any preconceived expectations of what life would be like in Canada, only that it would be an improvement over what I had left behind. The only certainty I knew was that I needed to return to university, after which the rest of my life would somehow fall into place. So I stayed focused on my education and work, and gave myself little time to ponder my decision to come to Canada.

But I was lonely. My brother and his wife had had a child the year we arrived, which enhanced my sense of family, but I missed my parents and worried about them constantly. I had difficulty making ends meet during my university years, and even though I was busy with jobs and studies, I was often quite alone. There were days I felt quite ill and deflated.

Moving to the Ottawa Valley opened my eyes to the country's diversity. So many immigrants come to Toronto assuming that Canada and

Toronto are synonymous. And then they go beyond the city and find a totally different world, both physically and socially. In some ways the Ottawa Valley seemed European to me, older than Canada, with it's handsome towns and unique valley culture. Although there was no Ukrainian element, I functioned quite well there; much of my adjustment had already been accomplished and I was beginning to think of myself as Canadian.

When I relocated to western Canada, it didn't take me long to discover the well-established Ukrainian community of Alberta. The contrast between the eastern and western Ukrainians is particularly fascinating. The Alberta Ukrainian community has been here for a century and they see themselves as an inseparable part of Canada's heritage. They still value the Ukrainian heritage, but they've pioneered here and their stories are woven into the Canadian landscape. When you ask them if they feel they belong here, there is no hesitation in their answer.

The Toronto Ukrainian community, on the other hand, is a post-war community, still very new, still very connected to the old world and the past. And even though they feel at home and have raised the next generation here, many still live as Ukrainians rather than Canadians, still limit themselves socially to their own community. In some ways they've made the transition; in others they continue to pine for the old world.

However, the world of their hearts no longer exists—we young, Ukrainian upstarts were ample proof of that, which made for some contentious times between us. They, who had anticipated we would be like the Ukrainian youth of their time, anguished over how contemporary and 'western' we had become. We, on the other hand, found them old-fashioned and critical of all the modern turns Ukrainian society had taken. On both sides there was uncompromising stubbornness laced with a temptation to compare and scorn.

In retrospect, we newcomers were more judgmental than we should have been. Whenever we got together during those first few months, the conversation invariably centred around the peculiarities of our hosts. It was easier to poke fun at their misplaced nostalgia and adulterated accents than it was to examine how our own insecurities might be prompting such harsh criticism when we should have been grateful for their support. Because we needed to retain some assurance of our own normalcy at a time when nothing was familiar, we chose to conclude that they were the ones hopelessly out of touch: in order for me to feel that I'm still normal and doing fine, it helps to find something wrong with you. In essence, what I'm doing is singling you out so I can protect my vulnerability and preserve what I know.

The Canadian-born youth of the Ukrainian community tried to communicate with us, and we criticized them terribly. You'd think we would have had enough in common to avoid such strife, but no, they postured for us because they were worried about what we might think of them, and we did likewise because we were intimidated by the fact that they belonged here and we were outsiders.

I'm not prone to offering advice, but I could suggest to newcomers that they shouldn't habitually measure everyone and everything against their own values. There is always the danger that what one's culture has taught one to discard might actually be of value in another setting. Newcomers mustn't be too quick to discard, and they must be prepared to meet people half way. People are not going to spend enormous amounts of energy on you just because you're newly arrived. They have their own lives, and if you're not willing to put forth something of yourself in a welcoming way, there's no reason anyone else should do so.

What is this country called Canada? First, it is not America, even though the Poland of my childhood made no distinction between Canada and America. But Canadians are subtly different. You can see it in our culture, which is much more than the sum total of English and French. There are so many other peoples who have contributed to make Canada what it is.

The most important thing about Canada is this: there is a place for differences. Most countries do begrudgingly allow for the existence of other cultures, but often these cultures are relegated to the margins of society. In Canada it doesn't have to be so. Here everyone can participate in and lend their voice to the mainstream.

If you look at countries such as France and Germany, there remains to this day a distinction between 'the French' (or Germans) and 'all the rest,' even though 'all the rest' are immigrants who reside there permanently and in large numbers. In Canada, that distinction is becoming less and less relevant. It doesn't mean the cultures are melding together here, but rather that they are learning to function better together. Even relations between the French and English, contentious as they might get at times, are still workable, and I have hope that Canada will survive this current, fractious era.

My hope is based on knowing that people from around the world will continue to come here, bringing with them their cultures and experiences and voices, and they will lend this to the building and shaping of the Canada of the future. Their Canadian-born children will be emotionally tied to Canada and hence they will have a greater Canadian voice than their parents had. I see how it happened with the Alberta Ukrainian community. Don't tell them they aren't as Canadian as Anglo-Saxons are. They feel their Canadianism every bit as strongly as anyone else. They also believe in and exercise their right to make demands for the betterment of the country.

Officially, the immigrants of Canada are mostly considered as members of their separate groups—the Ukrainian Canadians, Polish Canadians, Indo-Canadians, and so on. However, when we're all put together in one large group, we form a significant portion of the population, which is why I see immigrants gradually increasing their influence on the way this country functions, both politically and culturally.

However, the movement towards the mainstream is not so much about assimilation as it is about the evolution of a new culture. Years from now Canadian culture will not be an Anglo-Saxon culture. And it won't be uniform across the country for a long time, if ever. But when it's metamorphosis nears the point where something definable emerges, I hope our Native people will be a significant part of it. Canada's history has never included these people, even though they were here centuries before the rest of us. Our genuine recognition of Native Canadian history will, in fact, help to legitimize Canada as a real country whose history and heritage goes back far beyond the recorded three hundred years or so. To walk side by side with our Native Canadians would be to cast off those vestiges of colonialism that have lingered this long simply because we've long considered Canadian history to be not much more than a colonial history.

As for me, I think I'm coming near the end of my own transition experience. From the beginning I took on the attitude that I had come to stay; I would be part of this society and would therefore find my place in it. I've made my adjustments and have arrived at a comfortable sense of place as a Canadian. There will always be differences because I wasn't born here, but I don't consider that a negative. And there are so many like me—Canadians who've started out somewhere else.

If I have any regret, it's the ongoing price I pay for being apart from our extended family. Although the distances are not what they used to be and I can now travel freely to Poland to visit, I will never have the 'over-the-back-fence' relationship with my clan that I would have thrived on. My parents considered coming to Canada once but my brother and I were still in university then and we couldn't afford to sponsor them at that time. Now we want them to come, but they dread the challenge of relocating at this point in their lives. They have their network of friends and function well in that society, and they don't want to be dependent on us. And to adjust to a new culture and language at this point in their lives...it might be impossible for them.

But that makes it more difficult for me because I feel that it's somehow my turn to take care of them, especially as they grow older. And it saddens me that I won't be able to do that for them. It's a heavy weight on my heart, always there, and I have no way of lightening the load.

But to go back, that would be impossible. There isn't a country outside of Canada I could call home. Perhaps my reasons for coming here were not well thought out at the time; I was young and reckless and threw much caution to the wind in order to turn my back on Poland. At great risk, I first rejected Poland, then chose Canada. But I've grown to cherish my place here, in the Canadian mainstream.

As much as my past has been about transition, my future is as a Canadian. To live outside of Canada at this point would be to live as a foreigner.

Martina ter Beek

Near Amsterdam there is a farm, a small, antiquated, labour-intensive farm that lies well below sea-level. Spring rain brings mud that oozes around your ankles as you work, sucks tenaciously at your rubber boots, turns walking into yet another chore. Your most-used implement is the wheelbarrow.

Near Charlottetown there is a farm, a large, modern, efficient farm that lies well above sea-level. Spring sun brings green pastures that fuel the herd that produces the milk that stocks the factory that turns out extraordinarily good cheese. The wheelbarrow is strictly for gardening.

This is the story of how Martina ter Beek came to migrate with her family from the one farm to the other, of how she transformed her cheese-making hobby into a business that consistently produces some of the most sought-after specialty cheese in North America. "We came for opportunity," says ter Beek, "And we have found it in abundance."

When Martina ter Beek and her young family drove past a picture-perfect dairy farm in rural Prince Edward Island, she knew instantly it would make the ideal home for them. "Don't get your hopes up," her husband cautioned when he saw her eyeing the 'For Sale' sign. "It'll be way too expensive."

The ter Beeks, visiting from Holland, had been touring around the island as part of their itinerary while vacationing with an uncle who lived in Kentville, Nova Scotia. "We had our four children with us; the youngest was only five months old. Earlier we had seriously considered emigrating to Canada, and when our plans fell through, we gave ourselves this trip as a consolation prize. And yet, as we drove around I couldn't help but keep an eye open for property on which I could imagine us living and farming.

"I was born into a farm family in 1949; I've always preferred milking cows and making hay to school and studies. My husband also grew up on a farm, so when we married it was natural to think of our future in terms of farming. Unlike many young, aspiring farmers in Holland, we were fortunate to have a farm to go to; my husband was his parents' only son so we ended up on his family farm."

That farm, however, was a mere 50 acres located in the shadow of Amsterdam, on land that had once been part of a swamp and was now being slated for eventual re-naturalization. "We had our limitations on that old-fashioned farm. Because the government had plans for the land, we were prohibited from replacing the old barn or making any upgrades. The land was low-lying and wet, and all the work had to be done by hand. Our most-used machine was a wheelbarrow.

"Our first trip to Canada, the trip that put the emigration bee in our bonnet, occurred several years before the one that took us to Prince Edward Island. We had two children then and we came without them, to visit my uncle in Nova Scotia. We fell in love with the area, and everyone was so friendly. My uncle took us around to visit people, and they made time for us. In Holland you just didn't visit unannounced. You waited until you were invited, and you never stayed for a meal unless by prearranged invitation. Here, the business of visiting seemed much more spontaneous, easygoing, and people seemed to have more fun socializing."

Back on Dutch soil after their sojourn, ter Beek began envisioning what their life and future in a Canadian setting might hold for them. The more she thought about it, the more unabated she became in her enthusiasm for relocation. A farm in Canada, she calculated, might well contain the solutions to many of her questions and uncertainties about their future and that of their children: how much longer would they be able to earn a decent living on their antiquated farm? Where, in congested Holland, would they be able to find, let alone afford, land for their oldest son who had already decided that he too, would become a farmer? Their own farm wasn't large enough to subdivide and they weren't ready to hand it down; they themselves were still decades away from retirement.

"I was almost too enthused at that point. My husband, Rijk, was somewhat more reluctant; he could foresee many hurdles, and his parents didn't even want to hear us talk about emigration. But nonetheless, we obtained our Canadian visas and took part in several tours of eastern Canada specifically arranged for people who were considering immigration. We ruled out Ontario because it was too expensive, and Quebec because we didn't speak French. We were unfamiliar with the west so that left Atlantic Canada, and we began looking for land there through an agent. Rijk came by himself one winter just so we'd know what we were in for. He ended up buying a cap to protect his ears and he wore two pairs of pants the whole time."

When their visas were due to expire before they had found a suitable farm to purchase, ter Beek reluctantly resigned herself to the probability that relocating to Canada was not in her family's future. "It didn't make sense to give up a home and a farm and income for the unknown, in the middle of winter and with a young family at that. So we let the visas go.

"We told the kids that instead we would all go on a holiday to Canada the following summer. Of course the cost was prohibitive, but my uncle invited us again so off we went."

While in Kentville, ter Beek's husband wanted to drive to Prince Edward Island to visit an acquaintance he had met on an earlier tour. That trip took them past the dairy farm on Highway 223 near Winsloe North, the one with the 'For Sale' placard gracing the end of its lane. Ter Beek insisted they have a look at it, and the following day a real estate agent took them to see the property.

"It was beautiful, the gently rolling fields, the large, well-constructed barn, the lovely house. We didn't see the cows because they were in the back field, but that was just as well: as Rijk had predicted, the place was too expensive for us. Still, I wanted to see it again the following day, before returning to Kentville, but Rijk said there was no point.

"We went back to Holland, back to our routine there, and quite some time later, the agent contacted us to say the farm was still for sale. So we ended up buying it after all, and re-applying for our visas. We bought 66 cows with the farm, sight unseen. We didn't dare reveal that to our families; they already thought we were being extremely reckless."

The ter Beeks sold their Dutch farm and moved to Canada in 1985. "We arrived on October 14 and stayed at a hotel until everything was arranged. We moved onto the farm on Halloween day. Well, Halloween is unknown in the Dutch culture, so of course when the kids came to our door, we were unprepared. I said to them, 'Why don't you come back for candy next week, and then you can play with my kids.' I bought lots of candy but no one came, which was understandable of course.

"Our containers also arrived on Halloween. We brought our furniture, toys, everything for the house, and some farm machinery. It was cheaper to have it shipped than to sell it there and restock here. But also, it turned out to be a wise move because all those familiar things—the household furnishings, the beds and toys—really helped the kids to settle in and feel at home. I remember my youngest son, about a year old, climbing up on the couch even before the cushions had been put on it and announcing, 'I'm home.'"

Both ter Beek and her husband had taken English in school, which helped ease the adjustment that was initially required. The children, typically, learned almost effortlessly through immersion. "Our younger children learned English from the television program, *Mr. Dressup*, and the oldest, then 14, was put back a grade when we registered him for school. However, in the same year they placed him back in his original class, with his age group."

The ter Beeks were adamant that they would not sit at home and wait for the community to reach out to them. "We went around to all our neighbours and introduced ourselves. They were most welcoming and began including us in their community activities, inviting our children to join 4-H and so on. At first we attended the Christian Reform Church in Charlottetown; the congregation is 99.9% Dutch. It would have been easy to stay there, but then we thought, if we're going to live in a community and be part of that community, we will worship in that community too.

"And so we joined the local United Church. We were warmly introduced and made to feel very welcomed; everyone shook hands with us. Our neighbours go to that church and over the years we have made many friends there. It's the right place for us to be."

36

In order to accelerate her proficiency in English, ter Beek decided to turn her home into a guest home for tourists the summer following her arrival. She arranged all of her children in one bedroom, emptied out the other rooms and rented them out. And she served her guests home-made cheese for breakfast.

"I come from a family of cheese makers; my brother owns a large cheese factory and my sister has a small-scale operation. A year before we left Holland, my sister had taught me how to make Gouda cheese, a mild, creamy Dutch cheese that's popular the world over. I had begun making it for ourselves, and to give as gifts here and there. It was strictly a hobby; I had no plans for a commercial venture.

"I made a batch within my first week on the new farm. I had brought my equipment in the container and used some of the 'starter,' a powdered bacteria culture, which I had carried in my luggage. I wanted to see how it would taste and age, which largely depends on the cow's diet, hence on the soil and grass. Cheese should age at least 14 days, but after a week we found ourselves nibbling away. And it was good, quite similar to what we had made in Holland."

The paying guests also proclaimed it to be 'good.' So good, in fact, that demand for her product grew to the point where ter Beek would eventually decide to forego her tourist home initiative and concentrate instead on a commercial cheese-making business.

"We had started making cheese in the dairy house, where the milking equipment is washed and kept, and where the milk is stored until shipping. But a health inspector had come by early on to nix that operation. He was actually on a follow-up visit: he'd left the previous owner with a list of things to modify or upgrade, and had come back to see if his instructions had been complied with. They hadn't, which meant there was much that needed to be done.

"He also informed me I would require a separate facility for cheese-making if I wanted a license to produce cheese for commercial sales. We had barely settled in then, so it was really too soon to decide whether we wanted to go from hobby to full-scale business. In the short run we opted to continue making cheese in the dairy house just for ourselves, our guests and friends."

A new cheese plant would also call for a significant financial investment, to which the ter Beeks were not yet ready to commit themselves. For one thing, there were other major expenditures on the horizon, one of which was a whole new milking herd. By 1987 the ter Beeks had decided the time had come to increase their milk production by upgrading the herd of Holsteins that had come with the farm. They learned of a quality herd for sale in Maine, and again made the purchase sight unseen.

"We bought 30 more cows over the phone. Since we couldn't inspect them beforehand anyway—we didn't have the visas required to enter the United States—we stayed home and awaited the tractor-trailer that was to deliver them. The owners were right behind them in their car; who could blame them? They weren't going to relinquish their herd to strangers across the border until they'd been paid. So they accompanied us to the bank and waited while we had a certified cheque drawn up."

In the meantime, ter Beek's Gouda was becoming increasingly popular with her friends and guests. As more and more people sampled and passed on the rave reviews, ter Beek had to concede that her hobby was at a turning point. Would she continue to produce a bit of cheese here and there for personal use, or would she apply for a sales license and turn her cheese making into a full-fledged cottage industry? She opted for the latter, and in 1988 had a small cheese plant built, which she stocked with all new equipment ordered from Holland. An underground stainless steel pipeline was installed between the dairy house and cheese plant so milk could be pumped directly from the storage tank into the pasteurization vats. "We made sure we had our blueprints and specifications approved by the inspectors—we didn't want to be building it twice." Her licenses to sell both on and off the Island were granted shortly after.

Today the quality products made by Island Farmhouse Gouda Inc. are in demand throughout North America, and ter Beek's plant has evolved into a popular Island tourist spot. Visitors can watch the cheese making process through a large viewing window; a second window offers visual access to the temperature-controlled storage and aging area, where shelves of cheese rounds are tenderly turned over every day "so they will age properly and maintain their uniform shape."

"I call my product 'hand-crafted.' Nothing is computerized; everything is done by hand, the making, turning and coating. We take special care with it."

In order to produce a domestic Gouda that is virtually identical to the imported product, ter Beek orders all of her supplies from Holland. "I order the spices, the rennet, the wax coating, even the coloured cellophane the cheese is wrapped in. The only item not imported is the milk.

"I use about 70,000 litres of milk a year, to make 7000 kilograms of cheese. Much of it is sold as mild or medium, but some of it does sit around and age nicely. Our busiest time for production is the summer season. We sell at craft fairs, to specialty stores, and to a large grocery chain. The occasional order of aged cheese might go to a beer festival. Of course we also sell from the factory counter, and our mail-order business just keeps growing.

"We offer mild, medium and aged cheese rounds in two sizes and a good variety of flavours including onion and red pepper, red chili pepper, peppercorn, and herb and garlic. Those who buy the five-kilogram rounds are usually people who've come from Holland or Germany. We've also started making a low-fat cheese which is just getting off the ground in sales, but it's what some customers really want."

Having been dubbed *The Cheeselady*, ter Beek remains unaffected by her new-found notoriety as the maker of extraordinarily good cheese. Her burgeoning binder of appreciative 'fan mail' is ample evidence of a product so good that customers throughout North America gladly endure the inconvenience of ordering and waiting for delivery, rather than run to the nearest delicatessen for an alternative product.

Summer means long, labour-intensive hours for ter Beek and her staff of two, but she makes it a point to put her feet up during the winter. "Winter is my quiet season. Rijk and I enjoy conversation over leisurely breakfasts—our morning meetings, so to speak. In the summer we're each so busy with our businesses that we hardly have time to find out what the other is doing. So in the winter we bring each other up to date and plan for the following year.

"I could be spring-cleaning my house, but I like being lazy in the winter, just relaxing and enjoying the sun and the beautiful view out over the fields. It's a view I'll never become indifferent to. When we first got here, the amount of snow astounded us. But the winters here are so pristine, so fresh, and drenched with sunshine. The fields are an endless blanket of sparkling, radiant white. And for us, coming from the gray, dreary winters of western Europe, that continues to be a real tonic."

Shortly after we arrived we said, if the neighbours don't come to us, we'll go to them and introduce ourselves.

I've never been homesick. In fact, that's made me feel guilty at times since I knew our leaving was hard on the ones we left behind, and they missed us terribly. We were almost too preoccupied with our new adjustments to be homesick—the kids' schooling, new farming procedures, getting used to different groceries, the banking system, and hundreds of other details. But for those left back in Holland it was a different story. Nothing about their lives changed except that suddenly six beloved people were gone.

In the spring following the move to our farm, we all travelled back to Holland for the 40th wedding anniversary of both sets of parents. Financially it was a considerable challenge, but we felt we owed it to them to be at their celebration. In retrospect it was the right decision; once they saw us again they realized we hadn't gone forever, and that occasional travel back and forth would be feasible. So they knew we hadn't walked out of their lives altogether.

I remember my Dad, on his first visit here, looking out the window one day and studying the rolling hills and trees, and he said simply, "You have a beautiful view." He found it easy to understand why we had come here—both of my parents did. My husband's parents had much more difficulty with our leaving, and that's been hard on us. We tried to make them understand that we weren't leaving because we didn't have a good life before, or that we were rejecting Holland, but that we wanted something better for ourselves and especially for the children. In Holland we were very limited by our inefficient farm, high taxes, and the chronic over-regulation that exists there in everything you do. Rijk's parents tried to understand but were nonetheless

BUT OUR CHILDREN, THAT'S
A DIFFERENT STORY. WE'RE THE
GENERATION THAT PAVED THE WAY,
THEY'RE THE GENERATION
THAT HAS BLENDED IN,
AND THEIR CHILDREN WILL BE
TRUE CANADIANS, CANADIANS
TO THE BONE.

very deeply pained by their separation from us, from their only son and their grandchildren.

Compared to the adjustments required of them, many of the ones we faced as we eased into our new Canadian skin were quite minor, sometimes almost trivial. Take our meal schedule as an example. In Holland it is the norm to eat your hot meal at noon. And the Dutch supper is similar to a Canadian lunch. But here, with our bigger farm, more cows to milk and so on, there wasn't time to put a hot meal on the table by noon. So we Canadianized ourselves and shifted these meals around, which was much better suited to our schedule.

One of our top priorities was to find a place for ourselves in our new community. We have always been a close family but in the early weeks, before we knew anyone, we leaned on each other a great deal and became even more close-knit. I think the immigration experience often influences a family that way. But in Holland we hadn't had much time to socialize either, so our situation here wasn't all that different. However, we didn't allow ourselves to become too complacent about our isolation. We knew that unless we became part of society in a genuine way, we would never completely reap the benefits of belonging to our new home. And that meant we had to come out of our own little world on the farm and reach out to others.

If you stay in your house and wait for others to come to you, it likely will not happen, whether you live in Canada or Holland or wherever. Shortly after we arrived we said, if the neighbours don't come to us, we'll go to them and introduce ourselves. That's what we did, and we were well-received. People wanted to know about us, they asked questions, invited us to functions, and over the years we've grown to be a real part of this community.

Only once, in all my years here, was I bluntly told that I wasn't an Islander and would never be one. But that was an isolated incident, instigated by petty nastiness, and although it hurt at the time I didn't dwell on it for long.

I've never regretted our decision to become part of our local United Church congregation. These people are our friends and our neighbours. Had we stayed with the Christian Reform Church, I'm afraid we would have given our neighbours the impression that their worship wasn't good enough for us, that we preferred the company of 'our own kind.' And we might have never completely fit into the community.

Language, fortunately, has never been a major problem. When my youngest was five he dislocated his hip when an older brother fell on top of him. We took him to the hospital and understandably, he was in a great deal of pain. I was comforting him in Dutch and the nurse was questioning him in English and, despite his anxiety and pain, he automatically switched back and forth between the two languages without hesitation. But kids have a remarkable ability to pick up languages, and my son's experience made me realize my children would have absolutely no trouble learning flawless English.

It took Rijk and I much longer to be comfortable in English, and even now we don't speak it perfectly. At first I just couldn't get a joke. Everyone would laugh, except for me. And for the longest time I couldn't have imagined telling a joke. Often a literal translation of an expression or phrase just doesn't work.

But English was never an intimidating obstacle for me. If I needed to make myself understood I would explain what I was saying, and if that drew puzzled looks, I would just try explaining myself a different way. Rijk once sent me to Canadian Tire for a motor part—the literal translation of the name of this part from Dutch is 'cable shoes.' I asked for cable shoes and of course they had no idea what I was talking about. So I explained about wires connected to motors using little things that look like shoes, and they said, "Oh, you mean 'wire ends.' "

I wasn't afraid to make mistakes and I made plenty of them. I consider myself to be somewhat shy, but you can't be too shy to speak; communication is the only way.

We still speak Dutch at home. It was important for us to have the children keep up their Dutch since some of our family don't speak English, and they would feel terribly deprived if they could no longer communicate with this next generation. And we knew the kids could retain their Dutch without compromising their English. We also realized a second language is always a valuable asset.

I guess I still do many things the Dutch way, how I prepare our meals, for example. And in some ways I will always be Dutch, and always be seen as Dutch. My accent will permanently remain a visible part of me. So if being a Canadian means having an invisible heritage, then I will never be a Canadian. But I don't think that's what being a Canadian is all about. I can be a Canadian even though I'll always be Dutch too—I lived the first 35 years of my life as a Dutch person. I couldn't erase that if I wanted to, and I don't want to.

But our children, that's a different story. We're the generation that paved the way, they're the generation that has blended in, and their children will be true Canadians, Canadians to the bone.

When you come to a new country, it's so important to come well prepared, to know exactly what you're getting into. I know people who didn't prepare themselves mentally and who have consequently had a difficult adjustment. It's also important to keep strong the ties between yourself and the family you've left behind. We have gone back for special occasions; it's costly, true, but also priceless.

I love Prince Edward Island, the beauty, the pace, the friendliness and caring of the people. Here people are polite and have time for you. In Holland people tend to be more brusque. If you get pushed aside on a street or in a crowd, no one apologizes. The Dutch have a serious congestion problem; here we live immersed in unspoiled nature. Charlottetown is only 15 minutes away for those times when we need to be there. My children, two of whom are married, all live on the Island. Life is quite perfect.

Canada has so many opportunities for those not afraid of working and giving their best. I was able to turn my hobby into a successful business that will take me right to my retirement. And Canada imposes so few limitations and restrictions as compared to Europe. As an example, when I applied for my cheese-making license, no one ever asked me if I knew how to make cheese. They just assumed that I wouldn't be applying for a license if I didn't. No one asked to see a diploma. That's a Canadian trait, I think.

The opportunities for my children are endless. My oldest and his wife now own their own dairy farm on the Island, a dream that would never have been realized in Holland. My only daughter and her husband, after a brief stint in Manitoba, have come back to the Island to grow potatoes. My third child hasn't quite decided on his future, and my youngest will probably end up on this farm. Because we immigrated, they can now own land, work the land and choose their livelihood and lifestyle.

But for all my wholehearted commitment to Canada, I haven't yet formalized my Canadian citizenship. It's not that I don't feel Canadian enough—my heart belongs to this country. This is, and feels like, my home. I think I'm procrastinating because I'm anxious about the exam I'll be required to take. And because our citizenship has no bearing on our everyday lives, it keeps being pushed down on our list of priorities. As landed immigrants, the only thing we miss out on is being able to vote. We certainly pay the same taxes.

However, if suddenly there were to be changes afoot that would threaten our lifestyle, then our Canadian citizenship would become an urgent and immediate priority. We are here to stay. Our land, our livelihood, our children, our whole life—the things we cherish are all here. This is the only place for us.

Lothar Bode

The bungalow roof reverberates the summer rainstorm's cadence like tautly stretched deerskin. Inside, Lothar Bode casts an ear to the storm while navigating comfortably through the narrative of his life's journey. Haste seems unbefitting; there are many storied waters to ply, divergent channels to explore.

A former German soldier, prisoner of war, bush worker, stone mason and teacher, his observations bear the razor-sharp acumen of those whose eyes have seen other worlds. Canada, he maintains, is opportunity. The opportunity to graduate from university at age 37 with four young children in tow; to be awarded the university's gold medal for exceptional performance in Honours History.

The opportunity to chair the Track and Field segment of the 1981 Canada Summer Games; to be inducted in 1989 into the Northwestern Ontario Sports Hall of Fame.

For the German teen who vowed to learn English while in a British prison camp, Bode knows much about seizing opportunity and embracing it for a lifetime.

Lothar Bode would be the first to define the path of his journey to Canada as convoluted. "I was born in 1926 in Eisleben, East Germany, in the same block Martin Luther was born several hundred years earlier. My mother died when I was 11; when my father remarried three years later, it seemed a natural time for me to start thinking of leaving home. I had more or less grown out of the family. Two years later I left for good."

The year was 1942 and the menacing tentacles of the Second World War had unfurled over much of continental Europe. Like many other teens of that era nudged into adulthood before their time, Bode had joined the Hitler Youth a few years

earlier and now was being enlisted to help relocate tens of thousands of Berlin school children to the safety of Poland and the easternmost borders of Germany. "In retrospect, I wondered why we were moving children out of Berlin when we were supposed to be winning. You privately asked yourself those questions, but didn't dare come to conclusions because you were tied to the system."

Six months later Bode was recruited to an anti-aircraft unit, traditionally not a training ground for boys under the age of enlistment. But the military, increasingly short of manpower, was turning to its youth corps to plug the gaps precipitated by heavy casualties. With his fellow teenage comrades Bode would now plunge onto the actual battle ground. In a peculiar move to lend this scheme a semblance of civility, the military decreed that the youth would continue their schooling by day and participate in the war by night.

"The military had become my home, my parent even. It provided me with everything. Yet I lived knowing things could go wrong. I witnessed indescribable sacrifice and constantly carried the burden of knowing I could be the next casualty. It's not an upbringing I would recommend."

The following year Bode began training as a pilot in Belgium. "But in the fall of 1944 our unit was grounded since there was neither aircraft nor fuel to keep us in the air. So I became a paratrooper and was sent into infantry service. In January, 1945, in Alsace, France, 109 of us went into battle and only 17 came out; we were decimated."

By now desperate, the ailing regime shoved the survivors back into service, this time on the Dutch border. It was there, three months before the war's end, that Bode was taken prisoner. He was 19 years old.

For the next three years he was shuffled from one British prison camp to the next. "Even though the war had ended I was held for another three years because in 1945 the Allies found themselves with over five million German prisoners of war. And you don't send five million men home just like that. So you put them to work in the coal mines, navy depots and agriculture. When you do release them you start with the old ones and those you can't get much work out of. Being young and fit, I was kept until May, 1948."

Bode's prison years began in Ostend, Belgium, and it was there he first showed his resolve to make the most of his time in captivity. "We were 56,000 prisoners including some who spoke English. Here was my chance to learn a new language. The incentive was there too; English newspapers were available from the guards and if I could read them I would know how Germany was faring. So I compiled lists of words in notebooks I had made by stitching empty cement bags together and each day I studied these lists. I also volunteered for work outside the compound, which gave me the chance to practise speaking with the guards. That plus the English I'd learned in school was enough to get me through the newspapers within a few weeks."

But Bode also spent his time trying to escape, and for that he was transferred to Colchester, England, two months later. There he served as an interpreter. His second transfer was to a small, solitary prison camp near Stonehenge in Wiltshire, where he befriended an officer who helped him land a job as the camp's payroll clerk. "He was a world-wise man and a linguist, having studied both in England and at the Sorbonne, and he spoke fluent German. We spent a good deal of time together conversing only in English during many long walks to Stonehenge."

As Bode's fluency increased, he was motivated to organize English classes for his fellow prisoners, some of which he ended up teaching himself. Sensing Bode's intelligence and his determination to put his incarcerated time to good use, his officer friend suggested he apply for a course in modern history being offered for young Germans who were reasonably fluent in English. Its purpose was to persuade the selected prisoners to begin embracing democratic ideologies.

Bode was promptly accepted and soon found himself immersed in the study of British-German relations and German history and foreign policy. "The discussions were often heated but always stimulating. Our final class trip was to London, the very seat of Britishness, an eye-opener for those of us who had grown up under a completely different system. There's no denying, when I finally came out of Britain it was as an Anglophile."

One of the few prisoners to return to Germany fluently bilingual, Bode re-enrolled in high school and obtained his diploma at age 22, but already was beginning to cast his eyes on different shores. "When

I left England I knew in my heart I wouldn't be staying in Europe. I had seen a much broader world and, in truth, I'd always been a doubter of German politics. For one thing, I could never understand why Hitler had declared war on America. But to voice those opinions during the war would have been to invite trouble. So instead I had observed and kept my mouth shut."

Though his hometown was now in the newly defined East Germany, Bode was able to live in West Germany with an aunt while he finished school. She had previously taught at a private school in Philadelphia from 1915 to 1920, and now offered encouragement as he began considering emigration. When three of her American friends agreed to sponsor him and the United States re-opened its doors to German immigrants, he was one of the first to apply. It would take another two years for his application to be processed. In the interim he apprenticed and obtained his credentials as a stone mason.

"Then my visa was cancelled because a new American law decreed that former members of the Hitler Youth could not become citizens of the United States. But in the meantime I had also applied to Canada and received a Canadian visa. Then unexpectedly the American law was amended so that I now could emigrate to the United States after all. So I ended up with two valid visas in two different passports and neither country knew I had documentation for the other."

Bode travelled to New York and lived with his sponsor in Pennsylvania for the next four months. "Then one day I was phoned by an American friend who simply said, 'Lothar, use your Canadian visa if you still have it, get a re-entry permit and leave for awhile. Uncle Sam has plans for you.' My friend's father was on the draft board, hence the inside knowledge."

Bode told his employer he had to visit a friend in Hamilton, Ontario, then departed for the Buffalo-Fort Erie border. Predictably, his request for a re-entry permit was met with suspicion: many Americans intent on dodging the draft were also seeking entry into Canada. However US border officials lacked the hard evidence they needed to detain him, thus issued the document and allowed him to pass. "The permit was just to keep the American door open. Assuming things worked out in Canada, I had no intention of returning to the States."

But Bode's difficulties were not yet over. In Fort Erie a Canadian customs agent was concerned that he had recently entered the United States on a valid visa, and was now presenting valid documentation for Canada. His scepticism was heightened by Ottawa's discovery, mere days earlier, of a passport racket at the Canadian consulate in Rome. So Bode and the busload of passengers he was travelling with were detained while immigration officials awaited direction from Ottawa. Three hours later word came that his entry was being allowed.

Fresh off the bus in Hamilton, Bode was recruited as an interpreter by a frantic immigration officer who had twenty Displaced Persons to process, not one of whom spoke English. Bode obliged and the officer reciprocated by finding him a brick-laying job. He started work the following day.

When he was laid off for the winter Bode headed north to Kapuskasing to cut pulpwood. "That's when I discovered the meaning of Canadian space. The train from Toronto went on and on. In the early evening I asked the conductor when we would get there and he replied, '8:30.' And I said, 'Great, another hour and a half.' And he said, 'No, 8:30 tomorrow night.'"

The following June, 1952, Bode landed a second job on the merit of his linguistic abilities. Hired as Field Organizer for the Lumber and Sawmill Workers' Union, he was sent to Port Arthur where more than half of the 10,000 lumberjacks in the region spoke fluent German and little English. "They were Ukrainians, Hungarians, Czechoslovakians and Yugoslavs who had spent years in German work camps. They had come to Canada as Displaced Persons or refugees and thousands of them ended up working in the bush.

"My mission was to visit the lumber camps to determine whether working and living conditions were being adhered to according to the collective agreement, and to process and settle grievances. Occasionally conditions were appalling: workers sleeping on straw and under the same roof as the horses, undrinkable water, that sort of thing. Many operators hired immigrants right off the boats so they'd be naive as to what working conditions were considered acceptable in Canada. More than once I brought in government health inspectors to close down a camp. It was a challenging job but at two dollars an hour, I was making big money."

Three years later Bode became the treasurer of his Local, which had built up its membership from 1,700 in 1952 to 11,000 in 1955 and was now one of the largest Locals in Canada. In the same year Bode rose to become the chief liaison for the lumber and sawmill Locals of Northern Ontario, which meant negotiating collective agreements with 54 major pulp and paper companies and sawmills. "My job was to prepare the negotiations and strive for reasonable goals. The work was staggering, but we managed to do it without a single strike."

In the meantime Bode had met and fallen in love with a young woman who was living in Winnipeg. "She was the sister of a colleague who had become a good friend. On our second date, in April 1953, we attended a symphony concert in Winnipeg, and when she came to Port Arthur for our third meeting, I proposed marriage. She said she'd think about it. She phoned from Winnipeg a week later to say, 'September 19 will be fine.'

"In June I left for Toronto on union business and was kept away until two days before the wedding. In the meantime Georgette had moved to Port Arthur, found us an apartment and made all the wedding arrangements. All I had to do was sign the papers at city hall and get a haircut."

By 1956 the stress of Bode's job was beginning to wear him down. The following year his doctor bluntly ordered him to quit his job. "He said if I didn't, I'd shortly be the richest man in the graveyard. So, although I had a family to feed, I began looking for less stressful work and a saner schedule."

Bode turned down offers in management from two large pulp and paper companies, opting instead to start his own business. "I'd always enjoyed bricklaying and had some skill in that area—I knew I could build a straight chimney—so I went into masonry. Over the next few years I employed up to eight people, always paying union wages. But we couldn't seem to break even and eventually the business dwindled to just me working alone. And of course there was never any work in winter.

"One winter I ended up making kitchen cabinets for a friend who had admired the ones I'd built for our own home. That made me decide to take a course in cabinet making, but when I went to register the class was already full." Instead, at his wife's suggestion, he enrolled as a part-time student at the Lakehead Institute of Arts, Science and Technology, and quickly discovered his propensity for literature and history. Although he knew nothing of Canadian history at the beginning of the course, he had secured that class's top mark by year's end. The following year he studied full-time and did masonry on the side to pay the bills.

By the end of Bode's second year his professors were encouraging him to transfer to university. The family moved to London where he enrolled in an Honours History degree program at the University of Western Ontario, his wife's alma mater. When he graduated in 1963 he was armed with the university's gold medal for history, a major scholarship for study at Harvard University, and 43 job offers. "Being a student was very fulfilling, but we were also stone broke, $12,000 in debt and had a fifth child on the way. So returning to Port Arthur made the most sense, and there I began teaching history, geography and German at Hillcrest High School."

Until Bode's appointment two years later to Assistant Head of the school's history department, the family's financial situation continued to be precarious; Bode calculated his salary in those two years to be less than that of a floor sweeper at the local paper mill. But in 1968 his situation improved when he was appointed head of the History Department at nearby Hammarskjold High School, a position he held until his retirement in 1983.

During his career, Bode was instrumental in helping to revamp the high school history curriculum and introduce experimental courses in philosophy, sociology and American History for the senior classes. Midway through his teaching years he travelled to France on sabbatical to study the European Common Market, and from 1965 to 1968 he served on the Board of Governors of Lakehead, by then a university, as the first representative of the Alumni Association.

As diverse as his working years have been, Bode nonetheless found time to round them out with a singular voluntary commitment to the sport of track and field. In Germany he had routinely competed in decathlons, and once settled in Port Arthur, decided he wanted to reactivate his involvement in the sport. "However, when the senior girls began outsprinting me in the 200 metre run, I realized my own competitive days were over."

Rather than withdraw from the sport altogether, he set about revitalizing the city's ailing track and field program and over the next 16 years helped transform it into a top-notch club. As coach he took several athletes as far as the national finals; three became champions. He designed and built a portable indoor track, and organized and presided over dozens of local track meets and several national competitions. He rose to the national executive of the Canadian Track and Field Organization and coached the Ontario track team at the first Canada Summer Games in Halifax-Dartmouth. He officiated at five national championships as well as the 1967 Pan-American Games in Winnipeg, and the 1973 Pacific Games in Toronto. Following the Pacific Games he withdrew from the sport to spend more time with his young family, but was vigorously recruited in 1980 to run the track and field portion of the 1981 Canada Summer Games, held in Thunder Bay.

By his own admission, it was a formidable undertaking, requiring a new track and field facility and 139 officials to run a full Olympic program, save for a marathon, over a five-day schedule. Formidable, especially since Bode's health had been seriously eroding in recent years. "I had planned to stay in the background during the Games, raking the sandpit, replacing the high jump bars, and so on. But then the track and field chairman resigned suddenly and I was pressed into taking his place. I have pictures of the event and I look like a ghost in them."

By the time he retired from teaching in 1983 Bode had suffered several minor strokes and two heart attacks. "I was selected for a quadruple bypass in 1986, when I was practically beyond redemption; I had been declining for so long. It's a miracle I'm well today."

Well enough to attend his induction into the Northwestern Ontario Sports Hall of Fame in 1989. Well enough to enjoy retirement with his wife on the outskirts of Thunder Bay. Well enough to enjoy his grandchildren, and content to have left the mark of an accomplished mason on the homes of his children.

"Opportunity abounds here. My parents had nothing after the war and the prospect for my future in Germany was poor. For one thing, I would have never gone to university. Here we've had a good and varied life and we raised seven kids and helped them get through university. That could have never happened in Europe."

My gratitude to them is difficult to put into words.
They have conveyed to me that in Canada there is a broad sense of
fairness, which transcends national and cultural differences.
That makes me passionate about Canada.

I came away from England with the attitude that if I could find one way or another to discover my place in Canada, things would work out. That attitude has served me well. It didn't work as well for me south of the border for reasons other than the draft; the American psyche is far less tolerant of the political views of newcomers. I've always been to the left politically, and when I spoke favourably about a democratic president the response would be an irate "What do *you* know about the American constitution and American politics?"

In Canada I've found support for almost everything I've ventured to do over the years. The first principal I worked for had spent three years in a German prison camp, which put our backgrounds at opposite ends of the spectrum. And yet he was a most agreeable, fairminded man, and he became a very good friend. He expected his staff to do their jobs, work hard, and he supported them 100 percent. Looking back at my many colleagues and professors, I was always readily accepted. I cherished this acceptance, especially when it came, as it often did, from people who themselves had made notable contributions to society. Several of my colleagues had served in the British or Canadian military during the war, yet they never judged my background nor made it an issue. I felt appreciated, and never excluded.

My gratitude to them is difficult to put into words. They have conveyed to me that in Canada there is a broad sense of fairness, which transcends national and cultural differences. That makes me passionate about Canada.

What also makes me passionate is the wealth of opportunity available, even now. In my day it was astounding. After less than a year in the bush I had the money to repay a loan from my sponsor, help fund my stepmother's passage to Canada and buy a building lot. And I still had $800 left over. That's opportunity! Unfortunately, and this is something many Canadians don't realize, the rate of inflation has increased by 1000 percent. In 1952 I bought a brand new, six-cylinder Chevrolet for $2200. Such a car would cost $21,000 today. Inflation has diminished opportunity, and yet the opportunity is still there if you're willing to look harder and put forth your best effort.

It is human nature that opportunity is often not fully treasured by those who have lived with it all their lives. They overlook it or take it for granted. That same complacent attitude also plagues the destiny of our natural resources. Perhaps we don't realize that this precious, finite wealth is being abused; perhaps we don't have the collective nerve to say it has to stop. We could be much more self-sufficient if we cherished these treasures and used them carefully for our needs. There's so much we can grow and produce here. Our food shouldn't have to be brought in from Mexico and other parts of the globe.

Several of my professors at the University of Western Ontario kept telling us that the important thing to understand in the modern world economy is that the United States is no longer self-sufficient. It has to supplement its resources from outside. That reality has resulted in a world-wide struggle for resources. And our Canadian resources are showing the strain. Look at our fishing grounds, for example. Not only are we there, but so are the Americans, Portuguese, Spanish, Germans, British, Japanese and Norwegians, all over-harvesting. It's no wonder our stocks are being depleted.

Our forests have suffered the same abuse. During my three years as a Field Organizer I travelled to almost every lumber camp between the Quebec and Manitoba borders, and I came to know the bush well. I observed what was there, what was being harvested and what was being over-harvested. In 1956-57 I carried out an extensive study of the forest practises of 25 or 30 timber producers and paper producers in the province, and presented my findings to the government. Some of the companies were outraged and the Ontario Deputy Minister of Lands and Forests resented my intrusion on the status quo. But the information needed to come out. Many companies harvesting the forests didn't give a damn then and some still don't. It's the same in other parts of Canada. And those trying to preserve the forests are branded as radicals, hippies and ignorant bums.

It's also happening with agriculture. Instead of nurturing a crop for harvest, we're basically mining the soil the same way we mine the forests. Witness the dust clouds on the prairies and the thousands of orchards in southern Ontario that have given way to urban sprawl. The people who abuse our resources and invent the lies to justify the abuse, these people I can look in the eye and say "You are stealing from my children as well as your own. What you are doing is morally outrageous."

We, as a nation of caring people, should be able to develop the dynamics to lay these special-interest groups low, to say, "You've had a free rein long enough. You've exploited these resources and taken from a heritage that doesn't belong to you."

The Native people have a saying: *The land and the forests belong to the generations yet unborn.* That is as it should be. Also with our water supply, which is becoming increasingly threatened as our burgeoning neighbour to the south thirsts for more than their own rivers can provide.

I believe a good part of our ills have come to us via the television. It spews out garbage, violence, murder and mayhem, and distorts our thinking. Many analyses of current political events are shallow or just plain wrong. And we Canadians just sit and digest what's fed to us, often from across the border. We buy into their messages rather than take advantage of the opportunities that exist for us here. We're lulled into believing, for example, that a global economy is best, even though we realize that such a system never favours the individual over the collective. We lap up everything American television dishes out, and we let it dilute our sense of nationalism. Then we wonder why things go wrong here in Canada. As a teacher I've been pulling my hair out over television for a long time.

When I immigrated I came to become a Canadian, not a German living in Canada. That doesn't mean I must relinquish all of my German culture—we go to the German delicatessen every week for *wurst* which I couldn't live without, and I enjoy German poetry and literature—but it does mean I should leave German political agendas behind. The political agendas of the old country have no place in the new homeland. If our focus for Canada is reasonably unified, then it follows that our cultural diversity as a nation will be our strength. All around us are fine examples of this diversity and strength. You see it here in the gradual acceptance of more sensible methods of forest management and harvesting that have been introduced by the Scandinavians. And the Italian community in this area has made substantial artistic contributions, particularly in architecture. And then there are the restaurants that bring the flavours of other countries to us.

I can say without hesitation that Canada is my home. Georgette has been the greatest influence on my last 45 years. She was born in Fort Frances and grew up in this region. She understood the people here and has shaped my thinking toward them. She has guided me in realizing that we are neither easterners nor westerners. She encouraged me to enroll in university, offered unwavering moral support and even tutored me through parts of my English courses. In a very real sense she shaped me as a Canadian.

My Canadianism has also been shaped by our seven children and their spouses. They were born here, had their schooling here and see the world through Canadian eyes. There will always be differences in our perception of this nation, yet we are unanimous in our thinking that life is good here.

When I die they can scatter my ashes in the bush. I'm satisfied with the way our lives have gone. It took me 23 years to make it back to Germany for a visit. That trip reinforced what I have known for a long time: that nothing exists there for me anymore except my ties with my extended family. (My immediate family members all emigrated to Canada in due course.)

Recently Georgette and I returned to Eisleben and toured the renovated medieval church of St. Peter's. There stood the baptismal font over which both Martin Luther and I had been baptized. I felt the connection with Eisleben then, not as a religious stir, but as a distant memory of my past. A past that now exists only to remind me of how far I have come.

Carlos Caçola

AVEIRO, PORTUGAL—HALIFAX, NOVA SCOTIA

It used to be that when Carlos Caçola entered a photography com-
petition, his fellow participants had good reason to cringe.
Over the years he's walked away with numerous awards of impor-
tance for work that's been called art as much as photography.
During his career he was recognized as a Master of Photographic
Arts by the Professional Photographers of Canada Inc., and rose to
the ranks of Canada's top photographers.
Until his retirement in 1997, Carlos, as he is known professionally,
worked his magic in his home studio or on a windy Maritime shore;
manipulated lenses, lighting, backdrops; created a world and then
froze it for all time.
But a vulnerable side persists as well. When Carlos speaks, quiet
notes of pain often hang suspended in the undercurrents of his voice.
The quicksilver hurt of a hard and impoverished childhood is there;
so are the eddies of regret at having forsaken a cherished homeland
in search of better opportunities on a foreign shore. And though
three decades have passed, a wellspring of loneliness continues to
linger just below the surface.

When Carlos Caçola was 13 years old, he decided it would be less traumatic to drop out of school than to stay and suffer the humiliation of failing the year. Always a keen student, he had been struggling since first grade to keep up without the bene- fit of textbooks, which his mother couldn't afford. "The system was supposed to buy books for the poor kids. But when you saw who was getting the free books, those whose parents worked in the army or gov- ernment, you knew the system wasn't working."

Fortunately an astute teacher understood the boy's dilemma and counselled his mother that if leaving school was to be the only option,

he should at least have the opportunity to work in a setting that capitalized on his considerable artistic promise.

And so while his friends continued their education, Carlos reported for work at one of the ceramics factories for which Aveiro is still famous. Unofficially, it marked the end of a difficult childhood that had been further exacerbated by disease and death.

"I was the second child in a poor family, born during World War II. I didn't suffer the direct ravages of war, but we often went hungry since our food was mostly being shipped off to feed the troops, both Allied and German. I know how hunger feels."

When Carlos was five he developed a progressive bone decalcification affecting one leg, and within a year was using a crutch to get around. "That same year my father contracted and died of tuberculosis, rampant in the country at that time. Because looking after him had taken all of my mother's energy, I didn't get medical attention in time and I ended up spending much of my childhood in pain, with a deformed leg. I also spent much of it alone since my mother was afraid I would hurt myself playing with other children.

"At school I tried to get my own books since my mother was busy struggling to earn enough money as a seamstress to keep my older sister and me fed. I was a child trying to be a grown man, doing things for myself that I saw other parents doing for their children."

At the ceramics factory Carlos was to train as an unpaid apprentice for six months, first in design work and later as a painter of ceramics. After only two months, however, his employers acknowledged his singular talent by putting him on the payroll. Meanwhile, because walking was becoming a near impossibility, he rode a bicycle back and forth to work. "By now my one foot wasn't even touching the floor when I stood and I couldn't straighten my leg." Pain was a constant companion.

One day when Carlos was 17, his physician observed him hobbling across the street. "He called me into his office and said, 'We have to do something about your leg.' And I told him I couldn't afford it. And he said to leave it with him, he would think of something. I had known him since childhood and considered him almost as a father.

"He had it all arranged a few days later. He had spoken to the owner of the factory where I worked and together they were going to pay for my surgery. When I asked how I could repay him, he said that he wanted me to paint a series of water colours for him. He had always been very supportive of my work."

Carlos travelled to northern Portugal for the complex surgery, which involved removing the head of the femur and attaching the femur to the pelvis using a platinum plate and four screws. He was hospitalized for a year. Even though the pain in his leg remained intense, he returned to work following his convalescence and also resumed his interrupted education by enrolling in night school. Mathematics, which had intimidated him in the past, quickly became his strongest subject. He soon discovered a flair for mechanical design and selected his course load accordingly.

But poverty continued to loom over him and Carlos could see no way to break out of its harsh grip. "At the factory I worked very hard since I was being paid by the piece. But it all went to my mother to help make ends meet. In my group of friends I was always the poor one, the one with no money in his pocket." Although his heart resisted, Carlos began thinking that emigration might be the only alternative to a lifetime of destitution.

In his early twenties he married a young woman he had met while convalescing in northern Portugal, and a daughter and son followed soon after. At around the same time he changed jobs at the factory. "My boss knew I'd always been interested in photography, and I'd borrowed his Voigtlander on numerous weekends. In the factory we had a studio where all the ceramics were photographed for the company catalogues. He offered me a studio job and since it meant a bit more money, I accepted."

But still poverty punctuated Carlos' every struggle, like a bitter aftertaste on his tongue, elusive somehow and yet always there. "Being poor gets its grasp on you and although you work to get out of it, you see your family slowly falling behind. True, you are not starving and you have a little apartment and some furniture, most of which you've built yourself, but you know in your heart you'll never get ahead. The only way out was to leave Portugal, it seemed."

Carlos' sister and her husband had immigrated to Canada some years earlier, and he now began taking steps to do the same. But he soon discovered his disability presented a major stumbling block. His permanent limp was a concern for Canadian authorities in Lisbon, who were suspicious that he might have been afflicted with tuberculosis as a child. Back and forth he travelled to Lisbon where he was subjected to one medical procedure after another. "I went at least six times, using up money I didn't have. Each time they stuck a tube down my throat and into my stomach to siphon some liquid for analysis. The last time I went I told them that was it, I would drop my application if they called me for more testing."

In all it would take four years for Carlos to be granted a special permit for a one-year conditional entry into Canada. If he passed a medical examination at the end of that year, he and his family would then qualify for landed immigrant status and be allowed to remain.

"I found those conditions stressful, especially since the immigration officials said I had to take my family with me. I pleaded unsuccessfully with them to let me go alone so I would have only myself to transport back in case it didn't work out. But my doctor said to go anyway, the colder climate would be good for me. So we arrived in 1963. My sister had to post a $5000 bond, a lot of money in those days, for our transportation back in case I was to get sick. But I passed the medical exam at the end of the year and she got her money back.

"For the first little while we stayed with my sister in Dartmouth while I looked for a job. I found that very trying, to have my family dependent on her like that. And she would say to me, 'Why are you so worried? You have a roof over your head and food to eat.' When we left on our own I was coping with many things, including learning English. I remember coming back to my sister's place many times ... just to cry."

But within a few months Carlos found viable employment at a Halifax photography studio. "I was very fortunate in that I was able to find work in my field right away, that I didn't have to start out as a labourer." Though largely self-taught, he attended several courses including an advanced course in portraiture at the famed Memramcook Institute in New Brunswick where he studied under the American Master Photographer and Instructor, Joseph Zeltsman. His colleagues were not long in taking note of his artistic abilities. In 1971 he captured three major awards in the Maritime Professional Photographers Association competition, including runner-up for *Photographer of the Year.*

However, his marriage had been floundering for some time, chronically plagued by his wife's fragile health and the financial and emotional duress of relocating and starting over. When she decided to return to her native Spain alone, Carlos was left to parent two preschoolers. "She just couldn't cope. We were so far from home, we didn't speak the language and she was not well. It was very hard on her and on me too, a single father to two youngsters in a land that was still alien to me."

The following year Carlos made the arduous decision to send the children back to Portugal for a time. "My sister had been a tremendous help in the year following my marriage breakdown, but she had given up her job to look after the children and I couldn't expect her to continue doing that. In the meantime my mother and stepfather were pleading to have them come live with them in Portugal. So I finally decided to let them go until I could get myself better established.

"I couldn't go back myself. I had too many debts to pay, all the money I had borrowed for our travels. And to be truthful, I would have been ashamed to come home defeated and poorer than I had been when I left. I would have been considered a failure, a quitter, and I would have seen myself that way too. So going back for good was not an option at that time. But I did go back to visit my kids as often as I could."

When Carlos remarried in 1975, his son and daughter returned to Canada. "In preparation for their arrival Phyllis and I bought a house and spent our wedding night installing a hot water tank, very romantic. During our honeymoon we refinished the house and fixed up bedrooms for the children. I was very lucky to find Phyllis. The children couldn't have had a better stepmother."

In 1981 Carlos became Dalhousie University's official photographer, a position of prestige, but one that also left him physically exhausted much of the time. "I was promised an assistant but that never materialized so my days were long and unpredictable. I might be called at 4:30, just as I was packing up for the day, to do a photo shoot at the president's house that evening. And often they'd need the lab work done early next morning to get the prints to the media on time. That's how it went. I'd be lugging my equipment across campus several times a day, and my doctor finally said, 'It's a miracle you're still walking with what you're doing to your leg and spine.'"

Although Carlos had done well at his first Maritime Professional Photographers Association competition in 1971, he didn't enter again until 1987. "The registration and conference fees were very expensive. Added to that was the cost of preparing entries, the supplies, developing, framing, etc. I just didn't have the money for that in the early years. When the kids grew up and left home it became financially easier, and then I started to compete again."

His colleagues likely remember 1986, 1987 and 1988 as the years he steamrolled back into the world of provincial and national competitive photography and came away with six top prizes including the Maritime Professional Photographers Association's *Photographer of the Year* award. In that time the Professional Photographers of Canada also bestowed upon him their highest honour, designating him as a Master of Photographic Arts. Although he kept his prominence low-key, Carlos was now indisputably among the elite of Canadian photographers.

By 1991 Carlos had also garnered his third *Award for Photographic Excellence* from Kodak Canada. Over the next few years he captured numerous Maritime and national awards in almost every existing category of competition including commercial, artistic illustration, and press photography in the category of sports. "I constantly strove to produce something different, to be unique and innovative," Carlos offers by way of explanation. "I think I was more a photographic artist than a photographer. You can be technically good, but it is the artistic part that helps create something different."

For all his artistic accomplishments, however, Carlos lived with the knowledge that his employer, Dalhousie University, had capitalized more on his skills as a technician than on his artistic talent. And in 1992, after more than a decade in their employ, he knew the time had come to make some choices. His health was deteriorating. He was 55 years old, severely restricted in his mobility and in constant pain. He could go on long-term disability, or he could strike out on his own, as an independent in control of his work conditions and schedule. He chose the latter.

For the next five years he worked diligently out of his home studio, quietly producing privately commissioned work that continued to dazzle. "I was finally free to control how my day should go, and it was a wonderful freedom. I worked around my limitations; I had a cart for my equipment and often my wife or son or son-in-law helped with the heavy work. On the days I was by myself and moving heavy props around, well, I knew I'd feel it the next day."

But in the spring of 1997 Carlos's health finally forced him to close his business for good. "Call it quits while you are still mobile," his orthopaedic surgeon had tersely instructed. "You've worked 47 years; that's enough." Although not thrilled to be so suddenly spirited into retirement, Carlos conceded it was his only realistic option.

"They now say that what I had as a child and teen was an advanced case of Perthes' Disease. I've had more surgery since I've been in Canada and we recently looked at the possibility of a hip implant, but my pelvis and femur are just too fragile. And as a result of the heavy load I imposed on the joint over the years, arthritis has become an added problem. On my longer walks I now have to use two canes in order to keep the discomfort bearable."

For now Carlos has reached an uneasy truce with his forced retirement. "I'm still adjusting. I always thought I'd be working for the rest of my life. In spirit I still feel young but there are times my body feels like a hundred years old. Some days I feel relieved to be finished with work; other days I wonder if I've lost my purpose in life."

And what does his future hold? Less yard work, for one thing, since the home the Caçolas had built for them in late 1998 has "a front yard the size of a postage stamp. So there'll be less grass to cut and snow to shovel, two jobs I don't do well." He'll exercise his camera as the mood dictates, and plans an eventual return to painting.

"I've recently turned 62 and I should be relaxing, finally. But when you grow up fighting for all your needs, it's hard to learn to enjoy what seemingly gets handed to you on a silver platter. That's what I'm trying to do now, just relax and enjoy what life has given me."

*Immigration is one of the biggest dramas of
a person's life ... I wonder if the material gains are worth
the separation, the suffering.*

If I knew then what I know now, I honestly don't think I would have immigrated. It's not that I regret being here, it's that the adjustment has been so difficult and stressful, and it's been going on for so long. I left my extended family behind and still miss them very much. My chronically ill mother always reminded me in every telephone conversation that she could die without seeing me again. That always burdened me with guilt and also frustration because there wasn't much I could do about it. I have been back to Portugal a few times but it's time-consuming and expensive, not like getting in your car and driving for a few hours.

I don't really understand why I still feel so strongly about Portugal. My childhood was not easy. Times were hard and we were very poor— and yet there are very good memories too. Most of our neighbours were also poor but we would invent games and play together. Maybe it's the sense of community, the acceptance I experienced there that seems missing from my life at times. Maybe the trauma of my childhood left a permanent mark that continues to affect my happiness even today.

Immigration is one of the biggest dramas of a person's life. As an immigrant I can't help but feel permanently displaced. I wonder if the material gains are worth the separation, the suffering. We have a word in Portuguese, *saudade,* which means intense homesickness. That is what I feel sometimes. It's not that I don't appreciate that Canada is a good country. And I know I've had freedoms and opportunities here that wouldn't have been available in Portugal. It's hard to put it in words.

Many of us Portuguese immigrants feel that our old country is like a mother who couldn't provide. We were forced to take our talents to another country, someone else's mother, for opportunities not available at home. Even today Portugal keeps on exporting its talent rather than finding ways to keep us home. I find that very tragic.

My wife is Canadian, and my children consider Canada their

home. My son hardly speaks Portuguese and my grandchildren don't know it at all. And yet, I am constantly reminded that I am an outsider here. I've experienced discrimination on the job and even though my work has been recognized and acknowledged, I know I've had to work harder than my colleagues just to stay on an equal footing. My English is pretty good but sometimes people pretend not to understand me on the telephone. But when I lose my patience and tell them they're annoying me, they understand me right away.

When I go back to Portugal I'm reminded that I'm an outsider there too. The country is not happy to have us back. They blame all sorts of things on the emigrants who swell the summer population, like rising costs and increased traffic accidents. And they make jokes about the way we speak Portuguese; they ridicule our accent and the way we inadvertently slip English words into our conversation. This type of derision I find demeaning.

That's why immigration is the biggest drama in life. We are divided. We belong neither here nor there. We are restless, always searching and longing. We are like trees that have been transplanted but some of the roots have been left behind. It's a very subtle kind of suffering, and maybe I'm more sensitive to it than others are. When I discuss it with other immigrants, most don't seem as affected by all this. Perhaps it's because they're afraid to talk about what's going on in their hearts.

I'm determined to keep at least some of my Portuguese identity. A few years ago I started reading Portuguese to spruce up my knowledge of the language. I'm part of a Portuguese society, I've found people to converse with and I've taught Portuguese language classes. I do Portuguese crossword puzzles and listen to Portuguese programming on the short-wave radio my wife bought me a few years ago. I've become very comfortable with writing Portuguese and for a while was a columnist for a London, Ontario based Portuguese newspaper. When I write, long-forgotten words just seem to come back to me.

I do love Canada very much, its natural beauty and its people. But I worry about the cavalier way our politicians seem to be operating and wonder if we're not entering a phase of pseudo-democracy. Portugal was under dictatorship when I left, but I see unsettling parallels when comparing their government's attitude 32 years ago with our government's today. Too often we see our leaders willing to sell dangerous technology and do business with dubious regimes that have abysmal human rights records. All in the name of job creation, our leaders say. Well, why don't they import less and let Canadians manufacture more of what we need, like toothbrushes, winter coats or whatever. To that, they answer that Canadians wouldn't work for low wages. But Canadians would. Just look at all the people working in minimum-wage situations across the country.

I wish Canadians would react a bit more passionately to questionable political decisions. We shouldn't always be so reasonable and tolerant.

I know there's much to be thankful for: my Canadian family, a new home, a fulfilling career, and the option to have taken early retirement. But I'm also resigned to a lifetime of unsettledness. A lifetime of wondering 'what if.' I think the searching will be with me always. Sometimes it fades away for awhile but it never leaves you completely. My mother's death a year ago brought it all back to the forefront again. I grieved her passing of course, but carried the added burden of guilt over not having been there for her in her final, fragile years. It's a heavy load for an immigrant to bear, and it doesn't seem to go away.

I would never consider immigrating again, it's just too painful. But I couldn't go back to Portugal either. It wouldn't be the same, and I couldn't go through the resettlement experience again. To leave now would be to re-open my heart to the same turmoils and anxieties. The tug-of-war would be as intense as it was the first time around. And, paradoxically, there would be much about my life in Canada that I would miss.

In a recent Christmas card to my cousin I wrote, in acknowledgement that we in the extended family had all grown up poor but had done well to better ourselves financially, "We may be suffering in other ways but at least we've managed to shake off the grip of childhood poverty." And his response scoffed at me. "You emigrants," he wrote back, "had it easy compared to those who stayed."

That left me outraged. The people back home all think I came over and immediately found the good life. They think they're the expert on the immigration experience, but they've no idea how I toiled and despaired during those early years. And they don't know anything about my loneliness.

Blessed are those who've never left home. They have the luxury of being blissfully oblivious to this constant vacillating of the soul, this yearning that never completely goes away.

Bernard Callebaut

In 1982, a young entrepreneur travelled to Calgary and in the heartland of black liquid gold, founded a fortune so unlikely that the locals placed bets on whether he would, or would not, survive. Today, Chocolaterie Bernard Callebaut is renowned for its rich, delectable chocolate packaged so exquisitely that patrons invariably are torn between preserving the outer jewel and savouring the treasure buried within. In the distinctive building that houses the operations for 37 North American retail outlets, the Award of Excellence parchments are tastefully arranged on a softly lit wall. The corner office wears its newness well, a fitting stage for Bernard Callebaut, who sits casually behind a massive desk, points out the handsomely framed photographs of cherished family, and endures a silk tie, confessing he rarely wears one.

"I've never been homesick," says the affable Callebaut, who is proficient in four languages. I've not had time for homesickness."

When the young Bernard Callebaut left Belgium for a year of studies in Switzerland, he befriended a student from Thetford Mines, Quebec, who said to him, "Le Canada, c'est un bebe, a country where you can still do just about anything you want." For Callebaut, who was vacillating between joining the family's century-old company and striking out on his own, the comment was germane enough to store for possible future reference.

Born in a small town 35 kilometres north of Brussels, Callebaut well remembers the home of his childhood, nestled snugly beside the family chocolate factory. "Chocolate is what I grew up knowing, but my family of entrepreneurs was not limited to this one product. My father ran the Callebaut Chocolate Factory, established in 1911, and on an adjacent plot of land his brother managed the Callebaut

Bernard Callebaut

Brewery, which the family had founded in 1850. At one point we were also making soft drinks and butter.

"I was twelve or thirteen when I started helping out, unloading trucks, mostly during the holidays and in the summer. At age sixteen or so I began working with the chocolate, but even then I wasn't considering a career in chocolate making; in fact, I was quite adamant that I would do my own thing. To his credit, my father never tried to push me into the business, instead letting it be known that he would approve whatever career I chose. I was grateful for his understanding; I could have been put in a very stressful position."

However, the thought of joining the family business did sit with Callebaut for long periods at a time, and following high school and a mandatory stint in the military which was served in Germany, he tailored his education to allow for that option. He returned to Belgium to complete an engineering degree, then spent a year studying management in Switzerland. "If I was interested in chocolate at all, it was in the production end; hence the degree in electro-mechanical engineering. The management course was to round out my education, after which time I found myself gravitating home to work.

"I discovered I liked working with chocolate, but I was feeling ambivalent about our business. My mother had been running the company by herself since my father's death in 1972, and it was becoming a burden for her. There were those in the family who were jealous of her, and I suggested, 'Sell the place, while we are all still on good terms.' We wouldn't be the first business clan to end up in the courts, communicating only through the lawyers.

"Our situation was typical of the way family businesses tend to go: the first generation founds it, the second enjoys the benefits, and the third, if it's not careful, screws it up. The day negotiations for the sale began was the day I started thinking of leaving Belgium.

"By then our company was manufacturing bulk chocolate in liquid and five-pound solid blocks for sale to chocolatiers throughout the world. My father had never intended the business to become overly large, but at the time of the sale we had 300 people on the payroll and an annual production in excess of 77 million pounds."

The sale of the family business to the Suchard Toblerone Group propelled Callebaut to a personal crossroads of sorts: what would he do now, and where would he do it? "I had decided by then that I liked the chocolate business. I began thinking I could start from scratch as my grandfather had done. After some thinking I opted to go into the handcrafting of small chocolates rather than the manufacture of bulk chocolate." Callebaut spent the following year in Antwerp learning how to make pralines, truffles and chocolate bonbons.

In that time he began shifting his sights to North America. "I found I no longer cared for the confining business climate of Europe, and my prospective market there was already seriously saturated. Belgium alone has about 300 chocolatiers today. What would be the point of being Number 301?"

After collecting information on several provinces and states, Callebaut flew to North America and began travelling around. "It didn't take me long to decide on Canada, a decision based more on idealism and impetuousness than business acumen. Having made that choice, I then travelled to all the major Canadian cities and discovered I liked the west, specifically Calgary. Alberta was teeming with entrepreneurs, mostly in oil and gas, who weren't afraid to take a risk. That type of business climate appealed to me. And also, not insignificantly, there was no European-style chocolate being manufactured there."

Callebaut, an avid skier and hiker, was instantly enthralled with the province's vast natural resources. "I figured any place as blessed by nature as Alberta was bound to have a good future, and I wanted to be part of it. Also, this was my chance to live close to the mountains.

"I'd brought some of my handmade chocolates for people to sample, and when they reacted enthusiastically I became even more convinced Calgary was the city I wanted to do business in. Without any further analysis I sealed my decision at that point, a brash and risky move in retrospect. But there is also risk in analysing your plan to it's minutest detail, in having it become so bogged down that you never get beyond the drafting table. No, I figured if people were spending a few thousand dollars on designer sweaters in this town, and they were, then they wouldn't balk at paying a bit extra for specialty chocolate."

Having decided on the province and city, Callebaut's next task was to pinpoint a location for his novel venture. "I was directed to 17th

Avenue, which is supposedly the upscale corner of town. There I happened to meet a woman who was in the process of closing her specialty kitchen and bath boutique. This was in 1982, an economically disastrous year for Calgary, the year soaring interest rates and a sharply decreased profit margin in the oil and gas industry had snuffed out many local businesses. Perhaps that depressed climate should have heightened my reticence to plunge in, but on the other hand, economic crisis also nets you opportunities in terms of cheap real estate and negotiable rents. And the expensive sweaters were still selling. So I decided to take over the kitchen and bath location."

After solidifying the lease and arranging for several upgrades on the building which was to serve as both factory and retail outlet, Callebaut returned to Belgium to purchase the necessary equipment and arrange for its shipment. "Then I came back to Canada in the fall, started making chocolate, and sold 700 dollars worth on opening day the following March. It sounds dramatic but really, there was no rocket science involved. The whole process was pre-planned and therefore pretty straightforward.

"That first day was a good day's work, considering we were selling a specialty product no one was familiar with. A friend in the business gave me some sage advice—to price my product low initially, and then, as the demand for it grew, gradually increase it to its fair market value. 'If your prices start out high and you're then forced to lower them,' he suggested, 'that'll be the end of your business.' So even though my product was expensive to make, I followed his advice. Of course there were no profits that first year, but then prospective retailers began expressing an interest in franchising in other parts of the city."

Although Callebaut walked a fine line between survival and bankruptcy throughout those early years, he remained unfazed by the whispers of those who thought he must be mad to think he could sell high-priced chocolate in the heartland of petroleum country. "Here, the main business is heavy industry, and if you say you want to make money selling chocolates, they look at you and tell you that's great, but privately they wonder how long you'll survive. One family confided years later that they'd once made bets around their dinner table as to whether I'd make it or go broke.

"But as an entrepreneur, you can't let these odds stress you out if you have a vision and are convinced it's a good one. My vision has stood the test of time: we sold $200,000 worth of chocolate in the first year and doubled that amount in the second. And yet, even with the $200,000 I had in start-up funding, we were nonetheless financially strapped for a long time. The chocolate business is not a cheap business to wrap yourself up in. For the first five years I had no car, but that was hardly a problem since getting around the city on a bicycle was easy enough. The real challenge was to hang in there long enough to start realizing some return on the investment."

Few would deny that Callebaut has adeptly risen to that challenge. Merely a decade later, he had established a handful of stores across the city, taken on a business partner and hopelessly outgrown the 17th Avenue location. "Although our original location had 3500 square feet of floor space, much more than we required when we started, we were now bursting at the seams. Our cold storage, office, staff change rooms and packaging plant were all off-site, a cumbersome way to run a business. By the early '90s we knew the time had come to relocate. In 1994 we invested $4 million and built a facility of 52,000 square feet at Victoria Park, just south of the city's core.

"We settled on Victoria Park simply because at the end of an average workday, 30,000 vehicles drive past our front door on their way home to suburbia. We designed our parking lot to make the commuters' stop quick and convenient, and they've demonstrated they appreciate the efficiency as well as the product: on a typical Valentine's Day more than 2000 customers come through the door."

For Callebaut, who's passion for chocolate includes eating a dozen or so pralines daily, there's nary a venture not possible in this world of black, decadent gold. "Twenty years ago North American chocolate was made overwhelmingly of sugar and usually reserved as a confection for children. But chocolate has undergone a transformation, and people have discovered that it can be deliciously rich and flavourful without being sweet. In some ways, chocolate parallels the evolution of coffee: two decades ago you could get a 15¢ cup of brown water called coffee. Today's coffee is far superior and therefore trendy, pricy and all the rage at the upscale coffee bars."

Callebaut's fine chocolate, it would seem, has decidedly followed, if not leaped ahead of, the coffee trend. Today there are 37 Bernard Callebaut retail outlets throughout North America, and Callebaut himself, at age 47, has won numerous awards and much recognition for both his chocolate and his entrepreneurial acumen. In 1994 he received the Small Businessman of the Year award from the Calgary Chamber of Commerce, and in 1996 and 1997 he captured runner-up 'Prix d'Excellence' awards at the International Chocolate Festival held in Montelimar, France. In 1998 he became the first North American to coup the Festival's coveted top prize.

Although Callebaut is not incessantly driven towards growth and expansion, his Victoria Park facility does have the capacity to manufacture the considerable inventory required for 100 stores. "I'm not obsessed with our growth but I do see the need to plan ahead for it. We don't have specific plans to establish a certain number of stores by a certain time; instead, we focus on steady growth and the nurturing of close working relationships with our retailers.

"All our stores are locally owned dealerships rather than franchises, which means that we make money on the sales of our product line, but don't demand the usual upfront fees and royalties. Once established, a store grosses an average of $300,000 to $350,000 annually."

Although Callebaut's schedule is stretched between marketing, promotion and planning, his favourite work hours are spent on the factory floor, making chocolates. "Up until a few years ago I made chocolates every day, and even now I help out during the busy seasons. But I also enjoy doing promotional work, like chocolate-making demonstrations, at the stores. As for the company's administrative end, I'm happy to leave that up to my capable partner.

"Fortuitously, she is the woman who was closing her kitchen and bath boutique on 17th Avenue back in 1982. She's an interior designer so she also handles the stores' look and the product's packaging and presentation. We buy packaging and ribbon in Europe, and hand-painted ceramics by the truckload from small Portuguese companies. We make only a small profit on them so that our prices are still reasonable, yet our product has a very unique and European look about it. And that has helped to set it apart from the competition, a strategy that's served us well."

Another strategy that's worked well for Callebaut is the emphasis on making employees a genuine part of the business. "When I was working on the factory floor, I discovered that often employees have good ideas but nowhere to go with them. I imagined how frustrating and demoralizing it would be to know you have a good idea but no avenue to an audience for your suggestion. After a while you would begin to think, who cares? In order to avert that attitude, I now hold a weekly meeting with my manufacturing and packing staff, during which time they can say whatever's on their minds. And I tell them, 'If you have nothing to say, that's fine; we can always play cards for a half hour.' Some excellent ideas have been generated by the staff."

Callebaut also places a high value on corporate flexibility. "Because we are flexible, we can effectively make a decision today and implement it tomorrow, which enhances our efficiency. I hope that, as we grow, we'll be able to retain a decent amount of flexibility, that we'll never become so bureaucratically cumbersome as to be straight jacketed into a certain protocol and a certain way of doing things with no opportunity for experimentation with new ideas. The trick to keeping ourselves flexible is to minimize the layers of people between staff and management, which we've managed to do up to this point."

In the same breath, however, Callebaut concedes that the time has come for him to begin allocating more of the management to others in an attempt to downsize his typical ten-hour workdays. "For years I worked without taking a holiday, and although I've gotten a bit better about that, I still tend to combine holidays with work-related travel. And I know the time has come to slow down a bit. My business partner had a mild heart attack a few years ago, which opened our eyes to the reality that we can't continue putting in marathon days forever. So now we're working on a plan to increase our management to a size that's comfortable for everyone, while maintaining the hands-on involvement that makes this a good company to work for and do business with."

One step Callebaut has taken to downsize his personal agenda has been to give up a part-time, voluntary position with the Belgian consulate. "Actually, for nine years I was the sum total of the consulate's office in Calgary—the office, in fact, was in my building. I helped people with their passports, visas, documentation needed to claim pensions, and so on. At first it was only a few hours here and there, but gradually the extra hours and evening receptions crept into my business schedule and made me realize I just didn't have the time to do it anymore. The only ongoing volunteer commitment I have at the moment is as a member of the association vying to bring the Olympic Winter Games to Calgary in the year 2010."

Callebaut also resists filling his evenings with social and charitable functions, not an easy task for someone so highly profiled. "I enjoy public speaking, especially about entrepreneurship and the chocolate industry, and I do the occasional charitable function, but I'm not a high-profile junkie. I'll go to the odd black tie affair and make chocolates for free distribution if it's for a good cause, but I'm not apt to become a slave to the social scene. I prefer relaxing with friends over a beer and a deck of cards. I enjoy the low-key camaraderie, which is all part of the balance I strive for in my life.

"My father's advice was to combine the useful with the enjoyable, and I've tried to do that. Whenever I travel on business I know I'll be working hard, but I also make sure I set aside time for relaxation, whether it's a three-hour hike or simply lying on my hotel bed and staring at the ceiling."

Like most entrepreneurs, Callebaut can't help but brim with ideas for the future of his enterprise. Unlike many, however, he refuses to be pressed into quotas and deadlines. "I have no particular need to make more and more money each year. Money doesn't drive me. You can only use so much anyway. I like luxury, but I'm not extravagant. True, I can afford a room at the Chateau Lake Louise, but I'm equally happy tenting on an ice cap on Baffin Island.

"Really, my goals are simple: to strike a harmonious balance between work and relaxation, and to continue making a top notch product.

"And to sell it wherever I can."

If you have a vision and you're good at your work,
people don't ask, "What did your father do?"

I've never experienced *heimwee*, the Flemish expression for 'home-sickness.' I've not had time for it. No doubt, knowing I could fly back to Belgium at will helped in that regard, but it never crossed my mind to return permanently. In fact, now I only go back for family or business reasons. Although I love reconnecting with my family and friends over two-hour lunches in a European cafe, there are also other places in the world to visit. And other places in Canada. This is a spectacular country and before I die I want to get to know it much better.

I came to North America primarily to start a business, but I wasn't long in Calgary before realizing this would be, quite simply, a good place to live. Calgarians are extremely open and welcoming; I was very well received, even though my name meant nothing here and I could as easily have been a criminal. People gave me the benefit of the doubt.

In retrospect, this was the perfect place to establish a company, although I couldn't have known that back in the early 1980's. Calgary is the home of entrepreneurs and people are not afraid to go out on a financial limb. Perhaps that comes from being so tied in to the oil and gas industry. I know people who've gone bankrupt and they just get up and start all over again. I like that optimism, that dynamic, frontier spirit. People here don't hesitate to say, "That sounds like a good idea. Let's try it." That's my operating philosophy too, and it's served me well and kept us fresh as a company.

Belgium, in contrast, is an old society with many unwritten rules and regulations that are nonetheless etched in stone. If you're going to operate a business there, you have to do it in the centuries-old tradition that is so often encumbered by parameters of age and custom. Socially too, structures are more rigid. As an example, every Sunday my family members were expected to show up at my grandmother's house where business was discussed over an aperitif. Well, that sounds romantic, but it also restricts your personal freedom and forces you to constantly defer to what others expect of you. Here, no one bats an eye

I'VE NEVER EXPERIENCED

HEIMWEE, THE FLEMISH

EXPRESSION FOR HOMESICKNESS.

I'VE NOT HAD TIME FOR IT.

if you pursue your own vision. My mother, sister and brother are very special, but I don't need to see them every week.

Canadians are quick to support and acknowledge you for your own accomplishments. They don't ask, "Was your father a wealthy man?" I have a friend, not yet 40 years of age, who is a reservoir engineer and recently became co-owner of a successful oil company. She'll be a millionaire in another year or two. Her father immigrated from Italy and worked for the city's garbage department, yet no one's ever suggested that her aspirations be hitched to the achievements of her parents. If you have a vision and you're good at your work, people don't ask, "What did your father do?"

That's my message to the prospective immigrants, mostly Belgians, who solicit my advice: don't dwell on what you don't find here, but look around and take inventory of everything offered that can't be found back home. You say you can't buy unpasteurized cheese here? To me that's trivial but if you can't live without it, perhaps it's best to stay in your own home town.

Don't be afraid to bring your dreams to Canada. There are still so many opportunities waiting to be reaped in this country, especially for young people with ideas. Alberta, for example, has an innovative program to help youth sell their ideas on the stock market without having to put up the bulk of the required capital themselves. That attitude and support ensures that entrepreneurship is not just limited to those with money, which is ultra important in a healthy business climate.

The immigration experience demands an expansion of your mental horizons. It would be impossible to hurdle the phase of transition between the old world and the new without such an opening up of the spirit. And that's what sets us apart: we've had the experience of changing our ways of doing and thinking. Sets us apart, yes, but isn't exclusively our domain. Living abroad for a time or even in another part of Canada can also give you the same experience, can also augment a mental openness to possibilities heretofore not considered.

Often the limitations we impose on ourselves are due to not having looked around enough in the world of other people. For example, in Europe language is considered an asset, and Europeans commonly are versed in two, three, or more languages. Here in North America, we tend to undervalue the benefit of a second and third language. We see a second language not as a valuable tool for communication enhancement, but as the imposition of another culture's influence on us. And any semblance of imposition in our society is quickly interpreted as an impingement on our personal freedom, on which we place a high priority.

We Canadians can be a bit bullheaded about language, which we read as 'French' or 'English' and use as a pawn in our ongoing struggle over the unity issue. And the unity issue—there's a problem that's been seriously hobbling our collective energies over the last two decades. I believe separation would be a disaster, both for Canada and for Quebec. If Quebec were to look beyond the emotion of being its own country, it would see that the federal state really does protect the French language at the national level. Just look at the federal parks, federal services, airports and the provincial education systems for examples of this protection. Would we still have the national will and the federal resolve to maintain this protection after Quebec separates?

From an economic standpoint, separation isn't great news for Quebec either. The birth of any country involves an economic alliance with it's geographical neighbours, and for Quebec, that would again come down to Canada and the United States. But the separatists aren't thinking about that; instead they're counting on voters to base their eventual decision on emotion rather than fact. And the politicians will keep hammering the people with referendums until they achieve what they want. I'm generally an optimist, but I have no idea how this issue can be resolved.

The separation issue aside, Canadian politics is much more refreshing than the politics of Belgium. There, if your family supports a certain party, you will too, and so will the next generation, regardless of the competence and performance of the people at that party's helm. Hence, ideologies are slow to change and nothing much happens from decade to decade. The political machine lumbers along, moving a little to the left, then a little to the right, picks up an extra party here and there, and all the while makes no difference in the lives of ordinary citizens. I'm happy to be away from that climate.

In Canada, however, if a party falls out of favour over poor performance, it gets turfed out without hesitation. Federally we've had landslide wins for both the Conservative and the Liberal parties in recent times. That kind of pendulum swing would never occur within the staid Belgian system. And look at what's happened in Alberta in the last few years. Although the politicians have been criticized and their motivations questioned more than once, they nonetheless have made good on their campaign promise to eliminate the deficit. That type of accountability fosters trust in the political system, and trust is what we'll need to take us over the hurdle of our debt. We have no right to even consider passing on the debt to the next generation. It's our mess; we're the ones responsible for cleaning it up.

But every country has its problems and ours, at least, have not yet quagmired us into stagnation. People here are still eager to make something of their lives, and the eagerness is generated by knowing it can yet be done in Canada. I like that mentality; it's a big part of the reason why I'm Canadian and here to stay. It's exciting, invigorating, and will probably keep me working until I'm 80 years old.

Dr. Ranjit Kumar Chandra

NEW DELHI, INDIA—ST. JOHN'S, NEWFOUNDLAND

The nondescript office at the top of the stairs is hardly the backdrop
one would envision for a world renowned scholar and scientist.
But then, there are many things about Dr. Ranjit Chandra
that one might not expect to behold in someone so distinguished:
the soft-spoken, tranquil manner infused with unfailing
graciousness, the smooth, unhurried smile and mannerisms,
the cherished friendships, the highly principled values.
A Professor of Pediatric Research, Medicine and Biochemistry at
Memorial University, also the Director of Immunology at the
Janeway Child Health Centre, Chandra has twice been nominated
for the Nobel Prize in medicine and in 1989 became an officer of
the Order of Canada. Remarkably, the eminent scientist on the cusp
of medical discovery remains equally at home as the country doctor.
"I still travel to Gander, Clarenville and Corner Brook to see
patients," says Chandra. "I feel I owe that to the province."

A three-day visit to balmy St. John's in the summer of 1973 convinced Dr. Ranjit Chandra to pull up his considerable stakes in India for resettlement in juvenescent Newfoundland. He clearly recalls his arrival the following February at Gander International Airport, in the midst of a howling Atlantic snowstorm. Descending to the tarmac, his wife and children eyed him with some consternation and wondered if he might have gotten their destination wrong.

"We had planned to come the previous September but by the time our paperwork was straightened out, Newfoundland was well into winter. Our Canadian visa was to expire on February 28, and rather than having to reapply and wait still longer, we decided to come on that date. It was quite an initiation."

To the thirty-six year-old pediatrician who had been brashly wooed

away from India's top medical research centre by Memorial University, the blustery eastern city on the edge of the gray, roiling Atlantic seemed a veritable world away from tropical New Delhi.

The youngest of three children, Chandra was born in the village of Mailsi in the province of Punjab in northwestern India, and spent much of his childhood on the move. "My father was a physician in the Punjab medical service so we moved from town to town. During my ten years of school we moved at least eight times, but I don't remember having any real adjustment problems.

"I especially recall the year I was in grade four, when I became part of a lasting group of seven, very close friends. Even though I ended up in Newfoundland and four others eventually migrated to Pakistan, we've managed to stay in touch throughout our adulthood, getting together every few years to renew our friendship. Unfortunately one of the group passed away eight years ago."

Chandra was in grade nine when his mother died, a tragedy that was to have a profound effect on his choice of career. "She had a severe skin ailment for which there was no cure. A new treatment cleared her skin but left her with complications, and she died of a heart attack. I remember thinking I would research this area and look for a cure, but as fate would have it, that's not the field I ended up specializing in.

"The other influence on my profession was my father. Starting when I was ten years old, I happily tagged along with him to his office or clinic, where I would sit in a corner and watch him do surgery or perform an autopsy."

From an early age Chandra had demonstrated a singular intellect, graduating from both junior and senior high school with the province's top marks in science. At the end of his pre-medical program at Khalsa College in Amritsar, Punjab, he finished as the university's top-ranking student, a commendable achievement made even more remarkable considering the university drew its students from a population base of fifteen million and had over one hundred campuses spread throughout the province.

"I worked hard but greatly enjoyed my student years. I never studied up until the minute prior to exams; instead, it was my habit to close the books two days before and go to a movie, play tennis or distract and relax myself in some other way."

Though soft-spoken and reticent, Chandra was recognized almost from the beginning as a brilliant scholar destined to make medical history. After graduating from Amritsar Medical College in 1960, Chandra moved to New Delhi where he spent the following three years at the All-India Institute of Medical Sciences, completing a residency in pediatrics and researching the epidemiology of infections in newborns. While there, he and a colleague discovered, and lent their names to, a disorder affecting the lungs, heart and sinuses.

"I was fortunate to be at the best medical institution in the country, which had just been established the year before I arrived. My work was fulfilling and I became quite immersed in it."

So immersed, in fact, that when he completed the required oral examination at the end of his residency, all three of his examiners conceded that they had learned much from him. For the next two years Chandra served as a lecturer in pediatrics at the Postgraduate Institute of Medical Education and Research in the northern city of Chandigarh, his interest in immunology gradually taking hold. In 1966, then the only medical scientist conducting immunological research in India, he established the now well-accepted fact that malnutrition is the most common cause of world-wide immunological deficiencies. This basic premise led to further research that would eventually earn him two nominations for the Nobel Prize in medicine, the first in 1984, the second in 1986.

In 1968 Chandra travelled to England for further training in immunology at the University of London, returning to the All-India Institute a year later. But, by the turn of the next decade he found himself seriously mulling over in his mind the feasibility of migrating abroad. "I was happy enough at the Institute, but they did have a somewhat British system of hierarchy in place, and there was a chronic problem of political interference, a problem that still persists throughout India. Unquestionably, promotions at the Institute were politically motivated and influenced. So, when the interference was at its height, I made the decision to leave for a few years. But I kept my house and lab because I intended to return to India.

"At the time that Memorial approached me, I also had several offers from England and the United States. But Memorial's package was the most generous, certainly in terms of status. In India, I was an Assistant Professor and I came to the Memorial interview anticipating that the best I could hope for would be an Associate Professorship. However, I soon realized how young Memorial's medical school was, and how they had a genuine need for a person with my background and training. So when the Associate Dean drove me to the airport after the interview, I told him I would probably not come without the offer of a full professorship.

"When that was offered despite the fact that I'd had no training in either Canada nor the United States, I felt it was a generous contract. They gave me a full professorship, directorship of a new clinical immunology service at the Janeway Child Health Centre, a research facility, responsibility for a clinical immunology teaching program, and more money than I had asked for. They also offered a position to my wife who had just recently acquired her degree in medicine."

In an unusual move, the Royal College of Physicians and Surgeons, the regulating body of the medical profession, also chose to waive the examination that is mandatory for all physicians seeking a license to practise medicine in Canada. Instead, they issued Chandra an honorary certificate that entitled him to practise medicine in Newfoundland for five years before writing the examination. "I didn't think I would move out of the province, but I thought, 'Why have this restriction of time and place?' So I wrote the exam the year after I arrived, which meant I was no longer restricted to the university for my livelihood; if I stayed, it would be because I chose to stay."

Although Chandra was fortunate to receive these choice concessions, he would also contribute tirelessly and extraordinarily over the next 25 years. As well as tending to his responsibilities at the hospital and university, he began working long, productive hours at the research facility, his daunting schedule seeping well into evenings and weekends. To the salaried research staff who began extending their own hours as well, Chandra quickly became known as an upright employer who encouraged and rewarded exemplary work habits. "My staff will testify that I've never been one to abide by a nine to five schedule. But

I've also ensured that they've gotten significant promotions, and, if they're away from home as many of them are, I see to it that they get a free trip home each year. The unpaid overtime they gratefully work in return more than compensates for the funds spent on their travel."

From the beginning, Chandra's research has been in the area of immunology, an area he has likened to detective work as compared to the 'mechanics' of surgery. "At a time when most researchers in immunology didn't consider diet a fruitful tangent to examine, we were able to confirm in our research what people have always suspected: that diet can influence the immune system. As our papers started to get published and people realized there was practical significance in what we were putting forth, international interest in our research began to grow."

As the interest increased, so did the funding from various government and corporate sources, and the number of scientists on his team. In the mid-1980's the World Health Organization, an agency of the United Nations, began casting its net upon the waters in search of a research facility to be designated as the World Health Organization Centre for Nutritional Immunology. Several potential sites in various parts of the world were studied and assessed, and in 1989 Chandra's research facility was officially awarded the designation. Currently it remains the World Health Organization's only centre for nutritional immunology.

"Part of our mandate is to run courses, directly from the centre, for health care professionals interested in immunology—physicians, nutritionists, dietitians, nurses. We've had a good response; people have come from Canada, China, Chile, Germany, India, Italy, Mexico, Nigeria, South Korea, Spain, Sweden, Thailand, the United States and Venezuela."

Over the years Chandra has been instrumental in popularizing the concept of nutritional immunology, with ramifications that are only now beginning to reveal the extent of their reach. "We have shown that there are many practical applications in this field, and we've created keen interest in the industry that develops feeding formulas for specific applications. They are realizing that if they want to develop a feeding formula for someone recovering from burns and at risk for developing infection, for example, they need to carefully examine the research in this area before they start mixing nutrients. We've helped three companies to develop specific formulas; two of these formulas are now on the market."

Much of Chandra's funding comes from Health Canada and other medical sources and foundations, but also from the pharmaceutical industry in the United States and Europe. Additional funding is also garnered from other universities that sub-contract to Chandra the specific components of their research which only his facility is equipped to conduct. Such contracts come from all over the world, including Kenya, Brazil, Italy, the United States and England.

Chandra has also made significant inroads into the field of over-nutrition, citing over-nutrition as being almost as detrimental to the immune system as is malnutrition. "There are many side-effects of over-nutrition and a high intake of fat; heart disease and cancer are two examples. But just in the area of immunity, we have found that even essential nutrients like zinc and Vitamin A, if given in modest excess, can begin to cause harm. Take zinc as an example. In 1980, the American Recommended Dietary Allowance (RDA) publication noted that up to two grams of zinc per day for adults was considered safe. In 1982 to 1983 we did some work to show that even 300 milligrams per day, about one seventh of the amount considered safe in the 1980 RDA guidelines was enough to cause problems with the immune system after only six weeks. When we published our findings, we asked where the figure of two grams had come from. And no one could answer. Our findings have since been confirmed by others, and the upper safe limit has been decreased."

But for many essential nutrients, the RDA remains an arbitrary dosage, and Chandra cautions that the multi-vitamin preparations available over the counter or in health food stores may contain essential nutrients in dosages large enough to cause harm over a period of time. "We have been developing a dose response curve for each essential nutrient over the past twelve years, using clinical trials involving seniors. We developed a multi-vitamin, and in a double-blind trial showed it to halve the rate of infection, pneumonia, bronchitis and the common cold among our participants. Our patent for the product has recently been approved."

Chandra and his team have also been the first to determine a causal relationship between nutrition and the management of HIV. "On a superficial level it might seem like a totally different area of research for us, but there is a common thread—how diet and nutrition affect resistance to disease." For this project Chandra is collaborating with Johns Hopkins University in Baltimore and with researchers in India.

Ironically, while Chandra's findings have been internationally recognized as an important development in the management of HIV, they have yet to be fully embraced in Canada. "We have evidence that nutrition therapy is an important adjunct to the management of HIV, but in Canada, if you say you want to look after the nutrition of a person infected with HIV, that would still be seen as fringe medicine.

"I've tried to convince Canadian scientists that this research has important implications, but they are currently more interested in developing a vaccine for HIV. I'm not saying anti-viral drugs aren't important, but for the people infected today, a good state of nutrition might well reduce the incidence of other complicating infections in them. So they feel better and our evidence suggests they will live longer, meaning they may yet benefit from vaccines still to be developed."

As President of the 1997 International Congress of Nutrition which was held in Canada for the first time, Chandra made certain that a session on nutrition and HIV was inserted into the agenda. "Hopefully we're waking up some people here."

Looking back, Chandra maintains that although the move half-way around the world to Newfoundland called for a major lifestyle and cultural change for the family, it didn't dissuade his enthusiasm for new beginnings and opportunities. "I was adaptable because I was young and just beginning my career; I didn't hesitate to try new adventures and take on new responsibilities. And I had four friends here already, which did make a difference. For a while I continued to entertain my original plan to return to India after a year or two, but it soon became obvious that with the changes occurring there, it wouldn't be in our best interest to do so."

Paradoxically, it wasn't until fifteen years later that Chandra began experiencing a deep-seated urge to return to India. Although his children had all become Canadian citizens, he himself had purposely retained his Indian citizenship in the off chance that he might want to go back someday. "I knew I needed my Indian citizenship to work in an Indian medical school—the country's very strict about that. And I had always thought there might be a reason to go back, so I never made the move to become a Canadian citizen."

Now, however, Chandra knew he had to weigh the options one final time, pitting his list of reasons for going against his rationale for staying. Having painstakingly done that, he made the decision to stay in Canada and promptly sealed it in 1988 by becoming a Canadian citizen.

The following year Chandra added the eminent *Order of Canada* to his long list of awards and distinctions, and was also designated as St. John's *Citizen of the Year*. By coincidence he was out of the country accepting another award on the day he was to be honoured by City Hall. "I had already committed myself to being in Germany on that same day. So my oldest daughter, Sujata, went to City Hall and received the award on my behalf."

A 1999 sabbatical found Chandra back in India, this time in the cyclone-devastated region of Orissa where he helped with immunization as a member of *Doctors Without Borders*, with whom he has been associated since 1971. (*Doctors Without Borders* was the recipient of the 1999 Nobel Peace Prize.)

Back in Newfoundland, in his typically understated way, he continues to juggle more responsibility than most people could fathom having over a lifetime. Aside from the research, and the writing that it generates—he has written two books, edited seventeen more, and penned hundreds of articles—Chandra continues to lecture at Memorial University and teaches occasional courses at several universities abroad where he is a visiting professor. As well, he continues to see patients at the Janeway Child Health Centre and the Health Sciences Centre. "Up until three years ago I was the only clinical immunologist in the province, but now one of my students, formerly from Egypt, has decided to stay on and assume some of the clinical work load."

Remarkably, Chandra, the scientist on the cutting edge of medical discovery, is also Chandra, the country doctor. "Since coming here I've travelled monthly to Corner Brook, Clarenville and Gander to see patients in these areas. I feel I owe that to the province, even though when I'm on one of those little planes in the middle of a storm I can't help wondering, 'Am I doing the right thing or am I out of my mind?'"

That Chandra can even envision, let alone find time for, leisure activity is testament to his tenet that balance and moderation in all things is the key to good health. While he concedes that he worked especially hard in the early years, as of late he has begun allowing himself the luxury of transferring his energies from lab work to overseeing and designating, from paperwork to the tasks of applying for funding and generating more ideas. And, true to his propensity for management, he ensures the pockets of time he has succeeded in creating for himself are efficiently used.

Chandra begins most days with a pre-dawn, hour-long walk. Several times a week he plays badminton with friends. He relishes the occasional game of tennis, enjoys dining with friends, mostly adheres to a vegetarian diet and worships regularly at the local Hindu and Sikh temples.

Above all, he remains a devoted family man, proudly doting on his son and three daughters, all excellent scholars. The eldest is a gynaecologist; her next oldest sister holds an MBA.

"They've all gone on to pursue their own lives," says Chandra with no trace of discontent. "But they come home for holidays, and then the house is still a pretty lively place."

The bottom line is, you must be prepared to work very hard,
whether you're a doctor, teacher or carpenter.
And you'll have to be good. If you're good,
people will always come to you.

There are many aspects to the process of 'settling in' when you relocate your family halfway around the world to an alien land. Although culturally there wasn't much here for us when we first came, St. John's has become an ideal place to be. There have been many opportunities for fitting into the city and making ourselves part of it. We can belong to an East Indian community that's large enough to socialize in, yet not so large as to have its own set of social problems. Most parents in these East Indian families are immigrants, and all, without exception, are professional people, many of them doctors, engineers and teachers. Of course, since this positions our community positively within

IT'S OBVIOUS THAT ALTHOUGH I SAY
I NO LONGER FEEL AS IF I'M IN
TRANSITION, I STILL EXPERIENCE
THE LITTLE MENTAL TUG-OF-WARS
THAT SEEM TO BE SO TYPICAL OF
THOSE WHO HAVE COME HERE
FROM SOMEWHERE ELSE AND
LIVED IN OTHER PLACES.

the Newfoundland community-at-large, it also helps to garner our acceptance within that larger community.

Predictably, however, my family also faced challenges specific to our decision to voluntarily exchange a culture in which we were the mainstream for one in which we are a visible minority. Our task has been to not only assimilate within our new setting but also to retain some of our own culture, the traditions and identities from which we cannot be separated. When we first came here there was no temple, and for years we worshipped out of an improvised facility. Only in 1995 were we finally able to finance and build a proper temple.

As for schooling, neither private nor non-denominational schools existed in St. John's, a peculiar situation that actually ended up working to our advantage. Here the system was such that if you were of a certain religious denomination, you were required to go to that denomination's public school. Since our religion did not coincide with any that had their own public schools, we had our pick of schools.

Language factored into our transition equation as well. I had taken all my professional training in English, but now it was to become our everyday language outside of the home. Of course the children have learned to speak it flawlessly and my command is about as good or as bad as it's ever been. But we didn't toss Hindi aside; the preservation of any language is an asset and this particular one was tied directly into our culture. So Hindi was the language we spoke at home.

Professionally there is also a period of settling in. Wading through the bureaucracy of a new job was simple compared to what we had endured in India. More difficult was the challenge to find and make my place, academically and professionally. Even though you come to a new institution with your credentials recognized, you also come not knowing anyone, and gradually you have to show them what you have done and can do. And although I'm a Canadian citizen now, it was and still is a fact that if you come from another place, and particularly if you are—I'll be very blunt—not white, it takes twenty-five to fifty percent more effort to be accepted at the same level. Even now.

My children haven't thought too much about this, but they will come to realize it in due time. And when they do, it will be a bigger shock for them than it was for me. Whereas I came here with the expectation that I would have to work harder just to be accepted at par with my peers, my children won't be as resigned to such unjust and ungrounded obstacles in their career paths. They shouldn't have to be, of course, but discrimination is still an unfortunate fact of life.

I'm not suggesting that prejudice occurs only on this continent. It happens when an Indian goes to Africa, and vice versa. Even within India, people from the north will be treated differently when they go to the south. It happens around the world, whenever people from one area move into another.

But I have accepted that reality quite well, recognizing that some of its deep-rootedness can't be changed, and doing my part to minimize the misunderstanding on which it builds its strength. I have cultivated many strong friendships among mainstream Newfoundlanders and Canadians, and as someone who has had much exposure and done much work at the national level, I've always made it a point to work with my peers in a spirit of cooperation.

Even here, however, I can give an example to illustrate my point about the impediments of subtle discrimination. In 1997 the International Congress of Nutrition was held in Canada for the first time, even though a group of scientists had been trying to bring it here for years without success. In 1985 I was asked to head up the committee that would be lobbying to bring this conference to Canada. I gave it my whole-hearted effort and when the elections for that conference were held four years later, Canada got 36 out of 45 votes.

So with the conference coming to Canada, an organizing committee began looking around for a conference president. We were sitting around the table and one member said, "Oh, we have this nice person in Vancouver:" another mentioned a "prominent person in Toronto," and someone suggested a "qualified person from Montreal." Finally a woman on the committee said, "Listen to us talking! What are we doing? We owe this conference to Chandra. We should at least have the courtesy to ask him if he would like to be President."

Up until then I hadn't planned to take on the presidency. But when this happened I said to myself, "I'll show them I can run this thing," and I did.

I don't experience much discrimination in my grassroots community, but I know it still drifts through academia. That's not acceptable, of course, but also not startling, considering such suppressive attitudes have prevailed over several centuries. However, the shifting demographics of North America will spawn significant change in societal attitudes within the next 15 years. In the microcosm of the United States non-whites now make up an estimated 35 percent of the population. Canada, too, has a significant ethnic population; as an example, there are probably a half million Chinese Canadians in the country today.

Although I lived here for 14 years before becoming a Canadian citizen, my period of transition was quite well resolved before that time. I had retained my Indian citizenship, not so much because I was torn as to where I belonged, but for the possibility that I might one day find myself going back there to work. In my mind I did vacillate back and forth for awhile, which I think is natural, but now I'm truly comfortable with my sense of place in Newfoundland, both personally and professionally. The people here are very warm and supportive. We have ten families on our cul-de-sac—Italians, Chinese, Indians and Newfoundlanders—and I'm friends with them all.

I'm also very fortunate and grateful to have had my work recognized by my peers, community and country. Of all the honours I've received, the *Order of Canada* is the award I prize the most. As a new Canadian, to be recognized by your country in such a meaningful way, it's great.

And yet, there is always that undeniable factor of being swayed back towards where you once were, what you once knew. A few years ago I was offered an excellent opportunity in India, at a new institute devoted entirely to research in immunology. They were even willing to overlook my Canadian citizenship, provided I would take steps to again become a citizen of India. I was sorely tempted. But I knew I couldn't expect my children to make the move with me; even though they've all been to India regularly, Canada is undeniably their home. When my wife also refused to consider returning to India, I forfeited the institute's offer.

So even though I'm comfortably at home in St. John's, there always remains the possibility of moving on. I keep resisting the notion of leaving Newfoundland but the reality is, there is a down side to doing research here. Because of our remote location and affiliation with a young, localized university, our research findings and requests for funding are easily and sometimes carelessly dismissed.

I once applied for a grant to an American Foundation and was rejected. The following year I went to Boston to assume a temporary professorship at the Massachusetts Institute of Technology and Harvard University Medical School. From MIT I submitted the same application for funding with virtually no changes made, and it was promptly accepted.

But that's not only my struggle, it's the classic Newfoundlander's scenario, and in some ways the Canadian scenario as well. Canadians are not very adept at promoting themselves and recognizing their own achievements. As for the Americans, they are a competitive society and will go out of their way to get what they want.

Shortly after I appeared on the *Maclean's* magazine 1995 honour roll, I received a telephone call from a very high-ranking American politician who wanted to know if I'd given any previous consideration to moving to the United States. She knew of my affiliation with Johns Hopkins University and suggested I might want to relocate to Baltimore. She offered to sponsor me, and two weeks later I had my green card in the mail. That's how fast they can work.

Well, I'm still in Newfoundland.

There is much about Canada that makes it a great country to live in—our health care and social programs, a low crime rate, a relatively uncorrupt political system. India, in contrast, has many problems—pollution, poverty, social issues, rampant petty crime, swollen bureaucracy. Every contact with bureaucracy takes four times as long, whether it is to buy stamps at the post office or procure a document from City Hall. Language is another barrier to efficiency; there are so many regional languages and dialects, and they all have different scripts.

But we have our challenges here too, unity being the most urgent one. I'm not sure how that hurdle is to be overcome. It would be difficult to maintain any form of unity and solidarity if Quebec separates, and yet to continually allot privileges on the basis of cultural background creates great ongoing strain as well.

Increasingly, I ponder my retirement. The question of where I will live is always on the forefront. Do I want to spend three or four months of the year in the country of my birth? Will I stay in Canada, where my children will likely be working and living? My 1999 sabbatical year in India, Spain and Switzerland has me currently thinking that I should start planning to divide my retirement years into four-month segments to spend in India, Europe and Canada.

It's obvious that although I say I no longer feel as if I'm in transition, I still experience the little mental tug-of-wars that seem to be so typical of those who have come here from somewhere else and lived in other places. But having ruminated on all that, I harbour very few regrets over the way my life has evolved. I can say without hesitation that there are still plenty of good reasons for immigrants to come to Canada. Here you will find opportunity in a less competitive atmosphere than you would in the United States. If you are a member of a visible minority, you will notice some prejudice, but it's not an insurmountable obstacle. Fortunately, covert racism is usually soundly condemned by the majority.

The bottom line is, you must be prepared to work very hard, whether you're a doctor, teacher or carpenter. And you'll have to be good. If you're good, people will always come to you.

Cyril Dabydeen

The poet, Cyril Dabydeen, presses his open hands together, brings them up to touch his lips and with his other-world eyes gazes off into the distance of his own evolutionary migration. When he speaks, his words quietly and eloquently paddle through the waters of his imagination, pools of fluid sagacity that empty simultaneously into the mighty Berbice River of South America and the rugged Ottawa River of the north.

Formerly Ottawa's Poet Laureate, Dabydeen is a teacher, a tenacious defender of human rights, the author of numerous novels and collections of short fiction and poetry.

Unconditionally he lends his thoughtful literary voice to the heart of his past and present, makes audible his hope for the future.

"There is a tension in my work that's based on the binaries of 'here' and 'there,'" says Dabydeen. "And that tension has become my source of strength."

That the decidedly Canadian Cyril Dabydeen deftly juggles the emotions of both his past and present worlds is evident in the elegant poignancy of much of his writing. Unique to his poetry and fiction is its seamless and simultaneous documentation of life in both rural Guyana and urban Canada.

"What I most want to say about Cyril Dabydeen's poetry," writes U.K. scholar and publisher, Dr. Jeremy Poynting, in the introduction to *Coastland,* Dabydeen's first book of poetry, "is that he has managed to keep hold of everything he has passed through at the same time as continually extending his range."

'Keeping hold of everything' without letting the past weave around in his psyche like an encumbering menhir might offer insight on how Dabydeen, the Guyanese child came to be Dabydeen, the intuitive Canadian writer.

Born in the Canje District of rural Guyana on the edge of one of the country's largest sugar plantations, Dabydeen grew up with the intermingling smells of the Atlantic seashore and sugar cane in his nostrils. "My parents separated when I was young; my siblings and I grew up with my grandmother and other extended family members. In a fractured and impoverished colonial society such as ours, extended families under one roof were the norm.

"In Guyana we were two major race groups, the African Guyanese who were brought here as slaves by the British plantation owners, and the Indian Guyanese who were imported to the plantations as indentured labourers after slavery was abolished in 1838. My ancestors came from India, probably from the western coast or from Uttar Pradesh.

"I have a vague recollection of my great-grandmother near the end of her life, sitting in a corner by herself, wrapped in her thoughts. I don't recall her ever speaking English, which is my only language: you don't get ahead in a British colony by speaking Hindi. I only ever learned a few Hindi words from her, the word for donkey as an example, which she hurled as an insult whenever she felt irritable. Such was her frustration in the so-called New World."

As a child Dabydeen was required to work in the corner store his grandmother operated to make ends meet. "I wasn't a child labourer in the factory sense but very early on we had to help out."

Although he had been raised in the Hindu faith, Dabydeen's ever-practical grandmother decided early on that he should convert to Christianity. Christian churches and schools, previously sown with the seeds of colonialism, had sprouted up all around and she astutely calculated her grandson would have a better chance at a good education and a decent future as a Christian. So at age 12 Dabydeen was baptized a Lutheran. "Somehow, though, I ended up going to the Anglican school. The huge St. Patrick's Anglican church was adjacent to the school and once a week you'd have all these students filing into the church to listen to a minister from England. Not much was relevant. Now the government has taken over the schools and infused the curriculum with considerably more Caribbean content."

Halfway through his teens Dabydeen began teaching, first at the Lutheran school and then at St. Patrick's Anglican school. "We were called Pupil Teachers; it was a very British system: some of the 'brighter' kids, and I use this term in quotations rather than self-indulgently, were trained very early on to become Pupil Teachers. We never attended high school but we had to write and pass the Pupil Teachers' examinations, and then continue writing and passing an upgraded version every year. They were very challenging; I was fortunate to be among those in the country who passed them. So I began teaching and continued studying at the same time. I had the value of education instilled at an early age."

The more conventional path to a teaching certificate would have been to complete high school and then attend teachers' college, but for the financially challenged Dabydeen, that was never an option. Instead, he home-schooled himself through the high school curriculum while continuing to teach the lower grades. Extremely motivated and with a maturity hastened by the harsh conditions of his childhood, Dabydeen immersed himself in his schooling and absorbed every last kernel of knowledge channelled his way by Oxford and Cambridge, the universities presiding over his studies.

"My exams were all marked in England and what I was studying was very British. I absorbed Shakespeare's *Twelfth Night* by reading the play over and over again. I digested entire novels serialized on BBC radio, including Jane Austen's *Mansfield Park*. I spent countless hours in front of the radio taking my own notes, a unique way to study.

"But there was nothing of Caribbean history or literature in my curriculum. An exam might call for an essay about a winter's day, for example. What did I know about winter other than what I saw on Christmas cards?"

And yet Dabydeen achieved consistently high marks in all of his courses. His weakest subjects were the sciences, understandable considering he lacked access to a laboratory. "I learned biology by reading the text over and over, but I never dissected the rudimentary frog. Instead, I studied the plants and animals in my rural surroundings. As a child I had seen my share of dead animals. When the family killed a chicken on special occasions, we, the children, would stand around and witness the ritual. Even now I can recall the smell of the carcass slipping into a pot of boiling water to be softened for plucking. It was a good smell."

Dabydeen knew early in life that he would be a writer. But as that yearning awakened within him, it also propelled him into a disturbingly paradoxical position: on the one hand, life in Guyana and the Caribbean was what he knew, valued and wanted to write about; on the other, his entire education had moulded in him the mind set that everything good and worthwhile, literature included, came from abroad. Dabydeen alludes to this quandary in "Ambition," an essay published in *Matrix* in 1995: "my imagination festered, my dreams and ambition lingering as I longed to be elsewhere, yet longed also to be here (in Guyana), always!"

"A general pattern for people growing up in a colony is that you look for your values abroad. In retrospect, I did benefit from studying Shakespeare and various British authors, but the difficulty lay in the lack of an equivalent number of Caribbean writers to study. When you study only the scholars and authors from overseas, you take on the values of that world and no longer look within, to your own values, for guidance. Frantz Fanon, a black psychiatrist from Haiti, examines this social phenomenon in his classic book on colonialism, *The Wretched of The Earth*, and concludes that colonial systems tend to breed self contempt. Some scholars would take it one step further and argue that it was deliberately done by the colonizers to keep the people down."

At the age of 19 Dabydeen was awarded Guyana's highest prize for poetry, the Sandbach Parker Gold Medal. At the same time he was noting that fellow emerging Caribbean writers of his own generation were migrating abroad in search of both publishing infrastructures and the fulfilment of their ambitions. In a move that foreshadowed his own departure, Dabydeen began imagining himself in front of a typewriter in a cold room somewhere in the northern hemisphere.

"My ambition to write was part of a cluster of motivators that drew me to Canada. Higher education, which was not a real possibility in Guyana even though we did have one university, was another motivator. So was the lack of publishers in Guyana."

That Dabydeen's eye initially fell on Canada had as much to do with a boyhood pastime as with any analytical discernment on his part. "As a kid I used to send for all the glossy tourism brochures on Canada— I'm sure they thought they were mailing them to a rich Guyanese contemplating a Canadian sojourn—and I would lose myself in the perfect photos of the Maritimes, the snow-capped Rockies, autumn leaves, fishing, all the well-known sights.

"I was accepted at universities in both Canada and America but since Canada was also a member of the Commonwealth, I chose to come here." Dabydeen enrolled in English at Lakehead University in Thunder Bay in 1970, completed an English degree two years later and a First Class Honours English degree the year after that. He supported himself by planting trees and funded his first-year tuition with prize money won in a literary competition shortly before emigrating.

His undergraduate studies completed, Dabydeen enrolled as a graduate student at Queen's University and embarked on a study of North American literature. He completed a Master's degree and began preparing for doctoral studies, realizing full well that job prospects for scholars of language and literature were dismal.

"That was one stressor; another was knowing my mother and siblings were having difficulty in Guyana which was struggling to come out from under colonialism. They were quite desperate to have me sponsor them into Canada; after all, I was the eldest child and the only one with a university education. And how was I going to sponsor them? By getting a job. So the PhD program became history."

Dabydeen then fast-tracked his way through another Master's degree, this time in public administration, calculating it would be an expedient ticket to viable work. "It was a tough year. More than once I asked myself what in God's name I was doing in a class on macro-economics. But it was an enriching year too; courses on the workings of the multinational corporations stimulated me, and I found myself chumming around with students in political science, economics, history and philosophy. My horizons broadened rapidly, and more and more I began thinking that English was narrow, perhaps even useless."

After graduating Dabydeen travelled to Ottawa in search of work. "We were 30 graduates and 27 found jobs. But not me. I had no 'real' work experience in Canada and no connections in Ottawa, which negated everything else. The education by itself didn't mean much, evidently."

Dabydeen worked at an Ottawa Holiday Inn until a senior bureaucrat and fellow Queen's classmate spotted him there and offered him a contract position. In his new job Dabydeen soon learned, despite what he had coddled himself into thinking, that literature had lost no relevance in his life. "I disliked bureaucracy. I was a square peg in a round hole. I hated having to quell my artistic energy in order to focus on writing mediocre reports. I began envying the artists in the streets for their freedom, and I wondered where I was headed. My personal writing helped keep me sane, but I longed to do it full-time."

After several similar short contracts, Dabydeen was able to find more appropriate work teaching English and communications at Ottawa's Algonquin College. He continued to harbour a simmering ambition to earn a doctorate; three times he applied to Toronto's York University, three times he was accepted into their doctoral program, three times he forced himself to decline. "I had to continue collecting a pay cheque to help my family in Guyana." And so Dabydeen, finally resigned to his more immediate responsibilities, abandoned all plans for furthering his formal education.

One by one his family began to immigrate as he was able to sponsor them or help pave their way. "The burden of sponsoring is exclusively the domain of the immigrant, especially the ethnic immigrant, and especially if that immigrant is also his family's eldest child. I carried the enormous load of responsibility and paperwork and waded through a spate of bureaucracy, sometimes all in vain. I sent for my second brother first; he was very skilled and had been the headmaster of a technical school in Guyana. Well, Immigration decreed that before he could come I would have to find him a job, which I was able to do after considerable searching. And then they still wouldn't let him come. It was during the recession of the 1980's and I guess they thought they'd better protect the jobs for Canadians.

"My brother eventually came as a refugee; so many Guyanese and Trinidadians did during that post-colonist era. As for my mother, I was able to bring her in through the family sponsorship class."

Although he was grateful for the teaching position at Algonquin, the college also provided Dabydeen with his first palpable brush with discrimination. "A permanent contract was always outside of my reach. I carried a full load but was always laid off during the summer.

I was naive; I didn't realize how important small 'p' politics was. I strove to be a good teacher and writer and assumed these efforts would serve me."

Disheartened with Algonquin, Dabydeen left in 1983. When Ottawa formed an Advisory Committee on Race Relations and invited applications for membership, Dabydeen was quick to respond. "Because of the Algonquin experience I could see the world through a different lens. Not that I couldn't see clearly before, but adversity helps you perceive the human rights issue in a more focused way. Coming out of colonial Guyana and being a minority person in Canada, I was inherently interested in human rights. When I was accepted on the committee I quit the dead-end bureaucracy job and began working as a volunteer."

When the city advertised for a paid committee administrator not long after, it was deluged with more than 500 submissions from across the country, among them Dabydeen's. Once selected for the position, he inadvertently found a familiar mental tug-of-war again percolating to the surface of his consciousness: on the one hand he looked forward to fulfilment as part of a grassroots effort to bring equal rights issues to the forefront of the municipal psyche; on the other he found himself once again pondering a yearning to abandon conventional work altogether in favour of writing full-time. He had been writing consistently and prolifically for most of his years, drawing from his experiences as a colonist, immigrant and minority person. (These themes still dominate the underlying currents of much of his work.) Already his fiction and poetry had appeared in several notable Canadian and foreign literary publications. Several collections of poetry and short stories had been published and he was now beginning to compile the collection of poetry that would become *Coastland*, published in 1989.

He had also just been designated Poet Laureate of Ottawa, a distinction he retained until 1987. But now, in 1984, the need for a pay cheque, albeit modest, and the more immediate urge to make a contribution on the human rights front, won out over the enduring passion to forego the world and commit words to paper. For the next five years Dabydeen managed the committee, learned much about grassroots politics and generally became entrenched in his work. "I worked with the police and the media, organized conferences, and guided the committee in their efforts on policy direction in areas such as employment equity and cross-cultural training. The position was simultaneously enriching and stressful; working on race relations and within a bureaucratic climate, there were many sensibilities to circumnavigate."

In the meantime Dabydeen was also active in the League of Canadian Poets and helped to organize readings across the country for Asian-Canadian writers.

In 1986 he produced *A Shapely Fire: Changing the Literary Landscape*, an anthology of twenty of the best-known black and Caribbean-born writers in Canada.

In 1988, in addition to his committee work, Dabydeen began teaching creative writing at the University of Ottawa, an occasional position he still holds. "I loved the work but I also saw this as an opportunity to be a role model for other minority people. Here was a minority person who was teaching not computer science, not English as a second language, but English literature. You still don't see many people of colour teaching English, and often the assumption is that if you speak with an accent, then you don't know the language well enough to teach it. So, yes, I was there to teach creative writing, but also to expose those misconceptions for what they were. Beyond this, I was in an environment of like-minded spirits, creative people. The sense of the higher self and imaginative boundaries grew in me."

From 1990 to 1999 Dabydeen also served as Race Relations Manager for the Federation of Canadian Municipalities, travelling throughout the country to dialogue with communities and foster cultural understanding and harmony. Yet, although he found his work to be stimulating and invigorating, he continued to dream of the day he would be able to write full-time. "So often I thought of quitting my job and just writing. But there was important work to be done in race relations, and financial considerations to be taken into account as well. And my immigrant psyche also factored into the equation. A fellow immigrant respects you when you have achieved tangible economic and professional success. Mostly that doesn't include writing. Tell an immigrant you're a writer, and you're liable to get weird looks."

Weird looks not withstanding, Dabydeen turned to full-time writing a year ago and has meanwhile joined the ranks of established Canadian writers. In recent years he has authored several more books of poetry, three novels and at least three collections of short fiction. His latest book of poetry, *Discussing Columbus*, published by Peepal Tree Press in 1997, continues to examine the journey of transition, having grown "out of a consciousness of a world made up of layers of journeyings and settlement, of the meeting of heterogenous cultures and the result of their mingling." His most recent fiction, *My Brahmin Days and other stories* (Tsar Publications, 2000) echoes a similar theme.

Over the years the prolific Dabydeen has availed himself to the literary world in many ways. He has given readings, served as a book critic and participated in literary conferences. Most recently he was appointed one of nine international judges, the only Canadian among them, to adjudicate the Y2000 Neustadt International Prize for Literature, a $40,000 US literary prize awarded by the University of Oklahoma.

But none of these ventures comes close to displacing the fulfilment of putting passions, observations and convictions into words. "I will always write. Virginia Woolf once defined writing as being the most humane of all professions, and I agree. To write successfully is to have a voice that endures. I know I can be, and have been, effective in the social arena but often when that work is over, it's done, quickly displaced by the next item on the agenda. In writing, one can have a voice that lasts beyond a lifetime."

Older now, he's still a "new Canadian"
As his plastic citizenship card fades
At the bus stop, in driving snow,
he's asked, "Where do you come from?"
— after living here
more than twenty years

—From "The Immigrant Who Remained Forever an Immigrant",
in *Stoning the Wind*, TSAR Publications, 1994.

And I am here with a vengeance

—From "As an Immigrant", in *Coastland*, Mosaic Press, 1989

I would describe myself as a writer and maybe, a social activist; writing has been a central obsession for most of my life, and some literary critics have said that in my writing they can see a strong interest in the poor and the underprivileged. That's not to say my writing is overly virtuous; I've been known to use satire and irony in generous doses. I've also been described as having that dimensionality in my writing that comes from having lived in more than one culture. The memory of another place remains strong within me: the underpinnings of ancestry, the denigration by the colonial rulers of our cultural accoutrements, and the way we indentured people subsequently betrayed ourselves too, by unwittingly discarding things Guyanese in favour of everything British. So pervasive was this that many of us grew up embracing things foreign without much thought to the consequences for our own society. Things have changed since then, however, catalysed by Guyana's struggle for independence in the 1960's.

But these were the sensibilities with which I came to Canada. I came with mixed feelings, wanting the education and wanting to write more than anything else, yet consciously avoiding the question of whether I was here permanently or temporarily. The two classic reasons people emigrate—economists refer to them as the push and pull factors—both applied to my case. I was pushed out of Guyana by the lack of opportunity for me there, and I was pulled toward Canada because of perceived opportunity in a bigger country.

I've always been stirred by the Canada of my imagination, the Great White North of the tourist magazines I used to send for as a boy, the notion of the Land of Milk and Honey, of a place where new and exciting things—like Expo '67— happened. Now, of course, and especially when I write, the pendulum swings back and forth between the binaries of 'here' and 'there.' I write from memory, which, to paraphrase the poet and novelist, James Joyce, is the imagination, the mother of the muses.

Not surprisingly, when I write about characters who are between two worlds, in transition, it's like writing about myself. An underlying biographical impulse is always there. Nowadays people cross borders and travel within borders so frequently that modern life has become one of transition. I am intrigued about how this migration and transition affects the human spirit and I explore these dualities through my characters.

I've now lived more years in Canada than in Guyana, but there are always the reminders that I, in a sense, will remain the newcomer. I am still viewed as an ethnic writer perhaps, although I know I'm moving closer to what is considered 'mainstream.' But the mainstream is somehow resistant to that evolution, instead designating as 'ethnic' the themes of other origins, cultures and experiences, especially as dramatized by a person of minority. The question, however, is this: can I not write about these sensibilities as a mainstream writer? Perhaps I can see Canada more clearly precisely because I came here from elsewhere. Perhaps the synergy or symbiosis of having more than one place in one's imagination can enhance rather than limit our understanding of Canadianism.

We tend to see Canada in its phenomenological sense—the rocks, lakes, wilderness, cities, coasts, and so on. However, Canada is also the landscape of our imagination, what we, who each come with our own unique perspectives, imagine it to be. This is the Canada of our writing, our poetry, our art, our music. There are some nationalists who don't agree; they see Canada from a rigid, conventional perspective. But for me the notion of Canada, and also Canada as home, exists in my heart and comes out in my creative work.

The sense of home for those of us who are immigrants and 'outsiders' remains elusive. Especially for people of colour. Canada is a wonderful place but in a sense its identity is also still steeped in colonialism.

Racially based injustices still happen, and you wish you didn't have to spend so much emotional energy fending for your right to belong. And again you find yourself pondering the notion of home, of belonging, of being accepted. It's an ongoing dilemma and sometimes I think that my only true home is what has been coined the 'portable home of the imagination.'

I've lived in my respectable Ottawa neighbourhood for over 20 years and I own my home, but sometimes it still doesn't truly feel like home.

But I must add, with some sense of paradox, that these feelings generally do not dominate my thinking. However, when little reminders of your place are put to you, they do jolt you right out of your Canadian comfort zone. You expect society to uphold the principles of equal access and opportunities, and when it doesn't, you're left feeling there isn't room for you. And it dawns on you that some have already done their thinking about you, and that is that; it's beyond your control.

I do think the structures and mechanisms are there to protect the rights of minority people but whether these structures are efficacious would generate a good debate. Having worked in race relations for the past decade, my suspicion is that not much has really changed in government. I am heartened, though, by the changes I see beginning to happen in the social and political environment, in hiring practices and so on. And more Canadians are beginning to realize that citizenship is also about recognizing diversity and the experiences of other landscapes that are part of an immigrant's baggage.

Now that I have a child, I feel this sense of urgency to bring closure to the issues I grapple with. And yet, the only way they can be resolved is when I write and through my writing. When I write I can wrestle intellectually and emotionally with the issues and the way I perceive them. I can create a forum for my voice and my concerns. I can ventilate my emotions. And in doing all that, I can help myself to gain new perspectives, grasp new possibilities for resolution.

A few years ago my daughter was very cognizant of her colour, of being half brown and half white. And because of the messages she was getting at school—this was grade one—she didn't want to be half brown. It's my hope that as she grows and matures, she will have the emotional wherewithal and social support to cultivate an unswerving sense of home. I'm optimistic for several reasons: I have great faith in the education system and how, on the cusp of the twenty-first century, it's helping to shape our changing vision of the country. The policy of multiculturalism, when not adulterated by politics and special agendas, can also bring many positive things to our young society. And the population mix is changing so that by the time today's ethnic children reach adulthood, the colour of their skin might have become completely inconsequential.

"Of late I am beginning to see a new piece in the puzzle, those individuals born in Canada of non-white immigrant parents (Black, Hispanic, Asian or African), whose loyalty to Canada is instantaneous; with them there is nothing contrived or made ambivalent by a 'foreign' heritage or sense of another homeland. And notions of place, self and identity suddenly become intertwined."*

That's how it is for my daughter. The most accurate predictor of her sense of place here in Canada may well be that she will have played in the snow as a child. This is her home. The only home she has ever known and quite likely where she will live all her life.

When I ponder all these things in my heart, I have a great wholesome sense of things to come.

---

* From "Citizenship is more than a Birthright" by Cyril Dabydeen, published by *The Toronto Star*, Sept, 1994.

Diane Dwarka

FYZABAD, TRINIDAD—WINNIPEG, MANITOBA

*A visitor to the Manitoba Department of Education and Training
Library might be forgiven for not taking special notice of the
librarian who unobtrusively navigates between the computer screen
and the rows upon rows of books, compiling a list of titles here,
a collection of references there. Nonetheless this is no ordinary
librarian: This is Diane Dwarka, singular proponent for
intercultural congruity and Manitoba's first Multicultural
Education Specialist. To know her is to sense her passion for the
power and potential of education, her dedication as a tireless
builder of bridges, quietly spanning the common ground of those
who think they live worlds apart.*

*For her extraordinary vision and commitment Dwarka has received
numerous citations, among them the 1996 YM-YWCA Woman of
Distinction Award and a 1997 Distinguished Alumni Award as
presented by the Red River College.*

F ew families follow their three-year-old children to a new
homeland, but such was the case when Diane Dwarka and her
family migrated from Trinidad to Ottawa in the spring of 1977.
"Our youngest child was in poor health and when my husband's
mother, who had immigrated to Canada ten years earlier, came back
to Trinidad for a visit in June of 1976, she convinced us to let her take
Dane back to Ottawa with them. We had exhausted every medical
avenue available in our country so we agreed, although it was a tough
decision to make."

The Dwarkas had been struggling with their son's health since his
birth, and at age three he remained unable to walk and talk, could

manage only a liquid diet, and had achieved few of the developmental milestones typical for his age group. "We had the country's best doctors conclude he was mentally retarded, and yet, as teachers, we assessed him objectively and knew it wasn't so. When I informed his medical team we were sending him to Canada for treatment, they told me I was wasting my money. And I told them, 'It's my money. Let me take that chance.'"

Six months later the Dwarkas travelled to Ottawa to visit their son, and noted a marked improvement in his condition. "We could see that Dane was already gaining ground, and when he re-bonded with us during that visit, we decided the time had come to relocate the rest of our family. Our other son and daughter were still young enough to adjust to a new situation without too much trauma, so the time was right."

The Dwarkas were young, skilled and mobile, and additionally blessed with a significant head start in their journey to Canadian citizenship—they had a support system already in place. "My husband's mother and siblings were all in Canada; in fact, on his side of the family we were the last to leave Trinidad. So we had the luxury of coming to family. We were also sponsored by them, which undoubtedly streamlined our application process and enabled us to come in April of 1977, only a few months after we had visited Dane."

As is the case for many immigrants, the Dwarkas' reasons for emigrating had less to do with personal economics than with their quest for new opportunity. In fact, they lost considerable financial ground in relocating. Both left behind well-paid teaching positions and although they came with glowing letters of reference, the Dwarkas soon discovered that teaching in the Ottawa area would be an unlikely option for them. "For the first time ever, the districts were cutting back teaching positions and amalgamating schools. It was suggested that we could probably get teaching jobs up north, but that would have defeated the primary purpose of our move—to be with our sick child and look after him.

"We were fortunate to find other good jobs almost immediately, my husband as manager of a McDonald's restaurant and I as an Information Assistant with the Malaysian High Commission in

Ottawa. I worked with the many Malaysian student associations throughout Canada and helped to promote Malaysia to Canadians. As teachers we both were experienced in working with young people and able to put this background to good use in our new job settings."

But their son's chronically poor health continued to be a challenge, especially when it deteriorated to the point where Dwarka had to take a leave of absence from her work to tend to his care. "One night his breathing was so bad that I ended up taking him to hospital and spending the night there. I phoned the High Commissioner in the morning and he was very compassionate. He told me to take as much time as I needed. I ended up taking Dane to the children's hospital in Toronto, where we stayed for a month. When we came back to Ottawa I had to stay home with him for several months because he'd had his jaws wired together. Times were lean but it was made easier knowing my job would be there when I was ready to come back."

In the meantime Dwarka's own parents and brother and sister had immigrated to Canada and settled in Winnipeg. When her beloved mother-in-law died in 1979, the Dwarkas assessed their options in Ottawa and subsequently began considering a move to Manitoba. "We weren't able to visit my aging parents very often and so we thought, why not move closer to them? Our jobs were easy enough to leave and Dane was beginning to do better. He'd had extensive surgery and was beginning to eat, and with speech therapy he was making notable progress. So in 1981 we decided to move again."

Dwarka remembers their early years in Winnipeg as being the most financially challenging period of their lives. Neither partner was able to find work immediately, yet Dwarka readily recalls the support received from her close-knit family and new-found friends. "I looked after my ailing mom for a while, which was a special time. We also became very good friends with people who lived up the street from us. They realized our financial situation couldn't be anything but strained, yet they also knew we wouldn't take a handout. So they asked my husband if he would help paint their house. And then they gave us some lovely gifts in return, a big ham for example. They would see our children walking home from school and call them in to pick up some buns or other treat. They made it really easy for us to accept their kindness, and they didn't think of us as being nobodies. They had senior administrative jobs, yet they accepted us for what we were. We've remained very close friends.

"My dad also made it easy for me by giving us some generous help to tide us over. For the rest, we didn't spend time dwelling on our difficulties; we lived within our means and made do with what we had. We knew the hard times wouldn't last forever."

Eventually Dwarka's husband found work, again with a McDonald's restaurant. A few years later he returned to school to take a drafting course and worked for a time in government services as a drafting instructor. Today he teaches drafting at Red River College.

After her mother's death in 1982, Dwarka took stock of her own career path and concluded she should return to school. "I enrolled in a library technology course at Red River College and shortly after my graduation in June of 1984 was hired on at the Manitoba Department of Education and Training Library."

Dwarka's mandate in her new position was to help develop multicultural library services not only for Manitoba teachers, but for the province's ethno-cultural communities as well. She was quick to discover her niche in multicultural education and in 1992, when the multicultural library services were amalgamated with the Department of Education's main library, Dwarka became the province's first Multicultural Information Specialist.

To that end she designs and conducts workshops for teachers to help foster understanding of other cultures, compiles the bibliographies and selects the resources that form the library's valuable collection on multicultural education, and serves as a consultant to the province's educators. "We serve all of the Manitoba teachers in our 854 schools, as well as the students and faculties at the four universities within the province. And of course the public is also welcome to use the library.

"There's a great need to learn about other cultures, and if you are a member of a minority group, a need as well to have your own culture validated. I believe we are helping our schools to move in that direction. The Manitoba Grade Four curriculum includes a study of different countries and cultures. Some schools still teach the unit in a kind of superficial 'show-and-tell' way, but others are well beyond that and show a real understanding of the cultures being examined. The Grade Nine curriculum contains a significant human rights component, which fosters understanding, appreciation and respect among the students. That's of paramount importance since some of our schools have a really mixed population.

"One very positive aspect of this job is that I have no regrets about derailing my teaching career to come to Canada. I still work very closely with teachers in a way that challenges me, and my background helps me understand their specific needs and questions. Sometimes when I make suggestions or refer them to certain resources, they're quick to figure out my training is also in teaching. So the combination of teaching and library skills has really worked well for me in this setting. Of course the work is ongoing, with the French schools, the Aboriginal schools and all of the ethnic people in the school system, so you never see the light at the end of the tunnel. You keep going, going, going, but it's immensely interesting."

But Dwarka has not limited her energies to her family and profession, although these commitments alone would amply fill most people's agendas. Instead, she seemingly thrives on the interaction and stimulation generated by the dozens of volunteer initiatives in which she has been or is involved. In fact Dwarka has been doing her bit to make a difference almost as far back as she herself can remember.

Even as a young teacher in Trinidad, she had sought out ways to make a contribution to her community. She taught Sunday School, served as secretary to her church and led various youth groups such as Explorers and Trinidad Girls in Training. She was secretary to the Parent-Teacher Association at the local, regional and national levels. For her outstanding work with the 4-H movement at all levels she was awarded a Michigan State University scholarship, where she earned a Rural Youth Leaders Educator's Certificate. She later became President of the 4-H movement in Trinidad, Tobago and Grenada, and hosted Trinidad's first national 4-H conference.

During the Ottawa years Dwarka bowed out of community service to focus on her son's ongoing medical needs, but in Winnipeg her commitment to volunteer work was re-kindled with a brush-fire of energy and enthusiasm. Today much of her committee work seems a natural and complementary extension of her career as the province's Multicultural Information Specialist. Many of her chosen organizations share the same recognizable theme—the nurturing of bridge-building across communities that at first glance may seem to have little in common, and the fostering of understanding among people who's misconceptions are often based on inaccurate information.

Without a doubt Dwarka relishes the balancing act of her volunteer commitments, which she orchestrates with the easy serenity of a master juggler. Simply stated, she makes time for an issue that she believes requires attention. "I was asked a few years ago to join the Manitoba Association for Multicultural Education, which promotes multicultural education programs within the school system. There's a real need for effort in this area since many teachers have little experience in teaching cross-cultural courses. It's not that they don't want to teach these courses, it's just that in their own teacher training they were never taught how.

"Anyway, I declined; I was just too busy. A while later they approached me again and asked me if they couldn't just twist my arm a bit, and I said, 'All right, twist it.' The result is that I've just served a term as president and still sit on the Board of Directors."

Dwarka's arm was also twisted at the 1997 annual meeting of the Canada Council for Multicultural and Intercultural Education, when she agreed to a term as national president. "It was a huge job," she concedes, "especially since the national office was in Ottawa and I'm in Winnipeg."

But the list doesn't end there. Since 1995 Dwarka has co-chaired the Coalition of Human Equality. She is also current president of the Trinidad and Tobago Society of Manitoba and of a national human rights committee. She is the immediate past chair of both the Council of Caribbean Organizations of Manitoba and of the Community Legal Education Committee. She continues to be a member of the Holocaust Awareness Committee. In 1994 Dwarka was one of 15 Canadian educators and the only Manitoban to be selected to participate in the *Educators' International Holocaust and Hope Tour* to Germany, Poland and Israel. "As a Christian I was never taught about the

Holocaust in Trinidad, and as a result I was never fully aware of the atrocities that were committed. It's so important for people to know this segment of history. And it's never too late to become enlightened. Since the tour I've done much reading and we've added a substantial volume of Holocaust material to our collection at the library. I've also compiled a bibliography which annually goes out to all the schools in time for Holocaust Awareness Week."

Dwarka has also offered a portion of her ample energies to her own church. When she first arrived in Winnipeg she joined the United Church in her neighbourhood and was promptly installed on several committees including the Christian Education Committee and the Church Building Committee. "When we came the congregation was just getting off the ground, meeting in a school music room, and I found it very comfortable, just right for us. It grew as our own family grew. When the music room became too small, we moved to the gym, then to another school and finally to a new church." Over the years Dwarka has also served on several regional and national church committees, including a national campus ministry committee. Currently she is a member of several committees including an anti-racism working group.

Not surprisingly, Dwarka's significant and ongoing contributions to her community and province have not gone unnoticed. In 1996 she was lauded by the YM-YWCA which conferred on her a Woman of Distinction Award. That same year she also received an award from the Trinidad and Tobago Society of Manitoba for her outstanding contribution to life and work in the community. In 1997 Red River College recognized her with a Distinguished Alumni Award which "honours graduates of the College who have distinguished themselves in both their chosen profession and the community."

Since 1997 her name has appeared in a number of Who's Who editions, including *Who's Who of Canadian Women* in both 1997 and 1998. In 1998 she received the B'nai B'rith Midwest Region Human Rights Award for her 'exemplary role in human rights in the Province of Manitoba.' And in that same year she was awarded the Premier's Volunteer Award for community service.

These recognitions reveal much about the drive, dedication and commitment that form a large part of Dwarka's character. But to suggest as much is to solicit a quiet smile and an understated response that plays down the relevance of her own pivotal role. Instead, she chooses to talk of the work yet to be done, and the distances yet to be travelled on the footpath of the human condition before cultural diversity and unconditional equality will be truly embraced. And, like many parents, she diverts attention from her own accomplishments by speaking proudly of her children. Of the daughter who has an Honours Degree in Commerce and is now the Chief Administrative Officer of Legal Aid Manitoba. Or of the son who studied computer science and is now a program analyst. Or of the younger son, Dane.

"Had we stayed in Trinidad, I'm quite convinced Dane would not have survived. He did not have a known disorder but rather a series of challenges that prompted them to pretty much dismiss his future. Well, look where he is today. He took computer analyst programming courses at Red River College and received the George Wallace Memorial Scholarship at his graduation in 1999. He still has some challenges with his speech, but if you listen carefully you can carry on a good conversation with him.

"It was also predicted he'd always be small for his age. Wouldn't you know it, turns out he's the tallest in the family."

Often when I sing the Canadian anthem,
it brings tears to my eyes.
It's just an emotion: This land is my land.
But is it really my land?

Ever since I can remember, I've had a positive image of Canada in my mind. Growing up in Trinidad, our CGIT (Christian Girls in Training) leaders were missionaries from Canada and they were always telling us wonderful things about their country. So we developed an easy sense of familiarity with Canada, based entirely on the stories and impressions they shared with us. When we reached university age, they talked up the Canadian universities, McGill, Mount Allison, the list goes on. And since Trinidad has only one university, it felt natural for many people, including my sister, to come to Canada for their post-secondary education. After graduation my sister went back to Trinidad to teach but eventually decided to return to Canada. Same with my brother; he married a Canadian-born woman from a small prairie town.

A lot of people think of Canada as the land of milk and honey, and for many it is. But my standard of living in Trinidad was comparable to the Canadian standard; my parents were business people and I never lacked anything as a child. My husband and I both had teaching jobs so we were doing well. In fact, we gave up everything to come to Canada and we count the years we spent trying to get back on our feet here as being among our most difficult. So it wasn't destitution and poverty that brought us here. It was our youngest child. We wanted the best possible chance for him and we've never regretted our decision to immigrate.

We were fortunate because we had a family support system already in place when we arrived. For those who come alone, and especially if they don't speak English, it must be very challenging, pioneering in the sense that life takes on a whole new concept and everything is foreign. For those who come without the language, it's so important to start taking language training right away; communication is a key factor to getting settled in, finding your way around and being able to express yourself.

Often people come here with a picture, a perception of Canada, that doesn't really fit the reality. When they realize this, they are further traumatized and might be tempted to follow a natural tendency to retreat within themselves. But that only drags out the settling-in period, which is never easy even under the best of circumstances. It's far better to find the courage and resolve to make a few friends, seek out those who've walked the same path, and lean on them for the first little while. There's much of our daily living to sort through when everything is alien: our currency, the concept of tax in addition to retail cost, getting children enrolled in school, visiting the doctor, the everyday challenges.

Every Canadian city has at least some system in place to support newcomers during their early years. In Winnipeg it's the International Centre. We also have a *Newcomer's Guide to Manitoba*. Every province offers a series of handbooks for immigrants, which is available in many languages. Each province also has an association for immigrant women, so important because women are treated so differently in some countries and they, especially, have many adjustments to make.

There are many other support services as well. For example, we have the Black Educators' Association, formed specifically to help parents deal with such challenges as their children's schooling and parent interviews. Many immigrant parents wouldn't think of going to the school to confer with their children's teachers, yet the futures of these children may well hang in that balance. So support in that area is crucial.

When we came to Manitoba our daughter was placed in grade nine, although her teachers in Ottawa had recommended she be advanced to grade ten. A month later the school decided she would be better placed in the tenth grade after all, and so she advanced to the local high school where she found herself as a new student who had missed the entire first month of course work.

Two weeks later she did poorly on a math test, so her father and I went to the school to meet with her teacher, who was less than empathetic with our daughter's situation. Essentially her message was, "why should the school invest extra teaching time in this child when she's just moved here from Ottawa and may well move again?" We suggested to her that her attitude was inappropriate; a teacher is there to help a child, whether the child is in the school for a day, a month, a year or a decade. And she realized she'd said the wrong thing, and apologized. She had unfairly based our daughter's ability on the two weeks she had spent in that particular classroom rather than on her background and previous performance. As for our daughter, she required a total of two hours with a tutor to bring her marks back up.

When it comes to deciphering our own emotions about our sense of place after two decades of living here, there are many layers to wade through. On the one hand we left much behind, but on the other hand we have always been forward looking, and we approached our moves with the same attitude. On the one hand I relish every trip back to Trinidad, visiting friends and feeling as if I've never left, yet knowing and accepting that it's not my home anymore. But on the other hand I still find myself saying 'home' when I refer to Trinidad, so I guess I will always carry something of my birthplace with me.

I feel as strong and fervent a Canadian as someone who was born here. I've adopted this land. And yet, often when I sing the Canadian anthem, it brings tears to my eyes. It's just an emotion: this land is my land. But is it really my land? If I have to stop and think about that, am I simply reflecting an equilibrium of sorts, with one foot here and the other back there? Or are my emotions spurred on by the fact I once had a home and a history elsewhere?

But a home and history elsewhere does not suggest that I can not or do not love and embrace Canada. I can, and I do. However, there will always be differences. For example, I will never speak like a Canadian who was born here, and I'm comfortable with that. But what our family has managed to do is make ourselves part of the mainstream, a necessity if you're going to survive economically and be an active participant of the new society. Still, we make it a point to maintain some of the cultural traditions of our upbringing. I still enjoy preparing our traditional foods from time to time, for example, but I've come to know and enjoy many different types of cuisine.

There are new Canadians who have great difficulty making the emotional break from their former homes. They mostly continue to live the way they lived in the old country. And although they are withholding themselves from the opportunities to be reaped in their new homeland, they can carry on in this manner indefinitely. But the trouble begins when they try to impose this cultural and societal atmosphere on their young people. It's a battle they can't win and often their approach backfires by alienating the next generation. When we come here we have to be prepared to accept that our children will grow up differently than they would have in the old setting. It's all part of the trade-off.

I love Manitoba. As our license plate suggests, Manitobans are a friendly people and we were made to feel very welcome when we first arrived—by our church, our neighbourhood, our community. Our neighbours threw a barbeque for us. But we were equally eager to find ways of our own to reach out to our new community, and one of the first things we did was to head up the Neighbourhood Watch program. I'm not suggesting that there weren't difficulties—a move is always unsettling, and tensions arise, tensions usually generated by uncertainty. What I am suggesting is that you can't just wait to be accepted, you have to reach out as well.

My involvement with my church and my work has given me many opportunities to reach out and make a contribution. There are many, many ways to build bridges among people who are inherently good but lack the knowledge they need to understand each other well. That's why my work with multiculturalism is so important to me. I've learned so much, about the Metis, the Aboriginals, the Jewish people, the minority cultures, and I've come to understand them better, respect their differences and appreciate their similarities. There are many who think multiculturalism is all about tolerance. That's a word I don't like. Tolerance is a state of tension that has nothing to do with acceptance. To tolerate someone is to communicate with them only when I have to, to be civil only because the laws of the land dictate that I must. To be tolerant of someone is to have no emotional stake in that person. It's not a great way to live, and not the ideal I strive for in my work and life.

I do see attitudes gradually changing and stereotypical notions breaking down, perhaps as more interracial marriages are taking place. Such a shift can only add to our country's diversity and strength as a people place. As a Canadian who loves this country, I harbour many concerns about the future, but see room for optimism as well. We continue to endure an ongoing brain drain, but at the same time we are steadily producing a new crop of professionals to plug the gaps. Our health care system is probably still the best in the world even though it suffers from troubling hemorrhages, in the closing of small hospitals and in cutbacks in staff, supplies and services. We're becoming more aware of the finite nature of our environment, even though we still drive too many cars and don't recycle as vigorously as we should. Too many of us either still don't care or aren't aware of the ramifications of endless consumption.

Life is what you make of it. We've had some minor dealings with racism over the years, but I chalk prejudice up to ignorance and have no trouble leaving it at that. Perhaps it's because my experiences have allowed me to develop an open mind. Perhaps it's because I've carved a niche for myself and feel good about who I am and what I do. When you feel good about yourself, it doesn't matter what other people say.

Gary Ho

TAIPEI, TAIWAN—VANCOUVER, CANADA

*Had Gary Ho, as a university graduate in Taiwan in 1970,
cared to try his hand at foretelling his future, predictions likely
would not have included a rapid rise to wealth through real estate
development, a conversion to Buddhism, a change in citizenship,
and the creation of the Buddhist Compassion Relief Tzu Chi
Foundation of Canada.*

Yet all of the above feature prominently in Ho's biography.

*In the nine years he has lived in Canada, Ho has, through his
Foundation, quietly generated several million dollars and countless
volunteer hours for charity and other community causes.*

*And although he likes to work quietly, well away from the
spotlight's glare, his efforts have nonetheless gained him
recognition as an eminent community leader and benefactor,
and a local hero—as designated by* Maclean's magazine
in 1996.

*"By serving others with a grateful heart, I light up my own
mind. And if I can bring joy to fellow Canadians, then
I am doubly blessed."*

If Gary Ho had not come to Canada in search of a well-rounded
education for his three young sons, the Buddhist Compassion
Relief Tzu Chi Foundation of Canada would likely not exist today.
And if the Foundation had not come into being, a myriad of
Vancouver and area service agencies would be without the support
they've come to depend on in a time of ever-increasing need and
declining public funds. The Vancouver Hospital and Health Sciences
Centre could not have established the Institute for Complementary
and Alternative Medicines, the first such centre installed in a North

American hospital. And British Columbia's Multi-Ethnic Marrow Transplant Society would likely not have been founded.

Although Ho would be the first to wave away any talk of legacy with regards to his pivotal role in the establishment and work of the Tzu Chi Foundation of Canada, the Foundation's record of benevolent support is nonetheless testament to one person's ability to move mountains. Gary Ho, without a doubt, has quietly moved a mountain in the short span of time he has called himself Canadian.

Born in China in 1947, Ho was just two years old when his parents relocated to Taiwan. "My growing up years were a time of financial struggle for my parents. Taiwan's economy was in a slump and my father had a low-paying job with the military. But even so my parents were determined to scrape together tuition money for my four younger siblings and me. Education was a priority; education was the road map to a better destination."

After graduating with a degree in electronic engineering, Ho spent a year in mandatory military service and then performed a professional about-face by turning his energies to real estate. "I had a group of school friends—we were all poor kids—and we had this dream of starting our own real estate company. Our country's economy was just beginning to make its up-turn and we wanted to try working for ourselves. So we rented a small office and opened our business, the four of us. We lived there too, since we were too poor to live elsewhere. The kitchen and bathroom were our bedrooms. Our showers amounted to a splash of water from the sink. That's how we started."

From that questionable beginning, and with the help of Taiwan's dramatic economic turn-around in the 1970's, Ho's prosperity soared. Within the decade he had become well entrenched as a real estate developer, having completed such projects as high-rise apartments, office towers, and a housing development containing 1500 single-residence units. The good life he had longed for was now assured. "Obviously I was on top of the world, convinced that business was king. Business drove the world and nothing else really mattered."

In the mid-1980's Ho's wife chanced to meet a former colleague, a woman once known for her self-absorption and now completely bathed in humbleness. When Ho's wife enquired about her dramatic change of character and perspective, the woman attributed it simply to her personal discovery of Buddhism. "This woman then asked my wife if we would help support her master, Cheng Yen, in the building of a hospital. Since we had already developed our own family tradition of sharing with the less fortunate, there were no reservations about giving to a worthy cause, but I wasn't enthused about contributing to Buddhism. I wasn't a spiritual person. I didn't want my contribution to end up supporting a temple. On the other hand, a hospital sounded like a good cause, especially this one since it would be in a remote and primitive area desperately in need of services.

"So we donated $50,000 US, a one-time gift with no further commitment on our part. To be truthful, I considered Buddhism a cop-out from real life. Buddhists, I thought, went to the mountain top to hide out from the rest of the world. And I had no interest whatsoever in developing my own spirituality. I was a follower of the god of business."

The Buddhists, however, wanted to show their appreciation to the Hos, and made them honorary members of the Foundation's board. The Hos accepted. The Buddhists also offered information on Buddhism in general and the hospital project in particular, but this the Hos declined. "We didn't mind supporting their work but we didn't want them preaching to us."

The following year the Hos were invited to a luncheon in Taipei for honorary board members where they met the master whose project they had supported, Chen Yeng. "In her address to us, Master Chen Yeng spoke about her work and her vision for the hospital. She explained that doing charitable work, not preaching, was the key to Buddhism. I was deeply touched. This was not at all as I had understood Buddhism to be."

Almost inexplicably Ho felt himself being drawn to the message of Buddhism. Gradually he immersed his intellect and spirit into the teachings and writings of Master Chen Yeng, and eventually committed himself as a follower. He also became deeply involved in the works of the Buddhist Tzu Chi Foundation, a charitable organization founded in 1966 by Master Chen Yeng on the principle of "helping the poor and enlightening the rich." [The Tzu Chi Foundation, which translates as the *Foundation for Compassion and Relief,* had its beginnings in the singular conviction that Buddhist teachings could be put into practise by bringing charity, medical care, education and culture to those most in need. On the premise that religion transcends race, nationality and political boundary, the Foundation has, in the last decade, branched into 25 countries around the world including Canada and the United States. Currently it has more than four million members worldwide. In 1993 the Foundation established Taiwan's Marrow Donor Registry, today the third largest bone marrow data bank in the world and used by physicians around the globe.]

In the years following his conversion to Buddhism, Ho was content to devote himself to his family, business, and the Tzu Chi Foundation. But at the same time he was also growing increasingly disenchanted with the quality of his sons' education. "In Taiwan every child who aspires to a university education has to pass entrance exams at the end of high school, so all schooling is geared to one's performance on these tests. Needless to say, the system was very competitive and lacked balance. It didn't recognize the need for children to have a normal, care-free childhood. And we got caught up in it too. I used to put a great deal of pressure on my children, and the pressure was on us parents too. Everyone wanted their children to do well and be successful. But at what cost?

"Meanwhile, we knew of some Taiwanese parents who had emigrated to Canada for the sake of their children's schooling, and gradually we began to consider doing the same."

When Ho and his wife travelled to Vancouver to visit friends and look around, they were so taken by their surroundings that they purchased a house before returning to Taiwan. "We had been to many parts of the world. But Vancouver, we felt, was the most beautiful city we had ever seen. My wife loved it at first sight."

The Hos calculated that the ritual of moving would be straightforward enough: they looked forward to the adventure, a home was waiting for them, and their business would carry on as usual in Taiwan. By this time independently wealthy and at arm's length from the day-to-day running of their companies, the family looked forward to a more leisurely and contemplative pace of life in Canada.

Master Chen Yeng, however, planted the seeds of other possibilities into their consciousness. "When we told her of our decision, she gently reminded us that the spirit of Tzu Chi was universal and that we would be carrying it with us to Canada."

The family moved in December of 1991. Ho hadn't basked for long in his new Canadian setting when he felt compelled to offer the spirit of Tzu Chi to his adopted community. "The master had not directed us to start a branch of the Foundation in Canada, only that we should continue to practise the spirit of Tzu Chi for ourselves. But practising is more than just sitting at home and reading the Buddhist *Sutra*. It also means translating the teachings into deeds that will help the poor and enlighten the rich. I felt moved to do my part."

Ho and his family began by hosting a series of tea parties for friends and acquaintances, many of them from prominent Taiwanese and Hong Kong families, and used the occasion to enter into a dialogue about the essence of Tzu Chi. "We talked about how it is good, when we have so much, to give something of ourselves back to the community. We discussed the merit of giving and serving with a grateful heart, seeking nothing in return. It turned out that many who were part of those early conversations also wanted to embody the principles of the Foundation."

From that inauspicious beginning in 1992, the Foundation has grown into a vibrant team of 600 volunteers who have brought new light and hope to many of the city's beleaguered charitable and service organizations. Many are themselves recent arrivals from Asia. In any given week Tzu Chi volunteers can be found visiting the various hospitals and seniors' homes armed with home-made cuisine, free haircuts and moral support. They deliver Meals on Wheels, lend a hand at AIDS Vancouver, clean city streets, and support outreach programs for urban youth. Ho himself is grateful to serve up fresh Chinese fare at a Salvation Army soup kitchen on a regular basis. Grateful, because "when you just write a cheque, you won't be touched."

But writing cheques to the Foundation is something many individual patrons do on an ongoing basis, enabling the Foundation, in turn, to contribute financially to the community as well. "We are fortunate to have 3500 members who give us monthly support. Our master directs us to spend these funds, which comes from people's hearts, carefully and wisely. We don't use any donated money for administration; as volunteers we look after our own administrative costs. We place our dollars and volunteers where they are well-needed and we don't expect gratitude in return. The master says we must not pressure our recipients into feeling indebted. We must give with a happy heart so that all they feel is our softness, like cotton falling on them."

Ho is quick to point out that not all volunteers are Buddhist. "You don't have to be a Buddhist—we have Christian volunteers as well. The only criteria is a desire to serve with selfless gratitude and to practise the spirit of compassion and relief among those less fortunate than we are."

To date, the Tzu Chi Foundation has contributed or pledged more than $8 million to an eclectic bevy of worthwhile causes, which have neither cultural nor religious boundaries. The University of British Columbia Entrance Bursary Fund and other scholarship funds have received significant support, as has the Vancouver Public Library system. Winter coats have been bought for and distributed among Vancouver street kids. And although the bulk of Foundation monies is spent in Vancouver—"our philosophy is to raise money locally and use it locally"—support is not necessarily limited to Vancouver nor even to British Columbia: in 1996 Tzu Chi donated several thousand dollars to the Canadian Red Cross for the victims of flooding in Quebec.

Not surprisingly, the Tzu Chi Foundation has on occasion come before the attention of the media, although Ho makes no effort to solicit such recognition; the public spotlight is not particularly in keeping with Foundation's philosophy of service for nothing in return. And although well-intentioned, it has been known to misconstrue the purport of Ho's words. "I was once interviewed by a reporter from a local daily and talked with her about our philosophy of personal enlightenment. I told her that all people are equal, and that inside each of us there beats a Buddhist heart, meaning that there is good and compassion in everyone. She quoted me in her article as saying that everyone should be Buddhist. So although I was emphasizing common ground, she in her misquote ended up polarizing us as a group that would impose its values on others. I'm sure people were offended, and offending others is the last thing we want to do."

In the few years that Ho has been in Canada, he has mobilized his dedicated team of Tzu Chi volunteers to venture into arenas not usually associated with passivity and introspection, the traditional tenets of Buddhism. Using the Taiwan Marrow Donor Registry as a model, the Foundation established the B.C. Multi-Ethnic Marrow Transplant Society in 1995. The following year gave rise to its most ambitious project to date, the founding of the Tzu Chi Institute for Complementary and Alternative Medicine. This project, if any, has epitomized the ability to move a mountain with the levers of vision, dedication and tenacity.

Ho's interest in the project was first sparked by a pediatric endocrinologist who felt that the relationship between eastern and western medicine merited further study. "He was also Asian-Canadian, and felt that we might be interested in sponsoring such a project, the first of its kind. Of course he piqued our interest. Asian people have long known the benefits of homeopathy and acupuncture, and most of us have benefited from these treatments at one time or another. That the western world was now proposing to examine, in a hospital setting, the effectiveness of these therapies as a complement to western medicine was a milestone for both disciplines. So in May, 1996, we were approached by mainstream medicine for financial support. Specifically, they were looking for $6 million, and I thought, 'We're only three years old. How can we possibly raise this money?' But nonetheless, once we had obtained the approval of the master and our Board of Directors, I told him we would do what we could.

"In early June we decided to organize a large fundraising dinner party for the Institute. We set the cost per plate at $1200, for which we asked people to pledge $100 per month for a year. And charitable donations are tax deductible, so you didn't have to be rich in order to be our guest. For the meal our members served humble vegetarian fare. We ended up with more than 900 guests for dinner and, with additional pledges received throughout the evening, raised $3 million. So we were able to give $1 million to the project right away, with plans to pledge $5 million more over the next five years."

The Tzu Chi Institute opened in October of 1996, a mere five months after financial support had first been requested. Already it's being heralded as an important marriage bed for the best of eastern and western medical traditions.

Typically, Ho downplays his own involvement in the project, choosing instead to see public gratitude consigned to members and volunteers of the Foundation. "Obviously we are grateful for the tremendous backing that allows us to tackle such ambitious projects, and we are fortunate to be so generously supported on an ongoing basis. We have 85 honorary board members who have each contributed substantially to the Foundation. All our donations come from individuals. People are eager to contribute when they know every penny will go right back into a worthwhile project."

Even so however, Ho doesn't lose sight of his conviction that raising money, even for a noble purpose, comes second to the ethic of personal enlightenment through service. "It is through service that we truly live the teachings of Buddhism. That we learn how fortunate we really are. That we discover profound gratitude for what we have and for the people we are blessed to serve."

In 1996 *Maclean's* magazine bestowed national attention on Ho by singling him out as an exemplary Canadian who is making a notable difference in his own community. Referring to him as 'the millionaire investor,' the publication lauded Ho's ongoing ability to reach so many people in need in so many relevant ways.

Ho remains nonplussed by the recognition. "We don't do what we do for fame and thanks. We do it for the opportunity to bring light to our own minds through service to others. We do it because, ultimately, it makes us happy too."

> *... when I told my master I was moving to Canada,*
> *she said, 'You can't just go there to enjoy yourself.*
> *You can't just partake of their welfare and environment.*
> *You must give something in return.'*

I can narrow my reasons for coming to Canada down to a single one: my children's future. In Taiwan, the entire education system for the higher grades concentrates on preparing the student for the mandatory university entrance examinations. Nothing else seems to matter much. Everyone moves straight ahead, absorbing the academic curriculum without glancing left or right at the many other opportunities for learning that exist but do not fall within the strict parameters of what is considered 'academic.' I had three sons in that system and as they got older I became increasingly concerned that they were not getting a well-rounded education, not being exposed to a global perspective.

Now, a western education is also academically sound but at the same time it is more culturally balanced. My children have had opportunities to do volunteer work as part of their school experience, and they've been able to take elective courses in their areas of interest. My son was introduced to his future career in this way. In his first year in Canada we enrolled him in grade ten, and it wasn't long before his teacher took note of his interest and talent in design and suggested he take architecture as one of his elective courses. In Taiwan, where such early exposure is not an option, he might never have discovered this discipline. But today, in Canada, he is a qualified architect.

Of course the word in our circle is that it helps to have Chinese parents if you want your child to be successful. Chinese parents view their role in their children's education, to which they give top priority, as being one of amalgamating, if you will, eastern and western traditions in education. We tend to push our children more, although I've learned from my master that there is danger in pushing them too hard, always demanding their top performance and not appreciating them for who they are. Nonetheless, my children receive tutoring in Chinese three times a week. English is no longer a problem for them; Chinese is the language they will have difficulty with if we don't help them keep it up. English will be their first language, but the added benefit of the second language will give them an advantage in the business world.

When we decided to move to Canada in 1991, I anticipated that my life would be one of relaxed contemplation. I would, for the most part, manage my businesses from Vancouver. There would be the odd business trip back to Taiwan every few months, but other than that my life would be comfortably paced. However, when I told my master I was moving to Canada, she said, "You can't just go there to enjoy yourself. You can't just partake of their welfare and environment. You must give something in return." She wasn't suggesting that I start a branch of the Tzu Chi Foundation, only that I should continue to practise the spirit of Tzu Chi in my own daily life.

But when I discovered there were so many others eager to apply their money and energies to worthwhile causes, it seemed natural to think about establishing a team of people that would help where help was needed, with 'service with gratitude' as its mission. And we have found contentment, gratitude and a new attitude of tolerance within ourselves because of what we do. It's not always easy of course, but we think positively and see what we do as being a prescription for a happy, fulfilling life.

It is also a way for us to make a contribution to the country and community that has accepted us as fellow citizens. Since many of us in the Tzu Chi Foundation are newcomers to Canada, our work is a tool we can use to root ourselves and contribute to our growth as Canadians. We can strengthen our dedication to our new homeland by working for and with our new fellow citizens.

We are not without challenges, of course. The needs of the disadvantaged keep increasing and government support for this portion of the population keeps inching backward. And in this supercharged information era, it's getting more and more difficult to reach out and really have an impact on someone. At one time a book might have had a profound effect on the reader, but not any more. And even when we are touched, the moment passes quickly because there are so many things vying for our attention. We turn on the news and hear of a famine and feel sorry and miserable for these people, and then after the newscast we say, "Okay, let's have dinner."

Sometimes a friend might tell me, "I don't want to give now, but I'll help once I've made more money." Some of these friends are always comparing themselves to people with more money than they have. You can always aspire to be as rich, as wealthy or as beautiful as someone whose means you envy, but that's a futile place to search for contentment. There will always be people who 'have' more than you do. I know some very wealthy people who cannot eat and sleep because they're so anxious about their stocks and fortunes. They suffer the anxiety of potentially large losses and even though they have more money than they'll ever require, they get caught on the treadmill of needing to make more and more. I, too, used to strive to make more and more money, always comparing myself to those with greater wealth. Then my master suggested I change my tack by looking in the other direction, at the people who have less than I do, in order to balance my perspective. And then I realized how blessed I am to have what I have, and to be able to use these gifts to serve others.

And yet, having said these things about our human compulsion to accumulate wealth and physical possessions, it remains relatively easy to solicit individual support for a cause when that cause strikes a chord with the people. Canadians are generous and readily share their wealth. Here you can organize a telethon and raise a few million dollars in a weekend. Here there is time for benevolence. We are not as driven to make and amass our fortunes as the Taiwanese are, perhaps because we have the protection of a good social safety net and because our taxes are high enough to dampen the motivation to earn more and more money. In Asia you struggle on your own and there is no system to catch you if you falter. So Asians are, out of necessity, more preoccupied with the idea of making money. Canadians have the luxury of living a more relaxed life, which is better for both body and spirit. I think we enjoy life more.

Canadians are also big-hearted when it comes to contributing their time. I'm constantly touched by the energetic volunteerism that goes on here. People continue to volunteer even when in their 70s and 80s. I've seen very elderly people deliver Meals on Wheels to other elderly people. And professional people—medical people, your child's teachers, legal and financial advisors—mostly treat you well. In Taiwan professionals tend to handle people brusquely; *they* are the undisputed authority figures and *they* exercise that authority without hesitation. But here professional people will take time to chat and dialogue with you; here they are more empathetic and supportive. We may think the quality of our health care system, for example, is wanting, considering the long waiting lists and crowded hospitals. But perhaps our perspective would be better shaped by comparing what we have to what passes for health care in so many countries of the world. I believe our eyes would be opened.

As for my own transition into Canadian society, our family didn't have much difficulty settling in when we first came. No doubt it helped that we spoke some English, knew quite a few people from Vancouver's sizeable Taiwanese-Canadian community and didn't have to worry about finances. And it helped that we could go back to Taiwan whenever we felt like it.

But also significant, we gave ourselves a mission to focus on which helped to integrate us into our new community as people with a contribution to offer. When you feel you are contributing you quite naturally take on the attitude that you, too, belong in that mainstream. When you channel at least some of your energy to the needs of your community, there's not much time left for feeling like an outsider.

We were well received in our neighbourhood and we liked Vancouver right away, its beauty, its multicultural flavour and the open-heartedness of its people. In America you are expected to learn, conform to and do things the American way, which is essentially a version of the British way. But in Canada your culture and religion are respected; Canadians are open-minded and secure enough to accept others who might not be the same in some ways. But then that's what Canada is recognized for around the globe, and Canadians receive preferential treatment in many countries because of that recognition.

If my generation is unique in any way, it might be that we possess a richer tradition compared to what the next generation, the first generation to be reared far from the original motherland, will have. Although I pass on some of my traditions to my children through extra schooling, I fully realize their tradition will be a watered-down version of mine, soldered to a western way of life. I don't really have a problem with that, and if I did, I would still have to acknowledge that what has happened for my children in Canada is essentially good. Here children seem to have more room, more leeway, for growing up. When I was brought up, the words of our parents were orders. You obeyed without question. But now I see my generation of parents showing more devotion to their children. True, we still want to preserve what we can of our tradition through them, but we also try to be more understanding of their needs and give them room for self development.

In Taiwan I used to be very strict with my children, until my master taught me that if I could instead be grateful for them, then I could appreciate and accept them more completely. Well, I've tried to do that and now I give them my blessing and teach them to love others. And to be honest, it's been easier working with my children in the Canadian setting. There is less pressure on both parents and offspring here. There is less competition and conformity. Here, you think for yourself. A parent doesn't always find that easy, but it's the only way a child can grow into a well-adjusted, happy, contributing adult.

I am blessed by what I do, and I am fortunate to be in a position where I can devote my time to compassionate work. I don't say this because I'm noble, but rather because the opportunity to serve continues to enlighten me and feed my spirituality. I look around me and see hundreds of people, not limited to our organization, moved to do the same. We're all doing what any decent person would do. And Canadians seem to do this readily. That's one of the reasons I'm proud of my new citizenship and cherish my new homeland.

I haven't been here long, but I've already learned much from living in this society.

Nena Jocic-Andrejevic

BELGRADE, FORMER YUGOSLAVIA—EDMONTON, ALBERTA

Nena Jocic knows the challenge of leaving home and cultivating a sense of place in a distant land. She's done it four times, twice to Canada. "I know what it's like to be a newcomer," she says, her voice deliciously spiced with peals of laughter one minute, yet overcome with unguarded emotion the next. "You feel the burden from your perspective and carry its weight in your head. You set it aside, focus on your goals and do well, but still it's there."
Formerly the Executive Director of Changing Together:
A Centre for Immigrant Women, *Jocic has applied the threads of her own experience and ensuing resilience to the tapestry of change and adaptation that every immigrant must take on as their own. A woman of warmth, resolve and spontaneity, Jocic speaks five languages, is an egalitarian to her very bones, and is far from finished with the sculpting of her own destiny.*
"I continue to learn, listen, and self-analyse," she says, "and to accept the obstacles I cannot change."

Of the many adjectives Nena Jocic might use to describe her complex early childhood, one would rouse an easy consensus among her listeners: *cosmopolitan.* Undisputedly, Nena Jocic was a cosmopolitan child. The day she was assigned to a sixth grade classroom in a suburban Edmonton academy was the day she entered her eighth school to begin learning in her fourth language, in her fourth country.

Born in the former Yugoslavia to a Slovenian mother and Serbian father, Jocic recalls the early, transient years with mixed emotions. "On the one hand we had pretty much everything we wanted. My father's response to his own impoverished childhood was to be a man of great ambition, and so he became a civil engineer. On the other

hand, we spent much of my childhood moving from one construction site to another. And my father, with neither rest nor contentment in his bones, always spoke of the day we would leave Yugoslavia.

"My mother's brother lived in Germany and when I was still quite young she travelled there to find work, hoping my father would follow shortly after. I went to live with my Slovenian grandparents until she returned a year later. In 1966 my father was finally able to emigrate and we followed him to Germany."

Two years later Jocic's father, ever in pursuit of greener pastures, arrived in Montreal and began travelling westward searching for work. He settled in Edmonton and then summoned his family to come join him. "Those early years in Canada were extremely difficult, both financially and emotionally. I had never felt poverty before but here we were, with very little, trying to start over in a new, alien land. School, which I'd previously enjoyed, now became a torment. In Germany I had been put back a grade because of the language barrier and that, combined with my early physical development, made me easy prey in the Canadian schoolyard. From my school mates' perspective I was a legitimate target because I looked different, wore clothes garnered from charity and spoke weird languages.

"At home I watched my mother struggling with her own isolation while she cared for my four-year-old brother. She had thrived in Germany and had found her niche there. She'd become very fluent in the language and worked in an exclusive children's shop. But now, with her very broken English, she was relegated to a lonely life and a bottom-rung cafeteria job where she fried hamburgers and washed dishes. I really felt her belittlement, and that's never left me."

Jocic and her mother struggled through their own private isolation and even though their pain was in parallel, their paths were distinctly separate. "I suppressed the way I looked and instead concentrated on my abilities and talents. Within the year I was on the Honour Roll. But I also became a renegade at home, challenging the traditions and customs, generally being insufferable. My relationship with my father was especially tenuous; he was strong-willed and traditional, yet he demanded from me what he would have demanded from a son. He damned the culture I was trying to find a footing on, but nonetheless expected that I would make it as a professional in the western world.

"As for my mother, well, because my parents were really 'pan Yugoslavs' who had come from different parts of the country, they had no interest in taking up the issues that were splitting Yugoslavia apart. Most Yugoslavs who were immigrating at that time did, however, so my parents refused to socialize with any of them. For my mother that meant added isolation, until she found a niche with a local Slovenian association, a neutral, apolitical group that provided her with an extension of her own people and culture."

Jocic endured two years of misery at King Edward School, then skipped grade eight and migrated to a high school across town, in the suburb of Sherwood Park where her parents had just bought a home. When she was 15, she decided she would journey to Slovenia to visit her grandparents. She found an after-school cleaning job at the university to which she commuted on her bike, and a year later, with the required funds in hand, begged for her father's permission to go.

"It was an unusual concession on his part, especially since the political climate in Yugoslavia was then volatile; Croatia was straining towards independence and terrorism had spilled beyond the country's borders and into Europe. It wasn't the greatest time for a teen to be travelling to that part of the world by herself. But my father decided that I could go, provided I tended to a matter concerning the house we'd left behind."

The Jocics had retained part-ownership in their Belgrade family home, which had been under construction when they emigrated. Now four years later, it remained uncompleted and the family was becoming increasingly concerned that they were being swindled by their business partner. Jocic could go to Belgrade, they agreed, where she would enlist the help of a friend and former colleague in rectifying the mismanagement of the house. In the process she would stay with the friend's family, perhaps even join them on their annual summer holiday to the Adriatic coast.

"When I arrived in late July after visiting with my grandparents they took me to their grandfather's farm in the mountains and that's where I fell in love with their son, Miki Andrejevic. After a few days we realized the feeling was quite mutual."

When Jocic returned to Canada she announced her intention to migrate back to Yugoslavia permanently, much to her father's consternation. "But of course reality took hold of me and I ended up coming back to finish high school and plan for university."

At the University of Alberta Jocic immersed herself in history, psychology and campus life. She became increasingly involved in the Slovenian Canadian Association, increased her involvement in multiculturalism and became one of the youngest Albertans ever to be appointed to the Alberta Heritage Council.

After graduation she reconnected with Andrejevic and in August of 1981 he came to visit her in Edmonton. "Miki flew in the day before Heritage Day, and I had the Slovenian Pavilion running full tilt. I dragged him along, and who should come by but Joe Clark, then prime minister. We had an easy conversation with each other, and why not? This is a democracy, so our politicians should be able to interact with us without any pomp and pretence. But for Miki it was quite an initiation. An impromptu conversation on the street with the leader of your country would have been unheard of in Yugoslavia."

When marriage was proposed during that visit, Jocic not only accepted but agreed to move back to Yugoslavia with Andrejevic. "Not necessarily forever, but for a few years. Miki had just finished law school and I was feeling adventurous, ready to try something new. I needed a new experience to expand my perspective, broaden my viewpoint on life. And the notion of going 'home' intrigued me. We were married in my parents' backyard in 1982, then left for Belgrade."

In an act of coincidence rarely seen outside of epic Hollywood, the Andrejevics' journey back to Yugoslavia ended on the doorstep of Jocic's now-finished, childhood home. "Settling into that house was easy; settling into Belgrade was somewhat more challenging. In some ways it was the same old immigrant experience all over again. I was ridiculed for my flawed Serbian, even by my family who thought the way I spoke was very 'cute.' Well, I didn't want to be cute and I didn't care for their lack of tolerance."

However, the Andrejevics soon snared choice jobs and Jocic rapidly came to realize that they could count themselves among Belgrade's privileged. "I became an interpreter and executive assistant to the

Thai ambassador and Miki was hired on as general manager of the Belgrade Philharmonic Orchestra. My job was wonderful; the embassy gave me a great deal of responsibility and treated me more as a Canadian diplomat than a Yugoslav 'local.'

"Miki's work was stimulating as well. He accompanied the orchestra on several European tours, and well known musicians frequented our house for luncheons and dinners. We enjoyed good salaries and were well connected. And so, the city of my unhappy childhood, the city I had hated with a passion for so long, became the place where I most wanted to live."

Political changes were already in the air in 1987 when the birth of their second daughter, by cesarean section, brought on significant personal change for Jocic. "Maternity leave wasn't an option in my job, but I needed time off to recover and spend with my children. So I resigned, but it wasn't easy."

The Andrejevics were also beginning to understand by this time that a migration to Canada was imminent. "In 1987 the ominous signs of war were already in place. We could never have predicted it would be so complex and bloody, but of this we were certain: the nation called Yugoslavia was in its death throes. Even the installation of a competent prime minister in 1989 couldn't avert the cataclysm of death and despair that was like a fire burning throughout the land. Already the leaders of the various religious and ethnic groups, who had mostly come up through the political echelon rather than the education system, had so firmly entrenched their own special interests into the country's agendas that any salvaging of nationhood was hopeless. It's perplexing that, in a country with such high education standards, the political leaders are consistently the ones who've had so little schooling. But then, if you look at some of the leaders we've had in this country.... Anyway, the time had come for us to leave.

"We returned in 1990, myself with great reluctance. I didn't relish the challenge of resettlement. I worried that I'd be in for an emotionally rudderless time, having come from cosmopolitan Belgrade to conservative Edmonton."

Typically, Jocic overrode her worries with a take-charge attitude that had her scouting around for challenging work as soon as her children were enrolled in school and her husband in courses to upgrade his limited English. She found her challenge in early 1991 at *Changing Together*, a publicly funded centre for immigrant women. Less than a decade old and already burdened with serious discord within its own government, the Centre was desperately in need of a fresh start and new executive director. Jocic plunged in without hesitation, determined to improve the Centre's effectiveness by injecting some urgently needed cohesion into the contentious relationship that existed between the staff and Board of Directors. "Board members were resigning and being replaced all the time—that was the Centre's first problem. Because there was so little continuity, the visions and priorities of the Board were fractious, tangential."

While the politics raged on, Jocic rallied her staff into service. "Our job was to represent immigrant women and advocate for their needs, a challenging mandate made even more so by the eclectic nature of our clientele. These women came from every possible background and social situation and all had poignant needs as they struggled to settle in. Many came from mono-cultural communities and now suddenly found themselves in the midst of cultures, beliefs and customs alien to their understanding. Many struggled with cultural transitions, which by definition implies a struggle with self identity. Many who had enjoyed important professional or social standing in their old country now discovered they had neither the language nor the tools to assume a similar place in this society. Many who came as refugees had nothing except for the finality of knowing they couldn't ever return. And for those women who had, up until now, left family and household decisions up to their husbands, there was the stress of taking on intimidating new roles within the context of their families.

"For the women in these scenarios and so many others, we provided the encouragement, support, orientation and skill development required to plough through that first difficult phase of transition. The Centre was a fitting place for these women to begin learning to relate to each other. A place to learn English, bring their children and mingle."

One of Jocic's key goals was to establish a program aimed at the prevention of family violence in immigrant families. "Because of my own experience within a family that tried to bend my will to their traditions, I understood especially well that the stress of immigrating, of starting over and trying to fit in, can lead to abuse within families. Knowing how tough things could get in my family, I could imagine how hard it must be for families coming from cultures even more traditional than mine."

If the Centre was going to carry through on a commitment to prevent violence in immigrant families, Jocic knew it would have to be prepared to deal with an entire host of peripheral, yet essential challenges. "Our program was designed as a prevention tool for the family as a unit, to spread awareness of what is and isn't abuse within the context of Canadian law. We weren't suggesting that family violence is more prevalent in the immigrant community, but rather that awareness of what is and isn't abuse is not as prevalent. Our task was to bring home the message that family violence is a crime in Canada and that newcomers need to be as aware of this as any other Canadian."

During her tenure Jocic had provincial and federal brochures on domestic violence translated into 17 languages. She also applied for and received a grant of $120,000 to develop a workshop curriculum on family violence and the law, which was then translated into several languages and piloted in the Alberta Vocational College's ESL (English as a Second Language) classrooms. At the same time, the Centre began a complementary education and awareness campaign through its counselling office; in the first year 150 clients received more than 700 hours of individual counsel.

"The program was designed to be non-judgmental and in that way, I think, reached many people. It basically said: these are the norms. It's up to you, with your group or individual counsellor, to find a way of interpreting them into your culture. Do that however you choose, but be aware that cultural practices should not be used as an excuse to perpetuate abuse or family violence."

By 1994, however, a physically and mentally exhausted Jocic paused long enough to take stock of her own life's journey. Though her dedication and vision hadn't faltered, she knew her momentum was being impeded by a Board of Directors that had little sense of solidarity on the significant issues and an overzealous interest in the day-to-day details. "I minded leaving so much important work unfinished, but once I'd reconciled myself to the impossibility of keeping both the Board and the staff happy, there seemed no point in staying on."

Within days Jocic had traded one world for another by accepting the position of Development Officer with the University of Alberta's Faculty of Medicine. Having left the storefront world of the new immigrant, she now found herself among the most well-heeled members of society. Her job was to heighten the Faculty's venerable profile and coax a wellspring of alumni dollars into its coffers. "I can do this," she told herself, and within the year had organized several successful public events that resulted in a donations increase of $200,000.

It wasn't long before she ran into problems. "I figured out pretty quickly that I didn't fit their profile as the right person to run in their very patrician circle with its elitist proprieties. Although I more than accomplished their objectives, they were never completely confident that I, a non Anglo-Saxon female immigrant with an accent, was the right person to schmooze with the upper-crusted, old-monied alumni. No amount of accomplishment on my part would have changed that perception. I simply didn't fit their mould. So I left in 1996."

Again Jocic gravitated toward a demanding, high energy job, this time as Manager of Development and Planned Giving with the Edmonton SPCA, and again she felt herself spinning out of control as demands grew and her typical work week expanded to eighty hours. "Looking back, I was being the good, obedient immigrant again, taking on many extra responsibilities, never saying no, doing twice as much work to prove what? My eating habits were atrocious, I began losing a lot of weight, and in late 1998 was in serious trouble with the ulcerative colitis I've battled for more than two decades."

Three weeks in hospital gave Jocic a rare time for pause and reflection. "I'd never been much absorbed by spirituality although I had recently begun to question my purpose and destiny in life. I began praying, reluctantly at first, and soon began experiencing a wonderful sense of peace. That serenity kept me sane a few months later when NATO began bombing Kosovo. My new country was now involved in the bombing of my old country. What a misunderstood, misguided atrocity.

"It's taken a lot out of me, trying to understand the rationale behind NATO's actions and coming up with so few answers upon which we could develop a protocol for dealing with future conflict. But I keep busy with my new job as Planned Giving Consultant for the Anglican Diocese of Edmonton and Athabasca, and with my volunteer work in social and human rights issues. And we stay in touch with our relatives. It's amazing how resilient they are in the face of hunger, hopelessness and wanton destruction. Here's a joke they told us on one of their phone calls when we could hear the sirens and gunfire in the background: what do you call broken, taped-up windows in Belgrade? Windows '99.

"I've done the immigration thing four times and it's a process of growing and changing that requires much soul-searching and self-analysis. There are no short cuts.

Based on my experiences and work with immigrants, I know that newcomers can't expect the mainstream to accept them if they aren't prepared to change something of themselves too. You adapt by learning to change while remaining true to the person you are inside. And that's how, in the end, you might achieve some semblance of contentment.

"I was the proud, flag-waving Canadian up until two years ago, proud to be in a country known for its peacemakers and peacekeepers. But then this terrible, heavy-handed thing happened and the perfect Canadian multicultural, multiethnic society I had built up in my mind came crashing down. I guess it was too ideal.

"I still love Canada, but in some ways I feel like an immigrant again. Maybe I always will. Still, I can't give up on my journey—I'm not yet finished with it."

Is my transition between the old world and the new over, completed?
I don't know; it depends on what day you ask. Once you've
known another place you carry that with you, forever.

It's tough being an immigrant's child. You grow up with people who know what they want out of this new life they've chosen, yet you're subject to all of their inconsistencies and pain as they struggle to reconcile their notions of 'home.' You plough your private way out of the old world and into the new, yet your efforts are so often stymied by the very ones who are struggling with their own transition. Go and make friends, my parents told me, but don't become too much like them. Don't forget our tradition and our culture, they directed while at the same time shunning all social contact with other Yugoslav immigrants. And so we thrust ourselves into the Canadian mainstream, at the same time holding back a part of our hearts. I was ready to take on the mantle of Canadianism long before my parents were, a discrepancy in our private journeys that made living together particularly abrasive at times.

My father, in those years, was a complex person with one foot set squarely in the old, traditional world and the other in the world of education, technology and political enlightenment. He was equally driven by both attitudes, on the one hand an absolute authoritarian who forced me to find the strength and resilience I required to resist his dominance, and on the other, an independent thinker who encouraged me to be the same. His plans for my future also straddled the fence between old and new: marriage, motherhood and an engineering degree should all be mine by the time I was 23 years old.

Living with my father in the new world was not always easy.

Like so many immigrant women, my mother would have never come here, had it not been for my father. As a young girl she showed real artistic talent but her family, although not poor, was not prepared to fund her education. "What's the point?" they told her. "You're just going to get married anyway." Nonetheless she kept her ambition alive and orchestrated her own training to become a superb athlete and the country's top female in singles sculling. Had a virus not kept her out of the European finals, she would quite likely have gone on to compete in the Olympics.

Now she was here in Canada, alone, out of her element, all of her considerable skills rendered insignificant because she couldn't speak English. Through the veil of my own suffering I could see, albeit as an impotent bystander, her intense, private despair: the despair of being pregnant again at age 40 and cut off from the world, of having to scrape food from cafeteria dishes, not because she didn't know much but because she didn't know *English*. By the time I finished high school I had a good grasp of the language but she was still struggling with it,

PEOPLE USE THE CULTURE IN

WHICH THEY HAVE BEEN BROUGHT

UP AS THE STANDARD BY WHICH

THEY MEASURE EVERYTHING ELSE.

AND IF YOU DON'T MEASURE UP,

YOU'RE AN ODDBALL.

embarrassed by it, so embarrassed, in fact, that she didn't want to come to my mother-daughter graduation tea.

Life in the new world for my mother was not easy.

In high school my closest friends happened to be male, which my father just couldn't wrap his head around. In his tradition, by the time you're a young woman, you're over here, the young men are over there, and any contact you make with each other is always with the ulterior motive of the relationship in mind. The concept of a platonic friendship with someone of the opposite gender was not in my father's vernacular. So, from his perspective, my entire social life was suspect. And yet these were the friendships that sustained me throughout those vulnerable years. One of the boys and I became like brother and sister. His family bolstered me when things were rough at my house, understood my trials and truly loved me. I learned much about this country from their perspective. And had it not been for the unconditional refuge I knew I could find in their home, I'm not sure how my story might have ended.

It still hurts to revisit the heartache of those years. We were all wounded and trying to adapt, each in our own way, together physically and yet solitary in our misery. And this is so often the plight of young, immigrant girls: struggling to find a balance between the old world and the new. Struggling to be an outcast in neither. You see these children becoming either very strong, or very vulnerable and susceptible to domination. Often they become both somehow. Most immigrant children of my era, myself included, are extremely resilient. They are able to argue a point, to push people to the wall and never take no for an answer, only to break down completely at home, in the family, where they feel they've never had any attention. And then, if and when the attention finally comes, they have trouble dealing with that too.

So much of the suffering takes place out of the public eye. We generally don't realize how much stress is foisted upon immigrant women. Aside from their own loneliness and isolation at home, they also take on the burdens of their children who struggle with school and peers, and their husbands who come home frustrated by discrimination or difficulty at the workplace. Many of these women have come from a society in which they were secure in their own well-defined place. Here these roles no longer exist for them. They've traded a system in which they very capably manoeuvred and advocated for their families, for one in which all the rules and mores have been changed.

That's why the work at *Changing Together* is so crucial: it provides insight into how this society functions, and gives women and their families the tools they need to lead fulfilling lives in the new world. Interestingly enough, it's the immigrants, those who come by choice and with means, who suffer prolonged heartbreak over the old country. For refugees who come without choice and often without means, the emotional severance is usually more swiftly executed. Returning to their homeland is not an option, in fact the homeland often no longer exists, so they shift their focus and their energies to the new world.

I was 19 when I was kicked out of the house. My parents felt I didn't share their vision and they didn't want me living there any more. I rented a small apartment and put myself through university. I did well, enjoyed campus life and felt confident that my hard work would come to fruition in this country where who you were had little influence on what you could be. However, an experience while at university left me feeling, for the first time since coming to Canada, that perhaps a privileged class existed here after all, and if it did, I wasn't part of it. I had met a young man and we fell in love. But his family didn't approve of me, of my social stature and background, and it eventually forced us apart.

We Canadians have lulled ourselves into thinking we don't have a class system, but that's a myth. Of course we have such a system. Each circle, each profession, creates and protects its own territory. In the arts, Miki's profession, there's definitely a glass ceiling to contend with. Miki heads up the Writers' Guild of Alberta and they truly accept him as their own, but there aren't many immigrants at the helm of a significant Canadian arts organization. The art gallery, opera and symphony boards of this country are not awfully keen on having an accented immigrant for their executive director. And do we have Native people in these positions? I don't think so.

Our government further polarizes us into classes through an unsympathetic taxation system that continues to chip away at the few concessions left for parents and families. With fewer discretionary dollars for families, and the advent of money as a prerequisite for involvement in sports, the arts or higher education, class-ism will surely be close behind. You may have a child prodigy in gymnastics or music or figure skating, but if you don't have the required finances, your child's participation is precluded. And then the entire country loses, since the talent pool no longer comes out of the general pool.

Having said all that, thank God we live in a country where we don't have to be part of a privileged class to make something of ourselves. That in itself is a priceless freedom, and more important to me now than it was at age 20. It helps to be monied and privileged, but in the mainstream it's not yet an absolute prerequisite for success. And it's our job to protect that freedom so as to preserve the legacy of opportunity it carries for all.

I spent the 1980's in Yugoslavia where I discovered that the difficulties of resettlement are universal. Immigrants tend to think their tribulations are exclusively hinged to the culture they're easing themselves into. But my experience during my decade away from Canada taught me that intolerance is a trans-national attitude, not exclusively the domain of Anglo-Saxon society as I once might have thought. People use the culture in which they have been brought up as the standard by which they measure everything else. And if you don't measure up, you're an oddball.

Staying in Yugoslavia was not an option after 1990, and yet I resisted returning to Canada. I came when the Meech Lake issue was in full swing, which was poignant for me since I'd just been through Yugoslavia's own devastating version of Meech Lake. Serbs, Muslims, Croatians, Catholics, Slovenes and Orthodox had lived together in peace for decades. But in the 1980's, division, special interests, and selfish agendas had risen like perfidious plumes above the landscape of the common good and engulfed the entire country in carnage. In the end a few politicians got the fiefdoms they wanted, but at the expense of thousands dead and millions displaced. Well, in Canada we don't have the casualties and it will probably never come to that, but the Oka crisis came dangerously close.

Our Canadian society is becoming more divided every year, and even within the groups there is discord. Does Quebec really think their Native people will be agreeable to separation? No, they are ready to protect their rights by all means if necessary. I suggest that Canadians who don't think our country is in for significant change after separation take a hard look at Yugoslavia's sad fate. There won't be the casualties but there'll be a society driven by bitterness, and that's bound to affect us all.

And the separation of Quebec will only be the beginning. The hurt and misunderstanding will snowball right down the line. I could say I believe western Canadians are being discriminated against by Ottawa. Try getting a job in Ottawa if you're from the West. For every 100 people Canada has in foreign affairs, two or three are from this region, yet Ottawa's bankroll is disproportionately padded with western dollars. I'm not sure this country's ever had an equitable relationship with all of its provinces, but even the semblance of balance has long expired. So I could say, casually, that I have things to be bitter about. Now do you see how people get bitter? And when enough people begin feeling that way, they approach the table of common ground and put their special interests on the agenda.

The Native situation worries me. We've been diverting our attention to Quebec for so long, to the exclusion of giving a serious ear to Native issues. I'm quite sure Quebec will go, but when they do their Native population is sure to protest. That's when we'll be hearing from Native communities clear across the country. The government knows our Native people can no longer be pushed onto the reserves and told to be quiet.

Getting back to our personal situation, Miki had a much harder time adjusting when we first arrived, and then when his work took him back to Europe his simmering emotions broke to the surface of his consciousness like a wound reopened. His sad nostalgia and guilt over being safely here while countrymen continued to struggle there was further fuelled by the stories and updates shared by a Yugoslavian friend who had only recently immigrated. He carried these burdens in his heart, and as a family we all felt the weight for a long time.

But in 1999 we were comfortably trundling along as Canadians. And then the NATO bombs started falling on Kosovo. Suddenly my

Canada was contributing to the further decimation of my Yugoslavia.
I was devastated. I was angry. Angry enough to join a protest campaign, even though I consider myself a pacifist. Angry enough to help
design a peace plan and take it to Ottawa. The actions of neither side
were just, and what was accomplished when all was over? What was the
purpose of this madness? If we know one thing, it's that we've lost
credibility in peace keeping. But who profited? Who won?

I know who lost—the Serbian and Albanian people in Kosovo.

Last year I was being interviewed on CBC Radio's *Cross Country Check-
up*, a nation-wide phone-in show on national issues, about Canada's
involvement in Kosovo. I was sitting on the couch waiting for their
call and my eye fell on a picture of our wedding cake lying on the coffee table. It had been a huge cake with the Canadian map iced on top,
beautifully created by my mother. On an inverted glass placed over the
Hudson Bay, she had positioned a tiny cake in the shape of Yugoslavia,
exactly to scale, 1/50th the size of Canada. Sitting there waiting, my
tears fell on the picture of my two homes. I don't remember what I
said in the interview, only that I was angry, angry for my Canada being
altered and my Yugoslavia already gone. If Canada has gained anything from this, I hope it's the wisdom that you don't just go into a
foreign land and impose your values and your structures on the people. No, if you really want to effect a positive change, you learn about
their culture and their methods and then you work with them to have
the change come from within.

There were some who felt I shouldn't have campaigned against
NATO involvement, that I was being partisan. But when people are
suffering and you know in your heart there has to be a better way, it
becomes your business. And I shed as many tears for the Albanians as
I did for the Serbs. But the hurt and the betrayal don't help on days
when I ask myself, Where do I belong NOW? Where DO I belong?

I think I belong in Alberta. I feel more comfortable here than anywhere else. Alberta is safe and it is, after all, the place of my childhood. It's green and it's clean and the landscape goes on and on. The
people are genuine; this place has a big heart. I'd find it difficult to
live anywhere else.

Is my transition between the old world and the new over, completed? I don't know; it depends on what day you ask. I'll always feel like an immigrant in some ways. Once you've known another place you carry that with you, forever. I've gone from one home to another and put down roots by adopting the special people I've met and embracing them as 'family.' It's my nature to turn strangers into family; I've been doing it ever since childhood, and it continues to help me cultivate a sense of belonging as I journey through life.

I cultivate that sense of belonging, not by relinquishing my own unique identity, but by becoming more aware of it in the various settings and stages of my life.

Nathan Kaplan

MEMEL (KLAIPEDA), LITHUANIA—MONTREAL, QUEBEC

The art on the walls of the Montreal home makes one thing clear:
Nathan Kaplan does not paint like a man in his twilight years.
Most of the pieces exude unabashed strength and boldness.
Some hit hard and make no apologies for the impact. [Woe that
the silent screams and helpless, upturned arms of the Holocaust
should ever lose the ability to jolt the comportment of civilized peo-
ple everywhere.] Others, like the series depicting fish-market her-
ring in, on and under yesterday's news, are unexpectedly playful.
"When I packed my suitcase for Canada, I included a note I had
written to the Canadian I would become to never forsake
my passion for art," says Kaplan contemplatively, his hale mind
and vigorous heart clearly pulsing in tandem. "And thanks to this
land of opportunity, it's not a price I've had to pay."

In the 1880's Nathan Kaplan's grandparents strolled through their Russian Lithuanian village and observed a bevy of Russian officials assembled behind a table in the marketplace. From now on Jews would be allowed to own land, they were told, and the land could be had at no charge. "My grandfather, tired of being a baker, was the first in the village to sign up. Nine other families followed suit and together they founded the farming village of Padubysa. I was born there in 1910, the third of my parents' six children."

At age five Kaplan often accompanied his father to the potato fields along the Dubysa River at the same time as the Germans were steadily advancing on Russian territory. One day his mother came running to the fields, yelling for the family to come home immediately. The military activity she was seeing on both sides of the river had filled her with panic. And so, while the retreating Russians were entrenching

themselves on the Kaplan property and the Germans were establishing a stronghold just across the water, the family grabbed a few essentials from their home and retreated to the shelter of the potato cellar. That night the shooting began.

"The next morning we awoke to find German officials in our house. One of them had been a business associate of my father before the war, the first of many coincidences, miracles really, that saw our entire clan of 13 get out of Europe alive. This official told us to leave the village immediately; the Russians would be back and further conflict was inevitable. He allowed us to take a few provisions from the house."

Halfway out of the village Kaplan's father veered from the path of retreat long enough to see if another fleeing villager might have remembered to retrieve the Torah—"the common property of the entire people," as Kaplan was to refer to it in his writings years later—from the synagogue. In their panic and haste, no one had. The Kaplans took the sacred book into their own safekeeping and resettled in Rasseiniai some 40 kilometres away, where they lived for the next four years.

Kaplan's father, an entrepreneur with considerable resilience, wasted no time getting back on his feet by establishing a successful lumber business. This brought him into frequent contact with the manager of the German Military Bank of Occupation, who had been an artist of note in Berlin. When the manager happened upon some sketches produced by the young Kaplan, he invited him to come to his office after school for art lessons.

"He introduced me to pastels and a method of copying pictures from magazines. I was six years old. He taught me for the next two years."

When Kaplan was 13 the family moved to the city of Memel, now known as Klaipeda, on the Baltic coast. Whereas his pre-school language had been exclusively Yiddish and his schooling to this point had been in Russian, Kaplan now found himself enrolled in a German school. An art competition for students was already underway when Kaplan registered, but he nonetheless submitted an entry and came away with the top prize.

"But by 1923 I'd gotten fed up with the school; the curriculum and presentation were very traditionally German and already the anti-

Semitic leanings were on the wind. One teacher, whenever he became irate with me, would say, menacingly, 'You're not even good enough to be a soldier.' Finally I decided I'd had enough. I would go instead to a Jewish school, specifically the Talmud Torah School in Hamburg."

Kaplan was fortunate in that schooling costs were not an issue for his family; they had well recovered from their earlier losses and now owned an estate, a farm and the lumber business. In fact, when his father's family who had emigrated to Philadelphia some years earlier, returned to Memel to persuade him to come to America, they took note of his prosperity and instead advised him to stay where he was.

At the Talmud Torah School, Kaplan enrolled in the usual cadre of academic subjects including language training in French, English, and Hebrew. He also signed up for art education and it wasn't long before his instructor recognized his singular talent. "The first time the teacher saw my work he told me to leave the class, go out on the street and bring him back a sketch. I went out and happened to see the Zeppelin flying overhead on its way to America, and I drew it, with the people on the street looking skyward. Many times after that I would spend my art class roaming around outside, painting what I observed."

When Kaplan faced expulsion a year later for extending his summer holiday into the first two weeks of school, it was his art teacher who intervened on his behalf, suggesting that if the youth should ever become a renowned artist, the Talmud Torah School wouldn't want the notoriety of having dealt with him ruthlessly in his formative years. Kaplan was allowed to stay.

At age 16 Kaplan returned from Hamburg to Memel just as his father's fortunes were again changing. The forested land the family had bought from the Russian government three years earlier was now being reclaimed by the Lithuanian government without recompense to the Kaplans. Again the family fell victim to the injustices inspired by the changing political winds of the decade. Again, and incredibly so, the elder Kaplan refused to be browbeaten, instead turning his energy to establishing a company to import oil from Romania.

In the meantime the younger Kaplan was being encouraged by both family and friends to pursue art studies in Paris. Several times he packed his bags and boxed up his portraits and landscapes, but each time the increasingly volatile political climate and the family's unstable economic situation held him back. Instead, he painted at home when time allowed and read voraciously through his handpicked collection of more than 300 books.

"I also became involved in photography and began doing my own developing. I painted a large self portrait but left out the eyes. I could never paint them to my satisfaction so I left them blank. The painting became a curiosity among visitors to our home."

As the months turned into years and the years wore on, it became apparent that Naziism was on the rise and that anti-Semitism was being quietly incubated among the masses. On March 21, 1939, Kaplan's older brother telephoned from Kaunas, a city 175 kilometres to the southeast, to warn the family that the time had come to leave Memel. A day or two later Kaplan received a fateful telephone call from a German friend with whom he had once served in the Lithuanian army. The friend had since become a Nazi and a member of the Gestapo, but had earlier vowed that religious differences and conflicting ideologies would never destroy their friendship. "One day I will call you, Nathan," he had then promised, "and I will say 'auf Wiedersehen.' And when I do, it will be a signal for you to run and get out."

"I was sick with a cold and tonsillitis when he phoned, so my youngest sister ran to buy tickets for my parents, three younger sisters and myself to take an electric car to Kaunas. There was no time to pack my drawings and paintings, and to this day I regret their loss. Once in Kaunas, we learned that a Canadian official would be coming from Copenhagen in search of people interested in immigrating to Canada and revitalizing the many farms abandoned during the Depression. The terms were that you had to have a few thousand dollars to bring with you, and commit to farming for at least five years. So my father met with this man and showed him the documentation for the land and assets he had just been forced to abandon. 'Get ready to leave as soon as your visa is processed,' the man told my father."

Three weeks later the Kaplans were on a train bound for Riga in neighbouring Latvia. Carefully avoiding Germany, they sailed across the Baltic Sea to Stockholm, boarded a second train to Copenhagen, and sailed down the North Sea as far as Antwerp. From there they obtained passage across the English Channel to Harwich, traversed the country to Liverpool and boarded the SS *MontClare* en route to Canada.

"My parents, three sisters and I arrived in Montreal on July 29, 1939, four weeks before the Second World War broke out. I can't begin to explain the miracle of our having made it to Canada with the family intact."

The Kaplans were among the last Jews to gain entry to Canada before the notorious decree of 1939 went into effect. While the heart of the Canadian commoner, inasmuch as it could have grasped the full implications of Naziism at that time, might have sympathized with the plight of the Jewish refugee, Ottawa was resolute in its position: Jews were not suitable for Canadian citizenship.

Even today Kaplan marvels at how perilously close his family came to being turned back into the maw of German brutality. "Canada closed its borders to Jews when we were halfway across the Atlantic, but because we had agreed to farm and had previously been issued our visas, they granted us entry. We came as landed immigrants but any Jew arriving after us as a refugee would have been rejected.

"Even our crossing proved treacherous in an insidious way that we didn't realize at that time. A German passenger latched on to us and became overly friendly, trying to coax us into starting a business with him. We later found out he was a Nazi spy when the Canadian authorities came to our farm looking for him. A German woman, also a spy we later found out, tried to establish a relationship with us by letting us in on what she called a 'secret.' 'Did you know,' she said coyly, 'that the ship's hold is full of gold?' She tried to convince me the *MontClare* was transporting England's gold to a Montreal vault for safekeeping during the war. I assumed it was all a joke, but years later I read in the *Montreal Gazette* that Canada had in fact stored the treasury of both Britain and Poland during the war. So her story had been true. Who knows why she tried to mix me up in it. I'm glad I kept my distance."

Within two weeks of their arrival the family had purchased a run-down farm with neither electricity nor water in Williamstown, near Cornwall, Ontario. Kaplan himself was sent ahead to clean and disinfect the house which had sat vacant for some time. With three stray bricks he fashioned a makeshift stove in the yard, brewed a pot of coffee and ate of the bread and salami he had brought with him. In the afternoon a bachelor neighbour came by and offered shelter at his home for the night, which Kaplan gratefully accepted since his house reeked of disinfectant. It turned out to be a night not for the fastidious; sandwiched between an iron bed frame and a hairy, stinking bearskin, Kaplan lay there holding his nose and counting the long hours until dawn.

On his own farm the next night, he found a piece of cardboard for a bed and balled his jacket into a makeshift pillow. The unlocked door troubled him, however; only after hammering a nail into the floor and wedging a board between it and the door did he feel secure enough to drift off to sleep. Sleeping with the door unlocked was unheard of where Kaplan had come from.

A few days later the family came from Montreal. "When my sisters saw the house, they wept and refused to enter, until my mother reminded them our other option would have been annihilation."

Before long a small herd of Holsteins grazed the Kaplan pastures and the family set about learning to milk them. "There was one cow that could only be milked by my sister, Fanny. She was an excellent pianist and the cow must have liked her touch. My hands, well, they were swollen for the next two months."

Although the Kaplans struggled to adjust to a livelihood and lifestyle heretofore alien, they lived in gratitude for the freedom to start over yet again. That's not to suggest the gratitude flowed unbridled at all times; the girls, especially in the proximity of the cows, were often wont to lament, "If my friends could see me now." True, the farm and home were nothing compared to what they had enjoyed in Memel. But the long-sought religious and social freedoms were theirs now more than they had been at any time before. And when Kaplan's older sister and brother and their families arrived from Lithuania by way of Japan some time later, their harrowing escape having been orchestrated by the Japanese Consul in Kaunas, it was truly time to give thanks for the circle completed and the privilege granted for a new beginning.

When a cousin from Philadelphia arrived unannounced for a visit and found them in the barn at milking time, he wept at what had become of their affluence. Through his tears he recalled that when the senior Kaplan had travelled to Philadelphia to visit a decade and a half earlier, his wealth had been such that he had bought two new Buicks to take back to Memel with him. Now he was milking cows in a dark, musty barn.

The cousin refused to enter and turned away.

"He is a fool," the elder Kaplan pronounced. "Does he not know that we are the luckiest of people?"

Over the next decade the clan worked together to cobble a living from the land. Although his heart was not in it, Kaplan often drove to Montreal, peddling eggs and produce. "The passion of art still reigned in my soul but our economic needs had to come first. I had no time for anything else." When Kaplan finally did resume his painting, it was not with the fine pigments and sable brushes of his past; no, the economics of the farm dictated that he would work with old toothbrushes and rags. Much of his work produced during the farming years paid homage to the predominant themes around him, the themes of nature, animals and farm life. Even today Kaplan continues to employ a rag to achieve certain effects in water colour.

In 1947 Kaplan travelled to Philadelphia to visit his father's family, and while there he met Etta Ginn, a Holocaust survivor also from Lithuania. They married two years later. In the meantime Kaplan was accepted at the finest art academy in Philadelphia, only to have his visa denied by officials who, seeing him as a lowly Canadian farmer, called his motives into question. His wife, however, spurred on his resolve to change careers. Montreal seemed to offer opportunities for a talented, budding artist; why not move to Montreal? And so it was decided.

"Since I was leaving the farm anyway, it seemed an appropriate time to sell it and have my parents move to Montreal too. We had tried to make a go of it and we'd stayed five years beyond our committed time. We used to wonder why all the farmers around us had big cars. Well, it was because they commuted to factory jobs in Cornwall or Montreal while their wives and children worked the farms. That was the only feasible way to farm. But I didn't want to farm, and yet we didn't want to leave my parents there by themselves. So selling seemed the best option."

Kaplan's first job in the city was in T-shirt design; the work's lack of challenge decreed he would not be there for long. He was then hired as a textile designer at a large textile factory owned by a Czechoslovakian family. His job would be to create repeat patterns for goods destined to become drapes and garments; his wage would be $25 a week. Kaplan wasted no time becoming a valuable employee. As was his nature, he would quickly complete his own work and then walk the factory floor to observe, learn, and help out wherever he could. Sometimes his initiative was appreciated; occasionally it was not.

"Generally they liked me, especially after I devised a way to salvage goods that had become flawed by excess ink during the stamping process. Normally these fabrics would have been sold as seconds, but once I'd covered the imperfections with a hand-painted stem here and leaf there, they were as good as new. Well, that saved them a lot of money so of course they were eager to have me take that on. But they were always suspicious that I would learn everything there was to learn from them and then go off and start my own business."

As Kaplan's talent for textile design became more apparent, customers began clamouring for his creations. His restorative work was equally impeccable, to which his employer responded with mounds of goods for him to repair at home, long after his day at the factory had ended. And although he worked diligently and constantly devised ways to use his time more efficiently, the response was always to pile on more work and impose deadlines that bordered on the impossible. For eight years Kaplan remained philosophical about his setting, gradually realizing that the time was coming for him to move on.

"One day when my boss gave me a repair job to do at home, I asked if I could have two days off to attend a family wedding in New York and finish the work when I returned. 'No,' she said, 'Do it before you go.' So I organized the job into various components and estimated a time for each step: two hours for this colour, five for that one, and so on. Then I set my alarm for the time I had allotted for one step, raced to finish before the clock and then rushed to the next colour. In the end I beat my schedule by an hour. And when I gave her the work, she gave me hell for being too slow the rest of the time. That's when I knew I had to leave."

Although Kaplan's wife urged him to turn to painting full-time, he

chose instead to concentrate on textile design and launched Nathan
Kaplan Studio in 1958. As the demand for Kaplan's creations
increased, the studio grew to employ 22 people and added several of
Montreal's large garment manufacturers to its client list. Interest was
spawned south of the border, generating a more exclusive clientele
and an invitation to relocate in New York. "It was gratifying to have
New York interested in my work. I was once watching a Broadway
show, only to realize all the dancers were wearing my designs. But as
far as moving there, we had two young daughters at that time and New
York wasn't the place to bring them up. Canada had served me well in
my life and career. Why would I want to leave now?"

 Kaplan continued to paint throughout his working years; today
more than 100 of his works hang in public or private collections.
Although his themes have varied over the years, the depiction of Jewish
life and tradition has featured prominently in much of his work.
Beginning in 1980, *Wooden Synagogues*, his collection of 18 ink drawings
commemorating the wooden synagogues of Eastern Europe destroyed
during the Holocaust, toured various parts of Canada and the United
States. His many commissions include the painted chapel windows of
the Jewish General Hospital and the Jewish Nursing Home in
Montreal. A painting entitled *Triptych* travelled the world from 1990 to
1994 as part of the exhibit, *A Coat of Many Colours*, which documented
two centuries of Jewish life in Canada. Today the original hangs in the
family's Montreal home; a reproduction is housed in the permanent
archives of the Museum of the Diaspora, Beth Hatfutsoth, in Tel Aviv.

Although he has been retired for many years, the 90 year old Kaplan
remains robust in his lifestyle and thinking. The home he shares with his
wife of five decades is filled with his drawings and paintings, many of
them bold, poignant and unexpected. Several works-in-progress rest
here and there. Elsewhere in the city, Nathan Kaplan Studio continues
to thrive under the management of his elder daughter.

Kaplan finds it easy to enrobe himself in a cloak of contentment,
the kind that comes only after struggle and gain, the kind that is based
on never forgetting where you came from nor what life was like when
you once lived there. Kaplan remembers his childhood Padubysa, his
beloved Memel, his new-found Canadianism in rural Williamstown.

He remembers his people, pays daily homage to the generations that have passed, embraces the generations present and yet to come.

On the occasion of his 87th birthday, he spoke of the miracle of his family's survival during modern history's darkest days and gave thanks for the growing clan gathered around him.

And he had this message for his country: "We are proud of you, and I think you have reason to be proud of us too. Vive le Canada! And thank you."

Hardly a day goes by that we don't feel grateful for our life here.

I have fulfilled all my dreams in Canada. I came from a country where the government systematically stripped you of your personal and religious freedoms, to one where these very freedoms form the basis of government. To a person who has stood helpless in the face of brutally abusive authority, the gift of freedom is the most precious of all.

The gift was evident within the first week of our arrival. I was walking back to the farm from the village when a car stopped and the driver asked if we were the refugees from Europe. Technically we were landed immigrants, but I told him yes. He said, "Jump in the car. We'd like to meet your parents." And one was a Jewish businessman from Cornwall; the other was president of the B'nai Brith of Cornwall. They told my parents, "You are home. You are not strangers here." We hadn't expected there would be Jewish families in the area, and it helped to make us feel secure.

The following week the entire community came out to welcome us. There must have been 50 cars, and they brought food, pieces of carpet, all the things we could use because they knew we had nothing. It was heartwarming beyond words. Some time later a neighbour asked us which church we attended. I told him we went to a temple. "But the temple is in Cornwall, 16 miles away," he said. And I told him we didn't get there often. "Why don't you come to our church?" he invited. "You can pray to your God there." This I would have never heard uttered in Europe.

One time the local minister and priest came out together to pay us a visit. "Are people treating you well?" they wanted to know. "Because if they aren't, we can address that from our pulpits." In many ways our community was our security blanket. We had come from a climate of mistrust among the people, and now to be accepted as we were by people who didn't even know us....

The spirit of Lithuania had been somewhat like that before the onslaught of the German presence. My father had a wonderful, enduring friendship with a priest. When a small Lithuanian city burned to the ground, this priest set about collecting money to rebuild the entire city, the church, the synagogue, everything. And when my father happened to be in Philadelphia in 1923, he read in the Jewish paper that his friend was in town soliciting support for his project. My father sought him out to join forces with him and they marched into the newspaper office to be photographed together, he in his Catholic garb and my father in his business suit. Seeing the two cultures in solidarity did much to solicit donations, and the city was able to be rebuilt a few years later. Both my father and his friend were honoured for their roles in the effort. Living side by side in this way was typical until the Germans came. Most people don't know it was this way, all the more reason that era's history should not be forgotten.

It's easy to see where my passion for freedom, for Canada, comes from. Here we have the freedom to speak our own languages, although we should make an effort to learn Canada's languages too, and we shouldn't use our languages in a public setting. When we do, the message to others is that we are deliberately excluding them. We have no right to slight or offend those who have opened their borders to newcomers. Sometimes we forget to be gracious.

Canada gives us the right to practise our own traditions. And rightly so. My Jewish holidays and family rituals are extremely important to me, and have no bearing on whether or not I am a good citizen. So the Sikh RCMP officer wanted to wear a turban as part of his uniform? Why not? If he's good enough to be a member of the force, then how he covers his head is incidental. Perhaps his children will choose to do things differently, and they will deal with their choices as they see fit. There's no denying that the step between the transition generation and the one following is significant in terms of orientation to the former homeland. Even the concept of homeland itself

becomes upended as the years go by, if not by the transition generation, then certainly by the next.

Canada is a land of opportunity, even now. But in order to really
seize opportunity, you mustn't watch the clock when you work. Work
as long and hard as it takes to get your job done well. People who are
on their way to being successfully established don't have time for
movies or the tavern, at least not in the beginning. In order to do well
you need ambition, eagerness and your ultimate secret weapon in this
country—time well spent. Don't waste it away. There are too many
opportunities to reap. As an example of one such opportunity, I was
asked to teach art when I first came to Montreal, and although I'd
never studied it formally at the advanced level, it was not a chance to
be passed up. The experience added to my knowledge, and I discovered I enjoyed teaching.

Perhaps if there is a difference between those of us who have moved
here and those who were born here, it is that our past experiences in
a former homeland, which was in my case dysfunctional, keeps our
eyes and hearts open to what really matters in life, what is really of
value. The details are not so important. Our western system often
incites us to pay homage to the baubles of life, thereby overlooking the
intangible gems of freedom and acceptance. When you've never
known the strife of persecution and spiritual imprisonment, you tend
to undervalue the rights and freedoms you've never been without, in
favour of a preoccupation with the minor details.

I will always be awed by the way this country upholds our right to
freedom of speech. Even a man like Ernst Zundel who denies the
Holocaust is given his right to speak and have his message examined in
an open and democratic fashion. We may find it difficult to swallow his
rhetoric, and yet it is precisely his moment at the podium that ensures
our voice will be heard as well. There is no greater security than this.

Am I 100 percent Canadian? If my Canadianism is to be measured
in terms of my east European traditions and experiences, in terms of
the home of my ancestors, then perhaps I am not. But if it is measured by my sense of belonging and acceptance, then every ounce of me
is thoroughly Canadian. This is my homeland and I love it with a passion beyond words.

There have been so many blessings. We've never gone hungry in our 60 years in this land. I've been fortunate to do well in a field that is known as a tough financial row to hoe. We have a thriving family that's vigorously interested and involved in many professions and avocations. And we live in a country that accepts our traditions to such an extent as to be considered unremarkable. That's freedom. That's Canada.

Hardly a day goes by that we don't feel grateful for our life here.

Dr. Yatish Kotecha

The late-June evening steeps in the lingering humidity of summer's first sweltering day. Shadows, like outstretched fingers, grow from the roots of backlit trees and lamp posts. Over there the hospital, its squat outline imposing solemn shade on the asphalt at its feet. Through the doors and into the physicians' lounge, all sleek and cool and antiseptic. Overhead a speaker blatters, emits staccato strings of little words beckoning people here and there, 'hurry please' or 'no need to rush.' Dr. Yatish Kotecha apologizes for the delay; he's admitted two patients today and they're worrying him. Could he check on them first?

Soft-spoken, unaffected, highly principled, Kotecha speaks thoughtfully, frankly, now and then interspersing his telling with a laugh so contagious it would perk up even the most delicate patient. As devoted a family man as he is a family physician, he strives to embrace and enhance life's equilibrium.

"I much prefer to be in the background," he says, "and hopefully I'm contributing there in my own way."

Yatish Kotecha has no difficulty recalling the first thirty-six hours of his life as a Canadian resident. In the early afternoon of October 26, 1988, the young physician disembarked from a flight from London and proceeded to Winnipeg's Holiday Inn. At age 33 and after having lived in England for almost two decades, he had come to practise medicine in Deloraine, a small town in southwestern Manitoba.

The mid-autumn day was brisk but pleasant, and after checking in at the hotel, Kotecha walked to the nearby Manitoba College of Physicians and Surgeons to notify them of his arrival. He was being

expected, they assured him, and would be picked up the following day by a delegation from Deloraine. During his stroll back to the hotel, Kotecha noted the weather seemed to be changing.

By late evening 15 centimetres of snow had fallen and the temperature had plummeted to minus 27 degrees Celsius. The following morning Kotecha learned that his ride had been stranded in Brandon; he would have to make his own way to Deloraine, some 300 kilometres away. A scramble for alternate transportation produced a bus that would be leaving in mid-afternoon. When it pulled away from the Winnipeg depot a few hours later, Kotecha was among the handful of passengers on board.

"I'll never forget that journey, the miles and miles of vastness covered in snow, blowing snow at that. A few passengers got on and off here and there. By about eight o'clock I was beginning to wonder where I would end up. Before coming out I'd studied the map, but really, I didn't have much of an idea where I was going. And now it was dark and the communities were getting smaller and farther apart. The village lights grew more and more sparse, and it was freezing cold. I was wearing shoes and a flimsy English winter coat, of reasonably high quality for British weather, but totally inadequate here. The hours rolled by and fewer passengers got on and off until finally it was just the driver and me.

"And I wondered where he was taking me. Every time he stopped I would ask, 'Where is Deloraine, are we there yet,' and he would say curtly, 'Go and sit down, I'll tell you when we get there.' This was repeated several times, I'll never forget that. I became very uneasy and I realized the vulnerable position I was in. I had myself quite convinced this stranger was taking me for a ride to nowhere with the intent to harm me. I was scared, to be honest.

"When we finally got to Deloraine at around eleven o'clock, I was shivering with relief. The people who greeted me took me to my lodging and said, 'You must be very tired and wanting to get some sleep.' And I said, 'No, no, I'm not tired.' I was just so relieved to see people again. So they asked me what I would like to do. And I asked for coffee and a bite to eat. I wasn't hungry; I just needed people around me for a bit while I collected myself."

For the boy who had grown up in tropical Uganda and harboured an enduring ambition to see snow, Kotecha now suddenly found that desire satiated. Born in Kampala, he was the third generation of his family to make his home on the African continent. "I was from a family of Indian merchants who were employed by the British to operate between the Africans and Caucasians. Hence, my parents and grandparents all spoke English.

"My father, though, had been born in India and from the time I could remember, his heart had been set on going back to open a cinema. As a result, I spent two years of my early childhood in India. My one vivid memory of that time was when I was returning from school and confronted by a rabid dog that was being chased down by police in our cul-de-sac. They were there with their guns drawn, and the dog ran me over as I tried frantically to get to my house."

When Kotecha was seven years old the family returned to Uganda, the elder Kotecha having built his cinema and subsequently lost all his money. "I'm going back to Africa," he had declared to his family, "and I'm staying there." For young Kotecha, the immediate implications of returning to his homeland were significant: unlike his peers he spoke no English and could barely manage Gujarati, the Hindi dialect commonly spoken in Uganda. He was also two years behind in his schooling, but that disconcerted his family only for the short time it took him to catch up at the boarding school where they enrolled him.

In his early teens Kotecha was routinely taught by educators from all over the world who were employed with CUSO—Canadian University Students Overseas. One in particular made a lasting impression, a Canadian who had come to teach French. "Andre was as keen to teach me French as he was to learn my language. We just hit it off together; he treated me like a younger brother and I looked up to him, this wonderful young teacher from far off, mysterious Canada. But in his second year he left suddenly and without explanation, which made me feel like I'd been deliberately abandoned. I was hurt and confused. Here was a guy I had grown very close to, looked up to, and now he had disappeared without saying goodbye."

It wasn't until Kotecha was finishing his senior year that the mystery of the Canadian's sudden departure was solved. "One day and without warning the principal called me out of class and into his office. He was four feet eight, and mean as anything; I was sweating, expecting the worst, even though I couldn't guess what I might have done to stir up his wrath. To my surprise he said there was a present for me. I was so scared I just took it from him and fled."

The gift had been left for Kotecha a few years earlier by the Canadian, who had been called home abruptly because of family illness. Before leaving he had hastily put together a package and note which he left in the care of a school trustee who hadn't considered its prompt delivery to Kotecha a task of paramount importance. Eventually it had been misplaced, only to be found by the principal a few years later. "So my friend hadn't abandoned me after all. When I came to Canada, I actually tracked him down and reconnected with him."

Education was a priority in Kotecha's family, and when Yatish turned 15 it was decided he would continue his studies in England. England was a natural choice. "I was born a British citizen because when my great-grandparents were first recruited from India to Uganda to work for the British, part of the deal was full British citizenship for them and their families. Well, Britain provided free college tuition in Britain for all its citizens, no matter where in the world they live. So for us the words 'England' and 'university' were synonymous."

The Kotechas had the added advantage of a connection already established in Britain; an older son had completed an engineering degree in Bath.

Kotecha soon discovered however, that getting into a British college as a British citizen would be anything but straightforward. "My brother had had no problem making his arrangements with the British Embassy several years earlier. But when my turn came, they scoffed at me, saying, 'You're a foreigner and therefore you'll pay for your own education,' which would have cost my family between 2000 and 3000 pounds sterling per year. They completely ignored my valid passport and documentation and had no intention of letting me enter Britain as anything other than a foreign student. I approached them several times with my papers but they weren't open to a change of heart."

Finally Kotecha realized his only hope for the British post-secondary education he was entitled to was to employ his brother in a reluctant act of duplicity. As part of the plan, his brother advanced the required foreign student fees to the college and then gave the receipt he was issued to Kotecha. Kotecha then presented the receipt to the Embassy officials who, satisfied that he had finally submitted to his foreign student status, allowed him to leave for England. Once in Bath, he took his citizenship documentation to the college registrar and promptly had his brother's money refunded.

Happily Kotecha found the boorishness of the Embassy officials to be in sharp contrast to the Britons with whom he had daily contact. "My landlady was really great, very supportive of a kid who was such a long way from his family and home."

Back in Uganda the leader, Idi Amin, had begun flexing his muscles and threatening the banishment of the country's non-African people. "The year after my arrival in England my father wrote a letter saying he figured the expulsion was imminent. Then I didn't hear from them for three months and the money they routinely sent me dried up. I was forced to begin looking for a job.

"On September 24, 1972, I was watching the late news when the newscaster announced, 'Here are the first arrivals from Uganda.' And suddenly, there was my whole family on television. I didn't know the implications of the expulsion for either Uganda or England, but there was my family, in the news. They were shown arriving at Stanstead, a military base about 300 kilometres away. And I just stood in front of the television set and screamed, I was so excited.

"My landlady helped me to collect my wits and assured me everything would be sorted out. The next day my principal contacted a social worker who took care of the logistics and gave me money to buy what I thought they might need. Then I went with a driver from the college to pick them up in the college van and before we left, the principal said, 'Make sure you bring them to the college first.' And when we returned that evening he was waiting in the cafeteria with the cooks, and they'd rummaged around in the food stocks and prepared an Indian meal, vegetarian, rice and curry. By our standards it was a simple meal but it was such a welcoming gesture, especially since they'd never cooked such a meal before."

From there the family carried on to Kotecha's landlady who had been busy with her own preparations. "There was never any question of money; she went out of her way to make my family feel at home. Eventually we got everyone settled in either school or work and within the year we were living in the house that would be the family home for the next two decades."

The following year, Kotecha went to visit his older brother who by this time had migrated to Canada. "He was at the Air Force base in Trenton, Ontario, and I hadn't been there long when I fell in love with Canada. I would have liked to attend medical school here, but the cost was prohibitive compared to a British education. In England I could get a grant for my education. Here, I would have had a staggering debt to repay."

Kotecha returned to Britain but following his graduation from Southampton School of Medicine and his marriage to a woman whose family had also been part of the exodus from Uganda, he began setting his sights on Canada in earnest. He toured various parts of North America with his bride and when she decided she liked Canada too, he began circulating his resume. A family practice in Deloraine, Manitoba, near the Canada–U.S. border, it turned out, was sorely in need of another physician. If he could come, the job would be his.

But at the Canadian Embassy Kotecha was confronted with the same pompous disdain he had earlier experienced with embassy personnel in Uganda. "Had it been up to the embassy people, I would have never been allowed into Canada. Simply stated, they were unfair. A Caucasian classmate with the same schooling and qualifications was given the forms and information she needed without a hassle. I went just after her but they refused to even consider me."

Even when Kotecha produced documentation to verify that his qualifications had been recognized by the Manitoba College of Physicians and Surgeons and that a position was being held for him, embassy staff remained steadfast in their indifference to him. "Then I obtained approval from the Canadian government and a one-year work permit, and still they refused to deal with me, saying they had neither heard nor received anything from the government. At that point I hired an agent. And he basically gave them an ultimatum: if my papers were not soon in order, he would go to higher authorities and have their jobs put on the line. Twenty-four hours later my visa was ready and a week later I was here."

Despite his novel initiation over the hills and plains of Manitoba, Kotecha immediately found Deloraine to his liking and sent for his wife two months later. "Initially she wondered what she had come to, especially since she arrived in December, but she too found the community very open and welcoming. They were as interested in us as we were in them. One might think nothing much happens in a small town, but the cultural diversity there was amazing. I understand this is not uncommon in small Canadian communities.

"One of the physicians I worked with had previously spent time in Malawi. We also had a New Zealand family on a teacher exchange. A farmer I came to know well had actually been to India, and we ended up celebrating two Indian holidays, Indian Independence Day and Ghandi's birthday, at his home. Ironically, we'd hardly ever celebrated these feasts in England. And when our children came along we adopted a surrogate grandmother with whom we are still close.

"Deloraine was wonderful, the people were genuine and it was a great four-and-a-half years of my life. But we were far removed from our own kin, and that was an ongoing price to pay. Our mothers did visit when our son was born, but mostly our families would fly to relatives in Toronto and phone us from there saying, 'Too bad you're so far away. We don't have time to come visit.' Food was also a problem, since my wife and children are strict vegetarians. It's easy to say that they should adapt to what's available, but for Indian people culture, religion and life are all processed as one, so vegetarianism is about much more than just food and eating. To change the diet is to change one's spirituality. I will eat meat now and then, though never at home; I started eating meat in England—it was either that or be a starved vegetarian.

"I would routinely drive to Brandon, a distance of over 100 kilometres each way, for groceries, often coming back after 11:00 p.m. There'd be so little traffic on the road and more than once I asked myself, what if my car breaks down or I get stuck in the snow? Although we resisted it for a time, we knew in our hearts the move away from Deloraine was inevitable."

In 1992 Kotecha and his family relocated to Brandon, where he established a private practise. "We thought we'd have the best of both worlds by living in Brandon, a safe comfortable place to bring up our children, and close enough to Winnipeg to go there regularly to partake of our culture. But those plans didn't really work out. We didn't get to Winnipeg nearly as often as we had anticipated, and when we did go we were reminded of what we were missing out on. For example, my daughter was taking ballet and had a performance in Winnipeg. She wistfully watched a group of Indo-Canadian kids performing traditional East Indian dancing nearby and wished she could be part of it too. It upset me to realize she couldn't participate in our culture because of where she lived.

"Brandon does have a few Indo-Canadian families, but they are of an older generation, speak a different language and come from a different background. It would be fair to say there were cultural differences between us."

Again the Kotechas were faced with the difficult decision of uprooting themselves from a community they had grown to call home. Leaving Brandon would be difficult, they realized, but there were gains to be made in moving to Winnipeg. And so the decision was made in 1996. The first and most painful step was to dissolve the medical practise. "In Deloraine I had been in a salaried position so when I left, it was basically just a matter of walking away from the practise. But here the equipment, charts, everything, was my own and I had to dismantle it piece by piece. My practise had been quite successful and taking it apart was very traumatic for everyone involved. My patients were devastated; a few of them cried.

"But now that we're settled in Winnipeg, we're happy we've made the move. We have become more involved in our culture and religion, and the children are learning Gujarati on Saturdays, at a recognized language school.

"I have good memories of where I've been, and I don't regret the years spent in Deloraine and Brandon. Our ties to these communities remain strong and it's our priority to keep them intact. When our old neighbours come to Winnipeg to visit their relatives, they come see us too."

*I look at my children and see them as Canadians,
and then I realize that Canada has become my home.*

When my brother immigrated to Canada some twenty-five years
ago, the Western World was eager to accept Ugandan Indians who had
been displaced by the tyranny of Idi Amin. Here was an opportunity
to acquire already-trained professionals who were entrenched in a
good work ethic. Canada recognized the opportunity, threw open its
doors and welcomed the exiled.

However, when I made the move to come almost two decades later,
the climate was not nearly as friendly and open. Immigration policies
had changed, and of course I was coming as an immigrant whereas my
brother had been a refugee. But part of the problem lay with our
embassies. Back in 1988 the Canadian Embassy in England, I'm sorry
to say, was staffed by people with prejudices. It seemed, from my vantage point, that you'd have no problem getting into Canada if you
were white, but people of my colour would be held back unless they
were really pig-headed and determined to get in.

Does this still go on? I don't know. But I do think our government
doesn't realize that the role it has established for the embassy is not the
way the embassy sees itself. The embassy is intended to be an instru-
ment of government that provides a variety of government services in
a foreign country. But some embassy staff—and perhaps their working
conditions contribute to this—seem prone to thinking they are really
important people, makers rather than administrators of policy. Of
course, you'll find those kinds of people in all walks of life. It's just
that in this setting there is much power to wield and much damage to
be done.

Deloraine was a wonderful town to come to and if we had been able
to attract some of our family members to come and live there too, we
might still be there ourselves. Life was interesting, satisfying and
serene. We were unconditionally accepted as part of the community
even though we were different in some obvious ways. The people of
Deloraine saw us as neighbours, not as Indians or Hindus or people
of colour. And they were genuinely interested in us. When our second

child was born, both of our mothers came from England for a visit. Our mothers are very much Indian, they always wear their saris, and in the evening they would go for walks around Deloraine. Well, the local reporter got a picture of them and it appeared on the front page of the community paper.

For our part, we made it a point to include our friends and neighbours in our traditions and celebrations. Everybody participated, there was mutual respect, and we learned much from each other. Like our neighbours, our door was always open. The community was always welcome in our house, and there was much camaraderie back and forth. The celebrations and dancing, whether we were celebrating Christmas or an Indian holiday, those were times I will always remember and treasure. I hope that kind of sharing will continue with my own kids and their generation.

When we left Deloraine I was quoted in a Winnipeg paper as saying that settling there was something we had never seriously considered. Really, that quote was taken out of context. What I was trying to say was that it simply wasn't my way to commit myself to any one place for the rest of my life, not England, not Deloraine. I was young, my children were very young, and I wasn't yet prepared to think in terms of forever. I know there's the perception that many in small communities do think in those terms, but that perception is not completely accurate. People do come and go. I worked with a physician in Deloraine who recently completed his training as a psychiatrist and who's now gone back there to work. But how much longer will he stay? And yet, another colleague, no longer living, had been content there for 35 years. It's a generational phenomenon too; people of today's generation are much more apt to be on the move. They go away to obtain their education and have their horizons expanded at the same time. Relocating for employment is also a common practise these days. And because communities are not as insulated as they once were, their diversity and vitality have increased, assuming, of course, they can maintain their population base.

I've become very comfortable with Canada as my choice of homeland. Before my children were born I used to think of England as 'home.' At one time I was actually lost in my own mind as to where I belonged. I travelled to India thinking I might feel at home there, but I knew right away that I never would. The influences of Africa and England had been much more significant in my life. Until quite recently, in fact, I readily shared with people that England was my home.

My mother's death in late 1998 had me again thinking about my life's events and where I was going, as the death of a loved one often does. And I came to realize that although I had readily moved from one home to another when I was younger, always with the emotional anchor tethered to England, the thought of moving now and as I get older has lost its appeal.

Now, the only notion I still have of England as home is that when I hear doctors talking about how, if the Canadian health care system gets any worse, they'll be moving to the United States, I think to myself, if it gets that bad I'll go back to England. There are too many philosophical differences between Canadians and Americans for me to even begin to redefine myself as an American, and I don't agree with American health care principles. Health care should not be for sale. I can argue with the government as much as I like about how much I'm worth, but that's an argument to be resolved between them and me. I think it's just plain wrong to take that argument to the level of the patient, which is essentially to insist they show me how much I'm worth before I treat them.

If we better ourselves financially on the backs of our patients, can we call ourselves a civilized society? I ask the question because my influences go back to my early days in Africa, where it was common for doctors to work several hours each week in voluntary service to the needy. Often they received some support from the very wealthy families, but the system worked because the principle of serving the needy was being practised.

Here we tend to think the big solution is to inject more money into health care. Money would resolve some problems, but Canada's real challenge is twofold: to increase efficiency within administration and to make the public more aware of what health care actually costs. People often assume that because they don't pay for a test or service, it's free, when in reality we all pay for it. And some health care people argue further that because there isn't a fee, the service is more easily undervalued.

At the moment Canada is not very doctor-friendly and there is a shortage of doctors almost everywhere. Brandon has lost ten percent of its physicians. But personally, I'm not preoccupied by whether I'm going to lose ten or twenty thousand dollars from my salary. There was a time, not in Canada, when I didn't know where my next meal would be coming from, but now I'm comfortable and able to provide for my family, and the money honestly doesn't drive me. Yes, it's human nature to strive for materialistic gain, but I would never trade the values I have for materialism.

I was brought up in a very regimented system: you did things a certain way and you followed the leader. In retrospect, I was likely educated at the expense of balance in my life. Here in Canada, whatever the pitfalls, people are more independent and think more for themselves, which I find appealing. However, there are things Canadians do that I still have no understanding of. We don't focus on the positives of our vastness and diversity; rather, we seem preoccupied with building boundaries around our own towns and cities, and we're better at bickering than we are at cooperation.

I don't understand why the French and English are destroying themselves. Most Asians in Africa can speak three languages, English, Gujarati, and Swahili. That's not considered an out-of-the-ordinary feat, but a way to integrate with each other. Here we have only two predominant societies but instead of learning each other's language and recognizing the benefits of doing so, each society seems convinced that the other's culture and language is being rammed down its throat. Well, my brother's children who grew up in Montreal speak fluent French and English, and the reality is that they will have a much better prospect in the federal and international job market than kids from Western Canada will.

I don't want to get involved in who's right and who's wrong in that struggle, but I can identify with the plight of the French. As a Hindu, I have the same struggle for restitution. For example, if my father was dying in a hospital, should he not have the same right to his religious practises as a Christian does? Even today there are no provisions in place for the conducting of Hindu rituals in the hospitals where I work. And I also think it's more difficult to drum up municipal support for building a temple than it would be for a church. Until I moved to Winnipeg, I used to practise my religion in my own home. But we always sensed a loss on Sunday morning when the community went to church and got together, and we had no community with which to worship.

I do think people coming here have to be prepared for a culture shock. At first I couldn't believe how rudely people talked, using words like 'shitty' and so on. But I've become desensitized, and anyway, colloquialism is hardly the basis on which to accept or reject a nation. I believe newcomers fare better when they've set realistic goals for themselves and are able to focus on these goals. They might be disappointed if they choose Canada simply because it's vast and rich. I also think newcomers have a greater chance of settling in if they can bring members of their extended family with them. For us, being without family caused a sizeable void in those early years. Now that I'm in Winnipeg, I know I can visit my brothers and sisters in Toronto or Montreal for the weekend if I feel like it. And just knowing I have that choice heightens my level of contentedness and sense of wellbeing.

Like other Canadian parents, I harbour hopes for the futures of my three young children. I hope they will be true to themselves and to others, and that as they grow up they will embrace the values and moral standards we are teaching them.

I look at my children and see them as Canadians, and then I realize that Canada has become my home.

Judith Lawrence

BALLARAT, AUSTRALIA—HORNBY ISLAND, BRITISH COLUMBIA

*One would not expect a puppet duo once venerated by the Canadian
preschool set to be living out retirement in a patchwork house
planted on a Hornby Island cliff just below where the eagles roost.
But with its myriad textures and rustic delights, that house seems a
fitting, final backdrop for the once-precocious Casey and reticent
Finnegan of* Mr. Dressup *fame.*

*"Yes, they're around here somewhere," muses their creator and
longtime puppeteer, Judith Lawrence, now on her hands and knees
and peering under a bed. Casey and Finnegan, let it be understood,
are no longer foremost in her mind. Neither is retirement. Instead,
a long and illustrious career in the arts has given way to the
Herculean task of mothering Mother Nature.*

*"I don't play bingo or bridge or any of those things," says Lawrence,
surrounded by books, plants, pottery, and the willow baskets she's
recently started making. "I'm more interested in learning new things
and involving myself with people and ideas."*

Judith Lawrence had lived in Canada a full decade before the deci-
sive moment to forego her Australian citizenship presented itself.
"I was looking for a reason to become Canadian," she says, "and
then Australia joined the Vietnam war and I said to myself, there's
my reason."

"I had been working with a peace movement, *Voice of Women*, which
was protesting Canada's involvement in the war—I knew Canada was
involved in a covert way, but at least we weren't sending soldiers off to
be massacred—and suddenly trading one citizenship for another
seemed the right thing to do."

Lawrence was barely 22 when she migrated to Canada in 1956, on
her way to the United States. "I'd always been interested in puppetry

and when someone suggested I go to America to check out opportunities in children's television, I figured it was a good idea. Children's television was non-existent in Australia at that time."

Even as a child Lawrence would put on puppet shows for her family and neighbourhood. "I remember my father saying, 'You'll never make a living doing that.' But after high school I trained as a preschool teacher and then began doing my puppetry specifically for that age group."

Lawrence had originally thought she might venture to England to explore television opportunities in puppetry, and when she shared this intent with a member of the American Consulate in Melbourne after having performed at their Christmas party, he suggested she reconsider her destination. "So I bought a ticket to sail to San Francisco instead, and then discovered I wouldn't be allowed to work in America without jumping through a bunch of bureaucratic hoops. I wasn't prepared to do that."

When a friend noted that her ship would be docking at Vancouver on its way to San Francisco, Lawrence decided to pay a visit to the Canadian Embassy. "I didn't know anyone who'd been to Canada, and I thought it might be an interesting destination. At the Embassy I was told a chest X-ray proving I was free of tuberculosis was the only thing required to obtain landed immigrant status in Canada. So I made the cavalier decision to go to Canada for a year, check out the situation in Canadian children's television, then move on to the United States."

After arriving in Vancouver, Lawrence travelled by train to Ontario, then south to Chicago to take part in an important puppet festival. There she met several prominent Toronto puppeteers who invited her to look them up should she ever find herself in their city. "That got me thinking that going to Toronto made a lot more sense than going all the way back to Vancouver, so I decided to accept their invitation."

A mere two months after having set sail from Australia, Lawrence began working with the Toronto group and remained with them for the next five years. "By the end of that period, I'd become established in the puppet circles in Toronto. I was also teaching at that time—in those days you could just walk in and say, 'I'll have that job'—and for a while I edited primary readers for Nelson's, a Toronto-based publishing company."

Although her experience was not in television, Lawrence came to know several people at the Canadian Broadcasting Corporation. One day a producer in the CBC Television's children's department, who had seen Lawrence perform, telephoned her at Nelson's to inquire if she might be interested in being part of a new children's television program being planned for the following season. "Of course I said yes, and was offered a one-year contract. At the same time they also hired an American puppeteer named Ernie Coombs, who eventually would become known in almost every Canadian household as 'Mr. Dressup.' We began our show, *Butternut Square*, in 1964. I was 30 years old."

So began the evolution of Lawrence's characters, Casey and Finnegan, who would, over the next two decades, become almost synonymous with the venerable Mr. Dressup. "The Casey and Finnegan combination wasn't created overnight, although I'd always had a dog puppet named Finnegan. But my other character on *Butternut Square* was originally an older woman whom I soon discovered I didn't like. Before long we decided to replace her with a child character; a child and dog were an obvious combination that had always worked well for me with the preschool set. So that's how Casey came about."

Although Lawrence didn't intentionally set out to furrow inroads into the then male-dominated world of the media when she created Casey, she'd always had a leaning towards feminist and social issues. "The jobs for women in television at that time were mostly as secretaries, script assistants, and in make-up and costumes. And all the characters in children's programming were male. Even my dog was male, come to think of it! Well, I wanted to make Casey androgynous so that all children would be able to identify with this child's character. So when children asked me if Casey was a boy or girl, I'd ask, 'what do you think? If they said 'boy,' I'd say yes and if they said 'girl,' I'd say yes.

"In those days there were so few characters for girls to relate to on television and in books. The material that was available was painfully stereotypical: Mom was in the kitchen with the apron on and Dad was at work or fixing things in the garage. So Casey's character was a bit of an anomaly, encumbered by neither gender-specific role nor mind-set in the program's story lines."

Casey was also unique in another way that held enormous appeal to children everywhere: Casey was not a perfect preschooler. "At that time children's characters were typically good and obedient, never questioning, never exploring issues on their own. Well, Casey wasn't a particularly good child; in fact Casey was downright difficult at times, which added a completely new dimension to the relationship of the show's characters. Two of our script writers had backgrounds in early childhood education and took their work very seriously. They weren't just writing scripts; they were reaching out to the children in the television audience. Every segment of the program was distinct. There were no formulas."

Meanwhile, Lawrence's involvement in *Voice of Women*, which also protested the testing of nuclear weapons, took her to a meeting in Vancouver, and afterwards she was one of several delegates invited to spend some time at another member's home on Hornby Island. "It takes three ferries to get to Hornby, the first to Vancouver Island, the second to Denman Island, and the third hops the narrow strait between Denman and Hornby. We came out in May and when I got off the last ferry, I found myself staring at the most beautiful vista I had ever seen. The landscape was rural and spilling over with blossoms of all varieties. It didn't take me long to decide I'd like to spend more time here, and when I enquired about property for sale I learned of a piece of land that was being purchased by a group. I was accepted as part of the group, and thus started coming back to Hornby Island every summer after that.

"My parcel of land had no building on it so each summer when I came out for two to three months, I worked at putting together a house and garden. I started with a little pre-fab Panabode house, then cobbled on a piece here and there until it evolved into the house I live in now. As for the garden, it kept getting bigger too, as it often tends to do in the country. At the end of the summer I'd be off to Toronto again, which I didn't mind because my work in Toronto made it possible for me to spend the summer months on Hornby, and my revitalization on Hornby got me through the rest of the year in Toronto. The trade-off was a fair one, and anyway, I was extremely busy in Toronto. There was no time for pining."

Back in Toronto, the popularity of *Mr. Dressup* grew quietly and steadily. "When the American children's program, *Sesame Street*, came on the air, everyone predicted it would be the end of our show. 'You're so bland and homey, and they're so jazzy,' people would tell us. But both Ernie and I felt that our daily little half-hour drama was unique, and not at all in the same category as *Sesame Street*'s fast-paced, three-minute segments. We felt we would survive, and we were right."

Not only did *Mr. Dressup* survive, it thrived for years as CBC Television's best loved, homegrown program for preschoolers. Yet, as her twentieth anniversary on the show loomed on the horizon, Lawrence found herself becoming increasingly jaded, not only with her own role, but also with the concept of television for children in general. "Although the consensus had always been that our program constituted quality television for children, one of the questions that began to nag me was whether television was even good for children in the first place. Parents would constantly tell us how much they appreciated the program, but the truth was, we were still hooking their children into becoming consumers of television who would inevitably leap-frog their way to other programming. And much of what's shown on television is a waste of time.

"I also had a problem with the way television has been manipulated into a marketing tool. To CBC's credit, there were no ads aired during our segment, but most other programming for children, cartoons and such, are fraught with marketing aimed at parents through their children. And the more I thought about all this, the more uncomfortable I became with my role. Eventually that drove me to opt for early retirement in 1990.

"The other reason I chose to retire early was because I was getting drained and I felt the program was getting tired. We had all been around for a long time, and CBC's support for our efforts had started to soften. I wanted to stop while I felt I was still doing something worthwhile."

Retirement to her Hornby Island haven ten years ago called for a dramatic shifting of gears, which Lawrence soon discovered was just the tonic she needed. "It was easy to find a niche here. Everything in this island community is run by committees. There were ample projects to delve into but I limited myself to two, the Heron Rocks Friendship Centre, established to promote environmental awareness among the people of Denman and Hornby Islands and beyond, and the local recycling committee. While I'd been mostly involved in feminist politics in Toronto, here the pressing issues are environmental ones."

Lawrence was promptly recruited to chair the board of the Friendship Centre, and in its directive found much to keep her vigilant. "Although our first mandate is to preserve a priceless parcel of island property donated by an elderly resident, we're very active in many environmental issues. We organize educational seminars for residents and we've also hosted a group of environmentalists from Japan who came here to explore with us our mutual interests and goals.

"Locally, logging and water are our two big issues. Hornby's got a lump of crown land in the middle, at its highest elevation, that can be leased out for logging at the government's whim. Well, that land is our watershed and the trees on it keep it from being washed out. We tend not to think logging can have such a catastrophic effect, but just look at what's happened on Vancouver Island. The first thing a logging company does is build a road. And during the wet season roads become rivers, and clear-cut hills become landslides. Our entire island would become a landslide."

The quality of the island's fresh-water supply and surrounding salt water also poses a perennial concern for Lawrence and her fellow environmental watchdogs. "Septic systems, many located too close to wells, become woefully inadequate when our summer population swells. When you get ten people using a system designed for four, you can literally smell trouble. We keep testing the water for pollution hot spots and pass on the results to the residents as well as information on what we can do about it."

But it's Hornby's recycling initiative, the only one of its scope in B.C., that holds Lawrence's passion and imagination. Run by an elected committee which she chaired for several years before becoming president of the island ratepayers' association in 1999, the initiative has demonstrated that recycling can, in fact, significantly reduce the volume of garbage. "I'm not a fanatic, but it's very interesting to me, garbage is. We do deep recycling in a way no one else does. We handle everyone's garbage, and produce much less per capita than the provincial average."

Established two decades ago as an alternative to the significant expense of trucking all garbage off the island, Hornby's recycling program has unleashed the enthusiasm of its residents. "Anyone who remembers the nasty dump Hornby had 20 years ago is glad that bit of history won't be repeated. Now we have a free store, recycle as much as possible, compost and consider the landfill a last resort. We have a system of user-pay, which has a built-in incentive to recycle. Residents take their own materials to the depot and sort and recycle them. It costs two dollars per bag for everything delivered as garbage." Accordingly, Hornby residents now generate far less waste and pay less for waste management than do most other communities.

Recently a community garden was established to bite into the depot's ample compost crop. But not just any garden, however. "I figured, if we're going to have a garden, then let's have it teach us things." And so the notion of a garden demonstrating the viability of permaculture took hold. "Permaculture means permanent agriculture, a concept started in Australia. I've taken a few courses and now incorporate it into my own gardens too. Essentially, you assess your environment and then decide how to work with it to grow your food supply." The depot's garden currently experiments with drought-resistant crops and also serves as yet another reminder to residents that water is sorely limited.

Environmental issues continue to ruminate in her consciousness even when Lawrence retreats to her own serendipitous garden which hangs on a cliff's edge just outside her home. "The trouble with being aware of all these things is, you can't switch it off. I don't think I'll find rest as long as clear-cut logging and unrestricted development can continue on the Gulf Islands."

Rest isn't what Lawrence has in mind anyway. "I don't play bingo or bridge or any of those things. I'm more interested in learning new things like basket making and wood turning, and involving myself with people and ideas."

Overhead eagles soar placidly and in the distance the outline of Vancouver Island is delicately etched against the sky. "I like living here. I can put my life experiences to work and still learn a lot about how to accomplish things and get involved with people. And that's good."

*I think that moving, while it gives you
enormous benefits and advantages,
also creates something unsettled in you
that maybe you never get over.*

The psychology of the immigration experience intrigues me, especially now, perhaps because I'm getting older. We've all immigrated
from somewhere not so very long ago. My father's family in Australia
migrated from England, and I recently discovered that my mother's
family were Jews evicted from Spain who travelled to France, then
England, and eventually Australia a century and a half ago. What on
earth would have propelled them to go there? In those days they didn't
travel as I did; they endured a ship for two months and then ended up
in an alien land from which returning was not an option. And then,
how would they have adapted, settled in? My grandfather although he
never got to go back to England, referred to it as 'home' for the rest of
his days. Immigration is a compelling human experience.

I'm in the fortunate position that I can go back to Australia for a
few weeks each winter, which helps keep my contentedness factor high.
I think just knowing you can retreat to what you ultimately knew first,
whenever you want to, makes a huge difference in your outlook. It
must be difficult for those who don't have that luxury. My weeks in
Australia also allow me a reprieve from the west coast, which is very
gray and gloomy in the winter. Then, when I come back, it's time to
plant my garden again and from that point on I know I'll be fine.

I think I'm Canadian inside—I *have* lived here for 40 years. My
artistic career has been very satisfying and fulfilling, for which I'm
grateful, and most of my political ideas have been formulated as a
Canadian and as someone living in Canada. But, in a crazy way that
can't be analysed, some fairly large part of me still feels quite
Australian. I think the pull toward Australia is mostly irrational and
emotional, in fact, it may not even be based on anything real any
more. Whenever I'm there I find myself saying, 'In Canada we do
things this way,' and I find myself being more Canadian than I

thought I was. And when the Australians routinely suggest to me that Canada is the same as America, I can get quite irate.

What I don't like about Australia is how it's becoming so Americanized. Canada has the same problem, but I would have thought the sheer distance between Australia and American might have served to thwart at least some of the American influence. The soft imperialism coming from the United States is already very noticeable in some ways, and it's being foisted on Australians without a murmur of protest on their part. Television is playing a big part in that process. After the local channel goes off the air at eleven or twelve at night, the next thing you know you're watching CNN and getting a weather report for Chicago, for heaven's sake.

But whenever I return from a visit to Australia, the 'what-ifs' nonetheless hover over me for a while. What if I were to move back? Australia offers a pleasant, easy-going lifestyle to which I still feel connected even after all these years. My siblings and their children are there, which augments my sense of belonging. Australians are a very direct people, rather blunt, rude at times and always eager to argue and talk. It so happens these traits are also part of my makeup, of what I feel comfortable with. Canadians, on the other hand, are more reserved and perhaps somewhat withdrawn. In truth, my personality traits are more Australian than Canadian.

When I was younger, my career dictated where I would go, and I had no hesitation about relocating for the sake of my work. My career and my sense of adventure brought me to Canada. Now that I'm older and not tied to a job, I have the freedom to make decisions not hinged on any career motivation. Perhaps that's why I ponder more about Australia these days. I can choose to make a decision, delay making a decision, or avoid making a decision altogether. I suppose I could decide to move back to Australia, but I happen to like it here too. I'm very much a part of this community, and the concept of community is important to me. So my dilemma is interesting; I resolve it by leaving it open-ended. I think that moving, while it gives you enormous benefits and advantages, also creates something unsettled in you that maybe you never get over.

But my community of Hornby Island is accepting and wonderfully diverse, quite remarkable, actually. When the last ferry leaves at six in the evening, as it does outside of the tourist season, we're on our own. The place closes in around us like a blanket, and that's somehow nurturing in a way that eludes explanation.

Before coming here I had always thought of myself as an urban person. I was very comfortable in Toronto, with my work, and my friends. Life had a solid, tangible feel to it. Yet, when I migrated to Hornby, I was amazed at how easy it was to leave Toronto and settle in elsewhere, all over again. And now I've come to believe people really do need to get out of the cities, at least for a time, and give some thought and effort to the types of issues I work on. In the city you're lulled into a false sense of security about the health of the environment when in fact, cities make the biggest environmental messes.

Unlike in the city, whatever you do here has an almost instant effect, good or bad. You can quickly become a very useful member of a small community. I like the feeling of knowing I can make a difference. On the other hand, living here has its challenges too. You are confined to smaller parameters and you have to hone your negotiating skills to deal with people positively and conduct your work in a way that has impact. Choose not to do that and you can easily become a forgotten pariah.

I worry about my community losing its diversity as time goes on, especially as the cost of living here increases and young people are forced to move off when they can no longer make a go of it. There are more older people here and many aren't inclined to become deeply involved in their community. They do their thing together and go on trips and use the community as their home base rather than their home. They're not emotionally tied to this area; it just happens to be a nice place to retire to. Frankly, even though I'm retired as well, I have to say that if Hornby was to become a monoculture, a retirement community not interested in any of the issues I find pressing, I would have to search for a new home. Where, I don't know. Probably somewhere in rural Canada.

Whenever I travel around and see how people live elsewhere, I realize how lucky we are here. Canada is all about wide open spaces, which

Judith Lawrence

CANADA'S STRENGTH ALSO LIES IN

ITS PEOPLE. IT'S A MULTICULTURAL

COUNTRY THAT DOESN'T EXPECT

IMMIGRANTS TO PRETEND THEY

HAVE NO ALLEGIANCE TO

A PAST HOMELAND.

I thrive on; perhaps that's the Australian in me coming out. There's a certain edge to living on this island that I like as well. When the sea is rough or the snow falls on you and the power goes out, you defer to nature and tailor your schedule accordingly. There's something serene about living close to the land, about knowing nature is bigger than you are. And Canada is teeming with the bounty of nature.

Canada's strength also lies in its people. It's a multicultural country that doesn't expect immigrants to pretend they have no allegiance to a past homeland. At the same time, those who choose to come here should be prepared to make an emotional investment in this country. It's not good enough just to have financial betterment as your motive. You need to identify what you can contribute of yourself to your new society. You can't just live as a recipient, a taker. You must be open to your new community without looking back, without making odious comparisons, which are usually not well received anyway. Look for like-minded people. If you make the effort, you can find them anywhere. In my travels I've never failed to find people who share my interests in permaculture, the environment and women's issues.

No doubt it's much more difficult for the immigrant who doesn't speak the language or who is a member of a visible minority. But, being a lesbian, I belong to a minority too, and know the universal challenges of trying to fit in when you're 'different.' The people on Hornby don't seem to be judgmental of my partner and me—we've been together for years—but it hasn't always been comfortable to disclose this part of who I am. I lived a closeted life and had to be very circumspect during the years I was teaching and working with children. Not because I am anything less than an honourable person, but because my career would have been ruined in an instant had my homosexuality been disclosed. There's still a large school of thought that maintains that anyone who's sexual orientation is other than heterosexual is a threat to children, which is ridiculous and also hurtful. And these same people also insist sexual orientation is a lifestyle choice. What rubbish. Who would choose homosexuality over the choice of living like everyone else? No one would; it's not exactly the most wonderful, comfortable place to be. I don't live this way because it's groovy. I live this way because my homosexuality is part of who I am, part of what was chosen for me in life's master plan.

And my task, quite simply, is to live my life on this land as honestly as I can, even when it's not easy, to continue learning and making whatever contribution I can to this place I call home. That's what it's all about.

Jim MacNeill

GLASGOW, SCOTLAND—MONTAGUE, PRINCE EDWARD ISLAND

*He's been described as a crusty publisher and a Gaelic speaker
who still fancies Highland music, the MacNeill kilt and the
occasional single-malt scotch. He's been revered by his readers for
lending a genuine and balanced voice to their grassroots stories,
issues and questions. He's been denounced by the business and
government elite who resent his proclivity for conducting
independent research in favour of the official reports
they filter his way.*

*Jim MacNeill, writer, commentator, adventurer and owner of five
weekly and monthly publications, is all of the above. He's snagged
almost every major award available to his string of publications,
including a special Atlantic Journalism Award in 1991,
and the coveted Eugene Cervi Award presented in 1994 by the
International Society of Weekly Newspaper Editors for a lifetime of
tough and thorough investigative reporting.*

*"I'll be sticking around," says MacNeill, 61, with a trace of
mischief when the talk turns to retirement. "I'm still having fun."*

It was the weather that brought Jim MacNeill to Canada, not so
much the Canadian weather but the interminable grey of his boyhood Scotland that made him pensive and restless for clear skies
and sunshine. "After high school I joined the navy and sailed to the
Mediterranean, where I discovered that skies could actually be blue
day after day. That's when I decided I would leave Scotland for a place
that had more agreeable weather."

Although born and raised in the city of Glasgow, MacNeill consid-
ers his ancestral home to be the Island of Barra, in the Hebrides along
Scotland's western coast. After completing high school in England, he
signed up for a mandatory two-year stint in the military and had the

good fortune to be among the few draftees selected for duty with the Royal Navy. He spent the first year plying the waters of the North, Baltic and Mediterranean seas, and in his second year was transferred to a survey ship to help update the coastal maps of western Scotland. "By coincidence we were sent to Barra to chart the cluster of islands there, a pilgrimage of sorts for me. Some charts had not been updated in 100 years."

The weather was one influence on MacNeill's decision to emigrate; perceived lack of opportunity was another. "You had to decide on your career path early on in your schooling, and then you committed yourself by doing an apprenticeship. I still wasn't sure what I wanted to do, and I wasn't overly happy with Britain anyway. Other parts of the world seemed more alluring."

MacNeill gave serious consideration to Rhodesia (Zimbabwe) and New Zealand before settling on Canada, sight unseen. "I'd heard and read much about Canada. My father, a merchant seaman for many years, and my brother in the merchant navy had travelled extensively for many years so I'd heard a fair bit about this part of the world."

He made arrangements to join a one-way shipping crew that was to sail to Chile; from there he would fly to Canada's west coast. "When those plans fell through, I found three guys who were going to Saint John to work in the shipyards and joined up with them. Then two backed down and the third decided he wouldn't go either. So I ended up flying over by myself in June of 1958. I don't think the others ever came.

"It was literally an economy flight; if you wanted food on board you had to pack it yourself. The flight cost me 66 pounds, and I had 45 more to put in my pocket, about 123 dollars at that time. The first thing I noticed when I landed in Montreal was the size of North American automobiles. One, in particular, had me wide-eyed until I realized I was gawking at an airport limousine."

MacNeill had every intention of working his way to the west coast but Toronto begged him to linger awhile. "I was walking down Yonge Street on my way to the Ford Hotel—I had found a coupon for it in a Thompson newspaper—when I noticed the blue skies and pretty girls and thought maybe I should hang around for a day or two. A few days later I figured it was time to start looking for a job."

MacNeill was to spend the next two years in Toronto. His first job was with the city, manually breaking rocks as part of a highways crew, but that was followed by work in insurance sales, which he discovered he enjoyed and had a knack for. During his second year he met Shirley Nicholson, a Charlottetown native who was working in Toronto, and when he proposed marriage a few months later, she accepted.

"We decided we would be married in Charlottetown since that's where all her relatives were, and mine weren't going to be at the wedding anyway. Then we would head to the west coast where we already had work lined up. However, those plans changed abruptly when my prospective employer was killed, coincidentally on our wedding day. So when our honeymoon was over we returned to Charlottetown without any solid plans for our future."

MacNeill decided he liked Charlottetown and convinced his bride that they should try to make their home there. She found work immediately, and although he intended to go back to selling insurance, he felt he should first broaden his circle of acquaintances in another job setting.

"I went to *The Guardian*, Charlottetown's daily newspaper, looking for a sales job, which they didn't have. Someone then suggested I try the Charlottetown Bureau of the *Summerside Journal-Pioneer*, where I found work in advertising sales and circulation.

"There were two of us at the Bureau; the other guy was a reporter/photographer with a large area to cover. I started doing reporting evenings and weekends to help him out, and discovered I enjoyed it. My partner didn't like photography much, so I began taking that on as well. And over the next few years I was gradually switched over to news."

During that time the two began planning the founding of their own weekly publication, "but then he went to work for the government, which left me as Bureau manager and holding the plan all by myself."

Undaunted, however, MacNeill forged ahead alone and in 1963 began producing *The Eastern Graphic* out of Montague in eastern Prince Edward Island, to this day the Island's only weekly newspaper. "A fellow had shut down his print shop six months before I started my paper so I bought his offset equipment and moved it to Montague. For the first while Shirley and I did the entire shot, the ads, editorials, every-thing, by ourselves. It was extremely labour intensive, a seven-day-a-week job."

It wasn't long, however, before MacNeill's target audience sat up and took note of his publication. "I'd learned a lot in my three years with *The Summerside Journal-Pioneer*, and I knew there were gaps in the information being fed to the public. So I began making it my job to pursue the stories that often went under-reported in other publica-tions. The real stories behind the officially reported government sto-ries were particularly excellent fodder. I got a kick out of sniffing out these stories. I still do.

"I believe newspapers are duty-bound to report what's going on. A newspaper has two functions: to provide information and to offer comment. Not only my own viewpoint, but that of others too. We have about ten regular columns, and our letters-to-the-editor section is huge. People know they can always have their viewpoint noted. They know that, regardless of how we treat them in the news or editorially, they can have their say too. And I think that's an important part of my work as a community newspaper person."

In truth, the iconoclastic MacNeill has always relished rushing in where other Island publications are loathe to tread. In 1993 he wrote three editorials slamming both the RCMP and the Island's judicial system, which had acquitted an RCMP officer of all charges even though he had failed a breathalyser test at the scene of an impaired driving accident in which a teen pedestrian had died. "I asked the question on everyone's mind: how could he be found not guilty?" MacNeill's columns evoked a dramatic response from both ends of the reactionary spectrum: on the one hand they garnered him the Atlantic Journalist of the Year award, and on the other they were soundly denounced in a speech by the province's chief justice.

Although his unorthodox techniques for pursuing and tendering the truth have occasionally been brought to question, MacNeill has managed to remain unfazed by the acrimony that has now and then been hurled his way. "I believe it's my job to question the establish-ment and their actions and expenditures, in my editorials. Public ser-vants should be accountable to the public. People have a right to know what they're up to. But yes, my approach has sometimes been a wee bit different.

"Take, for example, the time Ottawa imposed a fifteen-year development plan on Prince Edward Island. We had so many federal consultants crawling around here that I was prompted to start a Consultant of the Week column. I outlined the featured consultant's background and qualifications—some of these guys were no more consultants than I am—and often I included their per diem rate. This information is readily available from the government. You just have to know where to look.

"We've also had a number of brushes with the legal profession, especially in regards to the way they look after themselves and the establishment. A few years ago two prominent lawyers pleaded guilty to assault charges, yet were given unconditional discharges, which meant no criminal records. Meanwhile, people were getting criminal records for lesser offences. I suggested in a column that they'd received special treatment and then, because I didn't want to let this slide away from public attention, I decided to run a box score the way they do on the sports page. In it I summarized and categorized the crimes that had occurred on the Island, included the number of convictions, and so on. At the bottom of the box I had the category, 'unconditional discharge.' And except for those two lawyers, that score was always nil. Well, even now, everybody remembers those incidents."

MacNeill also refused to shy away from the Confederation Bridge issue, choosing instead to make the issue almost as large as the bridge itself. "From the federal point of view, the premise that the bridge would be constructed was a done deal even before any feasibility studies had been conducted. What they dished out was pro-bridge propaganda, on which they figured Islanders would base their vote in the 1987 plebiscite. They didn't see the need to give us the information we needed to make an informed decision."

Determined the plebiscite would not be a worthless exercise solely for the purpose of appearances, MacNeill hammered out an exhausting 46 articles on the project. Using the Access to Information Act, he obtained and ploughed through a veritable mountain of documentation in order to help Islanders arrive at a balanced viewpoint of their own. He studied ice reports, environmental impact reports, funding reports and feasibility studies, poring over them time and time again until he'd thoroughly digested their contents. Then he started asking questions. At one point he realized he was missing one consultant's report and when authorities tried, unsuccessfully, to withhold it from him, "that's when they saw a ranting, raving Scotsman."

"I admit to having been somewhat partisan on this issue but I was trying to accomplish fairness. The government abused its power by giving Islanders a seriously one-sided story. Because my resources were too limited to cover the entire issue, I was put in the position of covering the side that was being completely ignored."

For its coverage on the fixed link, the *Eastern Graphic* was designated a finalist for the prestigious Michener Award for public service in journalism in 1988. "We lost out to Southam's and the CBC, so I didn't feel too badly."

Although MacNeill wouldn't categorize the *Eastern Graphic* as a renegade publication, "I've always thought it's our job to be a mirror reflecting back to the community what is happening there. And if there are shady corners, it's up to the paper to reflect a little light into them."

Today the venerable *Eastern Graphic* is 38 years old and the flagship of MacNeill's fleet of five successful publications. In an era where weeklies are considered a dubious investment and dailies continue to be swallowed up by media corporations that seemingly have no philosophical difficulties with compromising journalism to protect the bottom line, MacNeill is utterly comfortable bucking the trend. The *Eastern Graphic* alone boasts a circulation of 6000, especially commendable considering the town's population is just 1800. "We sell a quarter of our papers in Charlottetown, probably because we offer details on the stories that aren't thoroughly covered in the province's one remaining daily paper."

The *West Prince Graphic,* which serves the western end of the island and shares very little content with its eastern counterpart, and the *Island Farmer,* have also stood the test of time. *Atlantic Fish Farming* serves the fish farming industry up and down North America's east and west coasts, and has the largest circulation of any Canadian publication aimed at that industry. And MacNeill's newest venture is *Atlantic Gig,* a monthly look at Atlantic Canada's burgeoning music scene. Barely out of the starting blocks, it already enjoys a circulation of 15,000.

Over the years, MacNeill's particular brand of feisty, yet balanced, journalism has not gone unnoted by his peers. "We've been recognized both provincially and nationally for pretty well everything from editorial to news to advertising." In 1991 MacNeill received a special Atlantic Journalism Award for his outstanding contribution to Island journalism in the previous decade. In 1994 he won the coveted Eugene Cervi Award, presented by the International Society of Weekly Newspaper Editors for a lifetime of tough and thorough investigative reporting, or, to put it in MacNeill's own words, "a lifetime of giving hell to government and authority." And the Atlantic Canada Journalist of the Year Award, for which he was in competition with all other media including radio and television, was conferred on him in 1995 by the University of King's College in Halifax.

Nonetheless, MacNeill has no difficulty recalling the inauspicious beginnings of his venture into publishing. "There were periods of nip and tuck. I was burned out in 1967, shortly after a large order of newsprint, bond paper and envelopes had been delivered. To this day we don't know what started the fire. When you're faced with replacing all your used equipment collected from here and there, it's a major financial blow. I spent a week shopping around in Boston, for equipment that cost far more than the insurance was underwriting. I was so dismally far in debt at that point that I couldn't even consider packing it in. The second fire a few years later wasn't as serious."

Ironically, the *Eastern Graphic* is now permanently housed in what was once Montague's fire hall. "We'd been through several rented locations when the fire hall came up for sale. This is the hub for much of our activity, although the printing is farmed out to presses in Amherst and Summerside."

There are colourful moments too, embedded in MacNeill's publishing past. "Our first offset printer was an ex-convict, once on Canada's Ten Most Wanted list. But he did an excellent job in a time when there were few offset printers around, and never gave me any trouble."

Over the years MacNeill has spurned requests from all of the Island's major parties to run for public office. "I have no desire to become politically involved, and if I did, everything we do here would be seen to be compromised. Not only that, but everything I've ever written would immediately become suspect." MacNeill has also doggedly resisted a media corporation's offer to buy his lucrative string of papers. "They offered $1.4 million. However, my son, Paul, will eventually take over the helm. But I'll always stick around. I don't foresee myself losing the ability to write a column and be of value."

If and when MacNeill does begin winding down, it's likely he won't take to blending in quietly with the office furniture. "I've always told my reporters to get out there and talk to the people and keep their ear to the ground. I'll be doing the same. Even now I try and talk to 50 people a day. The conversations are not long, just long enough to touch base. That's how I continue to find the stories others miss."

In keeping with this mission, MacNeill has recently embarked on a quest to walk the entire Island and write about his findings and musings. "I walk the roads, the old rail beds and the beaches, meeting people and chatting with them. I write about history, issues, whatever I hear. The feedback has been overwhelmingly positive. Recently I visited two elderly brothers who ran a general store the old-fashioned way, one calling out the prices while the other punched the numbers into an ancient cash register. Three days after my column appeared in print, the older of the two suddenly died. The story turned out to be a unique tribute to him, and elicited a tremendous response from the readers.

"I figure it'll take me two to three years to do the entire island, perhaps considerably longer, given my current progress. Recently I walked 500 yards and spent four and a half hours with one Islander, then crossed the road and spent another four hours with his neighbour."

At that rate MacNeill may well spend the next ten years walking, observing, chatting and taking the pulse of the Island's people, his people. It's a decade he'll spend without a morsel of regret.

When you make the decision to live in Canada,
that in itself brings on the responsibility
of becoming a Canadian and at least
attempting to understand Canadian ways.

Coming to Prince Edward Island was one of the lucky breaks in my life, and it's been my home right from the start. In fact, I was the one who convinced Shirley after our honeymoon that we should try and make our lives here. I've never been an outsider; the only time I was ever called one was in an outburst by a woman who, angry with the paper over something or other, dismissed me as being 'from away.'

This island is a great place to live. The water is always near, and even though I no longer sail, I like having it right there, in the middle-ground, all the time. There's culture and live theatre, and we're handy enough to Toronto if we need to step out for any reason. But whenever I'm away for more than a few days, I begin to feel a compelling need to hurry back.

The music is here too, our own special brand of Maritime music, and so are the Irish and Scottish roots. We have a rich Scottish culture that goes back five or six generations to when the Scots first migrated here. That's what I've come into, a very friendly, familiar environment without the centuries-old animosities that still burden the people of the British Isles: Catholic versus Protestant, Scottish versus Irish. Here you can sit in a pub and enjoy a pint and good conversation, and your background is of no consequence, which is as it should be.

I know it's been said that you're not an Islander unless you were born here, but that's definitely not been my experience. However, I did come prepared to meet people more than half way, which you have to do if you're going to find your own place in your new community. The insurance company I worked for in my early Toronto days had hired a number of young Britons, and as far as they were concerned, they were simply enduring life in a British colony. They limited themselves to things British and stayed well away from the mainstream. They offered nothing of themselves to Canada and couldn't wait to get back to England.

Well, if you're going to immigrate, you have to be prepared to make a commitment to your new home. That doesn't mean you relinquish all your previous ties and interests, but it does mean you welcome new experiences and keep an open mind. People don't usually leave a country because they think it's the greatest; no, they migrate to a new home because they have some dissatisfaction with the old. And yet, to hear some of these immigrants talk, you'd think they'd left the best place in the world.

When you make the decision to live in Canada, that in itself brings on the responsibility of becoming a Canadian and at least attempting to understand Canadian ways. It didn't take me long to feel that Canada was my home, perhaps because I brought with me a sense of commitment, a sense of there being no turning back. I would be living here for the rest of my life.

I don't recall being dragged down by homesickness. I'd been with the navy so I was already used to being away from home. But I do remember my first Christmas in Toronto. I had invitations from friends to spend Christmas Day with them, but I didn't want to impose myself on their family celebrations until evening. So, having the day to wile away by myself, I decided I would go out for lunch. But all the restaurants were closed—that wouldn't be the case in Toronto today—and so I just walked all afternoon. At five o'clock I was wandering past the Swiss Chalet at Yonge and St. Clair just as they were opening. There were people who had been waiting in line, and we all went in and had an enjoyable Christmas dinner together. I still harbour the strongest feelings for that Swiss Chalet. They made Christmas for a lot of people that year.

Years later I wrote about that experience in one of my Christmas columns because I realized how sadly alone people can be at that time of year. I always send the paper to my family back in Scotland, and that particular column has stuck with them over the years.

The Canadian coldness wasn't a problem for me because it was dry and infinitely easier to take than the Scottish dampness that worked its way through your woolens and chilled you to the bone. I've always been invigorated by the Canadian winter, although come April I now find myself getting a bit antsy for spring. I don't take a winter holiday; Shirley and I have our differences on that one. If anything, I'd like to go north or to see the remote parts of Canada I've not yet visited.

I've been lucky to have had newspaper conventions take me on many cross-country travels over the years. Whenever we could, we took our five kids along and tried to spend a bit of time getting to know the area and people we were visiting. I think that's helped to nurture in them a special understanding of Canada and a sense of solidarity with the many fellow Canadians whom they've met over the years. I know it has in me.

On the whole I think we're a caring and accommodating society that's prepared to see other points of view, but we're doing an excellent job of splitting ourselves up over the unity issue. I believe separation is inevitable. Each time there's a referendum in Quebec, the number of people who want out of Canada climbs. Much as I dread Canada going down that path, I'm compelled to say that, as a Gaelic speaker from the Hebrides who experienced first-hand the lack of understanding that Edinburgh and London had for our culture, I can empathize with Quebec.

However, these issues are always a two-way street. Quebec's education curriculum, for example, is basically not offering any coverage of Canada. I was visiting a friend in Manitoba who was billeting a 16-year-old Quebec student on an exchange. He knew nothing of Canada. He thought Quebec was the only province with its own flag. We took him around the prairies, stopping at the Saskatchewan legislature and so on, and even he, himself, came to conclude his knowledge of Canada was sorely limited. And we said, "You must have learned something about Canada in school," and he said, "Not really."

Wanting to investigate further, I commissioned a freelancer to analyse the Quebec curriculum. She concluded that Canada was mentioned appallingly few times in the Quebec classroom. I know this happens in reverse too, although not to the same extent. And this is part of the problem.

The media also contributes to the problem, not just the Canadian media but the Quebec media as well. The two can cover the same happening and come up with totally different stories. And so often, emotions over silly little issues become so strong that they rise up to overshadow the more important concerns. Take the desecration of the Quebec flag that occurred in Ontario a few years ago. That got unbelievable coverage in Quebec, over and over again, to the extent that everyone in Quebec thought everyone outside their border was burning and stomping on the Quebec flag. No doubt other incidents have also been overplayed by the media on both sides. But the tragedy is that if separation occurs, it will have been based on emotion, which is often rife with falsehoods. When we become blinded by our emotions, we are left vulnerable to stupidity.

Our way of doing things politically also has me feeling jaded from time to time. Frankly, our best people are generally not in public office, neither federally nor provincially. Fewer and fewer people become politically involved on the premise that it's the right thing to do. And why should they? They'd only get skewered by the status quo. So as a result, the government becomes more removed from the people, and from there it's not such a giant step towards abuse of power, decline in accountability, alienation from societal issues, and less acceptance of responsibility. It used to be that ministers resigned over fiascos in their departments, but that protocol is now considered obsolete.

Islanders, and Atlantic Canadians too, have their own particular grab bag of problems. Our small size is a drawback in dealing with Ottawa. Interestingly enough, the islands on the east of the Atlantic have fared significantly better than those on the west. The Channel Islands are decidedly better off than we are, both economically and culturally. They gained independence in the 1940's and run their own affairs internally. They also have a great deal of say in other affairs that concern them. There's much we could learn from them. But what do Maritimers and Newfoundlanders do? We look to Ottawa for our solutions. We've taken the position that we can run to Ottawa, cap in hand. We play our role and they play theirs. Well, that also makes us a lot easier to dismiss.

Essentially, Prince Edward Island is an experimental station for Ottawa. Did you know that every Island child, unlike any child in the rest of Canada, is issued a social insurance number at two weeks of age? Normally it's issued when someone wants to start working; that was it's original purpose. But Ottawa wanted to pilot-test it for use as a national identification program, and so we're stuck with it. The possibilities for gross misuse are astounding: once someone has access to a child's social insurance number, it can be safely used to collect benefits for at least ten years, until the child starts looking for work.

When my kids were little, the school forms would routinely ask for their social insurance numbers but I absolutely refused to divulge that information so carelessly. I've written several editorials about it and spoken with members of Cabinet, but the rule remains in effect. It'll be with us until Islanders use their vote to show their disapproval.

But despite all that, Canada is an interesting, exciting country. Canadians can have unbelievable variety in their lives. And the more you travel, the more you become aware of that rich variety in culture and language, and in how people are living in their own corner of the country. That awareness is an advantage immigrants also bring for themselves when they come to Canada. And it's an advantage for Canada too, to be peopled by those who've seen and experienced other worlds and can temper their attitudes accordingly.

I remain convinced that Canada could easily handle millions more people and become a better country for it. Immigrants add vibrancy to our culture and boost the economy. They create jobs and investments. True, the problems also increase in complexity as our numbers grow, but the benefits far outweigh the setbacks. And if you look at the recent history of this country, the Dutch farmers on the island, the Italians, Portuguese, Caribbean and Asian people in Toronto, you'll see that we've gained economic growth and cultural diversity as a society.

As for me, if I was to do it all over again, I'd still settle in a small Canadian town. I think you can become more quickly established in a small town, especially if you're prepared to take whatever job you can, and work up to what it is you aspire to do. Small town people take you as an individual more readily. In the big city you're just part of the herd looking for a job.

Yes, I'd likely come to Prince Edward Island again. It's my home and I've come to know it well. All around me I see its beauty. I look forward to further discoveries as I walk its highways and back roads, beaches and rail beds.

POSTSCRIPT: *Tragically, Jim MacNeill died very suddenly of a heart attack on May 16, 1998, while returning to Montague from Halifax where he had just received an Honorary Doctorate from the University of King's College. He was 62 years old.*

Dr. Romulo Magsino

LUCENA CITY, PHILIPPINES—WINNIPEG, MANITOBA

The campus is typically Canadian—grey, square-shouldered buildings planted within a nondescript landscape, here a tender sapling, there a grassy knoll on which to find repose in the company of a literary classic, or wrestle with the basic principles of organic chemistry.

The office of the dean is just inside the entrance, to the left and through the reception area. This is the academic habitat of Dr. Romulo Magsino, eminent scholar, educator, and now Dean of the Faculty of Education at the University of Manitoba. Gracious, and meticulous in his contemplations, Magsino speaks in understated tones, sprinkles the essence of his commentary with quiet, introspective laughter. Ever-conscious of his own beginnings, Magsino remains fascinated with the human condition, seeks to interpret and understand; knows the evanescent present, with its answers and questions, is bound to past and future by the enduring threads of humanity.

Romulo Magsino was halfway through his doctoral studies at the University of Wisconsin when an ad in the school paper flagged down his attention. "I had been planning to return to the Philippines after completing my degree, but here was an ad for a teaching position at Newfoundland's Memorial University. I had no idea where Newfoundland was but I said to my wife, 'Wouldn't it be a fine experience to teach at a North American University for awhile?'"

Magsino submitted his application to Memorial University and then promptly shifted his focus back to his own studies. "There was no urgency for me to get a job. I was on a full fellowship at the University of Wisconsin, as I had been for my Master's Degree, and I still had my doctoral dissertation to complete."

A short time later he was called for an interview, and then, while still in the middle of his own research and writing, received notification that the job at Memorial was his. The year was 1972.

Born in the Philippines in 1941, Magsino had demonstrated early on his voracious appetite for all things academic. After receiving Arts and Education degrees from Luzonian University in his native city, he taught at the local high school for a year and then, deciding he wasn't yet finished with his own education, enrolled in Manila's Ateneo de Manila University Graduate School of Education. While there he applied for and obtained a fellowship to complete his Master's Degree at the University of Sydney, in Australia. With that degree in hand, he returned to Lucena City and began teaching at his alma mater.

The following year he applied for and was awarded a scholarship to pursue a Master of Arts in Education at the University of Wisconsin. By now married, he took leave of his wife and infant son and, temporarily, he thought, set out for North America. His family joined him in Wisconsin a year later, just as he was completing his Master's Degree and beginning doctoral studies.

"All this time I had been thinking my stay in North America would be temporary, that I would be returning to the Philippines where I knew I had a teaching job waiting for me at my old university. A newly established university in Manila was also interested in having me on faculty, so I knew I had several possibilities in my homeland.

"But Canada, and Newfoundland in particular, intrigued us and we theorized that I would be able to finish my own dissertation while teaching at Memorial. Like many theories, that didn't work out; family and career consumed all of my time. At the end of my first year I hadn't written a single chapter. So I asked for and obtained a six-month leave of absence from Memorial, and returned to Wisconsin to finish my doctorate. Meanwhile, my father-in-law had fallen very ill so my wife, pregnant with our second child, returned with our son to the Philippines for several months to be with her father and attend his subsequent funeral. Our daughter was born in the Philippines; the family rejoined me in Wisconsin as I was finishing my dissertation. At that point I could have returned to the Philippines or to my job in Newfoundland."

Although their hearts were still firmly planted in the Philippines, the Magsinos began giving consideration to a more long-term move to Canada. This was the era of Filipino president Ferdinand Marcos, who was enforcing martial law with the muscle of a repressive military regime. Rights and freedoms, including freedom of speech, were being stifled throughout the country. "My academic specialty was the philosophy of education, the analysis of political ideologies and philosophies in relation to education. I had learned how to evaluate, assess and critique. If I was going to be true to my calling in the Philippines, examining ideas and speaking according to my own findings, I would quite surely have ended up in jail. Essentially, there was no future for me in my homeland.

"So I returned to Newfoundland and took on a second one-year appointment, after which my position became permanent. It was a decision not lightly made. I had always assumed I'd be returning home to offer some contribution to my country. Even back then it was apparent the Philippines was suffering a brain drain. But if you can't practise what you've been trained to do, well, sitting in jail on the basis of principle is not effective either. We told ourselves that we could always decide to go back to the Philippines at a later time. And so we left it open-ended."

However, during the next several years, family and career took precedence over homesickness and patriotic yearnings, and when the Magsinos came to re-evaluate their plans they discovered that the opinions of their children, now numbering three, factored significantly into the equation. "My children were growing up and becoming socialized in the Canadian context, and it became difficult for us to think in terms of transplanting them back to the Philippines and starting anew. They had been to the Philippines many times to visit their relatives and although they always had a great time, Newfoundland was home.

"As well, I had been promoted to the level of associate professor by that time and there were no guarantees I'd achieve an equivalent appointment in the Philippines. These factors helped to solidify our decision to become permanent residents of Canada. And so we became Canadians in the late 1970's, but with mixed feelings because there was still such a strong emotional link to our families in the Philippines."

The Magsinos tried to ease that particular void in their lives by becoming immersed in Newfoundland's sizeable Filipino community. "When we arrived I was surprised to find a Filipino community already here, considering it's so far away from our end of the Pacific. The first Filipino to immigrate to Newfoundland came in 1959; many professionals were wooed by the Newfoundland government, especially those in education and medicine." Magsino studied the province's Filipino community to such an extent that his findings culminated in a series of academic papers published by Memorial University. For his efforts both academic and grassroot, he was selected in 1982 as one of five 'outstanding Filipinos in Canada' to receive the Mabuhay Award, presented by the Filipino Association of Canada.

But Magsino didn't limit his work and relationships to Filipino Newfoundlanders. "Quite easily I grew to love Newfoundland, the people and also the pace of life, which could be whatever you made it. I wasn't too crazy about the climate, but certainly my life as an academic was very enriching and satisfying. There were many possibilities for conducting research, and the university, not wanting us to become too isolated in our local setting, provided generous funding for travel to conferences. Really, I would have been content to stay in Newfoundland.

"But my wife and two older children wanted to move to central Canada. My wife wanted to be closer to her relatives in Toronto who had immigrated after we did. Every year we would drive up to visit them, which took three tiring days. We also figured our flights back to the Philippines would be less cumbersome if we were more centrally located."

As the Magsinos were mulling over various options and possibilities, a former colleague now at the University of Manitoba telephoned to say his employer was advertising the position of Department Head in the Educational Administration and Foundations Department. Would Magsino consider submitting his application?

"Based on my family's desire to relocate more than on my own, I said, 'why not,' and that's how I came to Winnipeg, in 1988." For the better part of the next decade Magsino worked quietly and diligently to strengthen the somewhat divided department in his charge. "The situation I came to was that this department had been formed out of a merger between two areas of study, so there were some solidarity issues to deal with. At times we had difficulty arriving at resolutions on program development and such, but I was fortunate in recruiting the cooperation of the membership, and like to think I made a contribution by helping them to develop a sense of unity."

By now well known for his skills as a successful moderator and effective team player, Magsino was asked in 1995 to take on the headship of the Department of Educational Psychology, which was experiencing similar challenges. Although chagrined that he would again be spending far more of his time on administrative duties than in the classroom, Magsino nonetheless accepted the position. "I agreed because I thought I might be able to help the department sort out it's difficulties, even though teaching has always been my first love."

All the while Magsino remained passionately involved with the Filipino community and again was able to successfully incorporate much of this involvement into his work as an educator. He studied the particular circumstances of being Filipino in Canada, did comparative studies in England, the United States and the Philippines—the Marcos regime by this time had begun loosening it's strangle-hold on the lifeblood of its people—and wrote endlessly about his findings. In America he researched the concept of multicultural education and in the Philippines he delved into the many parameters of education with respect to human rights.

Magsino also became involved in several Canadian Filipino associations, including the Manitoba Association of Filipino Teachers, but is quick to emphasize that the efforts of those groups are not exclusively for the benefit of Filipinos in Canada. "We work to ensure that all of Canada's minority people are motivated and stimulated to participate fully in Canadian society, educationally, politically and otherwise. The ideals we promote fit well in the Canadian context— liberty, freedom, justice, well-being, and social and intellectual values. We also make it a point to participate in the affairs of the province so that ethnic people can contribute to and be seen as part of the community-at-large. The idea is not to isolate ourselves but to make ourselves known to the community, thereby creating links for the benefit of the entire community."

Magsino himself has always made it a point to practise the message he puts forth. Making his home in a Filipino suburb would have been easy enough to do; there are an estimated 40,000 Filipinos in Winnipeg, clustered in various parts of the city. But the Magsinos chose to be closer to the university for logistical reasons, and wanted their children exposed to as broad a horizon as possible. "It's a natural impulse to have your residence near those who are familiar to you. So there's a tendency to settle in the same place, the Maples area north of the city, for example. However, ghettoization has not really been a problem in these neighbourhoods, in part because Filipinos place a high priority on their children's education. That in itself spurs more interaction with the mainstream and counters the tendency towards isolation."

Over the years Magsino has become widely recognized as a leader and visionary by the Filipino community, but never more so than on the day in 1996 when he was installed as the University of Manitoba's Dean of the Faculty of Education. "It's an honour to be the first Filipino Canadian to become the Dean of Education in a major Canadian University."

But even as he joins the upper ranks of academia, Magsino remains acutely aware of his roots, and of his responsibility to the thousands of new Canadians who look up to him as a role model. For that unswerving dedication he received further national and international recognition in 1998 as an outstanding Filipino Canadian.

"I have the luxury of being comfortably established and knowing my personal future is bright. But equally important, my accomplishments also send an important signal to minority people that if they work hard there can be a solid future for them in Canada."

There is a place for centralization and commonality,
but also for differences that are significant. This thinking is
pretty much in line with our stance on multiculturalism,
that we should value the people of other cultures
and the cultures of other people.

For security you naturally tend to associate with your own people. And when you come to a new country, there is the tendency to turn to your own people, especially if you are a member of a visible minority group. But if you choose to live totally within that isolated context there is the danger you might not be fully functional in the new environment, to the detriment of both the individual and the country. The Trudeau government first recognized this when it introduced a multiculturalism policy in 1971. Although the policy has undergone numerous revisions and its implementation has been chronically problematic, it was originally intended as a means to encourage full and equal participation in Canadian society.

According to the Trudeau regime, minority groups need to have their identity validated before they can be expected to participate fully in Canadian society, and in order for this validation to occur there must be support for their cultures. The policy further postulated that support for culture and cultural sharing would go so far as to solidify national unity.

There were those who interpreted the policy as being limited to the notion of cultural retention, but I saw it more as having a three-pronged objective: equal participation, a sense of unity, and some cultural retention and sharing. If you promote all three, then you have an ideal arrangement for society and you eliminate the reasons for denigrating or repressing the cultural aspirations of minority groups. To promote cultural expression is to show respect and acceptance, which then reduces the tendency to ghettoize, and encourages full participation in Canadian society. Only then can we ensure that everyone is equal before the law regardless of what references you use. To be equal is to have access to the same opportunities.

But the implementation of the multiculturalism policy in those early years limited its thrust to cultural retention, probably because that was the most tangible way to proceed and perhaps the natural starting point for fledgling policy. In the process, the government neglected to give equal emphasis to the other two objectives and thereby lost valuable opportunities for the promotion of national unity and equal access to education and employment. I've always argued that the policy itself has not deserved the criticism it has received over the years; instead, criticism might best be directed at the lack of effort to implement all three principles behind the policy.

From our end, ethnic people must realize that they need to be more active in their participation within the national context. It is not enough to learn about and celebrate one's own culture and country. It is not enough to rely on affirmative-action initiatives as the sole means to viable employment. Filipinos do have an advantage over other ethnic people in that they already speak English and come here fully westernized. They are also very achievement oriented, to the point where many in the Philippines sell off parcels of land to pay for their children's education if need be.

How you find your place in Canada is also determined by your motivations for coming here. Many immigrate of their own free will for the opportunities they expect to find here. When you're motivated to that degree, you are driven to do whatever it takes to succeed. Such were my motivations, and I don't think I'm very different from thousands of others who have migrated here.

But there are also those who have been pressured by their parents—'I'll stay here, you go to Canada.' The personal motive in these circumstances is not strong enough to overcome the sense of loss, of questioning the wisdom of having come in the first place. There are also those who may have been highly motivated initially, but whose experiences in the early years were so difficult that they, too, grew to regret their decision.

The lack of standardization in education requirements causes real hardship for some new arrivals. An education degree obtained in the Philippines does not allow you to teach here. Many who come from other parts of the world with degrees in engineering and medicine as two examples, have great difficulty getting their careers off the ground here. The double whammy is that not only is their training not recognized here, but going to university to upgrade becomes an impossibility when all one's time is spent just earning enough money to provide for the family and to make ends meet.

So doctors become hospital workers. Teachers become sales clerks. That's often the pattern. And eventually, with enough browbeating, these people come to lower both their expectations and self esteem.

Personally, I've been fortunate to have been spared these challenges. I've always been very self-reliant and I was quite internationalized in my thinking by the time I arrived in Newfoundland. No, the part of my transition that's been most problematic relates mostly to the ongoing difficulty I have placing my intrinsic Filipino values, which I still prize, within a Canadian context. For example, I would like to pass on to my children certain values with regards to sexuality and respect for their elders. But the influence of their environment is extremely difficult to oppose, and so my wife and I have had to make some difficult adjustments to their new-found attitudes. The typical Filipino values chastity before marriage. And children are expected to be mindful of, although not necessarily deferential to, their parents' guidance. They acknowledge the wisdom of their elders. Here, that's all very different, and many Filipinos are struggling to come to grips with it. I personally know of people who profess to have given their children the range of freedoms available in Canadian society, and yet as parents they remain torn and concerned. In a sense, they feel they've had no choice but to relinquish their influence over their children, an exceedingly difficult position for any parent.

Concerning my own situation, it's interesting to consider whether or not I've fully made the transition into Canadian society since I still hold my Filipino values so dear. At what point do I say that I'll forget my past and totally embrace the North American way of life, and do I have to arrive at that point in order to be fully Canadian? Personally, I think I'm richer for my background, and also for the flexibility I have in my thinking and activities, which allows me to operate in the mainstream. However, because of my background, pressures do remain. The Filipino community in Canada sees me as a leader and expects me to demonstrate how one can successfully incorporate

Filipino values into the Canadian way of life. So in a sense, I'm straddling both worlds and probably always will.

But for my children it will be different. There will be no particular
pressures on them to uphold or live according to traditional Filipino
values. They will carry on as full-fledged members of Canadian society,
with all its western ways and lifestyles. But for the generation that's immigrated, it's almost impossible to leave the transition period completely
behind.

I don't see the Filipino community in Canada as becoming completely transformed even though there will be two distinct groups a few
generations from now: those who've been born and bred here and
become totally Canadianized, and those who will have just arrived. There
will be tensions between them; the former group may not look kindly
on the latter for their imperfect English and 'old-fashioned' values.

A few decades ago the American notion of multiculturalism was
that of a melting pot: everyone would eventually lose their ethnic culture and identity to become homogenous Americans. It was a silly and
simplistic notion that never got off the ground. Instead, in the 1970's
there was a surge of third and fourth generation Americans rediscovering their ethnic roots and culture. Will this happen here too? It's
always easier for ethnic people to rediscover their ethnicity; no matter how well integrated they are, they will always be part of the whole
in a special way rather than in the ordinary way.

Three or four generations from now there will have been some
intermarriage; already there are a good number of mixed marriages, to
the point where there is a club in Winnipeg for intermarried couples.
But intermarriage is not happening that quickly, especially since many
Filipinos live in their own communities, and some of the city's schools
in these areas are 80 percent Filipino. At the same time, it's not
unusual to see Filipino youth dating members of other communities.
But dating is one thing and marriage is another, since marriage would
call for some sort of compatibility of the different cultures.

I haven't experienced a great deal of racism here, but I would say
little pockets of prejudice do exist. The Newfoundland population is
predominantly Anglo-Saxon, and my children were pretty much the
only visible minority kids in school. There were some incidents where

they were called "Chinkies," but that was before multicultural education became intrinsic in the curriculum. I'm not sure if such incidents would happen now. My children have done well in school, and
the truth is that when you do well the colour of your skin matters less.

We still have cases of uncouth people who will pull their car up
beside yours at a stoplight and yell denigrating comments. But that says
more about them as individuals than it does about Canadian society. I
do believe that the more educated people are, the more informed they
are and the more apt they are to accept others for what they are. As for
racist groups, there's not a whole lot to be done with them.

When I think about the difficult issue of Canadian unity, I regret
that Canada chose to reject the Charlottetown Accord. As a result, our
grappling with unity and distinctiveness has become even more cumbersome, and separation has become a significant possibility. We
wouldn't lose anything by acknowledging cultural diversity, and perhaps it's simple-minded to treat everyone exactly the same. People are
not the same. Regions are not the same. There is a place for centralization and commonality, but also for differences that are significant.
This thinking is pretty much in line with our stance on multiculturalism, that we should value the people of other cultures and the cultures
of other people. Our notion of unity should be based on these tenets.

At the same time, certain principles and arrangements cannot be
compromised. We cannot have every province doing its own thing if
we want to maintain parity and equality as Canadians. We have to
find a real balance, which is a task for government, difficult, but not
insurmountable.

Regardless of how the issue is resolved, the Quebecois and the
indigenous people have a strong case for the preservation of their
uniqueness, which they feel is being lost to the English culture. They
have historical claims to their distinctiveness. Immigrants, however,
do not have the same claim. We chose to come here. We cannot expect
government to make the same concessions for us. We must acknowledge to ourselves that by coming here we become part and parcel of
the whole society we have chosen to join. We can bring important cultural aspects with us, but we should expect to make compromises and
adjustments along the way. At the same time, there's always a place for

respecting and giving expression to certain significant elements of yourself that are drawn from your culture.

I encourage newcomers to retain some contact with their own culture. But at the same time they must expect to participate in civic affairs if they want their voices heard; the political system is the domain of the people who participate in it. If immigrants don't participate actively, if they withdraw into their own shells, then they cannot make a difference in terms of government policies.

I feel I have been able to make a contribution and at the same time maintain very close ties with my cultural community. One can have many roles, can chart for oneself an enriched life with many dimensions. Canada is full of opportunity and possibility.

I feel passionate about Canada but have some anxieties about how we are allowing ourselves to become more and more Americanized— the Free Trade Agreement, the art and culture we are constantly exposed to, and even our judicial system in some respects. I feel very Canadian in terms of being certain I don't want us to give in to American influences.

Even though I studied in the United States, I can't help but feel somewhat uneasy with the American presence in the lives of Canadians. For 50 years in the early part of the 20th century the Philippines was under American rule. We were told this was for our own benefit, that we would profit from American activities and tutelage. Growing up, I learned more in school about American history than I did about the history of my own country. Now, as an educated person who's had the opportunity to study history as it really unfolded, I realize we were exploited in many ways. The American government kept us agricultural and used our natural resources for their industries. They sold the finished products back to us and made our economy dependent on their manufacturing. They set themselves up as the model for everything, even culture, and as a result we imported their way of life without question. Our own values were diminished and we began accepting things very alien to our tradition. There was no attempt by the American government to cultivate anything distinctly Filipino; everything was to be Americanized. In the end we oversold ourselves to the American culture.

And so, because of who I am, I stay vigilant and hope Canadians are not voluntarily going down the same path. Not that the American culture is inherently bad; I have many respected American friends and I'm grateful to many Americans for my education. But the American culture is not *our* culture. I feel very passionately that we must stand our ground.

I love Manitoba, even though I still have a special place in my heart for Newfoundland. That's a difficulty: the more places you've lived in, the more ties there are to tug at your heart. But Manitoba is home now, where we will stay after my retirement. We talk of travelling often to Newfoundland, of perhaps wintering in the Philippines. But this is where our friends are, and our children too. This is where we can have the best of all worlds. And this is where, when the time comes, my remains will find their resting place.

Dr. Mary Majka

CZESTOCHOWA, POLAND—MARY'S POINT, NEW BRUNSWICK

*Her laughter is like music rippling from a delicate wind chime,
her quick wit delightfully to the point, her unaffected niceness
almost legend. This is Mary Majka—Mother Nature's powerhouse.
Trained as a physician, she is an eminent naturalist; a scholar who
has lectured the world over; a photographer and writer; the recipient of numerous awards and distinctions; a tireless advocate for
the environment. She hasn't had time to let any of it go to her head.
Her home at Mary's Point overlooks the panoramic Bay of Fundy
stretched out like an endless summer day, its transparent water
languishing against the glistening mudflats that are manna for
untold numbers of migratory shorebirds. The ocean's rhythms play
in the background, a fitting harmony for Majka's narration.
This is her world. She, with all her heart and soul, is it s keeper.*

Mary Majka doesn't usually sleep on bridges. That is, unless
the bridge in question is a local heritage landmark in
danger of being vandalized. Such was the case several
Halloweens ago when Majka feared the Sawmill Creek Covered Bridge
near Moncton might fall victim to quirky hooligans with matches in
their pockets and no regard for local history. Majka's response was typically in keeping with her take-charge attitude; she grabbed her sleeping bag, drove her car onto the bridge and settled in for the night.

Born in Poland in 1925 to a Czechoslovakian countess and Polish
school principal, Majka was a perfect fit for the profile of Canada's
ideal immigrant. She was young, energetic, bright, healthy and
skilled. Both she and her husband, Mieczyslaw—"'Mike' since we've
been in Canada since no one can pronounce his Polish name"—had

both recently graduated from the University of Innsbruck's medical school. Designated as Displaced Persons (DP's) after the war, returning to the ruins of Poland was not an option for the couple.

"We could go to any country that was taking a quota of DP's as determined by the United Nations Refugee Organization. We chose Canada because it seemed a more open society. Countries were vying for people like us so we had a choice of destination, but really, it wasn't a very compassionate system for people with lesser qualifications.

"We came in 1951 on an American troopship yet to be refitted after the war. Men to the right, women to the left. We were taken down, down, down, to the lowest level where it was so hot hell flashed before my eyes. We were at least 80 women in the room and because of the steamy heat we soon stripped off our clothes. In our white underwear in the steam, we looked like angels.

"My berth, the only one left when I arrived, had a red Exit sign and the crew's intercom system hanging over it. They constantly talked back and forth; I wasn't sure I'd make it to Canada.

"Then everyone got seasick. Our washroom had all the sinks in a row, followed by all the toilets. Many made it only as far as the sinks. They became plugged and flooded over, and water sloshed on the floor. When the ship rolled and the water swirled to the other side, we all jumped on the toilets.

"The next day they announced we would have to work for our food. I reported to the ship's hospital. They didn't need doctors so I said, sure, I'll be a nurse. My husband mostly handed out Dramamine. I worked with the children. Many had diarrhea because of the food, and anxiety of being separated from their parents. We were herded like cattle. It wasn't humane."

In Halifax the couple was put on a train for Hamilton, Ontario. "Mike had an uncle there and he had reluctantly agreed to receive us. But he wasn't very happy with us imposing on him so we struck out on our own after a few months.

"My husband did an internship in Hamilton, and in 1954 our first child, Christopher, was born. I became a full-time mother and have no regrets about not having practised medicine in Canada. We wanted a family and I wasn't that young anymore. In retrospect, my life as it has unfolded has probably been much more interesting and diversified."

Although the Majkas were eager to make themselves part of their new community, their efforts were met with indifference. "Our accent seemed to be a real barrier and, as much as we wanted to be accepted as Canadian, we could not get beyond being seen as foreigners. It was frustrating, discouraging.

"Then Mike was accepted as a resident in pathology at the Westminster Hospital in London, and we saw it as a new opportunity. That was in 1958. Our second child, Marc, was born ten days before we moved."

The family rented a home in a favourable London suburb and, anticipating a fresh start, happily settled into the neighbourhood. But acceptance, they soon discovered, would remain stubbornly elusive. "Try as we might, Canadians just weren't interested in us. Our only real friends were immigrants. We still had no real, meaningful contact with Canadians.

"I remember one day Chris was stung by a bee. An elderly neighbour consoled him. The next day I thanked his wife and told her how her husband's kindness had helped to make Chris feel better. 'Yes, George, he is like that,' she said disapprovingly. 'He talks to everybody, even the black boys on the train.' And I understood what she was telling me."

One might have expected things to improve when the Majkas moved to a housing complex specifically for physicians. They didn't. "I was never accepted by the wives of the physicians. My neighbours would ask me, 'how's the baby' but the conversation never went beyond that. We were outsiders. Mike was accepted on a professional level by his colleagues, but socially we had no contact with them."

When Majka's husband finished his residency in 1961, the couple began scouting around for opportunities in other parts of Canada. They received offers from hospitals in six provinces, including New Brunswick's Moncton Hospital. "New Brunswick sounded good because we were already very much involved in nature then. And we were ready to try something new." At that point the Majkas had lived in Canada for ten years.

In Moncton they found the craved-for acceptance almost immediately. "True, we were from a different part of the world. And we spoke to our children in Polish. But instead of thinking of us as foreigners, they saw us as being interesting, a curiosity almost. They went out of their way to make us feel at home."

The Majkas opted for a cottage on nearby Caledonia Mountain and became the mountain's only inhabitants. "Here nature was served to us on a platter. That first winter, we rented a house in the city but I enjoyed the cottage more. It was rustic, with a wood stove and outhouse. I loved the challenge of living that way. I didn't need to worry about what to wear or how to act. After that first winter we remodelled the cottage, rebuilt it actually, and put in water so we could live there year-round."

Majka marks the year she moved to the cottage as the start of her intimate relationship with nature. "I have always loved nature and had taken extra biology courses throughout my schooling. We had also been part of a naturalist club in London. Now, with my eldest in school and my youngest in tow, I was able to hike the mountain and explore it freely, studying, observing."

Majka soon found herself being invited to her son's class to talk about the migration of birds. "Chris committed me when he told his teacher, 'my mother knows a lot about birds!' But I was well received and ended up repeating my presentation for the entire school." Majka's reputation as an animated presenter who could translate the wonders of nature into everyday language soon spread. Before long she was inundated with requests from area schools. "I became a very busy volunteer but I could see there was a need for this kind of first-hand exposure to nature, which could not be gotten from books."

At around this time Majka was invited by a Moncton television station to appear as a guest on a locally produced cooking show. She was to share some Polish dishes with the host during the half-hour segment. "I ended up doing a few programs with her, and one day she phoned me saying she had been to the dentist and couldn't do the show. Would I do it for her?" Majka complied, and although she no longer remembers the segment, she does recall the studio was pleased with the results.

"That got me thinking, maybe I could do a show on nature." Majka took her proposal to the station's manager. He suggested she audition, which she did. "A few days later he phoned me to turn my television on, and there was the audition. That's how I got started."

The show, *Have You Seen?* aired from 1967 to 1974 and rapidly gained popularity. It wasn't long before the capable Majka was given free rein by her producers. But there were other opportunities to seize as well. When Majka discovered there was no naturalist club in the area, she and Mike rallied a small group of friends together and started their own. "There were environmental things starting to concern me. I wanted to educate people about nature, how it works and why we must leave it alone. In Europe I had long observed that many things in nature struggle when we interfere. I didn't just want to talk about birds and nature but also about the real issues like the protection of habitats.

"Those concepts were still brand new at that time. Terms like 'environment' and 'ecology' were unknown. In a way I was pioneering, and because I wasn't working elsewhere, I was free to concentrate on this work. It was also good that Mike's work was not affected by what I was saying, because I was becoming quite outspoken. At times people thought I was mad."

Though her viewpoints were challenged at times, Majka rapidly gained a reputation as someone who knew her field. In the late 1960's she joined the Atlantic chapter of the Canadian Society of Fish and Wildlife Biologists, the only woman among the membership. In 1968 she was invited to visit the newly established Sunbury Shores Art and Nature Centre in St. Andrews, N.B. That visit culminated in a scholarship to attend an Audubon camp in Maine, an experience which was to further enhance her already considerable knowledge of the sea and shore.

Later that year Majka volunteered to help conduct an interpretive program for children at Sunbury Shores. During one particular outing she took a group of children to visit a working beehive. She knew these bees to be very docile and recognized a unique opportunity for the children to observe them up close. She spoke calmly about bees in positive terms and encouraged each child to approach the hive quietly and unobtrusively.

"They all trusted me and came forward without fear. My message was, if you approach nature in that way, not disturbing and not harming, then it won't harm you."

Unbeknown to Majka, a man had been standing at the edge of the group, silently observing her. After her session he introduced himself as president of the National Audubon Society and offered her a second scholarship, this time to the Society's naturalist training program in Sharon, Connecticut.

Following her training and now fully qualified as a naturalist, Majka returned to New Brunswick and was recruited by Fundy National Park to develop a nature program specifically for children. "They had seen my television program and, like me, believed that to expose the younger generation to nature and to teach them the importance of preservation would be a sound investment in our future. At that time the parks were offering only adult-oriented interpretive programs. Children could tag along, but the information was really for their parents."

So, over the next four years, Majka set about developing and operating Fundy Park's nature centre for children, the first of its kind in Canada. "It went so well that I proposed to Parks Canada that it be a pilot program for possible expansion into other national parks. But they felt the education of children was a provincial jurisdiction and also saw it as a glorified babysitting service for parents who dropped their children off and went on to do other things. My argument was that these were exactly the children most in need of this program. Those who came hiking with their parents were already getting the exposure and didn't need me as much."

In the meantime Majka was also involved in a myriad of other projects. She taught outdoor education programs for the Moncton and surrounding school districts. Her writing and nature photography were being widely published, and she spent a summer on the University of New Brunswick's Saint John campus, teaching an outdoor education course for school teachers.

In 1972 she teamed up with wildlife biologist David Christie to found the New Brunswick Federation of Naturalists, an organization that is currently more than 400 members strong. Together they edited the organization's publication *NB Naturalist*, first from 1976 to 1977, and again from 1985 to 1994. But it was their mutual concern and love for the shorebirds at Mary's Point on Shepody Bay, near Fundy National Park, that drew them into a working relationship that has endured over the years. "David is like family," Majka explains simply. "He and I are like two horses pulling the same wagon."

Majka had long known that Mary's Point lay on a major route for many species of migratory birds. Located on the upper Bay of Fundy, its extensive mudflats provide a rich food source and respite for the hundreds of thousands of birds annually in transit. But Majka also knew the area's ecosystem was being placed at risk by the beach goers who roamed the beaches and sand dunes at will, often with horses and unleashed dogs. Some roared around in all-terrain vehicles; a few brought their pellet guns.

In 1974, the year the Majkas and Christie bought a cottage at Mary's Point, they decided to pool their energies and lobby for the point's protection. They began by conducting area migratory bird counts for the Canadian Wildlife Service. Very quickly their findings gained national attention, culminating in the Wildlife Service's purchase of 250 acres of shore land including Mary's Point. And so the Shepody National Wildlife Area was established. For Majka and Christie, it was a major coup.

When an adjacent property came up for sale in 1976, the Majkas and Christie snapped it up, painstakingly restored the house which had been vacant for 40 years, and moved in three years later. "I wanted to devote more of my attention to protecting and interpreting the Wildlife Area so I knew living next door full-time would be an asset."

Always agreeable but doggedly persuasive, Majka worked with various groups to address what she saw as the Wildlife Area's vulnerabilities. "Although the dogs and vehicles were by now gone, more and more people were coming to see the birds. This was good but we had to take measures to protect the ecosystem from increased pedestrian traffic." A 1984 government grant to the New Brunswick Federation of Naturalists was used to construct a parking lot and trail to the beach. In 1985 and 1986 the Canadian Wildlife Service installed a viewing platform and interpretive exhibits.

Majka's diligent work and lobbying, with Christie as her colleague, paid off in spades. In 1982 Mary's Point was designated as a Ramsar site, a wetland of international importance. Five years later the Shepody National Wildlife Area gained global recognition as Canada's first Hemispheric Shorebird Reserve. And still the improvements continued: 1992 saw the addition of an interpretive centre and salt marsh boardwalk, and in 1995 a woodland trail was built.

Incredibly, Majka hasn't limited her energies solely to the preservation of nature. "I also was doing this conservation of historic things," she understates. In fact, she established the Albert County Heritage Trust in the mid 1970's, which helped to restore various old buildings including a bank that's been reincarnated as a museum, and three covered bridges including the Sawmill Creek Covered Bridge.

Through her projects and various grants, Majka has offered seasonal employment to local labourers and students, sometimes as many as 20 positions in a summer. The Wildlife Area employs guides and interpreters, and the Heritage Trust has supported several projects over the years, including a coastal cleanup program, demonstration organic garden, and recycling project. Add to this the economic impact of the thousands of tourists who come each year to witness one of the world's most dramatic avian migrations, and one begins to appreciate that individual initiative and resolve can indeed give rise to the reverberations necessary to move mountains.

Majka's many recognitions include a Canadian Healthy Environment Award in the Lifetime Achievement Category presented by Environment Canada in 1996, and an Honorary Doctor of Science degree from the University of New Brunswick in 1998. Lofty laurels, but Majka isn't ready to rest on them yet although she does concede the time is coming to slow down. In the same breath, however, she shares details of her latest project, the restoration of a long defunct shipyard at nearby Harvey. Despite a funding snag that's followed on the heels of New Brunswick's change in provincial government in 1999, she remains adamant the project will be completed eventually.

"It's an important landmark and its story must be preserved. The largest wooden ship ever built in New Brunswick, the *Annie Wright*, was constructed there a century ago, along with at least 25 other wooden sailing vessels. The federal government was going to pay to have the wharf demolished but we talked them into letting us have the money for repairing it instead. We restored the wharf and had a researcher working here until our provincial funding dried up."

But lack of money won't dissuade Majka. Two years ago, before any funding had been confirmed and even while she was still at the 'flirting stage' in her negotiations with various granting organizations,

Majka has already begun working on the crumbling wharf. "I'd hired five workers and ordered 2000 tons of rock and 200 railway ties," she says matter-of-factly, hinting that her method and propensity for getting things done are at least tantamount to her vision and resolve. It's an approach that has served her well over the decades.

"Looking back, I guess I could say that I've lived my dreams. And if I've accomplished a lot, it's also because I've been so fortunate. I've had the privilege and advantage of financial independence. And the luxury of doing what I've always felt passionate about."

When you look very deep into the soul of this country,
you find a much more open, free and easygoing way of
behaving, working and thinking.

I have come to that time in my life when I can say that I've lived most of my years in Canada. I am no longer a newcomer and haven't been a European for many years. I was born in Poland and at 14 was forcibly relocated to Austria where I spent seven years, first as a worker during the war and then as a student. But I no longer belong to Poland and Austria. My roots were pulled many years ago.

Perhaps I'm still a mixture of Canadian and immigrant, but my alliance is with Canada. Immigration always calls for a transition, a transfer of loyalties, from one world to another. Superficially the worlds may not seem so different but in a deeper sense they always are.

For example, European society has been shaped by a long history of wars, famines, disease, and such. Although it's been modernized, in many ways it's still basically the same as it was in the Middle Ages. Culturally, there remains a strong link between the past and the present.

Canadian culture, on the other hand, has been built on a very different history. It has always had to be more malleable, adjusting to and allowing for the views and influences of other cultures as more newcomers arrived. Some might have tried to keep Canadianism homogeneous in the early days, but that effort would have been futile. What Canada could offer, which the old world could not, was the chance for everyone to start anew, fresh. When you look very deep into the soul of this country, you find a much more open, free and easygoing way

JUST AS THOSE WITH CANADIAN

FOREFATHERS WANT TO

RETAIN FAMILY CUSTOMS,

TRADITIONS AND FOOD,

SO TOO DO THOSE WHO

COME FROM OTHER PARTS OF

THE WORLD.

of behaving, working and thinking. For people coming here, that was, and still is, a compelling opportunity.

It's not all easy, of course. When we lived in Ontario, people had absolutely no interest in us. They weren't hostile, usually, they just didn't want to be bothered with us. Perhaps it was because so many immigrants were converging on southern Ontario and people were having difficulty adjusting to the influx. There's always a reason for discrimination.

What a contrast when we moved to New Brunswick. People were warm and welcoming, and we were accepted for what we were, on our own terms. We soon decided we would stay here, if for no other reason than this. We wanted to be part of this country and contribute to it; finally we had found a community that wanted us too. Even our children could sense the difference. Here people are genuinely interested in how you are doing. When I hurt my foot recently, people were concerned. When Mike had a hip replaced, they showed concern.

I often mention this to people who say, "there is nothing for us here, we have to go to Ontario." But I imagine things have changed there too in the last 30 years, due in part to the influences of all the immigrants who did settle there. And this is part of the contribution made by those of us who came decades ago: we paved the way, eased the way, for those who came later.

Also, Canadians have slowly come to realize that much of our society is based on the talents and values that were brought by the hundreds of thousands of immigrants who came after the war. I think those influences have mostly been positive. We need to keep reminding ourselves that most of us have come from somewhere else. Our whole culture and lifestyle and richness has come from somewhere else. What is Canadianism, if not an amalgamation of values and traditions garnered from all over?

Sometimes it's easy to think that the best of what the world has to offer is what we have here, in the western world, at this moment in time. That we westerners know best. But we need to retain respect for the cultures and differences of others, no matter where on the planet they live. It's wrong to conclude that just because someone might not know the specific things we know, they are below our level of enlightenment. Even the Third World citizens we perceive as being primitive have knowledge that we'll never have. We need a keener sensitivity to each other's differences.

I think newcomers to Canada shouldn't try to assimilate right away, and they shouldn't be forced into uniformity. Just as those with Canadian forefathers want to retain family customs, traditions and food, so too do those who come from other parts of the world. It's important for people to keep in touch with their past, to value it. Up until recently Canadians didn't seem to cherish anything that was old. Old buildings had to make way for new. Old things were dismissed as old-fashioned and carted off to the dump.

Newcomers should also try and combine whatever they bring with what they receive here. I think I achieved that. I'm very happy I was able to integrate what I was taught and knew in Europe with my Canadian life. Whenever I travel and lecture, I always include photographs and information about our life here. I guess in a small way, especially when I visit Europe, it's my way of taking back to them and sharing some of what I've received here.

I think we personally have probably also managed to augment the respect and impressions Canadians have of Poland. Canadians look at us and they understand that Poland is a country made up of people just like themselves. Our son, Chris, has also helped to heighten the awareness of Polish culture and dance through his writing and performances.

I am now the experienced old immigrant who has been here for ages. I often help newcomers try to understand the differences they see here. What I tell them, in gentle terms, is this: don't compare and criticize until you've lived here for a good while. It's very easy to say, "It's not as nice here, the flowers don't smell as nice, things don't taste as good." You only make yourself miserable and cheat yourself out of new experiences. You have to have lived here a few years before you can really see beyond the superficial differences. Is it really that important for the bread to taste exactly the same and for the butter to be unsalted?

When we arrived in Halifax in 1951, we passed by the luxurious Hotel Nova Scotia on our way from the immigration pier to the waiting train. In our dreams we could not have imagined that one day we might be wealthy enough to stay there. But when Chris was about ten years old we took the boys back to Halifax for a holiday, booked ourselves into that hotel, and realized a dream.

In 1999 we realized another dream when we took our 16 year-old Polish foster child to visit the newly opened Pier 21 Immigration Museum in Halifax where we retraced the steps of our beginning in Canada. Since she, too, is an immigrant I wanted to relive this with her, and was delighted that she took such interest in the exhibits and audiovisual presentations. I'm gratified that already she's used some of the material for school projects. And I'm also pleased that this important chapter of Canadian history is being preserved for all to experience.

For the thousands and thousands among us who passed through Pier 21 and did well in Canada, it stands as evidence that when you work hard and strive to fit in, your dreams can and do come true here.

Terence Marner

*The black portfolio's zipper separates with a definitive buzz,
a nylon bumblebee in hasty acceleration. The artwork of Terence
Marner spills out, rich liquid colour unfurled in thick fluid lines on
prints bearing names like 'Dark Night' and 'Suffering.'
Honeycombs of molten steel solidify against oily-black depths
that speak of inner and outer space. Here and there a dash of
crimson, ellipse of magenta, rivulet of dark cream. "I have a strong
interest in shape and relationships," says Marner, "and I've come to
see these images as meditational."
An artist, educator, film maker and writer, Marner has juggled an
illustrious and varied academic career with parenting and with a
deeply spiritual journey that keeps him watchful, curious, and
ever mindful of life's ephemerality.*

Like so many others who have foregone one home and set out for another, Terence Marner's decision to come to Canada had more to do with opportunity than with a bucolic notion of Canada as an end in itself. "One's reasons for relocating are never clear-cut. I'd be interested to find somebody who's actually sat down and clearly thought, 'I want to immigrate to Canada,' and there'd be no further story behind it."

Marner's own story of migration and resettlement tells of a near circumnavigation of the globe that eventually brought him to the heart of the Canadian prairies. Born in Lancashire, England, in 1937, he graduated from the University of Durham in 1959 with a Fine Arts degree. In the year that followed he had his first art show, obtained a graduate degree in Education, and netted a position with the local art gallery. Shortly after his marriage in 1962, Marner and his wife accepted teaching positions at Morogoro Teacher's College in Tanganyika, East Africa.

The move to East Africa was never intended to be permanent, how-ever, and by 1964 the family was ready to return to England so Marner could re-enter the British work force and simultaneously pursue graduate studies in film production. But he soon discovered a chronic impediment to his plan: by the time the British job postings were relayed to his desk in East Africa, the positions had long been filled.

"The system was very frustrating. By this time I was in charge of art education policy for all of the schools in Tanzania, and it seemed fool-hardy to forfeit all that and return to Britain jobless, especially since Veronica and I now had two young children. We'd left England with every intention of returning and now we couldn't seem to get back in. Our government had encouraged us to go out and teach in the Commonwealth, yet they seemed unable to effect our transition back into British society. That's when we started thinking of alternatives.

"In East Africa we had befriended a number of Canadians working for CIDA (the Canadian International Development Agency). They encouraged us to consider moving to Canada and gradually helped us realize it might be easier to build our future in North America. I began applying to several Canadian universities and landed a fill-in position teaching art education at the University of Saskatchewan's Regina Campus. We saw it as a good opportunity."

The Marners flew to England to pack up their belongings and pur-chase a custom-ordered North American car, which they shipped to Montreal. "Of course it had never been heard of in Canada, and has-n't been since. I think I imported the only model."

Leaving his family behind in England, Marner travelled ahead to Montreal, picked up his car, and spent the next three days driving to Regina. "I remember my first glimpse of Lake Superior, which I'd learned about in school geography. It was a gorgeous blue and I was filled with the optimism of new beginnings. In a place called Deep River a large sign for 'Export,' which in Britain is the best bitter beer you can buy, beckoned me to pull over in anticipation of a cold, quenching drink. But the man behind the counter asked, 'small or large pack?' and then seemed horrified that I had misconstrued he was selling alcohol."

No sooner had Marner arrived in Regina and parked his car when a former Scotsman, recognizing the British license plate, came forward and introduced himself. "He said he'd immigrated several years earlier and welcomed me to Canada. Meanwhile, a lively parade was in full swing, and in an open car sat an elderly gentlemen in a white suit, and with a white goatee and long white hair. He was surrounded by several lovely young women, and I asked the Scotsman, 'Who is he and why all the fuss?' And he replied, 'Haven't you ever heard of Colonel Sanders?' So went my introduction to North American culture."

When his fill-in position ended the following summer, Marner transferred to the University's Extension Department and began teaching Fine Arts and Visual Arts to night-school students. "In 1968 I began teaching an introductory course in film appreciation, a first for the university and basically an experiment. The demand for the course was unquestionably there; I had more than 120 students registered for each semester. Eventually several began making their own films, which was pretty exciting."

But Marner had also grown discouraged during those first few years. He found it difficult to create a niche for himself in what was then a relatively small visual arts community, a community that was split between the university and the city.

"I was well aware that one or two individuals regarded me as 'that guy off the boat who calls himself a painter and took one of our jobs.' In fact on one occasion the accusation was put to me directly. Thankfully Regina has changed much in recent years. Today there are several communities of artists, and an immigrant would probably have an easier time finding a niche in one of them."

The Marners had always been very involved with their church and it was there they turned in their search for community. "We found the church community here very open and welcoming. We got together with several other young families and recruited a priest from the University's Jesuit College to celebrate Mass with us. Each family took turns preparing the liturgy, which could include reflective readings from any number of sources, Dag Hammerskjold's diaries, for example. We had a great deal of freedom. Instead of preaching we would engage in discussion. Afterwards we'd share a potluck dinner; sometimes I'd bring a film to view and discuss. It was a spiritually satisfying experience for our family."

Marner, who had grown up in a non-practising Calvinist house-hold and converted to Roman Catholicism at the age of twenty, has never shied from an active and vocal role in church and spiritual matters. As a lay (non-clergy) preacher fresh out of university and with a natural bent for history, literature and grassroots spirituality, he was not easily intimidated by the detached traditions of a centuries-old institution. After university he served for a year as editor of a diocesan newspaper, creating several editorials that managed to consternate church officialdom. In one issue that particularly riled the diocesan bishop, Marner brashly espoused that choirs be extracted from church "like bad back teeth. They needed reminding that they weren't there as exclusive performers. I challenged them to sit among the congregation and get those people involved."

In Regina the Marners were delighted to discover that their church was less encumbered with protocol and more intuitive to the mood of its people. "And the community was more responsive. At one point the Bishop invited me over to discuss Vatican II and the clergy's changing role, and I thought, 'Here I am, a 31-year-old layman discussing church issues with the bishop.' This would never have happened in England, behind the 'spaghetti curtain' where the church was still very Italian."

But England still tugged firmly at the couple's hearts and when Marner was promoted to an assistant professorship and granted tenure in 1970, obtaining a leave of absence and enrolling in graduate studies at the London Film School seemed a logical next step. To finance the family's fare back to Britain, Marner held an exhibition and sale of his paintings. No sooner were they settled in London when a unique opportunity fell into his lap. "As part of my application to the school, I had written a film critique, which had been passed on to a London publisher. They proposed that I interview several film directors and produce a textbook on directing. No doubt I was selected because they planned to market the book in North America and figured a British Canadian would be able to write for that market. Of course I was interested.

"The book was published in 1972. And I thought, how ironic, here I've come to study film and I end up writing a textbook on the subject." Marner's second book, this one on art direction, was published the following year. Meanwhile, he'd completed his graduate degree.

"At the end of the two-year term we returned to Canada. I must confess that although we'd missed Canada for the first year, we probably would have happily re-settled in England had that been an option. But I couldn't get a job in England in the film industry because I wasn't a member of the union, and I couldn't join the union until I had employment. In Regina, on the other hand, I had both a job and tenure waiting for me.

"So we returned to Regina. But again I found the settling in period very difficult. My salary continued to come out of the Extension Department's budget, but my job had been transferred to someone else during my sabbatical. So I was relegated to the task of organizing non-credit evening classes. I was 35 years old, with a fresh degree and two books under my belt and, really, they didn't know what to do with me.

"It seemed that my work and upgrading over the previous two years carried little worth as far as my employers were concerned. What a sad contrast to the excitement of living and working in London. Needless to say, my health suffered."

Again the Marners looked to their church for respite and moral support. "At around this time we became involved in Marriage Encounter, a course the church offers to help married couples refresh their relationships. We'd been married about 12 years and it was just the right thing for us at that time. Before long we found ourselves handling the program for the entire diocese. We also thought this would be an excellent orientation for engaged couples and so we began offering Engaged Encounter courses, a new first for the church. It was fulfilling and we met many wonderful people."

Back at the university, Marner was eventually able to have his nebulous position transferred to the office of the Associate Dean of Fine Arts where he began teaching film studies. The following year the Dean suggested he design a degree programme in film production. "I realized I couldn't tackle this alone so I called on a colleague who had helped teach my first film studies class. Together we developed a proposal, had it accepted and enrolled our first students in the fall of 1977." For the co-founder of Canada's first film school west of Toronto, it was a momentous and deeply satisfying occasion.

In 1982 Marner spent a sabbatical at New York University as an adjunct professor in their film school. "I would never move to the United States, but I did find my colleagues there more open and receptive, and less threatened by newcomers and new ideas. When I was compiling my textbook on film in Britain in the early 1970's, the directors I approached for interviews had always responded graciously. As I took note of their Oscars neatly arranged on rosewood buffets, I often wondered if I would have had the same ease of access to Canadian directors, writers and artists, considering my lack of publication credentials at that time. Canadians would have been more hesitant to trust their reputations to an unknown writer. Despite the fact that we share much cultural heritage with the British and the Americans, we seem to have this thread of pessimism in our national character that makes us more cautious and inward looking, perhaps even pessimistic.

"But the Americans, like the British, have enough self-assurance to see the value in another's work, another's opinion. As an example, I had my students at New York do an exploration of the problems inherent in the university's film department, which just happened to be one of the best in the country. The faculty could have easily chosen to resent and dismiss the criticism, but instead they studied the video and took it seriously. So seriously in fact, that they showed the tape to senior administrators and eventually procured five new faculty for the department."

When Marner returned to New York University during a second six-month sabbatical the following year, he was offered a permanent position in the film school. "It was tempting; it could have transformed my career. But I declined. We had four children by that time, and we couldn't imagine bringing them up in New York."

While south of the border, Marner had befriended an Episcopalian minister who, upon learning of Marner's eclectic spiritual background, suggested he consider serving as a builder of common ground among the Christian denominations. Marner returned briefly to England to meditate on that possibility, then travelled to Regina to resume his academic duties. "Coincidentally the church asked me a few months later to sit on a newly-formed ecumenical commission, which I eventually ended up chairing. It was an exciting new direction, for the church and for me personally. Ecumenism was already happening informally, especially in small towns where people worked together regardless of what their respective clergy said. The difference now was that they'd received a carte blanche from their churches to carry on."

Over the last 15 years Marner has explored new ways to search out and understand the common ground that lies between Christian and non-Christian faiths. He has become increasingly interested in the eastern as well as the ancient traditions of prayer and meditation. "It's satisfying and relevant work, and it sustains me in my own life's journey."

In the decade leading up to his early retirement from the university in 1996, Marner continued to teach, lecture abroad and produce films. In the process he was instrumental in establishing the foundation for a solid film industry in Saskatchewan, which he readily admits was ground-breaking work. Keeping it healthy continues to be a challenge for the industry. "It's always been difficult making your living in film production in Saskatchewan, and I've seen much financial and marital strain among my former students who wanted to stay and work in the province. The markets for our films have largely been controlled by outside corporations and interests, thereby fluctuating with enough unpredictably to keep us all on our toes. If the corporations decided regional productions were important, we had work. If they decided regional productions were a waste of money, then the work dried up. My most successful students worked only 30 to 40 percent of the time. Even now. True, Saskatchewan's film industry has grown and there's a lot more money in the pot these days, but there are also many more film makers to share that wealth."

Irrespective of the many hurdles that often accompany neophyte industries, Marner has tasted much fulfilment in his still-evolving profession and continues to do so even in retirement. In recent years he's been exploring the potential of computer imaging as a complement to the traditional forms of painting. He experiments with art as a medium for meditation. He's also produced a CD-ROM on multimedia production, and *Gifts of the Heart*, a half-hour documentary for television. He continues to paint and in 1999 held a successful photographic show in Regina.

"I continue to redefine myself. There are plenty of new paths to explore."

If you're part of an extended family from Saskatchewan,
chances are you've got relatives all over the place. And you
belong in a way we can never conceive of belonging, which gives emphasis to
what I mean when I use the term 'exile.'
We are constantly aware that we live in exile.

When we moved to East Africa many years ago we discovered that the first steps you take to leave your culture are the key ones. After we'd made that initial move away from Britain, everything else was relatively easy. And yet, even after 30 years in Canada we still retain a strong sense of connectedness with Britain, with our beginnings and early years there, and also with the culture that continues to permeate the way we see and do things. We've retained a strong emotional tie, but that's not to suggest we've sat on our hands and despaired decisions that were made along the way.

A trip back to England a few years ago was a pilgrimage in the purest sense. We travelled to Northern England, to my hometown on the west coast and Veronica's on the east, and retraced the steps of our youth. We went to Durham, which we still consider our spiritual home, and to Holy Island on the east coast, to visit the ruin of a monastery built in or around the 7th century. And, amazingly, we happened upon a book on the history of the spirituality of the north of Britain, which had been written by a couple from the Pennines, near the area we come from. I looked through the book and recognized so many of the places listed. And I realized, these spiritual places are us; we identify with them completely. Somehow this book paralleled much of our own experience and gave it further understanding.

The historical highlight of the trip was our visit to the graveyard of my mother and brother, on a promontory overlooking the Irish sea. Archeologists had just discovered that that particular promontory has been continually occupied for 20,000 years, meaning that people have lived there since the ice receded. In a poignant way I felt privileged to have my mother and brother buried in the land where people have been dying for two hundred centuries.

But I also feel a sense of loss when I think about history, because

SOMETIMES A FRIENDSHIP WITH
SOMEONE OF THE SAME BACK-
GROUND CAN FEEL COMFORTABLE
BECAUSE YOU KNOW YOU CAN
SHARE THE SAME REMINISCENCES,
THE SAME SENSE OF HUMOUR,
THE SAME USE OF LANGUAGE
WITH THAT PERSON.

there is so little of that history, my personal history, here in Canada. I don't know how to resolve that other than to say we're used to being exiles. Now, one could go to the high realm of spiritual rhetoric and say we're all exiles on earth, all in transition, all going through the various stages of the great impermanence. But my personal exile, I believe, has to do with the intermittent sense of disconnectedness I experience, a sense that the concept of pure and permanent contentment with where we're at continues to elude us. It's not necessarily negative: taking on an impermanence about our life has also made it exciting and stimulating.

We're comfortable enough being exiles; after all, we exiled ourselves to East Africa for the adventure of teaching in a foreign land. Then we were exiled by our country, not because it didn't like us but because of its inadequate process for re-entry. So we know exile and have grown almost comfortable with it.

And yet, there remains a lingering gap in our psyche, a bit of emptiness in our emotionality. It's as if we've somehow been chosen to uphold the subtle, intangible differences between those who've lived in Saskatchewan all their lives, and those who've migrated here. If you're part of an extended family from Saskatchewan, chances are you've got relatives all over the place. And you belong in a way we can never conceive of belonging, which gives emphasis to what I mean when I use the term 'exile.' We are constantly aware that we live in exile.

Even Canadians who relocate from one province to another can still say they have relatives elsewhere in the country. We, on the other hand, are cut off from family members of our own generation. Those born and bred here always have someone there for their children, for themselves. And they have a sense of belonging that we can't possibly have. They have absolutely no reason to leave. They've got their roots— in family, friends from childhood days, church, every aspect of their community.

A few years ago we began pondering the possibility of a move to the west coast after Veronica's eventual retirement from teaching French immersion. We had grown weary of Regina's long winters and our four children had all left for homes of their own, none in Saskatchewan. (Ironically, our oldest son and his wife, and our only grandchild, have ended up in Britain. Here you have a kid born in East Africa and raised and educated in Canada, who completed a PhD in Britain and is now happily living there, with no plans to come back.) As empty nesters we'd reached another stage in our lives, and again we had come to the point where being on the move seemed the natural thing to do.

But when you start thinking of being on the move, you invariably end up reflecting on what you will be leaving behind. And Veronica and I asked ourselves, what are the bonds that would keep us here. Who are our friends, what do they really mean to us, and would we be able to find for ourselves a new community of friends once we'd moved on. Well, friendship is a many-layered concept. Often friendships are based on the similar circumstances of one's profession, being in the same office at the same time, but these friendships often dwindle when the circumstances change. I, for example, don't have much desire to go back to the campus.

Friendship is often also culturally driven. Sometimes a friendship with someone of the same background can feel comfortable because you know you can share the same reminiscences, the same sense of humour, the same use of language with that person. The culture you have in common is the medium that binds you together; if you feel comfortable on a cultural level, then you can overlook a great deal of other character differences that might exist. The truth is, were you to find yourselves back in the old country, you might well have no time for each other at all. But here the friendship thrives because it's based on the common culture.

There's also a fuzzy kind of friendship based on the warm relationships we have with people with whom we feel comfortable, but these are not deep enduring friendships. As an example, we breakfast at the local A & W two or three times a week, with a group that all comes in roughly at the same time. Over an endless pot of coffee we ask about each other and catch up. I know I'll miss that if we leave but also feel we can recreate it elsewhere.

I know I'm generalizing, but my gut feeling is that women have more confidantes, friends they can open up to and share with. I envy that. Men will not make themselves vulnerable to other men in the same way.

Instead, they'll go running or play sports together, buddy stuff. Well, I'm not a buddy person. So with very few exceptions, the friendships Veronica and I really value are those that involve both of us.

We have also thought of going back to England, especially with our son there now, but that gets us thinking of the many benefits we've reaped from living in Canada. This is physically a wonderful country and I'm passionate about its landscape. And there's a sense of freedom here that's quite different from Britain. Here I can do what I want; I'm not impeded by the social history to which I once belonged. Our youngest daughter is an accomplished horsewoman and at one time we owned a horse and were very involved in the shows. That would never have happened in England; aside from the costs there being phenomenal, that whole territory belongs to the gentry.

And there's also much more religious freedom here. The Roman Catholic church is open, you can be as involved or not involved as you want. Although we feel our spiritual history is in Britain, our spiritual journey coincides more with what's happening here. I see more bridges being built between different religious traditions, and continue to be part of that focus myself. I've learned, and keep learning, from Buddhists, from Hindus and Muslims. I know of a Tibetan monk who's frequently asked to speak in the Catholic elementary schools in Edmonton. Here society is wonderfully open and comfortable with spiritual diversity.

All this emotional vacillating had been going on for a long time when Veronica was diagnosed with breast cancer in mid 1998. Suddenly our focus and perspective were totally shifted. Suddenly we were in the position of needing the very community about which we'd been so half-enthused. Well, the support we've been extended has been tremendous, beyond what we could have imagined. The experience of Veronica's excellent treatment and community succour during her recovery has given us a wonderful reassurance about where we live. How fortuitous for us that we hadn't actually moved to Vancouver Island or anywhere else, where we would have had to deal with this largely on our own. No, this community has been good to us and truly, at this moment, we have no sense of longing for other places.

Instead we've become more focused on nurturing each other and our community ties. We continue to be busy in our church and we've become quite involved with a Buddhist group which has further intensified our feelings of belonging.

The other day I was looking out my back window on our lovely, expansive view, and I thought: maybe I'll go to Victoria someday, or maybe I'll just go as far as the mountains. Or perhaps I'll go just a bit further along on the prairie. Then again, maybe I'll just stay here.

One needs to work out one's destiny wherever one is. And right now I can say, I'm fine where I am.

Dusko and Svetlana Mitrovic

SARAJEVO, BOSNIA—TORONTO, ONTARIO

[The Mitrovics initially settled in Fredericton, New Brunswick in 1994, where the story of their harrowing escape from Bosnia was first told. Three years later, after struggling in vain to find permanent, viable employment, the couple made the reluctant decision to relocate to Toronto. There they continue to be immersed in the challenge of starting over.]

Well past sunset, the sweltering heat retains a tenacious grip on the day's waning hours. In the third-storey Fredericton apartment, short on both ventilation and insulation, a fan pushes sluggishly against air that's as warm as a recently vacated chair cushion. Dusko is tense this evening, his talk is chipped, his brow painfully contracted. Repeatedly he glances away, at his hands, or furtively at Svetlana as if for reassurance.

There are stories to tell; the telling is harrowing. Laughter comes more easily to Svetlana. She keeps watch over Dusko and frequently casts him a reassuring glance. Dusko narrates heavily, resignedly. In contrast Svetlana dances through her sentences with humour and optimism, belying the steely determination that saved both their lives.

They speak hesitantly at first, self-conscious of still-new English. And then the stories come, one after another, frenetically rolling over each other in a bid to be heard. Subplots spill out in compelling tangents. He recalls how he intentionally destroyed his glasses in a desperate bid to survive; she faked a pregnancy to flee Sarajevo.

Now it's past midnight and there is laughter and lightness in the air. The terrible trauma has been relived, and in its telling they have survived a second time. But the weight of their future, of starting over, also thickens the air. For although their horizon has begun to glow with economic promise, contentedness may take considerably longer to find.

Prior to the Bosnian war, Serbs, Croats and Muslims had lived peacefully in Bosnia for as long as Dusko and Svetlana Mitrovic could remember. Of Serbian descent themselves, they had lived their entire lives in Sarajevo and never given much thought to the ethnicity of friends and family. But the Bosnian war changed all that. The Bosnian war hollowed out their world until there was nothing left but a lifeless carapace, a monument to the forces of greed, corruption and power gone awry.

For Dusko and Svetlana, life in Sarajevo in the early 1990's bordered on the idyllic. Both had graduated from the Faculty for Agriculture; now both were employed with the Research Institute for Agriculture, Dusko as an entomologist, and Svetlana as a research assistant in genetic engineering. They were married in 1990; he was 28, she was 25. They shared a well-furnished apartment and Svetlana started post-graduate studies the following year.

"We had the information, music and all the western influences," Dusko recalls. "True, it wasn't democratic, but not at all like Russia either. We had passports and the freedom to travel. There was plenty of room for normal living. We weren't interested in politics and it didn't interfere with our day-to-day life.

"We were so naive when the war started in April, 1992," says Svetlana. "We couldn't imagine it would amount to anything, especially in Bosnia where the races were so mixed that race was a non-issue among the people. We could've easily gotten out at first but we saw no need to; we were sure it wasn't going to last."

The argument that the Bosnian war should never have happened is compelling. For years Serbs, Croats and Muslims had all shared equally in the governing of Bosnia, each with one-third representation in the presidency and senate. In recent times, however, the government had struggled unsuccessfully to procure official status internationally as an independent country. Weary of the effort, its solidarity and collective thinking slowly began giving way to individual interests. Any attempt at effective leadership was stymied by chronic bickering.

In early April the exasperated Serbs suddenly withdrew their participation from government, throwing Bosnia into crisis. Now severely crippled, it became dangerously vulnerable to the many rebel factions all too ready to install their own agendas. And even though Europe and the United Nations finally voted to recognize Bosnia's independence just two days later, the irreversible haemorrhaging of the people and landscape had already been triggered.

"All summer long we met with friends and made plans for what we'd do when the war ended," says Dusko. "There was lots of talk and hope because the international community was focused on us. We were living from one UN meeting to the next and following the situation so closely. There was lots of talk and hope and then—nothing. By July we were trying to leave."

Meanwhile, the front line had been brought to the streets of Sarajevo, and snipers ruled. Each ethnic group used its quasi-military muscle to maintain a toehold in the city. Screaming shells flew helter-skelter with no regard for civilian safety. All residents were equally in danger. Over the following months no part of the city, nothing, was left intact. Work for Dusko and Svetlana ended abruptly when their Institute was burned to the ground. Their car was stolen. Their apartment also fared poorly.

"We were listening to the radio, we were always listening to the news, when a shell hit the kitchen and completely destroyed it," Dusko recalls. "That radio was our lifeline but it also saved my life, literally," adds Svetlana. "Had I not been in the living room listening to the news, I would have been in the kitchen and that would have been my end."

On September 25 the Mitrovics were having lunch in the ruins of their apartment when someone knocked on their door. "It was the Muslim army looking for me," Dusko says. "Actually, they weren't a real army at all, more like armed street gangs with no training. My choice was to go with them or die.

"I knew it was coming. There was no way a man of fighting age could stay out of the war in Sarajevo. Sooner or later some army would come for you; it didn't matter if you were of their ethnic group or not. The Muslims came for me even though I was a Serb. I'm sure I was reported by a Muslim living in our building. He was probably sick of going to war each day and seeing me stay home. I tried to hide but you can't when you have to go out looking for food.

"So I was sent to the front line each day and came home at night. There was no uniform; I wore my jeans. The whole thing was pathetic." Seeing the war as a pointless bloodbath and detesting his own forced involvement, Dusko began spiralling slowly into deep despair.

In the meantime Svetlana coped by making it her mission to collect the documentation that might one day help deliver them from their hell. She went to what remained of government offices and police departments in search of their birth certificates, passports, criminal checks, anything that would help verify their identity. "I was persuasive so they gave me my documents," she recalls. "For Dusko it was harder. My father used his government connections to get Dusko's papers."

Already Svetlana was setting her sights on Canada. "America was too involved in the war and from their point of view all the evil was being perpetrated by the Serbs." Svetlana revealed her intention to Dusko during a particularly violent episode of shelling as they cowered against their apartment wall. "Dusko!" she called out over the deafening cacophony of war, "We are going to Canada!"

"Here it was the middle of war and she had this mad idea we would go to Canada," says Dusko. "For me it was totally pointless. Each day I would come home dodging sniper fire and she would show me more papers and say, come and see, I got this and I got this. Really, I had nothing to say to her. It was too hopeless."

Winters in Sarajevo are much like winters in Canada, and the winter of 1992 became a marathon of hardship. Their apartment in ruins, they retreated to a friend's basement flat which was considerably safer. Svetlana's parents also joined them there. Without electricity, water, and adequate heat, the focus turned to survival and nothing more. Svetlana walked several kilometres daily to fetch potable water from a communal tap. Furniture was used for fuel to cook UN rations. Various humanitarian organizations occasionally delivered a care package sent by family in Serbia. "But the packages had trouble getting through," says Svetlana. "The Seventh Day Adventists helped and since they were seen as a neutral group, they weren't harassed too much and thus saved many from starvation. The Catholics and

Orthodox also helped but they were more often stopped and questioned since they were not considered neutral.

"It wasn't safe on the street," Svetlana recalls. "And all the familiar faces were long gone—to Europe, America, Zagreb, Belgrade. They had gotten out in time. The streets had been ruined by grenades and were filled with garbage and chunks of buildings. There were no trees left; they'd all been cut down for fuel. Dogs and cats roamed everywhere."

In December Dusko was transferred from the front line to the army's headquarters within the city. "I couldn't bear the front any longer so I took a chance and broke my glasses. Without them I couldn't see well enough to be of much use at the front. The officers weren't pleased but didn't have much choice about moving me. So for the next four months I was a bodyguard, praying I wouldn't get shot, and standing for hours. Standing, because you can't march when there's shelling everywhere. Still, it was a vacation compared to the front."

Later Dusko mended his glasses well enough to continue using them.

"I was a bodyguard until April. Then a well-connected Muslim friend recommended me for work in another unit as an agronomist. The army had decided to begin producing its own food. By May I was growing their potatoes and vegetables."

Although much more to his liking, this posting presented a new peril. Now further away from his work, Dusko was forced to commute daily by bicycle through the sniper-infested city. "It was an hour each way. At times I knew I was a target."

The following November Svetlana seized an opportunity to escape Sarajevo. The UN had organized a convoy to transport the sick and elderly to Serbia and Croatia. "I was so desperate to get out that I forged a document saying I was pregnant and at risk, and they accepted it." When Svetlana stepped on the bus she knew she was leaving behind every vestige, every material shred of her previous life. She had become a refugee.

"Leaving Dusko was the hardest thing, and yet we knew that doing nothing meant certain death for both of us. Still, I was sure I'd never see him again, and my parents too. And once I was out it seemed even harder, knowing what was going on, just sitting and waiting."

In fact, passively waiting was the last thing on Svetlana's mind. As soon as she arrived in Belgrade she went to the Canadian Embassy and presented herself as a refugee. She and her husband wanted to go to Canada, she told them. Then she travelled to her family's lodge in Montenegro to await word from the Embassy. She also began a singular mission to stay in touch with Dusko and help bolster his resolve to survive another winter, this time without her. "I needed him for Canada," she explains simply.

Many letters were written; occasionally one would make it through. Dusko and Svetlana also had friends at both ends who were amateur radio operators. "I would go to the station with cigarettes or some gift to help pay the bills," Svetlana recalls, "and they would contact the operators in Sarajevo. We had to talk about Canada using a code we developed before we separated." In code Svetlana was able to make Dusko understand that the Embassy required his photograph as part of the processing documentation.

"I went to the only photography studio still standing and paid 15 German marks. I put the photos in an envelope and sent them out with a convoy; I had little hope that they would even make it to the outskirts of Sarajevo. But the convoy left two days later and she got the package as quickly as if there had been peace in the land. Who knows why we were so lucky."

In February of 1994 Svetlana received Embassy documents that had to be signed and returned. At that point she was forced to reveal that Dusko was stranded in Sarajevo. "A woman at the Embassy told me they couldn't do anything more until Dusko came to Belgrade. Unless I wanted to go to Canada alone. I said, No, No! and promised he would be in Belgrade in a month or two. She agreed we could wait a while without losing our space on the priority list."

By this time Svetlana knew their chances of being accepted by Canada were good. All she needed now was Dusko in Belgrade. There was only one option, she realized. She would go back to Sarajevo and bring him out herself.

On April 1, a cease-fire was declared and UN peacekeepers opened the crucial bridge that connected the Serbian-controlled part of Sarajevo to the Muslim section. Svetlana's parents were finally able to make their escape. But for Dusko the soldier, crossing was forbidden.

Svetlana, however, saw the bridge as a last chance for her husband's survival. As a Serb civilian she could freely apply to visit Serbian Sarajevo without raising suspicion. Once there she would obtain permission from the Muslims to cross the bridge to visit her husband, one of their soldiers.

"I had to go back to plan Dusko's escape with him," she explains. "This was the right time, the only time. He wouldn't survive a third winter under these harsh conditions. This was his only hope."

Dusko, meanwhile, had become obsessed with plotting his own escape, but each of his very limited options seemed suicidal. If the Muslims didn't shoot him as he was fleeing their side, the Serbs in their camp would surely have assumed he was Muslim and killed him on approach. "I think I was probably half crazy at the time," he recalls. "When Svetlana wrote that she was coming, I wrote back and told her, 'Don't be crazy. It's too dangerous.'

"But I did have one friend I could still trust; he was on the Muslim front line and he wanted to help. He planned that I would run from a specific location on his front line to the Serbian trenches, just 150 metres away. I was to pay the Muslim soldiers 500 marks to hold their fire. I had to trust them, there was no choice."

To raise the money, Dusko sold their remaining possessions, including his mother-in law's antique piano which had miraculously escaped injury. Even in the selling there were risks, however. "You never knew who was going to buy from you, whether he would try to steal it or kill you, or both."

Svetlana, meanwhile, had obtained her necessary passes and arrived on June 13. She had not seen Dusko in eight months. They were given three days together. Seventy-two hours. Four thousand, three hundred and twenty minutes. Time took on a veil of surrealism.

"We were so happy to see each other again, but only for three days and then..." Dusko's voice trails. "We were so sad. And petrified. I refused to report for duty; I just didn't care anymore. And...if I was half crazy before, I was completely crazy when she left."

But in those fleeting hours Dusko and Svetlana had solidified a plan, their only hope, their one chance in a thousand. They would give it their best shot. Or die trying. Dusko outlined the location from which he would attempt his run. Svetlana would go to the Serbs with this crucial information and persuade them to hold their fire. Assuming the Muslims in the trenches would not betray him and the Serbs in their foxholes would comply, all that was left to chance were the minefields strewn across the 150-metre stretch of no-man's-land. The date and time were set. June 19, 1994. 10:00 p.m.

Svetlana departed. "When I got to the Serb side I went to the army officials and told them about Dusko, when and where. They said, 'Oh my God,' because of the mines. I was like Mata Hari, working both sides."

When June 19 arrived, Dusko was picked up at the appointed time. At the trenches, however, he was horrified to discover his point of departure had been moved 400 metres up the front line. "The soldiers I paid had been transferred there so that's where I had to deal with them. There was nothing to do except go or back down. Backing down was not an option.

"I don't think I ran. There were too many obstacles, bushes and burned-out houses. I couldn't see a thing; it was too dark. I kept thinking about the mines and zigzagging. I was wet with fear. It took maybe two, four, fifteen minutes, I don't know. And then I saw the Serbs, their weapons temporarily at rest, watching my progress and waiting for me."

But instead of the freedom he had thought imminent, Dusko was promptly arrested and subjected to seven days of detention and interrogation. Then he was forcibly recruited into the Serb army. The war was still on, the Serbs needed soldiers, and he would do.

Although he was now reunited with Svetlana whom he saw daily, he soon discovered the Serb army was not much different from the army he had just fled. "It was the same crazed mob mentality; all the losers and criminals were there, acting out their fantasies of power."

A month later Dusko again turned to his glasses in a last desperate bid for deliverance. "I knew there was nowhere to fix glasses in Sarajevo. I figured they would send me to a border town and then I would somehow make it across the border. Whatever happened, I wasn't coming back to Sarajevo."

When Dusko walked into the office of the military physician to report his shattered glasses, he suddenly found himself being greeted by an old friend from pre-war days. "Sasha was from another town and had lived in Sarajevo while studying medicine. When the war began we hid him at our place for a while and kept him fed until he was able to escape.

"When I saw him, I took my intact glasses out of my pocket and put them back on. Sasha understood, and wrote an order for me to be admitted to hospital in Belgrade. Then we drank a litre of shlivovica (whiskey) together."

The following day Dusko took a seat in the back of a bus headed for Belgrade. Svetlana, who was free to come and go, stepped on a short time later and sat near the front. "We didn't want to be seen as a couple," Dusko recalls. "There was always the risk that at the last minute someone might figure out what was going on."

In Belgrade they scheduled interviews and medicals with the Canadian Embassy. "We were jubilant but we still had to be very cautious," says Svetlana. "Dusko could have been found and sent back at any time; however, since there was a cease-fire on at that time, the military was pretty slack which no doubt worked in our favour."

The couple borrowed money from friends for the bus fare to Montenegro where they would await the call to leave for Canada. It came three months later. "We were ready," Dusko recalls. "We had been ready all the time."

A UN group arranged for their bus trip to Budapest. From there they flew to Zurich, then Toronto and finally, on November 18, 1994, they touched down in Fredericton.

> *When the Mitrovics were first ushered into their*
> *fully furnished apartment, Svetlana spotted the microwave oven,*
> *same as the one left behind*
> *in their Sarajevo home.*
> *And finally wept.*
> *For the burden of life and loss.*
> *For gratitude, intense beyond words.*
> *For regret, unspeakable.*
> *For the weight of starting over, light as a blossom petal,*
> *heavy as late-winter snow.*

Even in my language I can't explain how terrible it was.

—DUSKO

Our hearts were broken.

—SVETLANA

[Dusko and Svetlana alternate their voices in this essay. Dusko's voice is indicated in Roman style lettering, Svetlana's in italics.]

War has changed us forever. It doesn't matter what side you are on, it is indescribably awful. It brings out the worst in people. When the Bosnian war started, there were no organized armies, just chaos and destruction everywhere. With the Muslims in the streets with guns and the Serbs in the hills with cannon, civilians were in as much danger as the so-called military. The scum and criminals were the first to take up weapons and start the war. The power of war, of being able to shoot and terrify people, is like a drug for them. During peace their lives are insignificant and now, for the first time, they feel powerful and important.

It was the same when I was drafted to the Serb side in 1994. It was the same kind of uncivilized people fanning the fires of conflict. They spoke the same cruel language and saw their own futures as being hopeless, so they didn't have much to lose. I remember thinking that if the war ever stopped, these people would just keep on fighting regardless. They don't see a role for themselves except in conflict.

I have been in three armies, the first in the former Yugoslavia where I was drafted into duty for a year. I hated every minute. Right now I'm officially a deserter from both sides of the Bosnian conflict, and I'm proud of it.

I refused to accept our situation as hopeless, even when it was. It was my way of coping. Going to Canada by myself was not an option. I desperately needed Dusko for Canada. I knew I had to go back and try to help him get out. His death was certain if we didn't try. Looking back now, our plan was totally crazy.

Our three days together were so sad. Our hearts were broken. Although we put together our plan, we were at our lowest point.

It was so hopeless there was nothing more to say. It was like a heart-breaking movie, nice to watch when you're not in it. Even in my language I can't explain how terrible it was.

Coming back across the bridge I thought, well, at least we have a plan. I was happy to be able to do something, to go to the Serbs and set it all up with them.

When I reported back to the army after three days away without permission, they interrogated me for six hours. They were suspicious why she had returned, probably because I'm a Serb too. I told them, "I had nothing to do with her returning to Sarajevo. You'll have to ask the UN They're the ones who opened the bridge." And they let it go at that.

Looking back, we were incredibly lucky and I just can't explain why. All that sniper fire and shelling we managed to dodge. And Svetlana getting all our documents and forging one for her own escape. Our friends with the ham radios. Getting my photo to Svetlana for the Embassy. And then meeting my physician friend who made the final escape so simple and straightforward.

We were also lucky to have stayed healthy. Stress can kill you or it can keep you in shape; in our case it propelled us. That first winter in our friend's basement apartment, we burned our furniture, hardwood floor, old shoes, clothes, books, whatever we could find, in a stove provided by the UN. In the morning I prayed my thanks that we were still alive. I prayed again when Dusko made it home safely each day, and again in my bed at night. And then the ultimate miracle. To have made it through a minefield with people reluctantly holding their fire at both ends...what are the chances of that happening? The prisons in Sarajevo are full, and 95 percent of the inmates are Serbs who've been caught trying to escape. And there are so many more who died trying.

The West had no idea what was going on there. The media reports were not accurate and they didn't care about us anyway, they just wanted to get their stories and get out. When I was growing food for the Muslim army, a foreign reporter came to me one day looking for a head of lettuce. There was some lettuce in the marketplace but he complained it was not fresh enough for him. That made me very angry. Their investment in us amounted to no more than a week's inconvenience and a story. They want to get it fast and get out, and give as little of themselves as possible.

When we first came to Fredericton we met other Serbs, but many of them carried on with the struggles and bitterness they had brought from Bosnia. And they limited their social circle to other Bosnians of their kind. These people, I think, will probably stay Serbian in Canada rather than becoming Canadian in Canada. For ourselves, we knew right away that wasn't what we wanted. We set out to befriend Canadians and become Canadian. We could never move back to Bosnia. That home doesn't exist anymore.

We are grateful to be in Canada but people tend to think of refugees as persons who had nothing in their previous life, people who come with gratitude in their hearts and no further emotional baggage. In fact, refugees are often educated people who had a good standard of living before the war, and who've seen that all destroyed. We knew all about TV's, satellite dishes, microwaves and universities before we came. Our libraries had the same good books. That always amazes people. Do they think we lived in caves? Sometimes they don't realize that along with our gratitude there has to come grief for the life we have lost. And there seems to be no shortcut to that process.

We're still working at starting over. And in our minds, to put our past life behind us as if it didn't happen, that will never be possible. We don't talk about it too often; we just try to get on with our lives.

Even though we had to rebuild our lives from the beginning, we had no intention of being a burden on Canadian society. The government supports refugees for up to one year after their arrival, but we were already working and supporting ourselves, paying our own bills, well before our year was up. It wasn't easy, but it helped us re-affirm that we were still as capable as we were before our troubles started.

Our first three years in Fredericton were undeniably hard, even though some wonderful people befriended and supported us. But we just couldn't find permanent work. Dusko worked on short-term contracts at the University of New Brunswick and I had seasonal jobs here and there. But then his contract wasn't renewed and we felt we couldn't face another year of uncertainty and maybe just sitting around with no purpose.

At first we were anxious about Toronto, about becoming invisible in a city so large. But then I landed a permanent position as a research assistant in a plant genetic engineering firm, a good job that would get us through the winter without the worries about money. And we discovered the city streets and their little shops and bazaars to be a great tonic for loneliness and emptiness. Toronto is good for immigrants. Here you don't stand out and you can walk down the street without feeling like you're the immigrant, the one who doesn't belong.

The following March, in 1998, I also found work with Svetlana's firm, so our move to Toronto was good, in retrospect. We weren't particularly anxious to open a new chapter in our lives, but it was just too dismal to think of another winter in our Fredericton apartment, without work and a sense that we were building a future. Now we have viable, fulfilling work and life seems almost promising in some ways.

I visited my parents in Montenegro a few years ago; we managed to save enough money for one ticket. That was very good for me, I had been depressed and having a hard time; just when you think you're managing to put the experience of your past behind you, it comes back to hang over you and burden you again. But it helped that I had been back there again; it shrank the distance in-between, somehow.

But then my father died in late 1999, which brought all that emotion back again. Except that now I'm even more confused, my emotions feel almost schizophrenic. My father died in Sarajevo where he had gone for cardiac care, and when I went back for his funeral, I realized that everything about that city had changed. Some areas were still completely destroyed and all our friends had long since gone. So I felt I didn't belong there anymore either and I came back to Toronto with a broken heart, grieving for the country of my birth as well as for my father.

We could never belong there again. We've changed so much, and fitting in would be impossible. We know that and we tell ourselves that. But, while our minds are in Canada, our hearts are still in Yugoslavia somehow. I can't explain it. We became Canadian citizens in 1998, but I would be lying if I said we felt 100 percent Canadian. Still, we were excited then. And positive. We were prepared to say we were not Yugoslavian anymore.

The only thing to do is to continue to work at being Canadian, remembering the opportunity Canada gave us to start over, being thankful and grateful.

I'm also making arrangements for my mom and my sister and her family to come to Canada, hopefully later this year. So I'm back to collecting documents again. Maybe when they come our hearts will feel more content and at peace.

I'm not sure we'll ever have children. I would find it hard to see them speaking English better than I do. They would fit in completely while I would still be adapting. They would be in school and taking part in society without effort, way ahead of their parents. I'm afraid it would be like having strangers in my own house.

There's still so much to work out. I think it's going to take me a long time to really feel at home here, if ever. Who knows? I don't know.

Marge Nainaar

*When Marge Nainaar smiles, her every facial muscle is committed
to the task. And Nainaar smiles readily. Ask about her sense of
place in Canada, in Saskatchewan, in Prince Albert and Canwood,
and watch her eyes light up. Ask about her past and she obliges with
a quick response, then eagerly jumps back to the present, to her life
as a Canadian. For the present is everything to this passionate
self-starter, this founding member and current general manager of
the Prince Albert Multicultural Council and Settlement Agency for
Refugees and Immigrants, this veritable woman of the northern
prairie.*

*"I would have never chosen this particular Canadian setting,"
Nainaar says with fervour. "But I'll be forever grateful that the
community chose us and made us one of their own."*

Had it not been for her husband's one year teaching contract,
Marge Nainaar would have taken one look at Canwood,
Saskatchewan, and headed right back to her home town of
Durban on South Africa's east coast. "I couldn't imagine how I'd sur-
vive here for a year, but we'd committed ourselves so here we were.
And after the contract was up we found we couldn't leave because the
people of Canwood had claimed us as their own. We've been here for
over 30 years. The people kept us."

Both Nainaar and her husband were second generation South
Africans. The impositions of apartheid aside, the couple was well educated, well employed and enjoyed a prosperous standard of living.
"We were both teachers and providing for our family was not a worry.
As for apartheid, it was all we had ever known so it seemed a normal
part of life. Racism and segregation had always been the law in our
lives. However, when we started our own family we began thinking that

somewhere there had to be a better system than the one that designated blacks and whites to their own neighbourhoods, schools and washrooms. The more we tried to make sense out of the system, the less sense it made. And so we became quite adamant that we didn't want our children growing up in that kind of restricted climate, which showed no sign of improving.

"Apartheid designated you as either black or white. When they wanted a further breakdown of your race, you designated yourself as either native; Asian, which we were; coloured, which included the offspring of anyone who had intermarried with the whites; and white. On some forms we were asked to designate ourselves as Indian. The whole system was ludicrous. Japanese South Africans, for example, were classified as white because of South Africa's significant trade relationship with Japan. Nothing about apartheid made much sense."

With emigration as their goal, the Nainaars set about applying for work abroad. "When Sundras landed a contract in Canwood in the north of Saskatchewan, we knew we'd clinched our ticket out of South Africa. That we knew nothing of Saskatchewan, let alone Canwood, was incidental; we were young and we would learn as we went along."

In the first week of August in 1967, the Nainaars and their three children flew into Winnipeg, which, although in sharp contrast with the affluent cosmopolitanism of Durban, offered an immediate emancipation heretofore only dreamed of. "Our baby was just six months old. While we stood collecting our bearings, an airport attendant noticed him and offered us a room where I could feed him. They presented a little carriage for our use and brought us something to drink. I was dumbfounded. Never in my South African experience had a white person been attentive to the needs of a black. But here, to be treated as equal, as part of the mainstream.... It was almost too much to take in."

Continuing on their way, the Nainaars boarded a small aircraft en route to Prince Albert, Saskatchewan. From her window seat Nainaar presided over the landscape below and noted that both towns and vegetation grew increasingly more sparse as the plane droned its way north. At the Prince Albert airport she surveyed the runway and solitary structure and initially concluded the pilot had made an unscheduled stop in the wilds because of engine trouble.

After an hour's drive through dense, northern forest, Nainaar spotted a cluster of buildings she thought marked the entrance to the town, only to realize a moment later that they, in fact, constituted the entire town. This was Canwood, formerly known as Canadian Wood, population 350. "I was distraught. The streets were dirt, there were no streetlights and our apartment was a tiny basement abode. I didn't think I had the skills needed to set up a home in the wilderness. In South Africa I'd had servants who attended to our domestic routine, not because we were rich and haughty, but because it was a way to employ the poor for whom there was no welfare system. Here, I didn't know where to begin. There were some tears shed."

However, Nainaar didn't allow herself to indulge in a prolonged gnashing of teeth. "Even if I had been so inclined, the people wouldn't have let me. They took to us and we to them. Sundras settled into his work and we turned our attention to the business of becoming part of our community. There was much to learn and at times it was overwhelming, but I kept reminding myself that this was better than South Africa, better than going to a park with your kids and seeing two benches, one for whites and one for blacks. In unpretentious Canwood everyone was truly equal. At first, because of my past experience, I found it disconcerting to be in a predominantly white society. But I'd made it a point to leave my own South African baggage behind, and I came with an open mind. If these people would have us, we wanted to be part of their community."

As the Nainaars began reaching out, they found people eager to reciprocate. By the end of September they had a kitchen full of vegetables from surrounding gardens and people eager to teach them the art of preserving. "I didn't know how to make pickles and I'd never seen frozen vegetables before.

"When people found out I knew nothing about winter, they brought woollies and warm clothing for the children. In South Africa you gave your used clothing to your servants, so when a woman came with a box of winter clothes I felt insulted and told her to take it away. And she asked me why. 'Because I'm not your servant,' I told her. 'Don't be silly,' she said. 'Here things are different. Everyone exchanges clothes. I'll take some of your clothes just to show you.' And she did."

Before long her neighbours were expressing interest in South African cuisine which posed a problem for Nainaar: she had never learned to cook. Undaunted, she wired her sister for a cookbook and then began making dishes relying on both her recipes and her memory of how her domestic help had prepared the meals. At the same time she was hungry to learn what constituted Canadian cuisine. As she grew more adventurous—"I wanted to learn how to make everything. What was a chiffon cake? Teach me how to make it!"—she enrolled in various cooking courses, only to end up winning local baking competitions and teaching cooking in neighbouring communities over the next eight years.

Though a qualified teacher in South Africa, Nainaar chose to devote herself to parenting and community work in the years following her arrival to Canwood. Over the years she joined many community and women's organizations, all the while carefully tending to her personal evolution from urban newcomer to bona fide prairie woman. In 1980 she became a town alderman, one of the first non-white woman to be elected to public office in Saskatchewan. During her three-year term of office she was instrumental in paving and lighting the town streets.

Gradually her evolution drew her to the work of the Multicultural Council of Prince Albert, at that time a loosely bound organization that focused on organizing cultural events. "We were an informal group that met in people's homes, but after a few years I began thinking we should have our own office. We were by then organizing Canada Day festivities and a number of folk fests, and I figured we needed the stability of a permanent location. So we rented a room in Prince Albert for $75 and I brought my own chairs from home as well as a large wooden tea box to serve as a table. My children bought me a typewriter from Sears. I didn't know how to type so I obtained a Gregg's typing manual and taught myself."

Out of that inauspicious and homegrown beginning, the Prince Albert Multicultural Council and Settlement Agency for Refugees and Immigrants has evolved into a crucial, government funded support service for refugees and immigrants. "You might think that Prince Albert wouldn't have much of a population mix, but we routinely have

Bosnians, Chinese, Central Americans, Poles, Iranians, Somalians, Sudanese, Haitians and people from Afghanistan and the Caribbean Islands participating in our resettlement programs. Although most of our clients are refugees, our services are available to all newcomers. We do the health cards and Social Insurance Numbers; we help with health needs, find accommodation, buy the furniture and enroll the kids in school. At one time our English classes were taught by volunteers; now we offer LINC—Language Instruction for Newcomers to Canada, a government program. Language instruction is a major first step for most newcomers. Once they become conversant in English, we help them find jobs, not an easy task in this day and age."

Although many would consider such a mandate as more than enough challenge, Nainaar, as president, sees her organization's mission as being much broader. "Our work is to assist anyone who needs help settling into the community, which explains why we also work closely with the aboriginal population. Many of the First Nations people in Prince Albert are recent arrivals from the north, and resettlement is traumatic for them too. The culture shock is there, as are the same needs that other newcomers have. They too need to learn about the city and the language. They're much like I was when I first came 33 years ago, and I can deeply empathize with their trials."

For her interest in and involvement with the First Nations population, Nainaar began receiving invitations to participate in various Native ceremonies and celebrations. "I wanted to learn more about our Native people so I could pass the information on to new Canadians. Newcomers should know about this country's Native people, should be taught to appreciate and respect their culture. Our council began its relationship with First Nations by accepting invitations to each other's activities; today we organize many joint ventures and sit on each other's boards."

This involvement culminated in an invitation for Nainaar to participate in a series of healing circles at the nearby Saskatchewan Penitentiary, a medium security institution with a disproportionately high Native population. "The circle is a wonderful tool for healing, much more effective than the Catholic confessions I used to endure in my South African days. It's lead by one of the elders and it's for the healing of all participants. It encourages you to open your soul and become as one with everyone. You feel the remorse of those who have done wrong, and their call to be healed. After my third time I felt very comfortable talking about my own feelings. The circle has done much for me too."

As Nainaar became more involved in the penal system, she wondered out loud why so many Natives were being incarcerated, in many cases for violations that seemed so trite. "Ninety percent of the inmates at Saskatchewan Penitentiary are Native. That doesn't speak too well of our system. And all in all, there are too many people who shouldn't be in jail—those who violate traffic tickets, don't pay taxes or smoke a joint. I don't think of these people as criminals but rather that they need healing. And prison is not known as a place to find healing."

Today, six years later, Nainaar is chairperson of the Citizen's Advisory Committee to the Saskatchewan Penitentiary, the Riverbend Institution and the Prince Albert Parole Office. When clashes occur, she works with both staff and inmates to explore possible solutions. Nainaar has also been instrumental in developing a unique community link with the inmates at the Saskatchewan Penitentiary, and she herself serves as the institution's community liaison. "My role is to organize events that will bring community people into the penitentiary to interact with the inmates. After all, that's the essence of any worthwhile rehabilitation program, to learn and/or rediscover how one might function successfully in a community setting. We've organized Metis festivals and drawn crowds of 1000, so people are ripe for this kind of interrelationship.

"In my early South African years, I believed offenders should be cast out of the community and shunned as part of their punishment. Well, I've grown too and although I've not come to a position of condoning or minimizing what they've done, I recognize that they're still human and in need of real opportunities for rehabilitation. When they heal, everyone benefits. If we keep them completely away from the community, what hope do they have of successfully re-entering society after their sentence has been served?"

Although the Saskatchewan Penitentiary was the first Canadian penitentiary to benefit from Nainaar's community liaison program, interest in the concept has since gone far beyond the prison's guarded gate. Nainaar herself has travelled to institutions in Ontario, Alberta and Manitoba to espouse an initiative that introduces a genuinely compassionate element to the rehabilitation process. Over the years her efforts and dedication have been such that she was selected to receive the prestigious international Wolf Project Award in 1996, given annually to an individual or organization for outstanding work in the elimination of racism.

"I was deeply honoured. It came as a complete surprise. I found out later that I had been nominated by the inmates at the Saskatchewan Penitentiary. I didn't even know such an award existed, and I'm surprised that they would have known. It's a very special recognition."

Nainaar's crusade against racism hasn't been limited to her work with Canadian inmates. Currently she is president of the Saskatchewan Association of Multicultural Education and sits on the executive of its parent organization, the Canadian Commission of Multicultural and Intercultural Education. "Our efforts focus on getting multicultural, intercultural and anti-racist programs into the schools. Even before I became involved with these organizations, I was taking myself to the schools to speak about other cultures. At first the children would stare at me and ask if my skin felt like leather and my hair like wire, and their teachers would be hushing them, very embarrassed. And I would say, 'No, don't hush them. If they can't ask questions, how will they ever know?' And I let them touch my hair and my hand, and then we talked about differences and similarities. That's why a live presentation is so much more effective than a video."

As one-time president of the Saskatchewan Multicultural Council and long-time member of Prince Albert's Race Relations and Community Issues Committee, Nainaar has concerns that Canada is showing signs of becoming overly sensitive to the presuppositions of racism, thanks in part to federal dollars and policies. "Some people will resent my saying that this country is not as racist as we make it out to be. Of course there's racism, but sometimes it's just too simplistic to chalk a feeling or incident up to racism. And the government, in their desire to make political hay in the racism field, is always quick to be appropriately horrified by anything that could be construed as racially driven. They reason that as long as they can project themselves as being on the anti-racist side, then they will be seen as honourable and in tandem with all good and decent people. But we need to understand that not everything that happens between people of different cultures is racially motivated. And that takes education. Education is the key.

"A lady standing in a bank line in Saskatoon was told by a young white man also in the lineup, 'I really love your tan.' And she rushed out of the bank and to the Human Rights office to say she had been insulted by a racist. When I was consulted on the matter I asked her, 'Don't you think it could have been a compliment? He really liked your skin colour. Are you ashamed of your colour?'

"And this is where children must be taught that it's okay to say someone is black. We tend to tell our kids not to talk about skin colour. We talk about wall colour, hair colour, and the colour of our clothes, but skin colour, that seems taboo. People will tell me, 'Ah Marge, that colour doesn't suit me but it looks great on you because...' And then they get embarrassed and I'll say, 'Yes I know, it's because of my skin colour.' Why should that be embarrassing to talk about? Brown doesn't suit me, but I look great in blue and peach. You might look dapper in red or brown. Why can't we say these things to each other? Here's where we have some work to do."

Although Nainaar continues to devote herself wholeheartedly to her work—in 1999 she hosted two major conferences, one for educators of non-English speakers and the other for immigrant serving agencies—she has taken measures to make her schedule less gruelling. A decade ago, well after her last child had left home and her husband had become principal of his Canwood school, she quit her daily commute to Prince Albert in favour of a small city apartment that has since become her weekday home. "It was too taxing, particularly in winter when Sundras was always worrying about me being on the road. I was getting home at 11:00 at night, only to be on the highway again by 7:00 the next morning. So now I stay in Prince Albert during the week and go home for the weekend. Sometimes Sundras will drive out to visit with me, and always we chat on the phone twice a day. It's a good arrangement, especially since I think of Canwood and Prince Albert as being two parts of my one home."

Although Nainaar remains invigorated by the people-oriented work she has chosen for herself, she does foresee the day she will scale down her community involvement and retire to the family home in Canwood to dote on visiting grandchildren. "I'm completely content in my north Saskatchewan setting. My loved ones, the work, the people, it's all very dear to my heart. This is where I belong. This has nothing to do with having been an immigrant, and everything to do with being Canadian."

When we first came to Canwood,
we saw people with a history here, and we had none ...
So we set about making a history of our own.

My transition time between taking leave of South Africa and coming home to Canada has long been completed. And although I haven't rejected my South African background, I have evolved, with all my heart and soul, into a Canadian. Of course, what you are is inherently based on your life experience, which for me includes my beginnings in South Africa, but no one could point at me today and say, "There she goes again, dwelling on her South African thing." No, I am Canadian, a woman of the Canadian prairie.

Certainly there was the culture shock when we first arrived, even though we had come from a western setting. To trade a city of two million people on one continent for a town of 350 in an agricultural setting on another called for many adjustments. Even language was an unforeseen barrier. We were used to British English intertwined with our own South African influences.

Shortly after we arrived a teacher invited us to her home for coffee. I was nursing the baby so I didn't go, but Sundras and the two girls had a lovely time and couldn't say enough about her hospitality when they returned home. So I telephoned to thank her, and I told her I looked forward to meeting her since my husband had said she was such a homely person. There came this silence on her end of the line. And I tried to carry on the conversation, continuing with 'homely,' but still there was silence. Then I thought that she mustn't have liked my family after all, and no longer wanted anything to do with us. It wasn't until several weeks later that I learned I had insulted her. In South Africa the word, 'homely' means 'homey.' I learned a lot of things the hard way.

I shudder when I think that we would have moved back to Durban had it not been for the teaching contract. That would have been the worst thing we could have done. Canwood gave us every opportunity for a fresh start, a new home, a place to call our own. Canwood was the place where, for the first time in our lives, we discovered we could truly be equal to everyone else.

A small town provides a good beginning for newcomers. Regardless of what skills they come with, they can learn people skills and find many ways of going about the business of becoming Canadian. I learned cooking, sewing and crafts, as well as pot luck, a social ritual I'd never heard of. We had never before taken food to someone else's home. Another custom new to us was the tradition that after the meal, the women go to the kitchen together and do the dishes. While I enjoy doing dishes at other people's houses and think it's a nice opportunity to socialize, I still have this notion that if I invite you to my house, you shouldn't have to do the dishes. So, as a vestige of my South African upbringing, I resist my guests' offers to help with the cleanup.

A small town can be a lonely place if you're not prepared to try very hard to find your own place within it. I'd like to teach people how to live in a small town. You have to show your neighbours you want to be part of them. I joined every women's organization in the area, eventually becoming president of most of them, which has been a learning experience in itself. When we first came to Canwood, we saw people with a history here, and we had none. At first I was overwhelmed with the feeling that we had no one here. I would go to meetings and feel overlooked, as if I didn't have a contribution to make. It was always, "Oh, I was in school with Stella," and "Stella's daughter will be a good one to handle that task," and so on. There was this history, this inter-connectedness among them, and I wasn't part of it.

I used to wonder, when the tasks were being delegated, why they didn't ask me; I had talent and experience. Well, the reason they didn't ask was because they didn't know I had relevant experience. I had to win people's confidence, to work hard and earn my place in the community. And I did work hard so that the community might one day say in a matter-of-fact way, "Oh, just leave that up to Marge." Now that would, and indeed does, instill a sense of belonging. And that's what we wanted for ourselves and our children more than anything.

So we set about making a history of our own. We had to work twice as hard to make people take heed that we, too, were here, and had a contribution to make. And 30 years later, we are an integral part of the community. Canwood was a good setting for our children in their growing up years, perhaps because we made a niche for ourselves through community involvement, but also, I think, because fate brought us to a small town. In the city we might have been quite lost for a long time. In a small town you get to know the people sooner, and they are eager to teach you the skills they know. In some ways your settling in becomes a kind of project for them.

I would encourage the government to send more refugees to the rural towns, where more people are wanted and needed, and where the townsfolk have time for newcomers. Sometimes I think the government has a tendency to lump immigrants together and send them off to the large cities, where the services supposedly are. But the long lineups are there as well. In Prince Albert, on the other hand, a newcomer can start language training right away.

I realize that in some cases, urgency is needed to remove refugees from their contentious situations abroad, and often this haste is extended to plunking them down somewhere in urban Canada. But if the talents and trades of the newcomers could be matched to a community specifically in need of those skills, the trauma of resettlement might perhaps be significantly reduced in many cases. Sending them to Toronto and Vancouver where they'll be forced to compete with so many others who have the same skills creates inordinate stress.

In some cases refugees end up in an area that has no need whatsoever for the skills they've come with. For example, Prince Albert does not have work for ship builders. To explain to people who are well qualified that we have no need for their skills, well, that's the difficult part of my work. And then to talk about retraining with those who only want to practise the skills they already have, and to help them deal with the fallout of their frustration, that's my biggest challenge. For those who feel their vantage point has been taken away, life becomes traumatic. They come with the mind set, 'This is my profession; this is what I'm going to do until I die,' and they never fully integrate, never fully rediscover that powerful feeling of belonging. But for those who feel their vantage point has merely been relocated, set back a bit perhaps, life becomes a challenge to seize and run with.

Newcomers need to remember that no one here owes them anything. If they sit back and wait for others to come to them with the job offers and prosperity, they'll be sitting for a long time. If I had wrung my hands and said to myself, 'Oh, woe is me, a poor black woman on the prairies all by herself,' I wouldn't be where I am today. You are not here to sit and watch others shovel out a path for you. You must do that for yourself. And self pity is not the way to do it.

Some people are adamant that our country is rampant with systemic racism. Sure, racism exists, but what purpose have we fulfilled by becoming so sensitive to anything that might hint of racism, to the point where a political chord has been struck in Ottawa and the move to 'eliminate' racism is on? Racism will never be eliminated. But now we have these race relations consultants all over the country, with their little business cards to prove they are indeed consultants. I'd like someone to tell me what a race relations consultant is, exactly. Is it someone who will try to suppress my way of thinking if it happens to be racist? Why is the government putting money into a venture that's aimed primarily at stopping how people feel? We know we'll never be able to shame or preach racism away. Quelling our emotions on racism is, at best, a short-term achievement. Education is the only way to achieve long-term change. Education about other peoples and exposure to them. That's why I go to the schools. That's why I let children touch my face and hair. That's why we actually talk about colour. Colour is not a dirty word. When people are genuinely interested in and comfortable with each other, the suspicions, prejudices and discriminations all eventually fall by the wayside.

Sometimes what is construed as prejudice is simply an annoying preconceived notion that can easily be laid to rest by dialogue. Every year, in the dead of winter, someone will ask me, "So, how do you like our winters?" People assume that since I'm a woman of colour I must therefore be a recent arrival. When I tell them that ethnic people are born in Canada every day, it's genuine news to them. And that's how we educate each other, simply by talking in a non threatening way. That's how we gain common ground. 'And yes,' I'll tell them then, 'I do like winter. Why else would I have lived through 30 of them?'

I was an immigrant for my first five years in Canada; then I became a Canadian. Truthfully, I've grown to resent people calling me an immigrant, as if I don't somehow have equal claim to this thing called Canadianism. Instead of dwelling on who is more Canadian, perhaps we should be a bit less reticent about wearing our Canadianism on our sleeves. We're known to be caring and laid back, positive qualities to be sure, but the time has come to be less complacent about the ever-increasing possibility of landing in the lap of the American psyche, and more passionate about our own future as a country united. The way to achieve that is to become involved in the country's issues.

Canada is a beautiful, bounteous country, but its greatest treasures are the intangible ones. Although our flag is poignantly beautiful, it is our humanitarianism and compassion that make this one of the best places to live in the world. People care, and so does our government, its flaws and shortcomings notwithstanding. We have the capacity to feel deeply, and we rally around each other when support is required.

When Terry Fox died two decades ago, the entire country wept. That's Canadian. In the years since, we've made him a hero, and honour his memory by carrying on his quest. That's Canadian. Our personal freedoms, and judicial, health care and education systems reflect our Canadian character. These systems are not perfect, but they're good and we continue striving to improve them in our quiet and understated way. And that is definitely Canadian.

Nguyen H. Trung

SAIGON, VIETNAM—MONTREAL, QUEBEC

The wall of urban heat surrenders at the lobby doors; inside the air-conditioners reign. To the left, sleek elevators wink their willingness to bustle you up, up, up to the top of the cloud-grazing tower. From the corner window on the 28th floor, the downtown corridor is a shimmering kaleidoscope of colour and motion, a distant choreography of people in flux. Against this backdrop, Nguyen Trung remembers the design of his own journey from a land besieged by conflict to the land of corporate wellness.

Today a banker with a remarkably lucid vision for service at the grassroots level, Nguyen whets his razor-sharp intelligence on the world of international co-operative finance, makes it compliant to the needs of ordinary humans.

"From here, I can be of service to people around the globe. And that may be how I'm making a contribution to this country."

W hen Nguyen Trung's parents decided to send him abroad in 1969, they had two urgent reasons for getting him out of South Vietnam. "I was a bit of a handful in those days and I hung around with peers my parents weren't too enthused about. Sending me away to study, they figured, would separate me from that influence and help me to grow up at the same time. But more importantly, South Vietnam was at war and those who weren't passing their exams were plucked out of the schools and universities to be drafted into the military. Since school wasn't my priority then, my parents lived in fear that I would fail my studies and end up on the front line."

Born in 1951 into a close-knit family considered to be among Hanoi's most privileged, Nguyen exhibited an innate social consciousness at an early age. "I've always been very non-conformist and, for as long as I can remember, I've had a tendency to connect with

people less fortunate than we were. So the bunch of friends I hung out with weren't always met with my parents' enthusiasm. To my mother's chagrin, I would skip school and go off for long jaunts in the country, sleeping in barns and talking to the peasants. I figured, with our connections among the top tiers of society, that I might be able to bring a bit more social justice to the country. You have such ideas when you're young and a student. But I knew even back then that what my family was about was not what the country was about. The country didn't live as we did, with our servants and trappings. My excursions into the rural landscape helped me to understand my country."

Although his parents were remarkably tolerant of his roamings and need for inner exploration—they themselves had rebelled against the tradition of an arranged marriage and chosen each other—their greatest worry was that he might stray from his schooling. "The highest priority for oriental parents is their children's education. That means you go to school and perform well, with no diversions. Your parents block the diversions from your life. They look after your finances and whom you will marry. Your job is to study."

Despite the fact that studying was not one of his favourite pastimes, Nguyen nonetheless finished high school with his marks among the top 200 students in Vietnam. "I attribute that to luck and the European system that lets you fool around all year and still do well if you can cram effectively at the end." As a result he was given official permission to pursue a foreign education. In those days government approval was required to study abroad, and approval was granted only to those in the top academic echelon. "The stipulation was that we would all study engineering, and we would all do well in our studies. The government's rationale was straightforward: regardless of how the war ended, engineers would be needed to rebuild the country.

"Most students went to the United States but I didn't want to go there; I'd had enough of the Americans in Vietnam. My parents wanted me to go to New Zealand since I had a sister there. But for me Canada seemed the right choice and that's what I set my heart on."

The authorities, however, didn't mince words telling Nguyen that Canada was out of the question: the decidedly anti-communist South Vietnam earlier had severed all diplomatic ties with Canada over its recognition of Communist China. Officially, the books on Canada were closed. Privately, however, Nguyen reserved his right to choose both his own destiny and destination. "I was determined that I would go where I wanted to go, and not be bullied into someone else's choice. When it came time for the authorities to hand out permits to the selected students, I happened to notice that a girl among us was receiving one for Canada. In reply to my questioning, office personnel said it was because she was the daughter of a senator. Well, to me that was unjust, and because I was used to hanging around with a vocal gang, I became so agitated that when they couldn't calm me down they invited me to leave and come back the following day when they would have 'more information' for me. They didn't want me stirring up the other students. The next day my permit for Canada was waiting for me.

"I had to be accepted at an engineering school before I could leave Vietnam, and I chose the Montreal Polytechnical Institute." As fate would have it, Nguyen was forced to drop out after only a week of studies. "I arrived on October 5, 1969 at the beginning of what was to be a very harsh winter. Already a month behind, I was trying to catch up to the other students and subsisting on a diet of eggs and onions, not because I couldn't afford better groceries but because I didn't know how to cook. Breakfast was three eggs and an onion, lunch was an onion and three eggs and supper was again three eggs and an onion. After a few days of walking to and from classes at the top of Mount Royal, I collapsed and was hospitalized for three weeks.

"My parents were naturally concerned and suggested I move to California where I had an uncle. But I was young, only 18, and had my pride. I wanted to do this on my own."

Nguyen spent the next few years studying computer science, decided that wasn't his forte, and transferred into economics. He obtained his degree from l'Universite de Montreal and was halfway through a Master's program in economics when South Vietnam collapsed. The year was 1975. "Going home was no longer an option. There was no home to return to. Suddenly there was an urgency for me to get a job."

At his neighbourhood Employment and Immigration Centre, Nguyen learned that the Bank of Montreal was advertising for a consumer lending officer. "I went to see them with a referral from Employment and Immigration; I suspect they interviewed me because they had to, not because they wanted to. They would have been looking for someone with a background in finance, not computers and economics. But I ended up being hired and sent to their staff training centre for management for the next six months. That's where I learned my banking."

Mere months after his first posting, Nguyen was asked to fill in for his branch manager who had become chronically ill. Nguyen did so seamlessly. His next posting was in the heart of downtown Montreal, as administrative supervisor at the bank's busiest branch in Canada. This was followed by a series of administrative positions at various Montreal branches. In due time his performance caught the attention of the bank's head office.

"The bank now had me pegged as a candidate with high potential. When they questioned me about my aspirations and I disclosed my interest in commercial credit, they transferred me to the branch with the second largest dealings in that area. From that branch's manager, a Scottish man who became my mentor, I learned my commercial banking activity."

In 1981 Nguyen was transferred to the bank's ailing International Banking Service Centre in Toronto and given three years to 'bring it up to speed.' Having accomplished the mandate eleven months later, he requested a transfer to Asia, which was refused when the bank decided instead to downsize and consolidate its operating units in Asia towards Tokyo. "So I went to my Toronto office every day to read the *Globe and Mail*, and twiddle my thumbs. And I began losing my momentum. I asked to be shipped back to corporate banking since nothing was happening internationally, but they said, 'No, you're too valuable for that. We're keeping you at the Centre.'"

Although Nguyen didn't mind living in Toronto—his daylight hours were spent at the office in any event—his wife, also a Vietnamese Canadian whom he had met in Montreal, was considerably less enthused. This left him in the awkward position of being pinned between his wife's desire to return to Montreal, and his company's resolve to keep him connected to their international operations, out of Toronto. Then came the directive that Nguyen would travel to the Bahamas on a special assignment. He would be given six months to bring the bank's Nassau house into order. When he asked for assurance that he would return to more challenging work than his Toronto responsibilities currently offered, vague rhetoric was offered in place of a solid promise. His questions were waved away and a ticket to Nassau was placed in his hand.

"And I said, 'What? I haven't even accepted the assignment and you've already bought my tickets?' And although the Bank of Montreal had been a wonderful employer, that's when I began thinking that perhaps my place was ultimately not with them."

When a senior official of the Montreal-based Caisse centrale Desjardins telephoned Nguyen's Toronto office in the fall of 1983 to say he had studied his application form and would like to meet with him, Nguyen was baffled. He hadn't submitted an application. On the other hand, if they wanted to talk, he was interested enough in meeting with them.

"I soon discovered that my wife had submitted the application after spotting an advertisement on the Desjardins position while visiting Montreal—since she didn't like Toronto we were spending every second weekend in Montreal."

Nguyen met with Desjardins officials during the Remembrance Day weekend and again at Christmas. In February of 1984 he joined their team as head of commercial operations. "I joined Desjardins without really comprehending its structure. Superficially I figured it was just another bank and I'd be working out of the head office. But before long I began to realize that, unlike the traditional bank, Desjardins was entirely driven by its member/clients and not by its head office. Its structure was thoroughly democratic, much like a reverse pyramid. And I really liked that complete change of culture."

Caisse centrale Desjardins is a unique banking co-operative within an 80 billion dollar operation that is today the sixth largest financial institution in Canada. In existence for almost a century, it has to date limited its Canadian operations primarily to Quebec, not out of policy as much as happenstance. Desjardins can attribute much of its growth and success to the 'quiet revolution' that, in recent decades, has signified the coming of age of Quebec's nationalist psyche. "We truly belong to the people. We have more than 5 million members in a province with 6.5 million people. We represent young and old, and are as attentive to the small, individual accounts as we are to the large portfolios, such as the province of Quebec, for example. Our membership is anything but exclusive. Our system is uniquely democratic: each Caisse elects a board, and from those boards various regional boards are formed, and from there a provincial board is selected. Our boards are not subject to undue influence since each member has only one vote, regardless of whether he has one share or one thousand.

"We are a hybrid of the traditional bank and the credit union. Unlike the credit unions, we are more cohesive, with all 1300 of our branches, known as Caisses, operating under the same system and guidelines. You can access your account in any one of our Caisses, and we offer the same standard of services as a bank does. We're much like a bank except we're more grass roots and run our operations with a cooperative spirit.

"Like the banks, we're authorized to deal in all banking activities, be it commercial, institutional or international. But unlike banks, our organization belongs to our customers. We are at the service of our members. We were created to be responsive to their needs and to generate wealth for them, not anyone else. We're not owned by stockholders, and we offer five dollar qualification shares to anyone who wants to deal with us. If we show a profit at the end of the year, a portion of it can be declared back to the members in the form of a rebate. Typically a rebate might mean a half percent relief on the interest rate of a customer's loan, which is already set at a very competitive rate."

When Nguyen was promoted to the position of Vice-president of International Banking Treasury Operations, he began working closely with Desjardin's co-operative partners in the international arena of commercial and retail banking. Unlike the traditional banks, Desjardins doesn't use its members' investments to create foreign debt and speculate in foreign investment; instead, it partners with foreign co-operative institutions intent on establishing a system of co-operative banking in their own country. "We partner with banks that have the same basic philosophy as we do. In Holland, for example, we work with the RaboBank."

By the late 1980's Nguyen had been well steeped in the world of international business and finance. He had witnessed and studied the impact of a co-operative banking system on several foreign nations. And as a former Vietnamese who understood the cultures of both his original and adopted homelands, he came to turn his attention, quite naturally, to the economic health of Vietnam. Simply stated, he found it wanting. Still hobbled by the recent ravages of war, Vietnam was in urgent need of economic and social retooling. For one thing, the country was still without a viable banking system for the masses, which Nguyen considered a major inhibitor to its growth and progression.

At about the same time he was approached by a friend in the Quebec Ministry of External Affairs who wanted to know more about Vietnam. The Ministry, it turned out, had fielded several requests from Quebec entrepreneurs interested in the possibility of doing business in Vietnam. As an international banker and former Vietnamese who still travelled frequently to Asia, could Nguyen provide the Ministry with an assessment of the current Vietnamese economy and potential?

"I said, 'No problem,' and on my next trip to the Philippines two months later, arranged a stopover in Vietnam to have a chat with some people I knew in government. And that's how this mutual interest between Quebec and Vietnam got off the ground. I saw this as a way I could make a contribution to both of my countries. The Vietnamese, though, had much to learn if Vietnam was going to be a successful player in the international business and investment arena. I coached them on the way the western world does business, and advised them that their own financial house needed to be put in order before they could hope for an exchange of investments with Quebec and the rest of the world. I'm not trying to minimize the intricacy of running a coun-try, but it's not unlike running a household. You cannot spend more than you bring in, and you must exercise financial discipline. You have to start relying on a tax base and have self sufficiency as your goal. And so I put this question to my contacts in the Vietnamese government: how many countries do you know that have succeeded in their growth and development by relying on the charity of other nations?"

Because the American embargo against Vietnam was still in effect at the end of the last decade, Canada was reticent about signing any pos-sible co-operative arrangement with Vietnam. Slowly, however, and always with the blessing of the federal Department of External Affairs, Nguyen sculpted an agreement between Quebec and Vietnam, an agreement that focused on the needs and aspirations of each side and that had in its undercurrent a deep understanding of both of the cultures involved. "I was careful to ensure that both sides were working with the same definitions. Nothing was left to interpretation and misunderstanding. You can talk until you become winded and it will have done you no good if your target group misunderstands what you are saying."

In 1992 Nguyen's negotiations, which he had conducted on his own time, without remuneration and independent of Caisse centrale Desjardins, resulted in a working and cooperative agreement between Quebec and Vietnam. The first agreement ever signed between Vietnam and a western government, it would focus on trans-national cooperative activity in hydro, transport and finance.

Nguyen saw the agreement as being a strong first step for Vietnam. What the country needed next, he reasoned, was a banking system, not a sophisticated one given the literacy rate of the masses, but one that would educate the people in basic finance and encourage personal empowerment at the grassroots level. Up until this point Vietnam's only banking system had been exclusively for the state's own enterprise. Undeterred by the scope of his vision, Nguyen began nudging the Vietnamese government into considering the notion that a banking system for the common people would strengthen the nation's economy. Taking his vision one step further, he proposed that a western co-operative banking system could, in fact, work in an eastern communist country.

"I invited them to examine our system although I cautioned them against copying it outright. Part of our success has been based on the nationalistic wave of the quiet revolution that had taken place in Quebec. The Vietnamese would have to look at their own unique situation and tailor their system accordingly. And that's where we could help out."

Desjardins, up until this point, had limited its international cooperation program mostly to developing a credit union here and there, more often than not in a remote part of the world. However, they had been impressed with the singular results of Nguyen's independent efforts with Vietnam, and gave Nguyen their blessing to bring his vision of a banking system for that country to fruition. "Up until now, what we had mostly done internationally was to offer technical assistance in the development of credit unions, which have no impact on how a country is run. But now we found ourselves shaping a country's entire banking system, from the top down and at the same time, through consensus building at the grassroots, from the bottom up."

In the years that have followed, Nguyen has, in his typically whirlwind yet painstakingly thorough fashion, succeeded in helping his Vietnamese counterparts establish several hundred co-operatives in Vietnam that have changed the way that country's people think about their finances. And although he's personally moved on to other projects in other international arenas—currently he is Senior Vice-president of Administration and Operations—he continues to be revered by many Vietnamese as the undisputed father of the project. The government of Vietnam, in turn, has shown its gratitude by placing a portion of its foreign reserve in the stronghold of Desjardins.

In other arenas Nguyen has had a long-time involvement with Oxfam Quebec and is currently that charity's treasurer. As well, and unrelated to his work with Oxfam, he raises funds for various small-scale educational programs back in Vietnam.

"I'm pretty happy with my life and I like living in Montreal. My work responsibilities are filled with many opportunities for learning, personal growth and fulfilment. I'm fortunate to be with this company, a people-conscious co-operative that shares much of my personal philosophy. From time to time I'm issued special projects and challenges, some quite different from others, on which I thrive.

" In truth, I'm a jack of all trades, and to be honest, I enjoy every minute of it."

If there's a country where we can all voice our opinion, it's here.

You grow accustomed to your setting. For me, setting is home. It is my family, my house, my neighbourhood, community, and the people I work and hang out with. Home is the multitude of customs and rituals that fill up my daily life. Home is the country I make my contribution to, owe my allegiance to. For more than half of my 49 years, my home has been Canada. This is where I'm content.

My 'back home' is Vietnam. Naturally I retain some emotion and allegiance for the country of my birth, but I have strong reservations about whether I could be happy living there now. For one thing, there would be culture shock. True, I look Vietnamese, am Vietnamese and speak Vietnamese, but I essentially was not raised in that culture. I grew up flexing my independence, left early, and have seen and experienced far more than most Vietnamese will ever see. Some Asian customs now seem overly contrite to me, the practise of always deferring to your elders, for example. When an Asian elder tells you something, you accept it unequivocally. Here, we would likely question it for rationale and evidence, and we wouldn't necessarily accept it if we weren't convinced for ourselves.

I can trace the way I think back to my childhood. My parents were quite indulgent in a caring way—my mother devoted herself to her children's well-being and education, and my father was an understanding, compassionate man. They set standards for us, to which they encouraged us to aspire, but they neither forced us into things nor forbade us from doing things. My eldest sister, studying in New Zealand on a bursary, met and married a New Zealander, which initially distressed my parents. But after discussing the idea and getting used to it, they came around and gave the marriage their blessing. I once dated an Asian girl who was not of my family's social standing. But instead of forbidding the relationship, my parents gave me reasons why this girl might not be suitable for me and then left the decision up to me. To be honest, much of the way I think and operate even now is due to the way I was raised. My parents could not have foreseen me as a Canadian, but the upbringing they provided has made an immense contribution to my comfort level in my new world. It's also contributed to the ease of my immersion into the process of becoming truly Canadian.

Up until Vietnam's collapse in 1975, I had always thought I would return to my native land. I was, at that point, just one semester short of obtaining my Master's degree, and I felt an urgency to return as soon as my studies were completed. I had an elder brother who had recently been killed in combat, and my parents were still reeling over the loss. Perhaps, I thought, using both my foreign experience and education as well as my position in Vietnamese society, I might be able to contribute to the restoration of order in my country. But then the country collapsed, and overnight Canada became the land of my future.

Apart from my three years in Toronto, I've spent all of my Canadian years in the province of Quebec. Quebec, as part of Canada, is my home. In my thinking and speaking I never segregate Quebec from Canada, although I acknowledge that I know much more about Quebec than the rest of Canada. If you know Montreal, you don't necessarily know the rest of Quebec. If you know London, you don't necessarily know Ontario. And if you know the western Ukrainian community, you don't necessarily know western Canada. That kind of diversity within our country is wondrous, one of our strengths. It is also the very reason we must, from our respective little corners of Canada, be cautious with generalizations about other Canadians. When we generalize it becomes easier to dismiss others, and by dismissing others we persuade ourselves into believing there is no common ground and therefore no vested interest outside of our own narrow horizons.

For me Quebec is the province I know well. We in Quebec lean more towards the European mentality. We have a bit of Latin in our psyche, a bit of emotion in our character. The road we take is not always clear cut. There is more of a vibrancy and spontaneity here, and we have been known to lead with our hearts. We are proud, we are nationalistic, and we care very deeply about our culture and our place in Canadian history. And yes, the question of separation is a preoccupation of ours, much as it has, in one form or another, preoccupied many Canadians for most of the last decade.

I think in some ways our wrangling over the separation issue is a sign of how fortunate we are in this country. We don't have wars to deal with, we don't have food shortages, we don't have life and death issues hanging over our heads. So instead we find other things to lament about and we speculate how our lives would be different if Canada's geographic contours were to be reshaped. However, with the help of politicians and the media, these speculations have grown to the point where they are polarizing our nation and creating some alarming misunderstandings.

Regardless of where our individual hearts are on this issue, the given is simple: if the boat we call our country sinks, we're all going to be in trouble. When I mention this to people, some will say by way of explanation, "Well, don't you sometimes feel mistreated because of your colour and race?" And I reply, "That would be no reason for me to sink the ship we all live on." And in that light, the minor mistreatment I receive from time to time is rendered almost irrelevant.

In our haste to feel slighted, we forget what a rich country we live in. We forget that our social net is so widely cast that almost everyone in need can find some form of support. We forget that people rarely die of hunger in Canada. I'm not suggesting our systems are perfect, but instead of building on our strengths we tend to spend our energies criticizing. Criticism, however, is not nearly as creative as is the quest for fresh strategies for improvement.

I'm more optimistic now than I used to be over Canada's chance of surviving the separation issue intact. For one thing, Quebec's current government is intelligent, and it's less radical than the previous one. And on a global level, countries that have become fragmented in recent years over political differences have not done well. We in Quebec need to stop leading with our emotions on the separation issue, and start thinking in terms of the economic ramifications of being a separate country. I've travelled throughout the province with my company and there are many people outside of the urban areas who have absolutely no idea what a separate Quebec would look like the morning after the referendum. They think things will stay exactly the same; we would have the Canadian currency, the Canadian economy and our Canadian passports, but we would have our own separate country. How simplistic and distorted. You can't have everything without giving something of yourself. But many people are not fully aware of the implications of an independent Quebec, and to be frank, our government hasn't done a great job of making them informed citizens.

How honest has the government been in its role on this issue? And how objective and honest has the media been in portraying the real issues of separation, the ones dealing with international business and finance? How thoroughly have they laid out how the Quebec and Canadian economies are currently intertwined and how this arrangement would be changed come separation? How well have they analysed how such far-reaching changes would echo at the grassroots level? Or has the media opted to spend more time showcasing isolated opportunities for polarization, and less time portraying, as objectively as possible, how the lives of Canadians in general and Quebecers in particular would be affected? We always seem to hear the issue in terms of 'us' and 'them.' Why not all of us together? Is it because we mostly hear the loud, harsh voice of a vocal minority? We have to understand that the media is powerful enough to galvanize the thinking of the population on an issue as emotional as this one. In Quebec the picture of the Ontario resident tramping on the Quebec flag has gone all over the place. Without a doubt the media tried to portray it as being indicative of English Canada's intent to stomp on Quebec. That kind of reporting is unfair and damaging to the entire country. Instead of compelling us to get together to explore our common ground, it makes us all more vulnerable to alienation. And alienation comes to you more readily when you think someone hates you.

If an English Canadian outside of Quebec says something negative about Quebec, does that mean all English Canadians share that sentiment? And if someone in Quebec says this province wants to separate, does that mean all Quebecers want to separate? Wait a minute, I'm a Quebecer and that's not what I want.

The sad irony is this: if you examine the things Quebec wants from Ottawa, aside from the cultural issue which does require careful handling, these things are much the same as what the other provinces want from the federal government. We're not that different in our needs. Is that not something we can build upon? Where is the glue that would bind us together?

We have a false perception that we are a nation of two solitudes. We are, in fact, made up of many solitudes. Must we be required to integrate completely for our survival as a nation? Must I be required to renege on my culture, on the past which has helped to shape me into what I am today? Or could we develop a mutual sense of respect that would be for the benefit of all citizens? And would this process not run parallel to a potential Quebec/Canada solution?

Here's an example of how I've retained an important aspect of my culture. Just look at my name: Nguyen Trung. Nguyen is my family name, Trung my first. I've never changed the order nor anglicized the name. Leaving my name as it was given to me at birth values my tradition and honours my family. I could have changed my name to Robert Nguyen, but for what purpose? Now, if some people see this as a sign of unwillingness to integrate, so be it. I believe that in a democratic society there is room among all the tolerance and open-mindedness for the little details we each have within our own respective cultures.

Often misunderstandings and misinterpretations result from feeling threatened, which is typically fuelled by false information. But we can resolve a good part of these difficulties by putting them out in the open and talking about them. If there's a country where we can all voice our opinion, it's here. We need to talk and we need to begin thinking plurally.

Can our future as a Canadian society be one of strength and solidarity as we enter the next millennium? The answer may lie in another question: are our politicians exercising their moral responsibility to enhance the well-being of the people who have entrusted them with their office? I define well-being as having a decent standard of living, decent employment, a reasonable tax load and a future for the next generation.

Our future includes newcomers, and to them I say this: you are now in a new country, a new setting. Be open-minded and prepared to accept change. If you come from an autocratic culture, do not interpret our freedom of expression as rudeness or a lack of social grace. And don't have your heart set on completely reserving the propriety of your native culture. You won't. If you could, you wouldn't be advancing in the new life you've come to seek for yourself. You will have to discover on your own what parts of the old you wish to preserve, and how you plan to do that within the new. Don't try to force your children to submit to your will. They will run with their new culture, and the system will be on their side; Canada is a country that promotes and respects the rights of children.

Even though my parents were very liberal in their thinking, I never questioned anything they said. I still can't argue with my mother. But my two young children have no trouble questioning me. I wanted my son to take piano lessons and he asked for a good reason why he should. I like that. It's all part of the difference between my generation, the one that walks the bridge between the old and new worlds, and their generation, which can never imagine home to be anywhere but here.

What I have chosen to preserve is my language. We try to speak Vietnamese in the home even though it's getting increasingly difficult as the children get older. And although both children attend a French secondary school, it is English they end up speaking at home.

When they first started school we had a teacher recommend that we force them to speak French at home since at that time they were shaky in French. I refused. Why would I choose to sever the link between these children and their grandparents, when I knew French and English would come to them in other ways? Well, they are now perfectly fluent in all three languages. As for the languages of the next generation, my children will be the ones to decide.

I've been to many countries and I have no doubt this is the best place to live. Europe has history and architecture, but after a while there, I begin to feel as if I'm in a tunnel, thirsting for both space and oxygen. Emerging countries like Latin America endure so much disparity. In the United States there is rampant ghettoising of the ethnic people. Then I come back here and I think, 'My God, can we not see the good life we have here? How can we work together to preserve this?'

Several years ago we took our children to Vietnam for three weeks, and they loved every minute. Much of it felt intrinsically familiar to them and they took to their surroundings almost immediately. But near the end of the visit my son, then six, looked up at me and said, "It's fun here Dad, but let's go home now. I like home better."

And I agreed with him.

Dr. Hiroko Noro

TOKYO, JAPAN—VICTORIA, BRITISH COLUMBIA

*The plate-glass window smiles on the concrete courtyard defined by
sensible right angles and strong, perpendicular lines. On its other
side, the window reveals the standard university office garnished
with familiar academic paraphernalia: files, books, a computer,
burgeoning letter trays, and a cache of notes and notices
haphazardly speared against a cork bulletin board.*

*Hiroko Noro, Professor of Japanese in the University of Victoria's
Department of Pacific and Asian Studies, and President of the
Canadian Association for Japanese Language Education, sits at her
desk, furls and unfurls her slender hands and ponders the path of
transition on which she has travelled for most of her life.*

*"I used to think I was rootless, even back in Japan. But I've been
transplanted and now I feel my roots growing deep in Canadian soil."*

A t first glance the diminutive and quietly articulate Dr. Hiroko
Noro hardly seems the powerhouse-in-the-classroom type.
But consider that her peers and students alike consistently
place her among the finest teachers on the University of Victoria cam-
pus. Know also that the University Alumni Association's Award for
Excellence in Teaching was bestowed on her in 1993, which prompted
her department head at that time to remark in a campus publication,
"... Hiroko Noro is to teaching what Wayne Gretzky is to hockey. In
either case the person seems to have been custom built for the task."
(*The Ring*, June 11, 1993).

Sitting at her desk in the C Wing of the University of Victoria's
Clearihue Building, and looking for all the world like a student herself, Noro, 46, easily remembers her very first teaching assignment. "I
was in grade one and the teacher asked me to explain addition to a
group of my classmates. I wasn't particularly outgoing, but I loved the

experience. Somehow the role of teacher felt naturally comfortable to me. Eventually I began tutoring, and throughout high school and university I had a steady stream of kids at my door.

Noro has another enduring memory of her early years in Tokyo, one that would set the stage for her decision, years later, to leave for Canada: "I'd never been comfortable with the patriarchal underpinnings of Japanese society. A Japanese woman is expected to be demure, soft spoken, and always agreeably deferring to men. Well, try as I might, I just couldn't mollify the voice in my head that kept telling me such a societal structure didn't make sense.

"Here we were, a sophisticated and complex people, and yet, much of our social and professional behaviours were based purely on the condition of gender. From childhood on, I had difficulty envisioning a place for me in such a society, and I knew even back then that I was a misfit among my own people."

An only child, Noro had been raised in the decidedly non Japanese tradition of following her own heart. "Be yourself," she was told by her parents, who gave her a liberal schooling in a setting where the best students were girls, and female teachers provided excellent role models for young women inclined to break out of the mould society had shaped for them. "My parents encouraged me to further my education, and took pride in my academic achievements."

Noro's first real clash with patriarchy occurred shortly after obtaining her Bachelor of Arts degree with a major in linguistics, from Aoyama Gakuin University in 1977. "To get into graduate school I had to submit to an interview whereupon I was asked about my personal aspirations and whether I might be getting married soon. A male candidate would have never been asked such an inappropriate question. And if there was room for only one student they would invariably always pick the male because 'he had a family to support'. The woman's studies, on the other hand, were considered a hobby, a way to stay occupied until she found a man and started her own family."

Nonetheless, Noro was accepted into Aoyama Gakuin University's graduate linguistics program. When she graduated with a Master's degree two years later, she knew the biggest hurdle was yet to come, should she choose to continue her formal education. "To obtain a

Ph.D in Japan in the Humanities was virtually impossible in the late 1970's. Because a Ph.D is not a requirement for teaching at the university level in Japan, most professors don't have this degree and are therefore unqualified to supervise a Ph.D candidate through the dissertation process. So most candidates complete the course work and then leave without the degree, to pursue a teaching career at one of the country's private or national universities."

Noro also knew her chances of finding viable work and job security in post-secondary academia were sorely limited. Japanese universities in the late 1970's were not teeming with female professors, and those who were fortunate enough to find work were often relegated to the position of lecturer, on the bottom rung of the twin ladders of job security and salary. It wasn't unusual for a qualified woman to spend ten years going from one part-time university teaching position to another before finally landing permanent, full-time work.

In spite of these deterrents, however, Noro entered her alma mater's doctoral program and spent the next three years fulfilling course requirements and trying to conform her research to her supervisor's academic interests. "The tradition in Japanese graduate study was that you 'belonged' to your supervisor, which meant the research you conducted was not of your own design but rather, a derivative of his work. I wanted to study the more pragmatic side of applied linguistics but my supervisor didn't agree, so it wasn't an option. He had high hopes for me as a prodigy of sorts and was determined to keep my work within the parameters of his own research. Our relationship had its tensions."

In her third year Noro travelled to Canada to visit a friend who was studying at the University of Toronto. "I loved Toronto, the people seemed friendly, and after scouting around at the university and meeting a potential supervisor who was supportive of my area of research, I began thinking of coming to Canada, not permanently but as a student intent on completing her education."

Not surprisingly, Noro's parents were aghast when they learned of her intentions to study abroad. "My parents had portrayed themselves all along as being liberal and individualistic, but now they suddenly had an entirely different message for me. 'A child is not supposed to leave her parents this way,' they chided me. Now they wanted me to stay home, get married and be a proper Japanese wife and mother. They were angry with me and I felt betrayed."

Although Noro had carefully saved the money required to underwrite her studies in Canada, her father nonetheless pressed $10,000 in cash upon her as she was preparing to leave, in 1982. "That made me feel even more guilty. Here he was, giving me a large sum of money when we both knew he was dead set against my going abroad to study. Maybe it was his way of salving his own anxieties about my venture."

Noro wasn't long in Canada before she realized her English wasn't nearly as proficient as she had thought it to be. In her first weeks, she grasped only ten percent of the average lecture. Even daily conversation was a disheartening ordeal. "I would go to McDonald's and order a burger and Coke, and end up getting a coffee. I felt frustrated and stupid. I had obviously come ill-equipped, and with a false sense of confidence based on the inadequate English instruction I'd been given back in Japan. Well now, here I was, coping badly with real English. If it hadn't been for my pride I would have probably quit my studies and retreated to Japan."

While the lack of oral comprehension was one challenge to contend with, sifting through an intimidating volume of required reading material proved equally onerous. Unexpectedly, however, she found support from her professors and fellow students. "My department had a high ratio of international and minority students, and, fortunately for me, the professors were very understanding of those struggling with English. Several classmates volunteered to lend me their notes and edit my papers. Their compassion for a stranger was truly amazing. They must have felt sorry for me."

To a bystander Noro would have seemed social enough; she was always quick to exchange greetings with her teachers and fellow students, and regularly attended social functions on campus or in the homes of her classmates. But deep inside she felt isolated, lonely, a world away from the society she knew. "I was given space in an office and on most days I would go there early in the morning to study, then go to classes, grab my lunch and supper at the cafeteria, work late and finally return to my rooming house. I could barely communicate with

the other roomers and one or two of them frightened me. One elderly woman was sweet and passive by day, only to run up and down the
halls in the middle of the night, knocking on everyone's doors and
yelling, 'What do you want from me?'"

Nonetheless, Noro continued to plug away at her studies and slowly
became proficient in English. She made a few lasting friendships. As
her comfort level with the values and mores of Canadian society grew,
she discovered that she enjoyed the ambiance of Canada's most met-
ropolitan city. In her third year she accepted a teaching assistantship
and began offering Japanese language instruction to non-Japanese
students.

"These kids taught me an important lesson: When learning is fun
and relevant, almost anything is possible in the classroom. And so I
began thinking seriously that teaching was something I could mould
into a fulfilling career."

In 1987, mere months away from her graduation and with her parents counting the days until her return to Japan, Noro happened to
notice that the University of Victoria was advertising for a Japanese
language instructor. "They were offering a two-year contract. I
mulled it over and decided I could easily handle two more years in
Canada. The job would also give me a valuable work experience to put
on my resume and take back to Japan with me. But needless to say, my
parents were both infuriated and disappointed."

Noro accelerated the completion of her dissertation, submitted its
draft to her advisor in August, and travelled west to begin teaching in
the University of Victoria's Department of Pacific and Asian Studies
in September of 1987. "I returned later for my final oral defence, and
to this day regret not going back again for my convocation. I guess I
was too shy to ask for time off."

Although Noro's transition from student to professor helped to
solidify within her a sense of being established in Canada, she found
herself unexpectedly facing isolation once more. "I thought my years
of being alone were essentially behind me. I had learned English and
was comfortable with Canadian culture. I figured I'd have little problem making friends and finding a place in my new community. But I
was wrong. The faculty members in my new department were all busy

with their own families and lives, and university protocol dictated that as a professor, I should refrain from socializing with students. So again the loneliness set in."

Things did not go smoothly in her first year. Being the lowest member on the seniority ladder meant that the work everyone was least enthused about was directed her way. "I was quite unhappy, and at the end of the academic year I began looking around for another job. Japan was still filed away in the back of my mind.

Two things happened to keep Noro at the University of Victoria. When reference requests from prospective employers began trickling into her department chairman's mailbox, her colleagues finally began acknowledging her as an equal. "And secondly, I started standing up for myself. I had to do some personal work on the equality issue too; I was always deferring to everyone else. It's not easy to be firm when you're a woman raised in Japan, even with my particular upbringing. Even now I find it awkward to address older, male colleagues by their first names. At the University of Toronto, graduate students used to call their professors by their first name, but I could never bring myself to be that informal."

Yet, even as her work environment finally began to improve, Noro found herself inexplicably dwelling more and more on the possibility of returning to Japan. In the summer of 1990 she flew back to embark on a three-month monitoring of her own pulse in the society she had once known so well. "I had since started a relationship in Victoria with a man originally from Czechoslovakia and I wasn't sure about my future with him. Maybe my trip back was a way to postpone having to deal with that. In any event, I went home to the considerable fallout of my parents' reaction to this man. 'Just suit yourself,' my mother said by way of dismissing me."

Noro didn't have to spend much time in Japan before concluding she would never be able to adjust to that society's notion of how she should conduct her life as a citizen. "Women were still expected to be retiring, and I realized I'd lost that characteristic somewhere along the way. So I came back to Canada, this time with the attitude that I was going to make my home and my life here."

In 1992 Noro married Frank Vitek and gave birth to a son. When she told her parents she wanted to bring him to Japan for a visit, they told her not to bother coming. "I was very hurt. My parents were being so hard and ungiving. But when my son turned one I just packed us up and went anyway, without first seeking their approval. My mother's curiosity about my son's looks overcame her, and when she saw him she bonded with him instantly and felt very grandmotherly towards him. It was a huge relief for me."

While Noro's heart-wrenching search for home put her on a roller coaster ride that went on for nearly two decades, her health has more recently placed her on another. Early 1998 brought a diagnosis of cervical cancer. Although it came as a shock—"There is no cancer in my family"—Noro wasted no time applying her trademark methodical approach to the management of her recovery and healing.

"My health has made me realize that it's time to put some of my energies towards me. A Japanese woman typically does not impose her own needs on anyone, but I now realize I've managed to grow comfortably beyond that kind of thinking. So since my surgery three years ago I've been on a mission to treat myself kindly. I've reduced my teaching load and now approach my health holistically with the help of homeopathic medicine. I've become acutely aware of the importance of regular mammograms and PAP tests. A routine PAP test saved my life and thanks to it, I'm now fine and back to normal."

Back to normal, and busy planning an upcoming international conference at the University of Victoria. With partial funding already procured, its unique focus will be on Japanese identity in western Canada. "We'll be examining Japanese immigration in both its historical and current contexts."

For Hiroko Noro, the young international student who began her journey in Canada struggling by day with only a smattering of English and cowering by night under the bed covers in a cheap Toronto rooming house, the life she's sculpted for herself is tangible evidence of how far she's come in less than two decades.

For both of us Canada has become home, the neutral territory
chosen separately many years ago, and now
mutually enjoyed and cherished.

I think I've spent much of my life struggling to fit in with my surround-ings, and yet, at an early age, comprehending intuitively that fitting in was not necessarily always in my personal best interests. As a teenager in Japan I was already critical of the role society expected from me as a woman, and decided instead to follow my own aspirations. My parents had always encouraged me to think critically and independently. As a result I knew in my heart early on that the future Japan offered me was not a destiny to which I could comfortably comply myself.

Even so, when I came to Canada in 1982, it was not with any thought of relocating. I was here for the sole purpose of obtaining my doctoral degree. I came as a Japanese who had temporarily ventured abroad to complete a course of study. That wasn't an unusual scenario in those days; many Japanese completed their education in a foreign country, with the majority returning to Japan after their diplomas had been issued. My friend at the University of Toronto, whom I had orig-inally come out to visit, did the same. In fact, she raced back to Japan as soon as her studies were finished. Typically, she had found it diffi-cult to adjust to the Canadian lifestyle and had limited her social con-tact largely to the international student body.

My personal journey and transition from one home to another started several years before I physically left Japan in 1982. I was badly out of synch with my graduate advisor, who expected me to tailor my research to his area of interest. Accordingly, I also became isolated from the other students, who were uncomfortable with, and perhaps threat-ened by, my resistance to being manipulated to fit a preconceived aca-demic and social mould. The long hours spent at school were demoralizing and frustrating. I struggled constantly to keep my vision from being derailed by the standards and values of colleagues who main-tained that what was good for them must surely be good for me as well. Life at home was not any more serene. I was still living with my par-ents. I was their only child, on whom they had pinned all their hopes and expectations. Throughout my youth they had supported my academic ventures but when my thoughts turned to studying abroad, they railed against the idea with all their imagination: You have studied enough; you should listen to your parents; you should work at finding a husband and starting a family; if you go to Canada you'll end up with a non-Japanese husband and *then* what will become of you?

In Toronto I felt equally isolated but in a different, perhaps more straightforward way since it's not unusual to feel alone as a foreigner in a foreign country. Right from the beginning, language was a problem. The constant barrage of English—from the radio, my professors, classmates and conversation on the street—pinged against my brain until it contained such a massive jumble of words that nothing made sense. It was as if I'd developed aphagia and lost my coherence even in Japanese. I was struggling to read English to the point of such straining that when I opened a Japanese book, I could no longer decipher the script and its vertical presentation. In those first six months I lost much of my ability to communicate in Japanese, could barely make myself understood in English, and had no one with whom to share my anxieties and confusion.

In the meantime my parents were phoning me every week, alternately pleading with me, then ordering me to return to Japan. We were always sparring on the phone, always talking about the same thing. The pressure was unbearable at times. In truth, I desperately wanted to go back. I was so miserable that I began feeling quite anti-Canada. I was critical of Canadian values and customs but didn't have the English to try and work it out with my Canadian peers. But my pride wouldn't let me go home in failure either. I didn't want to give my parents the last word and sentence myself to a lifetime of regret.

I must acknowledge that I did receive genuine support from Canadian friends in the form of help with my studies, but our relationship was not such that I could open my wounded heart to them. In retrospect, that was mostly my doing; I couldn't communicate, and I kept to myself. A Japanese woman is not supposed to burden others with her trials and problems, and I was very Japanese in my thinking.

I should have been less stubborn and proud, less afraid of failure. I wish I'd been able to ask for help. Canadians are generally very kind, even to a stranger, and I should have allowed myself to lean on them a bit more.

A month after my arrival, I became very ill with a flu and pneumonia. Still, I never told my friends, never sought medical help. I didn't want to impose myself on anyone. Now I realize how stupid that was; I could have died. When my friends found out later, they couldn't understand why I hadn't phoned them for help. And I didn't have the English words to explain to them how the deeply rooted tendrils of my Japanese conditioning coloured all I did, observed and interpreted.

In reaction to my isolation and misery I began rediscovering, even glorifying, the Japanese culture I had rejected—even loathed—for so long. I became supremely critical of all things and values Canadian, and joined in solidarity with other foreign students who were flailing their way through a similar private journey. The two other students who shared my office were from Thailand and Guyana. The Thai woman, especially, was very nurturing, and I was much in need of her comfort. In the refuge of our office we shared our biased and polarized concerns, criticisms and complaints. No doubt many of our observations and evaluations were grossly skewed and unfair, but that often seems an integral part of the birthing process into the new world. Because the new is so alien and therefore intimidating, there is a tendency to cling to the security of the old, familiar world, even if that world is less than ideal. You hang on to what you know and further pump up your security by denigrating what you haven't yet given yourself time to understand.

To say that my first half-year in Canada was challenging is plainly an understatement. But then suddenly, almost miraculously, my head cleared and English began to make some sense. Suddenly the reading comprehension was there too and although I didn't become a speedy reader overnight, I was able to pick up my pace considerably. My Japanese came back and I felt as if an excruciating rite of initiation had finally been completed. And now, with my increased comprehension, I was finally able to grasp something of the complexity of Canadian society which had, up until now, passed me by completely.

My Canadian friends tended to be older and one in particular treated me as a child. It's well known that Asian women tend to look and act younger than their age, and this woman who was about fifteen years my senior treated me as if she was my mother. She and her family took me to Canada's Wonderland, children's movies, kid stuff. They would routinely phone me or come to my place to see how I was doing. At first her attention was exactly what I needed: someone to nurture and mother me. But it was not an equal or peer-driven relationship, and in my second year I began to find it stifling. I gradually put some distance between us and eventually we went our separate ways.

My second breakthrough occurred when I met a Japanese student who even today remains my best friend. I'm not, by nature, a chatty person, but I recall that the first time I opened up to her and spoke of my loneliness and misery, it was as if a huge weight had fallen away from my shoulders. After that we spent an hour or two on the phone every evening, going over the minute details of that day's routine, and we became extremely close. The most difficult thing about moving to Victoria was leaving her behind in Toronto. We're still in touch today, and if I have a problem or anxiety, she's still the one I'm apt to phone for comfort and support.

In my second year I began enjoying my life in cosmopolitan Toronto, and increasingly developed an appreciation for the Canadian way of life. I was going back to Japan once a year to visit family, and with each visit I rediscovered my incompatibility with Japanese society. It's difficult to describe my ephemeral emotions about Japan and Canada. I would feel an overlapping haze of nostalgia for one and criticism for the other, and then suddenly these emotions would flip-flop, leaving me confused, rootless, rudderless, back to the beginning of my transition. I belonged neither here nor there, even though I kept assuming, without a great deal of enthusiasm, that I would return to Japan after graduation. I'm not sure why. I knew full well that I'd never fit in there to the point of contentedness. But could I find contentedness here? Or was I simply retreating to the familiar because of intimidation by the unknown?

In one of the more memorable ironies of my life, I discovered the University of Toronto's Asian Library at around the same time that I became a Teaching Assistant in Japanese language instruction. Purely for pleasure I started reading my way through the collections of

Japanese literature and history. As I went from one book to another I began discovering the treasure of Japanese culture and tradition. How could I have been so unaware of these books, growing up in Japan? I began rediscovering my language, which I had never studied formally, and grew increasingly proud of my heritage.

I was also enjoying my teaching experience, and it began to dawn on me that here was something I could do well and enjoy as a career.

Moving to Victoria felt a lot like starting over. The foreignness, the isolation, it was all in front of me again. I had a much smaller pool from which to draw new friends and so, as in the beginning, I found myself spending most of my time alone. Although there is an Asian population here, I was often stared at and asked about my accent. In Toronto I had never felt like a minority person, not even in those first six months. Toronto was wonderfully stimulating and cosmopolitan, and even now I look on it fondly as a 'hometown' in my past. Tokyo is my other hometown.

In Victoria I couldn't settle in and my mind kept wandering to the notion of a permanent return to Japan. In 1990 I did go, to test the waters one more time. And quite definitively it came to me that I had changed to the point where I was beyond resettlement into Japanese society. That was my turning point. I came back to Canada knowing I was going to make my home here. No more dancing on the fence.

And yet. . . in the summer of 1997, after 15 years in Canada, I found myself weeping at Tokyo's Narita International Airport. I had flown to Japan to bring my widowed mother to Canada permanently, a happy move that would add to my rootedness in Canada. But at the departure gate I suddenly found myself thinking, 'There goes my last link to Japan.' The sense of loss that crashed over me took me completely by surprise.

I thought I had finished labouring through my journey of transition. I considered Canada my permanent home. My husband and child were here, and I was comfortably settled in. But obviously there was still an attachment I couldn't completely explain.

Part of my heart will probably always remain in Japan. Ethnically speaking, I'll always be Asian. But I can't live there any more. Many of my expatriate friends echo the same sentiment: Japan is not a country to live in, but rather, a country to visit. Like a wonderful artifact, it is a country whose rich heritage and complex society is to be savoured and then best put back on the shelf. And I think I'm reconciling myself to that.

My husband and our child have helped to gel my sense of place in Victoria. Frank came to Canada as a refugee from Czechoslovakia, so he's ventured through many of the same challenges that I've experienced. He has no interest in Asia but until recently kept open the possibility he might eventually move back to Prague, although I wondered how we would have managed that as a family. Prague, to me, would have felt like someone else's choice, not my own. And he would have felt the same if I had dragged him to Japan.

Now he doesn't talk much about Prague any more. His parents have both passed away and only a brother, aunt and uncle are still living there. And last year he was diagnosed with lymphoma, so our focus these days is on our health and getting the most out of our lives.

For both of us Canada has become home, the neutral territory chosen separately many years ago, and now mutually enjoyed and cherished. It is the only place on earth to which we can lay equal claim as our home. Because of my immigration experience, I feel I've grown more tolerant of other perspectives. I try not be judgemental. I see a commonality among the many cultures of the world, and I believe people's goodness or badness has nothing to do with their culture.

Canada is a fair country, home to a tolerant and meritocratic society. Here, someone who comes up with a creative idea can find a fulfilling niche. It doesn't matter where you were born or to whom you were born. We're a little socialistic, trying to distribute the equity among the people. There is no obvious ruler and even the less fortunate have some say in the system.

If we lack anything as a society, perhaps it's a sense of history. However, that's not even necessarily bad; countries with a long history tend to have a more complex psyche and can be more difficult to live in. Canada is an easy country in which to live.

When I first chose to study abroad, my friends were critical, called me a traitor and accused me of abandoning Japan. Now they congratulate me and say, "How wonderful for you that you live in Canada."

Dr. Bridglal Pachai

UMBULWANA, KWAZULU-NATAL, SOUTH AFRICA—HALIFAX, NOVA SCOTIA

Dr. Bridglal Pachai is not afraid to tackle the juxtaposition of his two beloved homelands, the former and the current. Unflinchingly he writes in My Africa, My Canada *of the tears imposed by apartheid in his early years, the pain of unemployment decades later. Slowly and deliberately he speaks, for the contents of his soul are not to be self-indulgently strewn about like pebbles at a creek's edge; instead they are contemplated on, weighed against, and pondered over, stepping stones across the river of his life.*

An eminent scholar and teacher, and the first non-white South African to earn a PhD in history, Pachai remembers his roots, pays homage to them with the waters of fervent Canadianism.

"If in later life I have felt compassion for the underdog, it must surely be because I was myself an underdog for so very long."

More than half a century ago a teenage boy hastened along the dusty road between the villages of Mount Partridge and Plessislaer, in the South African province of Natal. Under the eye of the setting sun he hurried to the gargantuan Sutherlands Tannery, where he would be one of only two employees on the night shift, recently added to fill the wartime's increasing demand for shoes. Before shift's end the following dawn, he would have bolted through the making of 1500 pairs of stiffeners, a component of the heel, and then stolen a few hours' sleep on a bed of boards.

Such was the burden of a youth who, born into an impoverished family in the village of Umbulwana in 1927 and forced to abandon formal schooling at age 14, was nonetheless bent on furthering his education through the solitary medium of correspondence. Amid the scoffing of

those who felt it couldn't be done simply because it had never been done previously, he worked by night and studied by day for three years, in that time achieving the equivalent of three years of full-time schooling. From there he went on to become a teacher, the first of any race ever produced by the village of Umbulwana and, eventually, the first non-white in South Africa to achieve a doctoral degree in history.

Undisputedly, Dr. Bridglal Pachai has a penchant for turning hardship into challenge. His father had migrated from India near the end of the last century, a laundryman who until retirement struggled to feed his family on a patch of land sloping down to the nearby Klip River. His older brothers had left school at an early age to take on menial jobs, and all indications were that he would do the same. "There was no tradition of higher learning in the family. My father's generation was that of the indentured labourer; the generation of his children was evolving into one of waiting on white tables. I saw myself going in the same direction."

Like other non-white children, Pachai had already digested a good dose of South African protocol at an early age. Where there was dignity and opportunity, there were whites. Poverty, illiteracy and an exclusion from the affairs of the country formed the arena for the blacks, which by South African definition included people of all other ethnic origins as well as the indigenous blacks. The wedge of apartheid driven into the country's recent history by foreign interests ensured that privilege rested solely on the side of the whites while blacks remained relegated to the bottom rung of the ladder of opportunity.

"We blacks formed the vast majority of the population, yet we were made to suffer the dregs of a system that upheld the supremacy of a people based on the colour of their skin. From my earliest years it was a system to which I could not conform."

"The colour line in South Africa was the ultimate act of self-interest, drawn by the white rulers to keep themselves on the side of power and opportunity, while the rest of the population remained dependent and subservient. In keeping with the rulers' strategy to rule by dividing, the ethnic groups within the black population were further segregated into separate schools and areas of residence. That's how I came to be first a student, and then a teacher, at an all-Indian school."

After completing his first undergraduate degree, Pachai decided that any further studies would be in the field of history. "So little was known of the history of South African people. What passed for history was the story of white conquests and superiority. Officially, there were no black heroes; black history was non-existent. Well, now I could do something about those falsehoods and omissions." As he had done previously, Pachai seized this latest challenge and transformed it into a personal mission. Here was a tangible contribution to be made to his beloved, if shackled, homeland. He could delve into Africa's real history, coax it out of hiding, discover singular bits and dusty pieces in the archives and among the people, and configure his findings into the puzzle of Africa's fascinating story.

But no sooner had Pachai receive his PhD from the University of Natal in 1963, all the while parenting five children under the age of ten and teaching high school, when he began to realize how much of an anomaly he had become as an educated black within the strangulating confines of apartheid. "Of what value would this degree be in a high school setting? And yet, there was nowhere else to go with it. Even at this level, the structure of apartheid beheld race as the absolute prerequisite for genuine opportunity. Whites could go wherever they wanted in this structure. Blacks were lucky if they could go anywhere at all.

Shortly it began to dawn on Pachai that he could no longer continue to live in South Africa. "There were few opportunities for me, but more importantly, Leela and I both knew there would be no opportunities for our children as long as apartheid reigned. Going away seemed our only option, and yet, if we were going to remove the children from their birthplace and extended family, then we'd better be sure we were taking them to a better life and citizenship."

Pachai began looking for employment and found it in the form of an appointment at the University College of Cape Coast in far-off Ghana. Getting the job was relatively easy; getting eight people, including his wife's youngest brother who had made his home with them, out of South Africa and into a country that had taken its anti-South African and anti-apartheid stance to international levels, was considerably more difficult. A window of opportunity arose when Pachai discovered that the university had an overseas address in London, England. He would adopt it as his own and spread the word that he had accepted a post-doctoral fellowship in that city.

"Ghana was a chance to experience life outside of the confines of South Africa's artificial barriers. Throughout my term there I felt a part of history in the making as the country struggled through its own political metamorphosis. In the process, much energetic discussion and debate was generated among the people."

In 1964 Malawi, on the continent's east coast, declared independence. When the fledgling nation established the University of Malawi the following year, Pachai was aggressively recruited to become head of its newly created history department. This would be his second opportunity to help shape a history department in a newly independent, African country.

In Malawi, as in Ghana, Pachai found much work to be done. His students, products of a colonial education that had long and systematically measured the history and affairs of the country in European terms, had difficulty shifting their focus to things African. Because they had never experienced a book that treated their own history with dignity and respect, they also denigrated African history as being quaint and irrelevant.

Throughout the next decade Pachai strove to infiltrate his department with nothing less than excellence, and continued writing and presenting his papers to international audiences. A weekly half-hour radio talk show, *History of the Nation,* emerged and eventually evolved into a book, the first of several Pachai was to write on Malawi. Along the way he became the first non-white to be accorded membership in the South African Historical Society.

As the 1970s dawned, however, the Pachais took stock of their adventuresome life and concluded the time had come to begin searching for a permanent home. The politics and growing pains of Malawi as an emerging nation were always in the foreground and as an eminent scholar, Pachai was often caught in the middle. "And our working visas could only be extended indefinitely, each time but for a short period. Our lives lacked overall permanency. We couldn't be birds of passage all our lives, nor did we want to be. The time had come to go looking for a place to call home."

At a conference in India in 1969 Pachai chanced to meet Dr. P.D. Pillay, a colleague originally from South Africa and now at Dalhousie University in Nova Scotia, Canada. When Dr. Pillay organized the February, 1973 conference of the Canadian African Studies Association, he invited Pachai to present a paper on African politics in colonial Malawi.

Nothing in his previous life could have prepared Pachai for the winter that awaited him at Gander National Airport in Newfoundland. "The real torture was having to claim my baggage from a cumbersome open trailer on the runway, struggle it into the terminal for customs clearance, and then haul it back out for the continuing flight to Halifax. I still think of the Gander experience as my Canadian baptism."

The Canadian winter aside, Pachai found much to be impressed with over the next few days. "I had come as a scholar but also as a person in search of a new home. Although I was a seasoned traveller by this time, the setting, organization, amenities and atmosphere of this conference were of a standard I had not experienced before. I liked what I saw in Halifax. There were some who cautioned me about the challenge of finding work here, but others encouraged me to apply for Dalhousie University's Senior Killam Fellowship which would translate into a one-year appointment."

Before returning to Malawi, Pachai looked up several former colleagues now living in eastern Canada and ruminated with them on his findings and impressions. As his departure time approached, he was able to conclude that Canada offered more than any country he had previously considered.

When the Killam Fellowship was offered a short time later, the Pachais began the painful process of taking leave of a country they had grown to love. Amid the goodbye parties and other events held in their honour, they arranged to rent the Halifax home of a Dalhousie professor who, coincidentally, was coming to teach at the University of Malawi. The important details tended to, they figured the rest would fall into place.

Newcomers don't usually end up purchasing a home within 36 hours of their arrival in a foreign country, much less those who come with a rental arrangement in hand. But the Pachais hadn't yet left the

'Arrivals' wing of the Halifax International Airport when they learned that the house they had anticipated living in was no longer available.

"To our chagrin, we had four days to find other accommodations. But fortune intervened, as it had so many times before. We had dinner at the home of Dr. Pillay the following day and happened to notice that the house two doors down from him was for sale. We went over that evening to make an inquiry and signed the papers at midnight."

Seeing his children, especially the youngest, readily adapt to a new life instilled in Pachai the resolve to do the same. The influence of television and the legendary generation gap caused worry; on the other hand he found himself, for the first time, in a predominantly white meritocratic society that saw the colour of his skin as being largely irrelevant.

As a Killam Fellow, Pachai was installed at Dalhousie University's newly formed Centre for African Studies and immediately found it to his liking. As in his previous positions, there was much to be done: courses to be designed and taught, committee work, books to be written, and an inventory to be compiled on what passed for Canadian black history. Perhaps it was fortuitous that a son of South Africa, the first real historian of the South African people, would be the one to take stock of Canadian black history and find it wanting.

Nearing the end of his first year, however, Pachai had a more pressing problem. The Killam Fellowship was coming to an end and job prospects were dismal. While Dalhousie University offered a reprieve in the form of a one-year extension, it also cautioned against the likelihood of a permanent position. The history department had a full slate of qualified staff and a vacancy in the short term was improbable. Aware that time was running out, Pachai broadened his job search. He applied for several positions and was given numerous excuses as to his unsuitability for the job. Though overqualified for the public school system, he pleaded for a teaching position and the chance to demonstrate his dedication to both his charges and his profession. He would be perfect, he thought, to fill a classroom vacancy in a predominantly black community not far from Halifax. The woman who interviewed him thought otherwise.

And then, as he was despairing his future and how he would manage to provide for his family in the face of unemployment, St. Mary's

University came forward and offered him the position of Co-ordinator of its newly established International Education Centre. Under his guidance, first as Co-ordinator and then as Director, the Centre gradually emerged as a place of excellence in Canadian multiculturalism issues and Third World development issues. Of his contribution and leadership, Pachai says simply, "It was an opportunity to serve in new areas."

Pachai had already noted that his Canadian university students seemed to know as little of the history closest to them as his African students had known of theirs a decade earlier. This observation pressed him to organize a conference on multiculturalism in 1977 which drew historians and scholars from various parts of North America. Buoyed by its success, he went on to organize a pivotal, international conference on Canadian Black Studies in early 1979. "Canadian Black history had traditionally been considered irrelevant in Canada and also in Nova Scotia, where Blacks had lived, toiled and died for three centuries. We knew the history of Africa and Asia, but we were ignorant of how these histories intertwined with our own. The conference, which garnered considerable public interest and support, helped to bring these deficiencies to the forefront."

All the while Pachai continued to lecture and teach. "I had to pause every now and then to take stock of who I was, where I had come from, where I was going and how I would get there. In Malawi I had taught myself Malawi history. Then I taught Malawians about their history. I ended by writing books about Malawi history. That experience was repeating itself in Canada."

By mid 1979 the International Education Centre had run into financial uncertainties and Pachai, coincidentally, had received an offer to assume a professorship in the history department of the newly established University of Sokoto in northern Nigeria. "In South Africa, there was not much a person of colour could do for nation building independent of what the white rulers decided or determined. In emergent nations such as Ghana, Malawi and Nigeria, however, the need for a helping hand could be answered by foreigners like myself. And in this spirit I chose to go to Nigeria, temporarily, even though there were many in Halifax who protested my leaving."

Five and a half years later, amid deteriorating conditions in Nigeria,

Pachai returned home to Halifax and became the first Programme Director of the newly established Black Cultural Centre. Immediately he felt at home among people dedicated to the advancement of black history and cultural awareness. "My role with the Centre felt naturally right. I had been raised in Africa; I had learned, taught and penned African history. I had been a student and teacher of Canadian black history. My experiences over the years had made me sensitive to the plight of minorities all over the world. Yes, I shared much common ground with those served by the Centre."

During that time he also wrote two books on Maritime Black history and was installed as General Editor of the successful book series, *Peoples of the Maritimes*.

Still, as much as Pachai has always had a rightful affinity for people of colour, he has never limited his service to this segment of the population. In 1988 he was installed as first Chairman of Literacy Nova Scotia, a then newly minted provincial initiative, and in 1989 was appointed to the Canadian Human Rights Tribunal. Also in 1989 and with the full blessing of his colleagues at the Black Cultural Centre, he left to assume the Directorship of the Nova Scotia Human Rights Commission, a position he held until 1992, eighteen months past the statutory retirement age of 65. The following day he was invited to become Ombudsman—"a term I've gradually succeeded in changing to 'Ombudsperson' "—with Nova Scotia Power Incorporated, one of the largest private sector firms in the province. "Essentially my duties were an extension of my work with the Human Rights Commission, except that I had now transferred out of the public sector."

The year 1994 brought recognition in the form of an Honorary Doctor of Civil Laws Degree from St. Mary's University for his contribution to human rights issues. The following year brought official retirement, although Pachai continues to hold adjunct professorships at both Dalhousie and St. Mary's Universities, consulting, teaching a course here and delivering a lecture there, all on a voluntary basis. In 1997 he was inducted to the Wall of Honour at the Black Cultural Centre, and later that year set out for Gambia on Africa's west coast to teach an eight-week course on the history of Blacks in Canada, an experience he repeated in 1999. In January of 2000 he was recognized by the mayor of Halifax Regional Municipality for contributions made to the community, and in July of the same year was made a member of the Order of Canada.

Of the many things one can state about Pachai, it must be noted that he has never shied from an opportunity to learn, even when that opportunity beckoned from the other end of the planet. His venerable career has been eclectic but always in harmony with the passions of his soul. Bridglal Pachai, it can be said, remembers his roots. His life's work has been homage paid to the humble beginning that propelled him, against all odds, to achieve heights heretofore beyond even the imagination of his people.

> *Canada defies limits: anything is possible.*
> *That is the lesson I have learned*
> *and the lesson I shall pass on*
> *to my children and grandchildren*
> *and to all I live with,*
> *work with and plan with.*

—Bridglal Pachai, *My Africa, My Canada*, Lancelot Press, 1989.

The positions I have held in Canada have been pillars of learning that have supplemented the knowledge I had before I immigrated and heightened my understanding of Canadian society with regards to multiculturalism, human rights, and the experience of minorities. It was and remains my challenge to learn from those who have preceded me in these areas, and to groom those who will follow.

Although my responsibilities since my arrival in 1975 have been varied, I have felt my individual positions to be neither fragmented nor disjointed. On the contrary, each has complemented and added to previous understandings and gleanings. Each has risen out of my involvement in society. You become involved, you see a need and then you explore ways in which that need can be addressed. And even as that need is being addressed, it gives rise to a host of other priorities and concerns which, when tackled, further enhance your understanding

THE QUESTION IS, HOW CAN WE

EVOLVE INTO A SOCIETY THAT

REPRESENTS THE REQUIREMENTS

AND INTERESTS OF ALL CITIZENS?

of how the parts fit into the whole, whether related to current society or history. You come to see how the provincial parts fits into the national whole and the national parts into the international whole.

I came with a background of being a minority person in an apartheid setting as well as someone who had studied the history of the South African people, not only the official version but the real history that had preceded it by centuries. In that spirit I began to delve into the Canadian historical experience, and accordingly, came to the understanding I have of multiculturalism in Canada.

Essentially, Canadian history has given rise to two strains of multiculturalism. There is grass roots multiculturalism and official multiculturalism, the former preceding the latter by many years. The former occurred as an evolution of Canadian society, without government interference, as the efforts of people from all over the world contributed to the growth and development of Canada. The latter, Pierre Trudeau's multiculturalism, which surfaced in 1971, hitched a ride on the coat tails of the former and quickly became part of the political agenda, the vote-catching agenda. Born out of government intervention, it was therefore naturally designed to serve government agendas. Because public support for official multiculturalism was unabated in those early years, the initiative grew accordingly.

But this rampant growth created a backlash when Canadians began resenting the seemingly disproportionate emphasis on multiculturalism. As a result, official support for heritage languages, cross-cultural initiatives and ethnic services and education found itself receiving mixed greetings from people across the country. In some instances the backlash translated into a sentiment against the minorities, ethnics and outsiders who, it was perceived, threatened the western European and Christian principles upon which this nation had been built. Not only was the nation's foundation being threatened, according to those now critical of the initiative, but the root cause of the undermining was being bankrolled by the federal government.

Predictably, the government scrambled away from multiculturalism and in the process nudged it down the ladder of priorities. Policy on race relations emerged to fill the void, but not without its own problems. The very term, 'race relations' has a ring of divisiveness about it.

Race has always conjured up images of struggle, bigotry and lack of justice, and the majority of Canadians don't want to be reminded that there is racism in our country. The minorities also have a problem with this concept; they don't always want to be lumped together and heard from collectively.

In summary, our government hasn't done particularly well in achieving a sense of unity and solidarity among its varied people. It has failed to reach beyond a policy of support for individual cultures, and fallen short of leading all Canadians in a direction that would hold meaning for all citizens. Where could we go from here?

Perhaps what is required is a complete revision of the system we use to educate ourselves about each other. Perhaps that system needs to be repackaged for a total society, including the majority who are easily turned off when it comes to issues of culture and race, and the minorities who are easily made to feel alienated. Our education experience should represent not a power struggle but a new, common direction for all Canadians. There's no denying that our society is changing and will continue to change. The question is, how can we evolve into a society that represents the requirements and interests of all citizens? That's what needs to be debated, hammered out, and ultimately sculpted into an education package for all of us.

The other crucial fact that must be understood is that unemployment and recession are not caused by immigrants. A recession is not created within a country. It is part of a complex process that happens internationally and often, as history has borne out, in cycles. Recession creates as much hardship for an immigrant as it does for a sixth generation Canadian. It's easy to pinpoint the immigrant as the cause of hardship, but that's both simpleminded and short-sighted. Were we instead to refocus on strategies to support small business, strengthen the human element in our industries, promote on the basis of merit, and create a more representative workplace, many economic hardships could be dramatically lessened.

Canadian multiculturalism has been understood, analysed, propagated and written about in an almost endless number of ways. I myself have compared and contrasted the theory and practise of apartheid, into which I was born, with the theory and practise of multiculturalism in which I now live. The exercise has been useful, perhaps even more so because I am not limited by the horizons of those Canadians of older vintage who have only the single yardstick of the Canadian experience with which to evaluate a system. And the reality I have learned is this: that in a nation's journey towards a common destiny, whether away from colonialism or towards true multiculturalism, the stepping stones are much the same—the stepping stones of power struggles and imperialisms, of exploitation, alienation, economic hardship and ultimately, compassion and solidarity.

When I served as Director of the Centre for International Studies at St. Mary's University, the emphasis was on two areas of study: Canadian multiculturalism and Third World development. I saw a commonality in these two seemingly disparate areas. On the one hand we have a Canadian development context, on the other, a Third World development context. The strategies for understanding and determining a proactive course of action in these two scenarios is parallel; in each case a new reality is being forged from the current one by way of a similar metamorphosis. We can learn much from the Third World as we grapple with our own maturation, so much in fact, that when I approached a Halifax cable television company about a program on this subject, they launched a weekly series, *Third World Development—Know Your World*, which I hosted for two years.

On a personal level, Canada has brought a multitude of opportunity. I came for opportunity, especially for my children, and although the employment situation was worrisome and the cause of private tears in those early years, I have found it in generous amounts. Not only the opportunity of fulfilment in my work, but in being recognized for my work and more importantly, for who and what I am. I cite two examples. In 1985, weeks after my return from Nigeria, I was invited to write a volume on Black history for the Maritimes peoples project and to serve as general editor for the series. I was deeply honoured to be welcomed home in this poignant manner. Any number of people born in this country could have been chosen, but instead, the offer was made to me, an adopted son of Canada.

In the second example, I had, over the years, befriended Dr. William Pearly Oliver, a distinguished black Nova Scotian, activist, educator and minister of the cloth. In 1986 I was asked to be the main speaker at a celebration of his 50 years of marriage and community and pastoral services. I was humbled. He had chosen not one born in Nova Scotia or even on Canadian soil, but a newcomer, a novice, one from the outside. For me it was the ultimate sign of acceptance by a fellow Canadian, and I will always remain deeply touched by the singular honour he bestowed on me.

My own transition years, if transition is being interpreted within the strict parameters of 'settling in,' lasted no more than the four years between 1975 to 1979. From the beginning I was comfortable in my community and social environment. I had come in search of a new homeland and, having found it and committed myself to it, was prepared to live in it with my body and soul.

I concede that I did have grave concerns about my finances and employment prospects in those early years. The then decline in the national economy meant universities had curbed their hiring, especially of seasoned teachers who generally cost them more than entry-level staff. The only appointments I could procure had neither tenure nor security. Supporting my family became more and more of an urgent issue, with children in school and university. I balked against leaving the land I had so wholeheartedly adopted, but when the position in Nigeria was offered, there wasn't much choice.

My move to Nigeria was never intended to be anything other than temporary, even though it still amazes me that I stayed away as long as I did. When I returned to Canada in 1985 the employment situation was still bleak but providentially, a very fine offer was made to me by the Black Cultural Centre. And with that offer came the last of my days of financial insecurity in Canada.

Even though my transition into Canadian society has long been completed, I, like so many others who have had beginnings elsewhere, still harbour a very deep attachment to Africa. It's a profound and persistent attachment, permanently etched on my life and thinking. However, Canada is unequivocally my home. I make this statement without reservation and ambivalence. Canada defies limits: anything is possible. That is the lesson I have learned and the lesson I shall pass on to my children and grandchildren and to all I live with, work with and plan with.

Canada, in spite of its multicultural irresoluteness at times, is proof of an important tenet I've held throughout my life: scholarship is scholarship. Scholarship knows no cultural and ethnic bounds, no definitions along the ludicrous lines of race and colour. And scholarship and education, I believe, give strength to the foundation of a civilized society, a society that can be home for a multitude of diverse people.

If I have made any contribution to Canada, perhaps it has been in bringing an important aspect of Canadian history to the foreground, and in the process, shedding some rays of understanding on our ever-changing interpretation of multiculturalism. In the land of my birth, there was not much a person of colour could do to contribute to the building of the nation. In the land I have come to embrace, all things are possible for one with vision, perseverance and a penchant for hard work.

NOTE: *Dr. Bridglal Pachai's autobiography,* My Africa My Canada, *has been used as a reference in the development of this chapter. Dr. Pachai is currently working on its sequel,* My Canada, My Africa.

Dr. Jan Prsala

Prague, Czechoslovakia—Armdale, Nova Scotia

Dr. Jan Prsala, founder of the Prsala Back Exercise Centre, *is probably his own best advertisement: The first thing you notice about him is his perfect posture. His clear, sparkling eyes also seize your attention, as does his insightful wit generously garnished with pleasing staccato laughter. As his narrative warms, punctuated by a graceful ballet of the hands, you learn that he has suffered and recovered from two herniated disks, that he nonetheless skis, plays tennis and hikes with the vigour of a man half his age, and that he was once a rising volleyball star. What silently emerges in parallel to the spoken word is his capacity for pushing himself to the limit (without which he would have never made it to Canada), for being inherently caring, for his wholehearted devotion to family.*

A coach and professor at Dalhousie University until his retirement in 1988, a man of languages and a life-long learner, Prsala is easily remembered for his dedication, compassion, and commitment to quality education.

"It took six and a half years for Canada to grant our citizenship," he recounts with a chuckle. "But we made it, and now we're here to stay."

Throughout his first decade on Canadian soil Jan Prsala's daily ritual included giving thanks at the family dinner table for the gift of Canada. "That's not to suggest everything was rosy right from the beginning, nor to downplay the difficulties of the early months: the second-guessing, homesickness and language barriers. But we knew from the start our two children would have a decent chance at a better future here, and we kept ourselves focused on that conviction."

Prsala's personal ambition to leave his native Czechoslovakia had anteceded the birth of his children by many years. From the time of

his own childhood he had harboured a simmering urge to migrate to the perceived greener pastures of North America. "My father had a friend in our village who had emigrated to the United States before the war. I was about seven when he returned with his sons for a visit in 1937. I remember noticing the boys, so self-assured with their newly acquired American mannerisms and clothing, and I envied them. During the war I resented my father for not having left earlier as well, when he could have done so quite freely."

Prsala was born in rural Czechoslovakia in 1930, the youngest of three children. "From the beginning my parents, who both spoke German, instilled in us the importance of foreign languages. Proficiency in German was especially crucial, they maintained, because one day soon the Germans would be crossing our borders and occupying our land. They vowed we would be ready for them, and so they forced me to learn German when I started school. Although I resisted with tears, their insight and our family's subsequent preparedness proved to be our lifeline when the Germans finally did arrive.

"But that didn't mean we liked being schooled in German, especially the way the Germans imposed their ways and regime on us. The war years were a hardship; food was severely rationed and its quality was marginal. However, we were fortunate to be spared from gnawing hunger because my father, a high school teacher and principal, knew many people and was a great barterer. He always seemed to have butter and eggs hidden in his coat sleeves. When the war finally ended, we were crazed with relief. I remember my friends and I throwing our German texts around and whooping with ecstasy."

Prsala's high school years were spent in the fragile interlude of freedom that followed, even as the burgeoning clouds of communism roiled on the eastern horizon. "I wanted to study medicine but that was a door not open to me since my father was a patriot known and harassed for his anti-Soviet passions. So I turned to my second interest, sports, which had been my passion throughout high school, and was fortunate to be accepted into physical education studies at the Charles University of Prague."

Two years after graduating as a physical education teacher, Prsala returned to Prague to teach at his alma mater and sign on with one of the country's top-ranking volleyball teams. He married, then abruptly derailed an aspiring career in elite athletics by herniating a lumbar disk. Although in extreme pain over the next decade, he nonetheless continued teaching and studying at the Charles University of Prague, and began making his mark as an extraordinary volleyball coach. "We were blessed with two healthy children and, had it not been for my back pain, life would have been quite blissful at that point."

And yet, deep within, Prsala continued to nurture the possibility that he might one day be able to procure for his children a better future abroad. "I wasn't a member of the Communist party and so was never selected when calls for temporary teaching positions came from Tunisia, Algeria, Iraq and elsewhere. The closest I came was at age 35 when Tunisia offered three temporary coaching contracts. To my surprise, I was the third candidate selected. With great expectation I readied my passport and underwent multiple inoculations against a cadre of diseases. Then, at the last minute Tunisia reneged on the third position and I was dropped from the list. I remember the agonizing letdown but look back on it now as a supreme blessing, the ramifications of which I couldn't have imagined at that time.

"Like my father, I was worried that our country would end up under a long-term communist regime completely controlled by the Soviet Union. We could see it happening bit by bit; the writing was already being manoeuvred onto the wall and life was becoming a little more claustrophobic every day. I desperately wanted to get my family out before the more menacing aspects of communism began intruding on our daily lives, but our borders had already been closed and, to be honest, I knew our chances of leaving were getting slimmer by the day."

Leaving illegally was out of the question. "Perhaps I just wasn't brave enough, but I knew too many people who had tried to leave and failed, with harsh consequences. A friend and his wife who knew the border area well had made meticulous plans to cross at an isolated area where the terrain was particularly difficult. An unexpected snowfall betrayed their intentions and slowed their progress to the point where they became easy prey for the border guards on their heels.

"Another friend succeeded in crossing the border into Austria and boarded a train to head further west. Unbeknown to him, the train would be travelling through a part of Austria that was being held by the Soviet Union at that time. When it was stopped to verify the identity of each passenger, he was taken prisoner and banished to a uranium mine where he endured hard labour and excessive exposure to radiation for many years.

"A third friend fell victim to a swindler who for a fee arranged his escape on a train, buried beneath a load of coal, and then told police at the border where they could find him.

"I couldn't justify such risks, especially since we weren't suffering at the hands of communism at that time. It would have made no sense to gamble my family's fate against such dire odds and consequences."

Yet Prsala doggedly held out hope for his family's deliverance to the outside world. He kept a constant vigil for any possibility that might hold promise and maximized his own prospects by tutoring himself in English and French. When his opportunity did present itself in 1966, it came as an offer from an unlikely source: the Canadian Volleyball Association.

"I happened to notice an advertisement in the paper. Through the Czech Sports Federation, the Canadian Volleyball Association was advertising a six-month contract for a volleyball coach. "I applied and could hardly believe it when I was selected. But there was no time for basking while the paperwork was being readied if I was going to optimize my lone chance of getting out of Czechoslovakia. I hired a tutor to help me with my English and French, and I was also desperately determined that my poor back wouldn't shanghai the contract. I went to several specialists to no avail, until one chiropractor finally held out some hope for my improvement. He began prescribing an excruciating, weight-bearing exercise but after three torturous months the pain suddenly gave way to strength and resilience in my back. The timing was quite miraculous."

While waiting for his contract to materialize, Prsala's exhilaration began giving way to bouts of confusion and self-doubt. Would his limited knowledge of French and English be sufficient? Would his accent irritate? Would he be able to manage the gruelling schedule that had been arranged for him? Would his family be allowed to join him three months later as promised by the Czechoslovakian government? Would the aircraft be safe? One week prior to his departure Prsala experienced the first of what were to be numerous bouts of anxiety. "But I dared not abort my plans. Instead, I prayed a lot and left everything in the hands of the Almighty."

Mere days before his departure, Prsala went on a pilgrimage to his hometown to say goodbye to family and life-long friends. "My heart felt clogged with intense, mixed emotions. What I had so long hoped for was finally happening. My people were saying good-bye temporarily: 'Good luck, see you soon.' But my goodbyes were final. Perhaps I would never see them again. Still, I couldn't tell anyone of my plan to defect, not even my wife."

On September 20, 1967, Prsala boarded a flight on the first leg of his journey to Canada. "I'd never flown before but once I was on the plane I figured since my plan was past the point of undoing, I might as well try to relax. Things would work out somehow." Rather than shrink from his alien surroundings, Prsala characteristically carried on with the same resolve that had kept him bolstered and vigilant throughout the preceding decade. "I knew I had to integrate and figured I might as well start doing so right away. In Frankfurt I had a few hours between flights and purposely struck up a conversation with an English speaking couple at the airport restaurant. It was only the second time in my life that I'd conversed with people fluent in English. On my flight over the Atlantic I wove my way through a fairly effective English/German conversation with a Canadian and a German. Then I dared to think that perhaps my contract might work out after all."

In Toronto Prsala was met by the secretary of the Canadian Volleyball Association. "His Yugoslavian accent put me at ease, as did his wife's Russian accent. They took me to their home in a huge car, and over the course of the evening we chatted and I had this perception that my English was getting better and better by the minute. I remember thinking, 'This is a piece of cake. Within a few months I'll be speaking like I was born here.' The next morning I woke up with my rudimentary English and realized I'd been deluded by several glasses of soft drink that must have been liberally spiked with alcohol."

The itinerary drawn up for Prsala allowed no time for acclimatization. The morning after his arrival he was taken to Ryerson College for his first three-hour presentation on volleyball theory. "I remember controlling my nervousness by doing deep breathing in a nearby park. Then it was time to face an audience of 200.

"Before leaving home I had prepared a handbook with my material in Czech on the left-hand page, and columns on the right-hand page containing translations into English and French. That morning it proved to be my life saver. After the first half of the session I was feeling guardedly pleased with myself, particularly when a former Czech who had known my father came forward and congratulated me. At the end of the session I was able to understand and respond to questions from the audience. Many came forward to shake my hand and offer their appreciation. Finally, after all my anxious moments of self doubt, I knew I could do it. A tremendous weight came off my shoulders."

The following day Prsala repeated his presentation to a group in nearby Hamilton, this time without the assistance of his handbook. From that point on he never had to refer to it again.

On his third day in Canada, Prsala flew to Vancouver where an onerous schedule awaited him. "I was ferried from one school gymnasium to another, doing presentations, clinics and demonstrations for people of various age groups and skill levels. As I grew more comfortable I began incorporating jokes and anecdotes into my delivery to make it more varied and entertaining."

Over the next several months Prsala took his volleyball clinic to every major Canadian city and numerous towns along the way, conducting more than 100 presentations to over 5000 participants. He travelled from Newfoundland to Vancouver Island, veering up to the Northwest Territories long enough to deliver his volleyball message to the native residents there.

"It was an extraordinary way to experience Canada and the trip to the north was especially memorable, but I soon became mentally and physically exhausted. The constant worry about whether the Czechoslovakian government would follow through on their promise to allow my family to join me in Canada was also wearing me down. Without them my plans were nothing.

"All of these stresses combined to spark the occasional anxiety attack, which usually struck with little warning during a teaching session and rendered me barely able to speak, feeling as if my head would explode. The last thing I wanted was to fall apart, so I coped by struggling for self-control long enough to announce a break and then taking a mild non-prescription drug to help me regain my composure."

As if the strain of speaking and thinking in English every day for weeks on end was not enough to test his mettle, Prsala began a circuit that would take him through French-speaking Quebec. "In addition to exhausting teaching sessions, I was also interviewed by the media, in French. Television interviews were the most daunting of all. Not only was I uncomfortable, but so were the hosts. It was particularly awkward when I misunderstood, and therefore responded inappropriately, to an unrehearsed question.

"In Quebec City I was one of three guests interviewed on an hour-long, television talk show. I was just beginning to relax after the show when I was ushered to a make-up room. The realization slowly pored over me that the previous performance had been a rehearsal, and now I would have to endure the real thing all over again. Looking back, I think I owe credit to the generous make-up for helping me to 'save face' or at least giving me a face to hide behind as I struggled my way through a second time.

"In Montreal I was the only instructor for a weekend-long volleyball clinic with 120 participants. Since about 25 of them could not speak French, I had to follow what I said in French with its English translation. Again the clinic was successful and well-rated, but again extremely stressful. I consumed more nerve-calming medication in Quebec than in any other province."

In early December Prsala returned to Toronto for a break during which time he soothed his shattered nerves by resting, taking long, rigorous walks on wintry streets and playing volleyball for a local team. He tried not to dwell on his most dreaded fear: that, even as their arrival time drew near, his family might be denied passage at the last minute.

Prsala began renting an apartment on December 22, the day his family finally disembarked in Toronto. "Words can't describe my relief and my joy. And then, on Christmas day so many generous and unexpected gifts arrived from my volleyball friends, more than my children had ever seen or even dreamed of before. In the surreal haze of the holidays that followed, we settled in as a family and savoured our reunion."

In January, however, reality set in. Prsala enrolled his children in school, then flew to the west coast for a month-long assignment, leaving his family who spoke no English to cope by themselves. "We recall that January as our month of tears."

Even though Prsala's volleyball contract was expiring at the end of March, he applied for and was granted an extension of his family's visas, a routine procedure now that they were in Canada. "Already distressed, my wife was even more distraught when I told her we would not be returning to Czechoslovakia. She had worked in international radio and when spring came and a new democratic government under the leadership of Dubcek was installed, she was adamant things had changed enough there to warrant our going home. She cried out of homesickness every day until August, when the news broke that Soviet forces had moved in to occupy our country. Thousands of Czechoslovakians, including her colleagues in radio were ruthlessly dismissed from their work and persecuted. Abruptly her tears stopped flowing, and it dawned on her just how blessed we were to have made it to Canada."

In the meantime Prsala had accepted employment with Dalhousie University's School of Physical Education and moved his family to Halifax. Halfway through his second year of teaching and coaching, an opportunity to complete his own education was unexpectedly proffered by a friend and former colleague at the Charles University of Prague. "I had come to Canada just one credit short of a PhD in biomechanics. I had completed the course work for this last course, on the history of philosophy, but left Czechoslovakia before my final exam could be scheduled. Now this professor was arranging for me to take the exam in Halifax in September.

"As soon as I realized the exam was in the wings, I began studying at six every morning, and after a day of teaching would revisit my textbooks again until well past midnight. Over the summer I studied 12 hours a day. And then in September, when my head was filled to overflowing with pedantry, and in Czech no less, the exam was indefinitely shelved due to political turmoil on the home front. However, as long as the possibility remained that I might still be able to write it, my only option was to spend hours every day reviewing the material, preserving the fragile equilibrium in my brain. We were looking after a friend's cat at the time and I remember envying it as it luxuriated in the window with nothing more on its agenda than to soak up the autumn sunshine."

In November Prsala, exhausted, was finally able to sit for the exam, which he passed with little difficulty. The university invited him to travel to Prague the following spring to have his degree personally conferred; he dared not accept the invitation. In turn, the university refused to mail it to him. "But my professor came through for me again. He convinced them the degree was rightfully mine, and I received it many months later via the Czechoslovakian Consulate. I'm greatly indebted to him; he risked his reputation for me, and in fact he was later dismissed for being 'unreliable.'"

Over the next decade Prsala taught, coached and gave volleyball clinics throughout North America. Between 1969 and 1971 he helped coach the Canadian men's national team and in 1971 he served as the team's assistant coach and manager at the Pan American Games in Colombia. That same year he published his first of two volleyball handbooks and sold 4500 copies.

In 1975 Prsala herniated a second lumbar disk and this time chose a combination of surgery, which was only partially successful, and rigorous exercise to enhance his rehabilitation. Seven days after starting his own back exercise ritual he was back in the gym and on the tennis court. However, he knew the time had come to give up coaching. Instead, he chose to shift his focus to the advancement of his academic career. Convinced more than ever that his modified approach to a healthy back was superior to conventional therapies, he selected spinal rehabilitation as his area of research. He went on to write a handbook and produce a video on back health, and designed a series of portable back exercisers for which he holds current Canadian and American patents. Although his methods were initially considered unorthodox by many, including the medical community, the results his long-suffering clients were able to achieve garnered him significant, albeit cautious, attention.

When several physicians began referring their patients to Prsala for back care, he opted for early retirement from Dalhousie University in order to establish his own back care institute.

Over the years he has successfully treated more than a thousand clients and today he is slowly wending his way to real retirement.

Looking back, Prsala finds it easy to pinpoint that aspect of life in Canada which has offered his greatest reward. "We came to Canada for our children's futures and they have done well; one is a pharmacist, the other a physician. We cherish the luxury of not having to worry about their destiny as our parents had to worry about ours. That means everything to us. What more could a parent want?"

The longer we stay here, the less we feel the pull back.

I could deliberate at length about our early years in Canada, but suffice to say they were challenging. Though Helena and I were thankful to have made it here safely when so many didn't, the homesickness and longing for things familiar nonetheless seeped beneath our skin and festered there into the dichotomous emotions of gratitude for new beginnings and grief for the life left behind. Almost involuntarily we endured intense bouts of irrational longing to return to Czechoslovakia, me to the point where I would find myself daydreaming of paddling home across the Atlantic in a kayak.

When you come with a family that speaks no English and a wife who is desperately homesick and you are homesick yourself, life is not easy. When the only English and French you know has been learned from a book or taught to you by someone who knows the language only in theory, and when your pronunciation and intonation are painfully distorted, life is indeed onerous. In retrospect, I'm convinced my language difficulties and the fact I was thrust in front of an audience from the day I arrived, brought on my anxiety attacks in those early years.

Financially there were worries too. My volleyball contract paid $300 a month, of which ten percent had to be forwarded to the Czechoslovakian government. The remainder, I soon realized, wouldn't take us nearly as far in Canada as it would have in Czechoslovakia. But we managed, and for all our challenges and daydreaming and loneliness, we never seriously considered returning to Czechoslovakia. Whenever things got especially rough, we kept ourselves tightly focused on our primary motive for leaving—the future of our children.

Dr. Jan Prsala

TRUE, HALIFAX DID NOT HAVE
THE THOUSAND-YEAR-OLD
HISTORY, CULTURE AND
ARCHITECTURAL BEAUTY OF
PRAGUE, BUT IT DID HAVE
CLEAN AIR AND TIDY,
TREE-LINED STREETS.

Reminding ourselves that the journey of our migration had been like a navigation around icebergs on a moonless night also kept us from wallowing in self-pity.

No, we couldn't feel too sorry for ourselves. Our apartment here more than matched our living conditions in Prague, where we'd shared a flat in a large apartment house with my wife's parents and also, for a time, her brother. That house had originally belonged to my in-laws but like many homeowners they had lost it to a greedy government and become tenants in their own home.

Our financial situation stabilized after I made it onto the Dalhousie University payroll. We acted on the good advice of a Czech friend and took out a 90% mortgage on a $46,000 duplex in the suburbs. We couldn't afford to live in it initially, but it got us into the housing market and by the time we sold it sixteen years later it had tripled in value. I don't understand why so many Canadians still opt to rent when, with a little planning and financial management, they could be building up equity in their own homes.

A milestone occurred when I cashed in my unused return ticket to Czechoslovakia and bought my first well-used car. It meant more to me at the time than any new car would today. It also congealed a sense of belonging in me, for I was now a participant in a distinctly North American ritual. My enthusiasm was not lessened by the lack of a driver's licence. In fact, I was so enamoured with the car at first that I would get up several times during the night to make sure it was still parked out front.

A year went by and the yearnings for our past life slowly began to recede. Already the notion of home had started to become ambiguous, as if we were seeing it through a lens slightly out of focus. No doubt our shifting emotions were accelerated by the political strife that had steamrollered over the landscape shortly after our departure, but also by the life we had begun to carve for ourselves in Canada.

True, Halifax did not have the thousand-year-old history, culture and architectural beauty of Prague, but it did have clean air and tidy, tree-lined streets. The children and I enjoyed the luxury of walking to school and to work. In Prague I'd had to rise at five in the morning, endure an overcrowded streetcar for an hour's ride, and then begin my workday in an unheated gymnasium just as the sun was struggling over the horizon.

In Halifax the ocean was rarely out of sight and we spent much of our free time exploring beaches and rocky coasts. In Prague we recreated in crowded and polluted parks and occasionally travelled by train to the greener, rural landscape. In Halifax you could go to a grocery store and fill your entire cart for about 22 dollars. In Prague food line-ups were the norm. We would stand in line for hours without knowing what was being sold, and often, when we finally made it to the counter, they'd be sold out. Because we had no refrigerator we repeated this time-eroding ritual every day.

Over the years the emotions our homeland once evoked in us have gradually given way to an inner tranquillity. The longer we stay here, the less we feel the pull back. Nineteen years after our arrival we made a pilgrimage back to Czechoslovakia and confirmed what had gradually taken root and grown steadfast in our hearts: that our decision to emigrate had been a wise one, our choice of Canada a blessing.

Nonetheless, time has also served to temper our views of Canada. When we first arrived our eyes beheld no shortcomings, no imperfections, in anything Canadian. We've become more objective, of course, but we still continue to marvel at the range of personal freedom that's laid on the doorstep of every Canadian. We don't have to belong to a political party to advance in our careers. We aren't required to attend meetings designed to evoke homage to the political ideologies of the day. And we can freely speak our minds.

But that's not to say we see no frays in the seams of our Canadian system. On the contrary, several things trouble us or, at the very least, leave us perplexed: the country's onerous debt, induced by unbridled government spending; the burgeoning number of people on social assistance even though the opportunities for work are there if you want them badly enough; the ease with which these systems can be defrauded; the disturbing disparity between rich and poor; the cavalier attitude towards public education; the subtle denigration of inter-generational connectedness among families which seems a uniquely North American trait; the elusiveness of deep friendship.

In spite of our best intentions and efforts, we've not been awfully successful in understanding nor conforming to this society's notion of friendship. We came ready to develop and nurture bonds in our new community similar to what we had enjoyed in Prague. But friendship here seems more vulnerable to being expropriated by the ambitions of power, money and pride. One might expect that an affluent society has the luxury of being less preoccupied with it's wealth, but in fact we North Americans seem disproportionately absorbed with materialism. Much importance is based on the virtue of 'having,' and the bonds of friendship often end up in tatters because of it.

We still grieve the loss of valued friends sacrificed to these ambitions. Perhaps our grief is more poignant because as immigrants we want to feel we are accepted and appreciated by our community. Especially for immigrants, the bonds of friendship, not just with 'our own' but with the mainstream as well, help to validate and solidify our sense of belonging.

Several years after my move to Halifax I was offered a position by the University of Manitoba. I was wooed by phone and by mail but had no desire to leave Nova Scotia. However, a close friend and colleague, originally from Winnipeg, saw this job as his chance to return to his home province and submitted his application. One day as we were chatting I reassured him I wasn't interested in the job, partly because I knew how much he wanted it. As soon as the words had been uttered, and from that day onward, he became a stranger. I was left confused and hurt. Had I inadvertently offended his sense of pride enough to spark the destruction of what I thought had been a strong bond?

Another valued friend and I were to team-teach a summer course together. He would teach two thirds of the curriculum and I would cover the remainder. We would both be paid accordingly. Then he asked to switch workloads because of his wife's pregnancy, and I agreed. However, an administrative error resulted in his being paid for what he'd originally been contracted to teach. I assumed he would eventually reimburse me and said nothing for a long time. When I eventually did broach the subject, he dissolved our friendship on the spot. It took several years before he returned what he had been overpaid.

Again I was left disillusioned and unsettled. How could a friendship be this disposable? French Canadians, I think, have a concept of friendship that's more similar to what we grew up with in Czechoslovakia: they are less formal and more gregarious in an unselfconscious way. Even their language is friendlier. And their friendships are mutually and unconditionally nurturing. But within our circle in English Canada, we, personally, have found such strong, enduring and unconditional bonds to be somewhat elusive. And that's been difficult for us.

Still, we have nonetheless been genuinely accepted by our many acquaintances and we've managed to forge a real sense of place for ourselves in our community. No doubt our past remains an inherent part of what we are; I suspect we will always have an involuntary toe-hold in the door of the home we left behind, even if that home now exists largely in our imagination. In that sense we'll always be set apart from those Canadians who were born here, who have amassed all of their experiential and emotional baggage in this country. But to this we are resolved: that Canada has our allegiance. Indeed, Canada has our heart.

Betty Ramshaw

LONDON, ENGLAND—NOKOMIS, SASKATCHEWAN

To know the prairies is to know its morning and evening light,
waves of subtle colour—aqua, rose, gold and brown—
that undulate in a random pattern over sprawling pastures
and grain fields stretched to the edge of the horizon. To know the
prairies is to know its unspoken creed, the creed of unlocked doors,
unconditional hospitality, neighbour helping neighbour.
Betty Ramshaw knows the prairies. A war bride, farmer, writer,
raconteur, former activist for employee rights and advocate for
continuing education for older adults, she has lived and embraced
the prairie creed for more than five decades.
"It's the people. I've never harboured bad feelings in all my years
here," she says. "That says something about the people. It's not just
me rolling over; I'm not the rolling-over type."

The first thing Betty Ramshaw learned to do when she came to Canada was drive the tractor. "My husband had a job grading the highways and he needed a driver since he had to control the blade on the back. I'd never driven anything before and the day I arrived he took me into the pasture with it and turned me loose."

For the plucky war bride, it was just one more challenge to take in stride. Born in London in 1925, Ramshaw had been raised in poverty in Bethel Green, the city's infamous east end. "My father was a fish fryer and worked twelve-hour days, six days a week. My mother sewed ten pairs of 'whites'—cricket trousers—every day at home. We lived in row housing until we were bombed out in 1940."

After only three years of formal schooling, Ramshaw was sent to work in a clothing factory and apprenticed as a tailor at age 16. She toiled in several factories and when the Second World War began raging across Europe she was directed into war work.

Ramshaw and her girlfriends regularly went to the Hadleigh barracks dances where they revelled in their popularity with the soldiers who outnumbered them ten to one. By late 1945 order was being restored across the continent and the British girls knew the dances, an idiosyncratic by-product of war, would soon come to an end. When the Hadleigh barracks hosted one of its last socials, Ramshaw—then Betty Stichbury—and her friends were there as usual. In the dark hall with the band at one end and the bar along its smoky length she met Art Ramshaw, a Canadian soldier, who fancied her so much that after their first dance he proclaimed, "I'm going to marry you."

"We had been given tickets on a raffle for a chicken and, you guessed it—we won the prize. Well, one thing led to another, he came to dinner, we fell in love and eight weeks later, on December 22, 1945, we were married in the little Saxon Church of St. Peters. Within the month my new husband was on his way back to Canada."

Before long Ramshaw's life had returned to its usual routine, the memory of her husband and their marriage reduced to a hazy dream. But a letter from the Canadian Embassy the following June wrenched her back into reality. Canada was calling for its war brides, some 48,000 of them, and Ramshaw was to sail on the SS *Aquitania* on July 26. She coped with the inevitable parting from her parents and brothers by busying herself with preparations. But the unknown loomed in front of her and weighted her heart with apprehension. "Dear God, help me" she wrote decades later in an essay entitled *Oh Canada*. "I was only twenty years old and had made a commitment before God to love and follow a man I could hardly remember."

However, Ramshaw was not one to wallow in despair and had every intention to carry out her commitment. Her family never questioned the wisdom of her decision; instead they extended their full support. "My brothers gave me five hundred dollars, every cent they had, for a return ticket in case it didn't work out. 'Give it a year and if you don't like it, then come home,' they said. 'And if it does work out, keep the money and put it to good use.' I felt safe with that. I put the money in the bank. Much as I loved England, I never intended to come back. The money eventually went to hire machinery and buy seed, after we'd lost several crops. We never spent it; it just dwindled away."

Impeccably dressed in a suit, girdle, stockings and high heel shoes, Ramshaw arrived in Nokomis, Saskatchewan on August 6 with visions of rose gardens, trees and green grass on the merry-go-round of her imagination. In contrast, the unoccupied homestead she was escorted to stood lifeless with it's bleached, wind-burned siding and blank windows. There wasn't a neighbour nor tree for miles. "Art was happy, he had been born in this house. But all I saw was brown, baked wood, cracked windows, dirt and desolation."

Nonetheless, mere weeks later the Ramshaws had the house presentable enough to live in. They then turned their attention to surviving the winter. "We bought two stoves, a McClearly Royal Charm—'Mac'—which turned out to be a woman hater, and a Quebec heater that wasn't much better. Art could light Mac with a piece of paper, a handful of wood and one coal. But Mac would mock my attempts by disdainfully puffing black smoke in my face. The house got so cold we couldn't sleep upstairs. We had a broken single bed and a buffalo rug on the floor. At night we moved the rug to the bed."

A year later Ramshaw's mother emigrated from England. Although grateful for family, her mother's arrival added to her emotional tailspin. "I was happy to have her but her marriage was over and she was depressed. She knew what I'd given up to come here and could see for herself I had nothing, no pots, pans, nothing. I was embarrassed and I worried that she was second-guessing my decision, which made me take a good, hard look at it myself. I didn't think I'd done a stupid thing but I didn't want her thinking it either. " (Ramshaw's mother settled in Nokomis and lived there until her death in 1994, at age 95.)

From 1946 to 1948 the Ramshaws struggled to eke out a living on the farm. They raised chickens, cows and horses in an aging, roofless barn, grew crops that mostly failed, and graded the roads. In 1948 Ramshaw gave birth to a stillborn child, and on a lonely winter day she briefly considered plunking herself down in a snow bank so she could freeze to death. "I had wanted this baby so badly. I had grown up in a factory environment, all those girls around, and now nobody. Even though my mother was here and everyone was nice, there were so few people. It was lonely. I needed the familiarity of my own. Maybe I had more growing up to do. The doctor *had* told me that if I wanted to be a mother I would have to start acting like a woman."

Ramshaw became pregnant again in 1949. Because she was deemed high risk and because life on the farm was an unending, futile struggle, the couple relocated to Moose Jaw. "Our daughter was born there and Art and I worked wherever we could. At one point Art was holding down three jobs, including one with Canadian Pacific Railways. I answered an ad in the paper for a position with the Prairie Cloak Company. They were going to make reversible parkas, plain on one side, plaid on the other. The owner said he'd pay me a dollar for each one I made, a good deal for me since I'd been factory trained and was fast. The first day I made 17. And he refused to pay me."

Instead, the owner installed Ramshaw as the plant's manager, with a wage of 53 cents an hour. With few other options available, Ramshaw was forced to accept. However, it wasn't long before she found the owner demanding favours from some of his employees. "In the English factories you put up with a lot of terrible conditions but not with that. I talked to the girls and told them they didn't have to put up with that. One day I was showing a girl how to use a machine and he came along and said something inappropriate to her, and I told him to leave her alone. He continued talking to her so I picked up a box and rammed it on his head."

Ramshaw was dismissed but rather than retreating meekly to her home, she reported her experience to the Trades and Labour Council. Shortly thereafter the factory was shut down. "But then people were upset because they'd lost their jobs. Labourers are so vulnerable without rights and protection."

After a string of jobs including tailoring at home and mending for a dry cleaning company, Ramshaw and her husband were ready to re-evaluate living in Moose Jaw. "Our second child, a boy, was nine months old when Art lost his CPR job on Christmas eve of 1951. We had to decide, were we going to live here and work for the city all our lives, paying rent, the bills, and having nothing left. Or would we go back to the country to work for ourselves. Come spring we returned to the farm.

"We bought 1000 chickens and 1400 turkeys and gradually built up a herd of cattle. I took in sewing and we planted huge gardens. Art said I would have canned the fence pickets if they'd been edible."

Slowly the Ramshaws inched ahead, but every available penny was put back into the farm. In 1953 they borrowed five hundred dollars to have electricity brought in. "You name it, we did it to make ends meet. Art used to clean barns for other people. I raised 500 chickens a year and could clean, pluck and package 50 a day. I made all my kids' clothes. The neighbours would give me the coats their kids outgrew and I'd turn them inside out and make new ones for mine. We sold 15 dozen eggs to a cafe every week, which went to pay for our daughter's music lessons. Our disposable income was $5.35 per week."

Almost a decade of hard work later, the Ramshaws had to concede that the land alone could not afford them a decent living, especially if they hoped to fix up their house and repay their debts. "Crops grew and failed, that was the reality of Saskatchewan. Grasshoppers ate their way through our lives, and throughout it all the wind just blew and blew."

In the 1960's Ramshaw's husband began working in the potash mines in nearby Lanigan. A second son was born. The couple cashed in a life insurance policy worth $4000 and began fixing up their house. "We put in sewer and water. The flush toilet was finally installed in 1968, on the day our daughter got married."

A few years later the Ramshaws decided to convert their home into a bungalow by removing its upper storey. The day after the extensive renovations were completed, the house caught fire. "Fortunately it was mostly smoke damage and damage to the woodwork. Our friends and family were a tremendous help in getting it all fixed up again."

In the early 1970's Ramshaw got her first taste of higher education when she began teaching tailoring and general sewing for Humboldt Community College. "A friend and I teamed up to do this together. First we had to take a one-week home economics course at the University of Saskatchewan's Saskatoon campus, which was rather boring. They tried to teach us how to do a bound buttonhole in a way that would 'only' take 15 minutes. I showed the instructor a way that would take only three minutes, the way I'd learned to do it in the factory. But she continued to teach it her way."

For the next five years Ramshaw and her colleague taught evening courses for beginners right through to advanced, at various locations within their sixty-mile territory. "The classes all went from seven to ten o'clock, and then we'd have the long drive home on these dark, country roads. Many nights we didn't get home until after midnight, which is why I finally gave it up."

In 1976 Ramshaw started training and working as a nurse's aide at the Nokomis Health Centre. Two years later trouble loomed. "I had been working my fifteen guaranteed days per month for about two years when I went in one day and found they had hired someone new and reduced my days to two per month. This new person was a friend of the Director of Nursing. When I asked him about it he said, 'We can get a dozen like you off the street any day.' I had no rights, plain and simple.

"We also had no pension plan. But one of the women on staff had worked at a unionized hospital and so we began organizing ourselves to become unionized. We had the first meeting at my house, and management kept driving by to see whose cars were parked in the yard. I told the women, 'Sign here because if you don't, you'll be unemployed tomorrow morning.' So they signed and that's how we got the union in. I became the shop steward.

"There were so many little injustices. I remember one woman who came to me with all of her slips; she wondered if she'd been entitled to a raise six months earlier. When I asked the Director of Nursing about it he said, 'She doesn't need it, she's got a husband. We gave the money to So-and-So who needs it more; her husband is an alcoholic.' The union fought it and the first woman got her raise. The second was allowed to keep her money as a gift.

"Then management called me up in front of the board, I hated those meetings. They were so angry with me. But I told them I was going to continue pulling for the employees rights. We kept documentation on everything and there wasn't much trouble after that."

Ramshaw retired from the Nokomis Health Centre in 1989. Throughout her working years, even when she herself had been the underdog, she had championed the cause of those more fragile and vulnerable. When her children were due to start school in a decrepit building, she was on the front line of the parents' group demanding a better facility. They had invited the local politician in for a tour, made sure the school looked and smelled its worst and hinted the press would be informed if nothing was done. Nokomis got it's new school.

When her youngest reached kindergarten age, Ramshaw decided the town had been without such a facility long enough. She organized a drama group to raise money for a teacher and supplies and rallied the townsfolk together to build equipment. Mere months later the area youngsters had a kindergarten to attend.

In the early 1990's The University of Regina established a seniors education committee to study the education needs of the province's older population. Ramshaw became involved at the local level and before long found herself on the committee. "When they started this, they didn't realize how important it is to have continuing education for older people. But for many this was their chance at a renewed connection with their community, and the concept caught on like a prairie fire. Distance learning, they called it. Bringing the courses to the people rather than the people to the campus. They began offering courses in each of the four areas around here, scheduling each course at a different time so participants could take all four in the same session if they wanted to. They're short courses, or a series of lectures or presentations. We've had courses on art, writing, computers, money management, theatre, just about anything. The idea is to keep communities together and seniors well. If people are busy they don't have time to sit around and be sick.

"There was this one man, Norman, who used to attend all the courses. We offered line dancing, he couldn't line dance so he made the coffee. We offered an art class, he bought all the supplies, sat and watched, and made coffee. The courses were his life. And he always used to say he wished he'd gone to university. When he died a few years ago he donated his body to science. He'd always wanted to go to university, and by golly, he finally got there."

Ramshaw became so involved in distance learning for older adults that she was invited to travel to Ottawa to further promote Saskatchewan's experimental model, which has since been adopted by several universities around the world. In 1996 she spoke at Talis International, an international conference and research seminar on older adult education at the University of Regina.

She's also become a guest lecturer at the Saskatchewan Institute of Applied Science and Technology, speaking to student nursing aides on love and sexuality in the elderly. "I remind them that the people they'll be serving once had credit cards, drove cars, and lived normal busy lives."

Ramshaw's personal education continues as well. She's joined a local writers' group and has written several essays and stories, some of which have found their way into anthologies. "I write mostly about my childhood in London, which was not an easy time. I don't write much about Canada; writers tend to ruminate on strife and struggle, and there's not enough discontent in my life here." She has also begun reading her work at various community functions and is in increasing demand as a guest speaker. "I'm asked to give motivational presentations to the veterans, and I go to schools and talk about the children of war."

Today the Ramshaws rent out their five quarters of land and, like many Saskatchewan farmers, live with the knowledge that the next generation won't be following in their footsteps. "Our daughter moved to British Columbia and our youngest son is an ordained minister. Our oldest son says he can make more money in a month as a mechanic than he can in a year of farming, which is true. Our grandchildren aren't interested, and even if they were, it would take hundreds of thousands of dollars just to buy the machinery.

"Our oldest boy will probably inherit the house when we go. All I want him to do is continue taking care of the flower bed in front, the one that contains my mother's ashes and will one day contain ours. What he does with it after that, I don't care."

When I first came here I thought,
this is the land God forgot to finish.

The hardest thing about emigrating was leaving my family, but as far as moving to another country, there were no great trepidations. There was the terrible sadness of leaving what you love and are familiar with, and one does love where one lives. But there was also a sense of adventure, new beginnings. We'd just gone through the war so we had this hope for a better tomorrow. I was in love and that was all that mattered.

Art had told me what it was like in Saskatchewan but it hadn't registered with me, so when I came I was truly shocked. The houses were all shacks, and not a tree around them. Nothing for miles and miles.

When I first came here I thought, this is the land God forgot to finish. It looked incomplete, empty. And there was no water, no electricity, no way to get around. But my husband had promised me he'd work like hell, and he did. We both did.

The hardships and setbacks we had over the next decades, and we had many of them, were not because *he* was a failure or *I* was a failure. No, they were due to drought, machinery that wouldn't work, the baby that shouldn't have died, things beyond our control.

The people here were great, right from the start. I remember the marvellous shower they gave us. All the men wore overalls and they had this darndest music with violins—Art plays violin too, if you can ever get him going—and everyone was stomping and hopping. Canadians are the worst dancers; they hippity hippity hop, they don't really dance. Everyone was wonderful and I've still got friends today that I made back then.

Being around all those welcoming people and meeting Art's family, I knew I was with good people and I would be okay. But yet, there was the loneliness to deal with too. It's hard to explain. I was lonely for England and yet I knew I didn't want to go back.

The poverty of my first decade in Canada didn't help. Not that I feared poverty, I had grown up with it. I can make clothes out of cast-offs; I can grow a large garden and feed my family. But the shortage of money was bad, a real slayer of the spirit. I never knew when a crisis might hit that would do us in, that would be beyond our control. When our daughter was nine, she had her appendix removed and the doctor demanded fifty-seven dollars. He was going to take it to a collection agency if we didn't pay. We borrowed it, I don't remember from where anymore.

When our children were very young I had pneumonia, but the doctor wouldn't come out because he knew we couldn't pay him. Art ended up borrowing from his mother to buy the drugs I needed. Being in these situations frightened me but they also made me more prepared after that. Debt is a horror; every cent you make is for the debt and there's no money for a lamp wick, and you ration your lamp fuel and when the day's fuel is gone, there's nothing to do but go to bed. I wouldn't want to go through that again.

The other thing that was difficult was to pretend you weren't poor. Even though everyone in the community was poor, you had your pride. My brothers never knew how poor we were. I always had something put away so that if they suddenly were to turn up, I could make a decent meal. My daughter said recently, "Remember when I was around ten and we still didn't have power and lived on cracked eggs and oatmeal that year." Every penny we made off the land went back to pay for the land. And when that was paid for we bought more, so there was never any extra money. The land was only paid off about 14 years ago.

I think if I brought anything to Canada, it's my sense of justice for people who work under difficult conditions. My mother toiled at home for pennies. I hear all these things about how nice it is for mothers to sew at home. Well, it's a sweatshop when all they're doing is using your machine, your power, your thread, your scissors, and paying you a pittance. I know what sweatshops are. So when I came here I was philosophically already in the left-wing camp. I never went around looking for trouble wherever I worked, but when I saw injustice or unfairness being inflicted I tried to do something about it.

I love Saskatchewan. Maybe it's because it's a poor province, and I know about poverty and being the underdog. Saskatchewan always seems left out, even in the national weather forecast. I think that's why I feel a kinship with it, and motherly towards it. I was strong to begin with, but this province has made me stronger. England is my birthplace and although I don't like people putting it down, I wouldn't exchange it for Canada. I look at it now and see that it's narrow and confining. There's no confinement here, no rules of class. I can be anybody I want to be, and I've broken many barriers and made many friends. In Canada I don't have to know my place; I belong anywhere within its borders.

When you first leave for a new country, you can't look back because every time you do you'll see something you miss, something that breaks your heart a little bit. Embrace your new country, settle in and do something with your life. As long as you harbour a possibility that you might go back, you won't settle in. You have to start thinking, 'I can't go back because it's no longer the way I left it anyway.' But some people have a harder time with it than others. I have a friend who's been back 22 times and is now finally feeling settled. We knew a lady who came out the year after I did, and she never stopped grumping—they didn't cut the meat right, didn't make the bread right, butter didn't taste right, jam had too many seeds in it, and so on. Maybe some people aren't completely committed when they decide to immigrate, or maybe they just have too much time on their hands.

By all means, bring what's in your bloodstream with you. Bring your culture and your little recipes and remedies, and your old wives tales too. Add to it what you can learn here. I still make roast beef and Yorkshire pudding, but I've also learned better cooking here. I've learned from the Italians and Germans and Ukrainians. That's what makes a new country. My eight grandchildren are a mixture of English, Swedish, Scottish, Icelandic and Cree. Art's family is British, so he and I are of the same particular paint pot. But we've added some colour to our pot and just look at the marvellous mix we have now. That's nation building.

I went back to England 21 years after I arrived, when I was 41. It was a sentimental journey; I wanted to see and smell everything one more time. And it made me weep. Then I went back in 1991, did all the touristy things, had a lovely holiday, and felt absolutely nothing. I no longer fit in, and I have no wish to go back.

I used to think God had forgotten to finish the prairies. But if you take a close look at the light and the beauty of the land, you'll see that it's perfect. If you live here long enough, you'll find it's grown on you and stolen your heart. At dusk you can see the colours in the sky; they're all around you but you don't really experience them until you've lived here awhile. The people are like that too. They're not prominent, but once you're here you begin to notice and appreciate them. And then you know you're among decent people and life will be good.

Dr. Roz Roach

*The rambling, two-storey brick home on a tree-lined Toronto street
sits shoulder-to-shoulder with its look-alike sisters. Brambly
bushes rise and fall around the porched entryway, evoking notions
of home, hearth and security. But Women's Healing Place is no
ordinary home for, behind it's doors, women are being helped to
discover the tools they carry within them to live their lives to the
fullest. Women's Healing Place is the brainchild of Dr. Roz Roach,
psychotherapist, academic, writer, tireless activist for equal rights
and opportunity.*

*In the sun-drenched sitting room with the cozy cushions, Roach sits
poised and elegant, a woman whose personal evolution has left her
supremely comfortable in her skin. She speaks ardently, sentences
tumbling out one after the other in rapid-fire succession, generously
punctuated with laughter as warm and encompassing as a favourite
woolen wrap.*

*"I feel at home in many places," she says. "I'm a citizen of
Planet Earth."*

D r. Roz Roach clearly remembers that when her Montreal relatives sent for her, she wasn't at all thrilled about leaving the
neighbourhood and countryside she had grown up in. Not that
she'd had an ideal childhood in rural Trinidad. Far from it.

"My reluctance was about not wanting to leave what was familiar: my
aunts and cousins, the sunshine, the crowded, noisy camaraderie,
my sense of place there. But it wasn't about fear of missing my immediate family. Although I was only 13, I wasn't very emotionally connected to them."

The youngest of five children, Roach had learned early on to be
independent, her own unwavering ally. After the death of her mother,

her father remarried and had six more children, the eldest three years younger than Roach. "After my father's second marriage I went to live with my grandmother and aunt, and although I was in my father's home from time to time, I never had a real relationship with the children of his second family."

In her grandmother's home Roach was not long in discovering that she, with her coarse black hair, black skin and African features, sat solidly on the bottom rung of the family ladder. "My grandmother was a woman of Spanish descent who had married a black African. I was the darkest in the family and she never failed to tell me so. Not just her, but all of Trinidadian society. It was a societal thing: if you looked a certain way, you were beautiful, and if you looked different, you were not.

"Here's what came out of the colonization of Trinidad: the darker you were, the uglier you were. The fairer your skin, the prettier you were. And the longer your hair, the prettier you were, the straighter your nose the prettier you were. That's the message we got from the British. The people who 'made it' were light skinned, I won't say white because there was so much mixture due to the mission marriages. In the days of my childhood, the societal struggle in Trinidad came down to this: the lighter your colouring, the better you were."

Because Roach began showing considerable academic potential shortly after entering school, she was awarded a government allowance to cover schooling expenses. Suddenly both her father and grandmother, who had heretofore been mildly indifferent to her existence, began expressing great interest in her. A tug-of-war ensued between them, both wanting the child in order to have access to the allowance.

"I knew it wasn't about Roz, it was about the money I had coming, which was intended for books and schooling. My father's wife, who was East Indian, made it very clear I did not need an education. I needed to learn to cook and clean and iron so that when I grew up I could get myself a man. She herself had no schooling, did not know how to read nor write, so education was not important to her. But I would protest and talk back, sharply and in-your-face. I would challenge her and then she'd be even more determined that I should not read. It was her way to keep me down. She kept me out of school for a year and taught me Indian cuisine, how to keep a spotless home and garden. She was extremely obsessed with cleanliness; that was her way of being a successful adult.

"I don't remember my father ever using my school money for me. At times my grandmother attempted to, on essentials like shoes, but never books."

For all the indifference and negativity Roach endured at the hands of her guardians, she did find refuge in one family member: an older brother she still cherishes looked out for her, and a favourite aunt was adamant she would have a good education. "Conrad was simply wonderful, always the optimist with a ready laugh. My aunt played a significant mother role, both directly and indirectly. For every time that I was told education was a waste of time, she was there to reinforce how essential and important it really was."

Religion further served to assign Roach to the back rows of the marginalized. "I came from a very Catholic family and every week we would go to confession. I would make up sins to confess. (How silly the notion that children sin. If sin is evil intentionally committed, then children and sin don't go together.) Coming from confession one day I started thinking, 'If I was to be run over by a car right now I would go straight to heaven.' It suddenly occurred to me that I could so easily step into the traffic, and I was idly pondering this thought when my mind suddenly exploded with the message: No Way! I wasn't going to waste my life this way. So instead I went home, sat on the back step and planned what I would do with my future."

In retrospect, Roach largely credits her survival to her own inner strength. Rather than internalize the neglect she was suffering, she chose instead to focus on the concrete fact that time was on her side. If she could bide her time and come away intact from a childhood of hurt and rejection, the future could be hers. "I remember the day I made a commitment to take responsibility for my own destiny. I had felt all along that I had come to the planet with a purpose, and I stayed very connected with that sense of purpose. I knew that if I could wait my turn to grow up and keep looking forward, things would turn out well. I did a lot of self-talk."

Staying connected to her sense of purpose also served Roach well during her student years in Montreal. "Why did we choose Canada? For economic opportunity, which included education. In the 1950's many Caribbean women, my Montreal aunts and cousins included, came here to work as domestics. They came not so much for the work as for the opportunities that would benefit the next generation. They came to open the doors, and they reminded me over and over that education was the key to a better life."

For all her personal fortitude and academic competence, it nonetheless took Roach a lot of self-talk to propel herself through high school. She felt alone and disconnected in Montreal, without a community to lean on and contribute to. "I was the black kid, the one with the accent, the one who didn't speak French. I felt as if I'd moved to another planet."

High school endured and completed, Roach enrolled in a nursing program at Montreal's Dawson College in the early 1970's. That was followed with studies in science at Vanier College and in family life education at Marie Victoria College. She began working as a nurse and practised in all areas of nursing, including psychiatric, to enhance her general understanding of the profession. "Even though I now still work as a nurse one day a month, I decided that nursing was not for me; people would take and take and take without giving back, and I couldn't replenish myself fast enough. But the experience did influence me to take an undergraduate degree in applied social science and behavioural science at Concordia University."

Roach financed her education with two nursing jobs at different Montreal hospitals. "I went to school all day, worked from 3:30 to midnight, and moonlighted at another hospital on weekends. I kept that up for about nine years; at times I thought I was killing myself slowly."

Although her motivation came from within, Roach found her resolve quietly tempered by the attitudes, inadvertent and otherwise, of acquaintances who felt her personal goals were set unrealistically high. "I had so often been told, not intentionally unkindly, by black friends or nursing colleagues that I shouldn't aim so high, that 'for a Black' I had achieved plenty and it was time to be satisfied. On the other hand, my accomplishments also threatened them. They wanted me to lower my goals so I wouldn't make them look bad or feel incompetent or inferior. They weren't comfortable with me having something they didn't have."

Occasionally the backlash was more unsettling. Roach recalls the time a hopeful companion, feeling rebuffed when she declined a date to the movies in favour of working on her studies, harshly derided her. "Take your papers," he snorted, "and use them to wipe your ass. You'll never get a decent job."

"It was another quiet and powerful motivator," Roach says fervently.

For the woman who had spent much of her life as a loner, succour came in the latter part of her nurse's training in the form of an extremely supportive husband whom she refers to as her partner. "After we met in the early 1970's he quickly became, and still is, my dearest friend. He's very much like I am, except that I'm spontaneous and a risk taker while he's more contemplative. From the beginning we've walked the same path, side by side, not one in front of the other. He was totally supportive of my work, concerned I worked too hard, and every night when I finished my nursing shift he would have my bath ready and my dinner waiting on the warmer. And he would ask what I wanted to wear the next day and get it ready, iron it if necessary."

Roach followed her undergraduate degree with training in individual and group psychotherapy at the Allan Memorial Institute, the first black woman and nurse to do so, then did her master's and doctoral degrees in medical anthropology and trans-cultural psychiatry at McGill University.

"The McGill interview was provocative; they asked me about Freud and I told them I didn't know about Freud but I could tell them about Martin Luther King. When I was accepted I made a commitment to myself that I wouldn't be their token Black; I rebelled against everything in the three or four years I was there.

"I never set out with the vision to become anything in particular. Each of my studies propelled me on to learn something more, to take a particular tangent. At Concordia I realized I needed to figure out my own self before I could be of benefit to others. That took me into psychotherapy training. While there I became very concerned about the use of medication in psychiatry and figured there had to be a better way to help people deal with their problems. That lead to my graduate work in trans-cultural psychiatry, studying psychiatry in different cultures and how these cultures heal people without using medication."

Her convocations came and went; however, Roach pointedly chose not to attend them. Instead, she opted to celebrate her accomplishments in ways more meaningful than the usual cap-gown-and-handshake affair. "Convocations don't mean anything. It's people with no real relationship to each other all behaving a certain way, dressed a certain way, to make it look like a celebration. And who determines the clothes, the rituals? And why? Why a silly cap and not a donkey cart? I prefer to celebrate in my own inner space, or with those who are special to me. It's about choice, and it's my choice."

After the birth of their son and daughter, Roach and her partner took to reassessing their lives in Montreal and found that although it was generally good, basic needs were nonetheless wanting. Racism was a quiet but powerful undercurrent, subtle and insidious, always there, every day. "The message we got all the time was: you aren't good enough because you are black. We were routinely left out and although excuses were made, we knew the real reasons why."

Roach's children were not immune either. When her son was four, a playmate told him he couldn't come to his birthday party because he was 'dirty.'

In the late 1980's the family began considering a move to Toronto after Roach was offered several career opportunities in that city. Even the children brimmed with optimism over the prospect of starting anew and discovering a sense of place in a city that seemed so culturally diverse. Within days of moving, however, Roach came face to face with raw, unmuffled hatred. On a crowded subway she felt an elbow jab against her ribs, first once, twice, and then again. "Excuse me," she said to the woman next to her. "You're hurting me."

Instantly the woman hissed, "Go back to where you came from." Startled by the ugly confrontation, Roach then startled herself even more by grabbing the woman by the earrings and yelling, "Don't you ever do that to me again."

There were other incidents as well, enough to make Roach and her family realize that, in spite of what they had hoped for in Toronto, they wouldn't be enjoying the luxury of slackening their pace and vigilance against the systemic scourge of racism.

Roach shared her perspectives on and experiences with racism in a compelling essay, *Walk a Mile in My Shoes*, which appeared as the cover story for the Summer 1995 issue of Homemaker's Magazine. She lectured both at home and abroad, and continued with her groundbreaking research in trans-cultural psychiatry. To that end she regularly travelled back to Trinidad to better understand how psychiatry is used as a tool for healing in different cultures.

In 1995 Roach broke more ground by founding Women's Healing Place, a safe refuge where women of all races and cultures can receive the support they require to address the challenges in their lives. With her team of highly qualified therapists, Roach offers family counselling, individual and group psychotherapy, facilitation and mediation consultation. Women's Healing Place offers an especially invaluable support system for women of colour, who often feel they don't have anywhere to turn to with their problems. "Many still think therapy is about mental illness or weakness, but it's really about wellness. We help you recognize your inner needs and wants, and we work with you in partnership to help you move to a higher place of well being. We help you recognize what makes you sick, what makes you screw up your life. We give you the tools to help you move through your difficulties. Our aim is to empower women to achieve their highest level of wellness.

"I've been doing psychotherapy since my nursing days, and I've come to believe that you can bring all people to a healthy state of being, but not all in the same way. Psychiatry, on the other hand, tends to put us all in the same groups based on our behaviour. Then we all get the same treatment, and of course it doesn't work for us. You and I might be exhibiting the same behaviours, but we've each had different experiences and travelled our own separate roads to these behaviours. How could the same treatment be effective for both of us?

"I've come to understand that one can't use a pat model for treatment; instead the focus must be on a holistic approach that encompasses the individual's life experiences and focuses on physical, emotional and spiritual wellness.

"You go to the psychiatrist and he says, you are this. And because you are this, you take five milligrams of that. Well, that's not the road to genuine wellness. Instead of prescribing pills, listen to my body language, my cultural background, my digestive system, my hormones. If not, you'll only end up treating the symptoms.

"I arrived at this approach by going into the system to get the training, to learn the system and make some changes on the inside, and to figure out what the hell went on there. I didn't go to fit into any medical model, and I don't.

"I also don't want my practise to be based on income. People come here without paying if they don't have the means. Not because I'm a saint but because I know where they're coming from. I try to balance my practise so that sixty percent of my clients pay and forty percent don't. We have a sliding scale for payment and also use the barter system. And we have short waiting lists; if someone calls for psychotherapy it means they're ready to do their personal work now. They need support now, not in six months time. So I refer them to another practise. If it's me they want to see and they prefer to wait, that's up to them."

Currently Roach also offers her expertise as a mediator to a number of women's organizations in need of retooling and restructuring, a difficult mandate that nonetheless brings her great satisfaction. As well, she advises the Attorney General of Ontario on domestic violence issues and writes the health page for *Panache*, a magazine for women of colour.

Although Roach has been blessed with copious measures of mental and physical energy, she purposely strives for a balance between work and non-work so as to maintain optimal personal health and well being. "I'm fortunate to have plenty of support—my family, my in-laws and several best friends. My partner and children are everything, and our home is a harmonious place. With my friends and my dear mother-in-law and sister-in-law, we have these lovely sit-down-on-the-floor afternoons where we just talk and reconnect."

And Caribana, Toronto's annual Caribbean festival, is Roach's special time to play. "It's my spiritual time, my time to reconnect with my soul through music, laughter, food, people and friends. It's my time to release myself in a way that feels good and meaningful. It brings out my creative side; I make costumes and chant and sing and dance on the streets with my friends. We laugh and celebrate and feast on our traditional foods. Then we come home to sleep and the next day go out and do it all again."

With her children now in university, Roach's thoughts do occasionally drift to retirement. (Not that it will be happening any time soon. There are still marathons to run and mountains to climb, and Roach has plans to produce a CD on domestic violence as a fund raiser for a proposed women's shelter in Toronto.) But with her partner there's talk of an eventual winter home in the Caribbean, although a permanent return to Trinidad is not being considered. "Whenever I go there to do my research, people ask when I'm coming back to stay. I laugh and tell them I'm here to work and party and reconnect. But I'm not torn between here and there. After the action's over, I know it's, 'Get on the plane, Roz, and go home.'"

> *If someone has an apartment to rent but you turn up with your black skin*
> *and the apartment is already rented, could it be that you were simply too late?*
> *If a teacher guides you to hairdressing rather than the sciences, couldn't he be just*
> *looking out for your best interests? If someone spits at you, could it be that you*
> *just happened to be standing where he wanted to spit?*
>
> — Roz Roach, "Walk a Mile in My Shoes". *Homemaker's Magazine*, Summer 1995.

I go back to the Caribbean every year to partake of the culture I missed so much during my early years in Canada. Fortunately, now I can experience it whenever I want to. After years of working myself to the bone and walking hand in hand with poverty, I now have the luxury of choice about where I want to live, work and play. And my conscious choice is Canada. Canada is the home I run back to after I've been abroad. If someone asks me whether I plan to go back home to live, implying that home is the Caribbean, I tell them Canada is my home. I've lived here most of my life; I've created my world and my space here. I brought my soul here and used it to develop and cultivate a Canadian space for myself and my family. I've earned my space here; no one is going to push me off.

I've worked all my years in Canada, sometimes two or three jobs at once. I've never been unemployed. I've learned both English and French. I've contributed two positive citizens, my children, to this country, and I see already that they're giving back to their community. I've been a volunteer, I still do volunteer work.

But sometimes people look at me as someone who has it all—a respected professional with a great marriage, healthy children and academic credentials—and assume that I came into the world this way. That I've not had to scrap for my survival and work hard for my achievements. I remember once being called to mediate for an organization that needed some help getting back on track after having been derailed by racism. As part of the process I asked two members of the organization, two women of colour who felt they had been poorly treated, to share with me their issues, their perspectives of the problem. Their response was: 'You wouldn't understand.' In their eyes I was too privileged, too removed from their situations, to have any hope of understanding them.

And although I didn't want to spend hours explaining myself to these women, I remember thinking: if you only knew where I came from. If you only knew there was a time in my life when I thought I would die of starvation. If you only knew that I ate a bowl of oatmeal every day for almost a semester, that I had two pairs of panties, I'd wash one and wear one. If you only knew that I wore the same pair of Farmer Brown overalls to school every day with different T-shirts, that I never received social assistance because it was never available to me. That I walked a long, cold walk to a friend's house every Sunday for a hot meal, then back to my place because I didn't have bus fare.

I know what it's like to struggle, to taste poverty, to not fit in because I look and talk differently, to be a minority. I know what the *isms* feel like, racism included. So often people conclude that I was born the way I am now, that I came here completely in charge and grounded, doing well and knowing how to take care of myself. But that negates the process of my journey: I've spent much of my life learning how to be.

Transition has been a part of most of my life in Canada. I was very sad and lonely during my first years, trying to figure out Canadian society. I didn't know who lived next door, couldn't speak like them, couldn't make myself understood—that went on for a long time. I didn't like feeling so marginalized and to counter it I spent a lot of time reinforcing in myself my goals and reasons for coming here. I knew I needed an education; I knew I'd have to go two and three times as far as others to overcome the difficulty of being black in this country.

It's a fantasy to think there's no racism in Canada. It's not covert and in-your-face like in America, but more subtle, pouncing from behind your back when your guard is down. That makes it more sinister, more insidious. And people have so many ways of putting it out to you. If someone has an apartment to rent but you turn up with your black skin and the apartment is already rented, could it be that you were simply too late? If a teacher guides you to hairdressing rather than the sciences, couldn't he be just looking out for your best interests? If someone spits at you, could it be that you just happened to be standing where he wanted to spit?

I never know when it will touch me, touch my children. As a parent raising black teenagers in Toronto, I have a lot of quiet worry about how my children are being seen. People don't know they're healthy citizens. My son is six feet and five inches tall, and when the police see him with his friends, they don't think of him in terms of Roz's son. They see him as a threat and ask him to move along, even though his white friends are left alone. That's discrimination. What can we do? It starts with the parents and the messages they give to their children. Sometimes in my practise I see parents talking to their kids about discrimination, denouncing it, but in the same breath supporting other forms of prejudice such as homophobia. Not that I'm putting homophobia and racism side by side, but if we're fighting discrimination, let's fight all discrimination.

In truth, although some people have done significant work in this area, society is not committed to initiating any real change. People continue functioning on the same plane day to day because they don't want to change the status quo. They are protected by their structures—power, religion, money, big houses, their own kind—and they like things the way they are.

I've done a lot of my own work to move to a place where I feel grounded and centred and balanced so that I can see the world and respect all people. That's a hard place to get to but a great investment, and one we should be prepared to make. Occasionally an incident happens where I feel I'm able to make a difference, perhaps have an impact on someone's attitude. Once when I was still nursing in Montreal, I was taking the elevator up to my floor to start my shift. A white woman stepped on, very nervous and clutching her purse. When we got off I walked to the desk and was greeted by the staff, so immediately she real-ized I was a professional and this was my environment. I could have left it at that, but instead took the initiative to approach her and introduce myself, and she told me she had been so afraid. And I gently told her that not all black people were bad, badness has nothing to do with colour. She apologized and her eyes filled with tears. She kept saying how sorry she was, over and over.

It takes an inordinate amount of work to change racist attitudes and perspectives. Women's Healing Place runs a series of summer camps for kids and I see these kids voicing the same observations, the same anxieties, I had when I was nine or ten. And they were all born here, a generation later, and yet they're still getting the same quiet, off-put-ting messages from society. I ask them how they can overcome these challenges and they say they don't know. I suggest we start by looking inward at what is good and strong within us, hold on to those quali-ties and keep telling ourselves we're okay. I help them develop and nurture their self-esteem, which they can then use to soar to a higher, better place. Perhaps, in these kids and their generation we'll see some dramatic advances in our quest for a truly equal society, where the colour of one's skin has no influence whatsoever on one's position and advancement in the community.

Education is a key factor in determining both one's destiny and relationship with community. I've always viewed my education as an inseparable part of my life. So when my son tells me he finds school difficult, I tell him, "You have to see it as your life, your job, your opportunity, not something you're forced to do."

Life is also about doing. When I was nursing years ago, I worked with a black woman, a nursing assistant who pondered going back to school to become a registered nurse. But she saw so many obstacles— she couldn't do math, it would take too long, and so on. I told her if I could do it she could too, one course at a time. I offered to help.

When I met her again two decades later, she hadn't managed to see beyond her obstacles, and she said, regretfully, "Girl, if only I had followed your advice twenty years ago."

I love Canada but I do have my worries. The erosion of our health care system concerns me. From a nursing point of view it's no longer about, "How are you doing," rather, "Here, take your pill." It's no longer about connecting with the patient and promoting wellness, but more about just doing procedures and moving along. The moments to talk and listen are gone. Well, if you can't connect to the patient's emotional needs, it'll be really difficult to care for the physical needs.

I also worry about Canada's future as a place for people of all cultures and ethnic origins. We brag that Canada is for all of its citizens, yet we know hardships are foisted on minority people because of a lack of understanding or wanting to understand. I worry when I hear people phoning in to radio talk shows to speak of the country's problems in terms of blacks and immigrants. That's simply not true. Don't talk about us that way.

I love Canada for the way it threw open its doors to all immigrants during the Trudeau era. Immigrants and their cultures were welcomed into every sector of Canadian society. But the sense of hope for equal opportunity and strength in solidarity that was born out of that era is slowly being eroded. We're becoming more fractured than ever, with regions threatening unity and special-interest groups straining our solidarity with their own agendas.

It need not be so. We can belong to our region and to Canada too, just as we belong to both our country and this world.

Sometimes when I'm abroad, people will hear my Caribbean accent and ask where I'm from. To say I'm Canadian often triggers the need for a lengthy explanation, so sometimes I simply say I'm from Planet Earth. It's a true enough response; I've been blessed to have touched so many places and to feel connected with so many cultures and peoples. I'm a citizen of the planet.

Leung Tom

CANTON (GUANGZHOU), CHINA—MONTREAL, QUEBEC

*West of downtown Montreal, Dorval Airport in the middle ground.
Speed along the concrete-walled Cote de Liesse, traffic whizzing by,
aircraft overhead, life in hand. Watch for the exit, now on the ramp,
through the underpass and into the factory parking lot where haggard
tufts of sunburnt grass protrude from wounded asphalt. Through the
door now, and into a pool of sudden quiet, air-conditioned serenity,
foundling cat asleep on a chair. Behind the desk sits Leung Tom,
community leader, inventor, owner and President of The Eastern
Group. Typically works a fifteen-hour day, refreshes with tennis,
golf, Tai Chi, meditation. No plan to retire, ever.*

*"I've lived in Canada for forty-eight years," says Tom. "I wouldn't
have it any other way."*

Leung Tom's father had lived in Canada for more than three
decades before he was finally granted permission to apply for
citizenship. He had migrated from China in the early 1900's,
one of thousands of young men who had come in search of work and
opportunity in an alien land. Unbeknown to these Chinese workers,
the overtly racist sentiments of the day would destine them to a life of
hard, menial work at below-poverty wages. By paying the mandatory
five-hundred dollar 'Head Tax' through which they tacitly conceded
their unsuitability for Canadian citizenship, they earned the privilege
of toiling in the laundries, restaurants and general stores of Anglo-
Saxon Canada, under demeaning conditions and with no hope of ever
belonging in the mainstream. They laboured for the Canadian Pacific
Railway Company, inching the new rail bed westward and through the
perilous Rocky Mountains. Many died there, needlessly sacrificing
their lives to the wanton carelessness of a company that valued profit
more than it did Asian lives.

The unjust hardship these men were made to endure in Canada is a well-documented, if lesser known, blemish on the face of Canadian history.

"What was blatantly discriminating," says Leung Tom, "was not so much that they had to pay a tax—today's immigrants also have to pay fees to gain access to the country. No, what was blatantly racist was that they were denied citizenship, and their wives and families were denied outright access to the country."

In fact, Tom is being generous in his assessment of the notorious Head Tax, which was flagrantly imposed only on Chinese males seeking entry into Canada. And in denying entry to their wives, the government effectively succeeded in depriving these men of any semblance of normal family life. Instead, it callously sentenced the Chinese worker to a lifetime of hard, destitute misery and chronic misunderstanding, and all too often, a lonely, pointless death on the altar of indifference.

Tom's childhood memories do not include his father. "I was conceived on one of his visits back to China, and by the time I was one year old, he was gone again. Shortly thereafter the Second World War erupted, which stopped his travel altogether. In 1947, when Canada finally reversed its ruling on citizenship, my father became a Canadian citizen and applied immediately to have his family join him in Canada. We were finally accepted in 1952; we arrived on Christmas Eve."

What is remarkable about Leung Tom's father is that he would choose to clothe himself in the citizenship of a country that had denigrated him and his race for several decades. But Tom thinks he understands the motives that nudged his father from outcast to citizen. "Inexplicably, he somehow came to see himself as being inherently part of the Canadian landscape. It felt like home here, if for no other reason than the fact that he'd lived in Canada for so long. And, not insignificantly, life in China during that era was also undeniably hard. People can't imagine the horrors we endured during the war. Death and destruction blanketed our very existence. My father knew that, and he realized that in Canada lay our only hope for stability and opportunity."

When Tom came to Canada, he was 19, tall and lanky, a youth with a singular bent and enthusiasm for all things electronic, and one of China's top basketball players. "My mother and I came to Oakville,

378

where my father was living at that time."

Tom couldn't speak a word of English but landed a job, albeit without pay, mere days after his arrival. "I walked into an appliance store looking for a job. Black and white televisions were just coming out and few people knew how to fix them. I told them I could fix televisions and they let me work there, without pay. I became one of their top technicians."

In those early months Tom also learned what it meant to be targeted as a visible—minority person on the streets of Oakville. But instead of internalizing the animosity and allowing himself to be victimized, he chose to tackle his antagonists by befriending them. "Young children would throw rocks at me on my way to work. Rather than cower from them or ignore them, I showed them how good *my* throwing arm was. Then we started waving back and forth to each other and using hand motions to communicate; I couldn't speak to them but we became friends. I never let these situations bother me, but saw them as a challenge which I could turn into something positive."

After eight months of working without remuneration, Tom enrolled in an engineering program at McMaster University in Hamilton, Ontario. "It took them about a week to catch on to my lack of English, and because they couldn't imagine how I would manage, they asked me to leave. But I pleaded to be allowed to stay and write the mid-term exams, after which time they could assess my work and make a decision about my enrollment. And they relented, saying, 'It's your money, your time.'"

Undaunted, Tom threw himself into an environment wherein he would learn through accelerated immersion. I mixed with people, studied with them, and I had an added advantage that put me in their demand—I joined the varsity basketball team. By the time the mid-terms rolled around, I was all set for them."

Tom transferred to Montreal's McGill University for his second and subsequent years, playing varsity basketball, and eventually graduating with an engineering degree specializing in electronics. But not without paying his dues: one September, after an exhausting summer spent juggling two jobs, Tom had just completed his course registration when he fainted on the spot. Forced to withdraw from university, he spent the following year in treatment for a persistent bleeding

ulcer. He was determined not to fritter away his convalescence, however, and used the little time he had between long bouts of hospital-
ization designing electronic equipment. When his ulcer had not
improved a year later, he travelled to Hong Kong and turned to
Eastern philosophy in his search for healing. "I went to learn meditation from a Tao Master and the results were miraculous. The ulcer
promptly healed itself; I was jogging just three weeks later."

After graduation in 1960 Tom married a young woman he had met
while at McGill, and began working for Canadian Marconi Co., a
large electronics manufacturing firm. There, he was to face his most
disconcerting encounter with prejudice. "Within a month and a half
the company had put me in charge of a department where the work
involved a high degree of technology hinged on various military projects. But then they suddenly reneged on the promotion, giving some
vague reason as to why they were moving me out of that department
altogether and into telecommunications and radar, areas with a lesser
degree of military sensitivity. I found out later the RCMP had done a
check on me—this was in the early 1960's and the Cold War was at it's
height—and because I still had a sister living in China, they deemed I
should not have access to military-sensitive technology.

"I refused to let it bother me. I would have hurt only myself, no one
else, by letting it fester. So I told them, "Fine, I'll transfer," and spent
the next decade in the telecommunications department. I never did
get back to the first department; I never managed to clear security."

In the meantime Tom was also spending much of his spare time
exploring new applications for technology and designing successful new
inventions. Today he holds several electronic and mechanical patents,
among them the patent for the world's first metal/wood golf club.

By 1971 Tom had advanced to the salient position of Chief
Engineer with Canadian Marconi Co., and although he enjoyed his
work and its accompanying intrinsic benefits, he suspected it might
not be enough to keep him motivated in the long run. The last thing
he wanted was to find his comfort zone in a rut. More and more, he
found himself pondering the feasibility of forming his own company.

"I knew that if I didn't take the plunge then, I wouldn't do at all. If
I postponed it until I was in my forties, I knew I'd no longer be able

to muster up the momentum needed to get a company off the ground. I also figured that if I acted now and decided in a few years time that it wasn't working out, I'd still be young enough to find viable employment elsewhere."

Tom also calculated that his chances of successfully operating his own company were particularly healthy in the early 1970's. "Marconi had just closed a precision castings division that had been consistently losing money over the previous half-decade. I offered to buy it from them. I didn't know much about castings, which is the manufacture of defence and electronic parts using moulds, but I figured I could learn, and I did."

From this beginning has risen *The Eastern Group*, a conglomerate of five manufacturing companies, each with its own specialty and mandate, mostly in advanced technology. The versatile Tom, as president, oversees the operations of each company, all located under one large roof in a Montreal industrial park. Much of his business is in commercial aviation, although he also manufactures golf clubs, specializes in telecommunications and at one time operated a real estate company. "Before the end of the Cold War, much of our work was in military projects. I had 350 employees then, but we've downsized to about 65."

While the end of the Cold War cost Tom many millions of dollars in lost revenue and spelled out significant change in his *modus operandi*, a deeply personal transformation also contributed to a dramatic re-evaluation. "Up until then, technology was really the only thing that had held my fascination, that mattered to me. Nothing else seemed to matter as much. But by chance a conversation with a friend made me stop and reconsider my priorities. I began giving thought to the possibility that perhaps there was more to life than inventing, designing and manufacturing. I found my interest in meditation being rekindled, and began to study it further on my own. I transferred my preoccupation with technology to a broader curiosity about life, its purpose, our purpose in the universe."

As one outcome of his personal metamorphosis, Tom transferred a significant portion of his energies to Montreal's sizeable Chinese community, and was not long in being lauded as a strong and dynamic leader with a penchant for getting things done.

"There are about 80,000 Chinese people in Montreal. We are the city's fourth largest ethnic community. When I came on as President of the Montreal Chinese Community United Centre in 1987, I saw several priorities to address, including the need to engage in some bridge building between the elderly of our community and mainstream Canada. We can't come to this country and just continue to live here like an ancient society off in a corner by ourselves. Yet, many of the elderly were doing just that.

"True, we have our cultures and traditions that have remained intact for centuries, but when we immigrate here we must accept that we are now also part of a young, changing society. We must recognize that we are, or should be, part of the impetus that's changing that young society.

"It's not good for the elders to continue stagnating in the past, and not good for the next generation either. It creates intolerable friction between the generations when one wants to preserve what is, while the other wants to change with the times. Therein lay my second priority: to work at alleviating some of the polarization that existed between the generations."

Since his inception as Community President, Tom has vigorously promoted the concept of common facilities for community use. He presided over the construction of a community centre which was completed in 1989. He has overseen the development of a Chinese cultural and business centre, "a place to express and celebrate our own culture, but also to invite other cultures to come in and share their traditions with us." Completed in 2000, it includes a school aimed at helping to ease the transition period for the children of newly-arrived Chinese immigrants.

"Academic instruction is being provided only until the children have gained enough proficiency in French and English to enter a mainstream school. True, it will be temporary segregation, but in the end these children will have a much better chance of finding their place in the mainstream. It's a difficult period for these youngsters just coming to Canada, not so much for those from Hong Kong who already speak some English, but definitely for those from Mainland China who often don't. There's a great deal for them to cope with, in terms of school. And mainstream schooling also creates added tensions for their non-English or French speaking parents, who can't help with homework, can't follow the curriculum, and can't confer with teachers. This school will allow families to find their bearings before taking the plunge into mainstream society."

Tom has also lent his energies to an organization known as *Overseas Chinese Congress of the World*. Established in 1997 during a Hong Kong meeting of 300 Chinese emigrants from around the globe, the Congress' purpose is to foster a spirit of cooperation and open communication among its eclectic membership. Designated as its organizer, Tom developed the constitution and set up a networking system that enables members to stay in contact and work together on projects as they arise. For these efforts and others, he has twice been featured in Chinese government publications featuring outstanding Chinese emigrants.

Today Tom could easily choose to ease up on his intimidating work schedule—typically he works fifteen hour days six days a week—and enjoy the luxuries of life he can now well afford. But retirement, he insists, is out of the question. "One doesn't achieve for one's own purposes. If one did, there would be reason to stop working and just be comfortable for oneself. But as an inherent part of the universe that is connected to all other living things, I can't just be here solely for the purpose of enjoying myself and using up the world's resources. So I won't ever retire."

Tom continues to feed his insatiable curiosity about life and its purpose by remaining acutely observant of his surroundings. "Wherever I go, I always find time to step inside a church and initiate conversation with the pastor. That's how I gain new insights."

Although retirement is not an option, Tom does make it a point to set aside time for relaxation. "I play golf and tennis regularly, I do Tai Chi and meditate daily. I may not have much time for recreation, but when I relax I can detach completely from everything else and make optimum use of my 'time out.' Thanks to meditation, I have no stress and therefore find it very easy to relax. Meditation has taught me to help myself and fear nothing in this life. I'm very healthy, happy and content. What more could I need?"

Tom's father died a decade ago at age 90, but his presence contin-ues to linger in the mind of his only son. "I know I have achieved more than my father could ever have imagined for me."

And yet, even as Tom stands among the select ranks of those Canadians who have achieved prosperity in a way that few can imagine, he has managed to retain and embrace the essence of his own Eastern roots.

His father would have been proud.

*If you treat yourself as a stranger from another land
and let people look down on you, then you
could allow yourself to become very homesick.*

Montreal is my city and I wouldn't live anywhere else. My city offers interesting people, a stimulating environment, great food, quality education and a sense of security you rarely find in a city of this size.

However, having been a Montrealer for several decades, the sepa-ration issue is never far from my mind and therefore must factor into any personal notions I might have of Canadianism. Separation is an extremely complex issue involving almost every aspect of what makes a society and a country run—the economy, politics, everything. Personally, I can't picture how Quebec would be able to disentangle itself from all of these systems without some very severe hardships and ramifications. So I'm not particularly worried about separation, although I remain aware that it's a strong sentiment in this province.

I see a pattern emerging in the way the separation issue comes to the forefront every so often, a pattern I describe as a 'ringing curve,' which is a term often used in electronics. You hit a bell, it emits a loud noise, and then it dies down. There may be some residual small noises but eventually it dies down completely, until something else hits it again. Every so often something in our history or state of affairs causes the social and political adjustment bell to ring again, which then rouses a flurry of interest, anxiety and activity, but after a while it qui-ets down until something instigates the next round.

Many people I know who voted for separation did so not because they want separation *per se,* but rather, they want some recognition, some acknowledgement of their distinctiveness. They are only too aware that the separation road would be a rocky one. We who live in Quebec know we enjoy many benefits channelled from Ottawa, including financial security and generous equalization payments.

We also know Canada is one of the best countries in the world in which to live. Here there are more opportunities than most people from elsewhere can imagine, even for those immigrating today. And much of this opportunity is being provided by employers who have earlier come from somewhere else. If you doubt that, just look at their names.

Whenever I speak with new immigrants, I suggest that their first priority should be to advance themselves to the point where they can communicate and connect with people. And how do you do that? By learning the language, the customs, the viewpoints of your new society, by walking the streets and studying people and absorbing everything you see. How do you find out that pens and screwdrivers are different? How do you find out what's available? By walking into a store and looking around. I used to walk evenings and weekends, always looking around. I would spend hours in the hardware store, just studying the inventory and the materials used in their manufacture. There are no limits to how you can educate yourself this way.

And in the process of absorbing your new environment, you learn to fit in, to become part of it. You learn to treat people certain ways, to pay your income tax, to not make noise late at night. You learn that you cannot criticize or judge your new society without first completely knowing that society. You learn that if you want to succeed, you will spend your time looking for a job, not watching television. You learn that you must be prepared to show plenty of initiative and start at the bottom.

I've never really been homesick. If you do things to help yourself fit in and you look at the meaning of your life in a more global way, then you don't easily give in to despair. But it's natural to feel lonely for the ones you leave behind. For me it was my sister. However, if you treat yourself as a stranger from another land and let people look down on you, then you could allow yourself to become very homesick.

All my life I have tried to make friends out of people who thought they were my enemies. In my early years in Canada, I knew that whenever I ran into a problem with people, it was usually because they didn't know me. I seemed alien to them. Once I got to know people and they realized we had common ground to share, the animosities and mis-understandings usually evaporated quite readily and permanently.

In our Chinese culture we are encouraged to look within ourselves to find answers to some of life's perennial questions: Who am I? Where am I in my life? What is my purpose in life? What is the mean-ing of life? When you have some answers to these questions, chances are you will be less vulnerable to homesickness and loneliness, and more apt to be better insulated from the anxieties and stresses of life.

When I was four and a half years old, my teacher told me, "If you can find out who you are, what you are and where you are, you will be able to solve anything." These are questions I haven't always known the answers to, but I've always had bits and pieces of the answers. Even when I came here at age 19, I had some awareness of where I was going in my life. And over the years I've grown spiritually to the point where more answers have gradually come to me.

I meditate every day; meditation helps me to grow spiritually, enhances my health, and gives me control over my life. I also offer a weekly class on meditation which has been taken by hundreds of peo-ple. I help people to come to a level of self-understanding through meditation to believe that they can learn to help themselves and con-trol their destiny. Westerners are often so preoccupied by what it is that Western society has traditionally valued—work and economic suc-cess, the car, the vacation, and the television—to the point where these values interfere with one's own natural evolution. The Eastern phi-losophy can help us to rise above these preoccupations and free our minds. And the Eastern philosophy is gradually gaining interest in the Western world.

There is much Canada has given me, but freedom has been it's great-est gift. Coming from a country with an abysmal human rights record, I can say that freedom is more important to me than anything else. In Canada I can do and say what I want without feeling as if someone is watching, monitoring. Canadians have so much personal space, not just in the physical sense but in every sense. There isn't a country in the world that offers more personal freedom than Canada does. We who have witnessed violations of human rights in other countries will never take these freedoms for granted. We know they are to be cherished.

I was ready to belong to Canada right from the beginning. I was ready to become wholly Canadian, to make my contribution, fit in and find my place. Whenever I travel to China now, I'm struck by the realization that I'm visiting a foreign country. China has changed and I have changed; even if I wanted to, which I do not, I could no longer hope to fit into Chinese society. I am a Canadian. Canada is my homeland.

Veselina Tomova

*The artist, Veselina Tomova, has a world-weary history.
Her voice is pensive; she weaves self-deprecating humour into her
narratives, laughs and sighs simultaneously. At her kitchen table,
she draws deeply from the view of the historic St. John's Harbour
just below her window, liquid sapphire cupped on three sides by
ancient, rounded hills. At her kitchen table, she draws deeply from
an idling cigarette, all elbows, darting hands and youthful vitality.
Her art is exquisite, the colours exuberant yet subtle, the painstaking
detail indicative of a perfectionist at work. Though she's lived in
Canada only a decade, her work has already been hailed by critics.
There have been shows, awards for the children's books she has
illustrated, and no shortage of business for her graphic design
company.
"I came for my future," she says, "and I've found my home."*

In late 1989 Veselina Tomova, a resident of Sofia, Bulgaria, began
preparing for a very special art show. Already a prominent local
artist and rising national star, she diligently created for a year and
then shipped the entire collection off to Cuba. "My friend, Vessela,
and the man who was then my husband were also creating works for
this exhibit. It took us a long time to do the mountain of paperwork
and to obtain official approval to attend the show. Nothing was ever
easy in Bulgaria.

"Why Cuba? Because it's also a communist country, so we knew our
request to go there wouldn't arouse undue suspicion. And because
flying to Cuba meant stopping in Gander to refuel. Cuba was our only
hope."

When Tomova was 14, and already firm in her resolve to be an
artist, she travelled to Sofia from her hometown in central Bulgaria to

enroll in a high school that specialized in fine art training. "I wanted the best education Bulgaria could offer." Following that, she obtained a bachelor's degree from Sofia's Academy of Fine Arts, and in 1983 came away from the Academy of Fine Art and Book Design in Leipzig, Germany, with a Master's Degree in Fine Art.

"My ex-husband, who was then my boyfriend followed me to Germany and enrolled in the same University. After I graduated I worked in Leipzig for two years as a book illustrator, and could have had a good life there. But at that time I had no reason nor desire to live abroad."

Tomova and her boyfriend returned to Sofia and married in 1985. "I wasn't born in Sofia so I couldn't live there as a single woman. I would have been deported to my parents' city in central Bulgaria, where there was no chance for a decent job. The only way I could stay in Sofia was to be married to a resident. So my boyfriend was nice enough to marry me."

Tomova landed a job as art editor with Sofia's Science and Art Publishing Company and over the next five years also participated in numerous juried exhibitions in Bulgaria and Germany. A son was born, and life was stable and prosperous. "We were in our early thirties, we had an apartment, a car, and we both had full-time work. I was doing a lot of extra freelance work and making good money; financially I was better off at that time than I ever will be here. But then in 1989 the so-called democratic changes started."

After forty years of rule under the same communist regime, Bulgaria was beginning to feel the winds of political change that had begun drifting over from the Soviet Union. In an unprecedented, reactionary move to the political rumblings that were rolling across eastern Europe, the Bulgarian government ousted it's leader and called the country's first free election. To an outsider it might have resembled a brazen leap of faith on the part of the government; in actual fact, it was a cleverly calculated move. The rulers knew, given their long-standing power, status and economic clout within Bulgaria's borders, that they couldn't possibly lose an election. Bulgaria had been the same for too long. In enduring the pre-election discord that was sure to come, they would seemingly offer the people a semblance of power, let them vote, resume the seat of power and offer the whole experiment up as an example of the dysfunctional nature of democracy.

But that wasn't how Tomova and those in her circle saw it. "We were all very excited at the beginning, thinking these changes would be far-reaching and for the common good. Everyone our age was part of the movement advocating change; we were all drawn in, you couldn't just sit on the sidelines. There was a feeling of optimism; we were having our first free election. Our borders opened up and, whereas it had been almost impossible to leave before, it now became relatively easy. A lot of our friends, even though they were excited about the election, grew increasingly uneasy about the fate of the country and chose to leave in the fall and winter of that year.

"But we wanted to stay and be part of this momentous change. We thought we would win the elections and everything would be perfect. How naive we were. Of course the communists won again, which brought an end to the so-called period of freedom, and the whole system collapsed.

"Ironically, the election process actually had been democratic. But the communists had been in power for 45 years so they were the ones with the experience, the upper hand, and the money for campaigning. Many older people couldn't imagine what life under any other regime would be like and so they didn't even bother to vote. My grandparents didn't vote and I got so angry with them, and they said, 'It doesn't matter who's in power, Bulgaria's going to stay the same.'"

On the contrary, Bulgarians soon discovered after the election that the country was anything but the same. "Before the changes there was order under a totalitarian system, through the mechanisms of repression and authority. There were restrictions to our personal freedom— you could be thrown in jail for speaking your mind—but at least there was order. After the election the mechanisms for control crumbled, leaving only dangerous chaos. The government was only interested in economic power; they had no time for law and order. In fact, they calculated that anarchy and chaos in the streets would keep the masses from organizing any strong, consolidated movement against them.

"And then they introduced a free-market economy, which meant each of us was really on our own. Those with money became the country's first capitalists. The rest of us had to buy all our services, including protection from crime, at over-inflated prices. The disparity between the rich and poor grew, and the police were ineffective because they were as scared of the hoodlums as everyone else. And so it became a matter of each person being preoccupied only with survival of self. That was just no way to live."

Tomova didn't take long to reassess her future. "Daily life became a depressing struggle and I just couldn't see any hope for improvement. I didn't want my life and my son's life to go this way. Although we had been caught up in the politics of change, I didn't want to be political; it's not my nature. And because we had worked for the opposition, we also worried about our safety. I just wanted to do my work and have a peaceful life. And that was no longer possible in Bulgaria.

"We had two options: we could give up our jobs and move far into the countryside where we could live peacefully but unemployed, or we could emigrate. The latter was a dubious option since it meant defecting; All the borders were now completely closed. But defecting was our only chance at a decent life. So we started planning the show in Cuba."

Discreetly the family scraped together their savings and borrowed from Tomova's parents-in-law to purchase airline tickets. "We couldn't sell our things, that would have brought us unwanted attention. We repaid his parents by leaving them our car to sell after we were gone."

Getting official approval to travel was one cumbersome hurdle; getting on a flight that actually did stop for refuelling in Gander was quite another. "The five of us—my husband and three-year-old son, my friend Vessela, her daughter and me—headed to the airport. When they saw the children and our tickets for a flight that was to stop in Gander, they immediately became suspicious and told us we couldn't go on that plane, it was full. They booked us on another flight with entirely different connections. I was devastated; after all this I wasn't going anywhere near a democratic country.

"What happened next was incredibly lucky. We had a friend who was a doctor stationed at the airport and we pleaded with him to help us; we were desperate. He conferred with the pilot of the original flight and, just as we were losing hope, the pilot agreed to take us. His plane hadn't been full at all; in fact, it was half empty.

"The rest seems anti-climactic now. In Gander we just walked off the plane, approached a policeman and told him we were defecting. He summoned an immigration officer who interviewed us and took us to a Gander hotel. A week later we were put on a bus to St. John's, went through our immigration hearings, and obtained refugee status."

Tomova and her family spoke no English and came with only two hundred dollars and a bag packed with sandals and beach things. "We were going to Cuba for a week. To take anything more would have made them suspicious."

Like other refugees, Tomova and her family qualified for a one-year government support program. "I think I was too desperate to be scared about my future. The Settlement Program was paying our rent and gave us one hundred and twenty dollars a week for food. But winter was coming and we needed so much. We didn't really know what kind of winter we were in for, but from what I'd heard, I knew we needed to be prepared. We needed an income. I was ready to do any kind of work, I wasn't picky."

Tomova's first job was with Breakwater Books. "I was again very lucky. They were looking for an illustrator for a children's picture book when I happened to walk in with my portfolio. As part of the contract they offered an advance of five hundred dollars, an awful lot of money for us at that time. But the day after I received the cheque, my son broke his leg, sliding. It was in a cast for three months. I couldn't get any work done with him around so I had to hire a sitter in order to get the book done. There went my five hundred dollars."

A Winnipeg publisher offered Tomova her next contract, to illustrate the children's book *A Dozen Silk Diapers*, which went on to win the 1994 Manitoba Publishers' Award for best designed children's book. That project was followed with a six-month contract to create a series of murals for Memorial University.

"Meanwhile, my personal life was falling apart. I had met someone, quite by accident, with whom I had fallen in love. But my husband, who speaks French, wanted us to move to Montreal where he thought there would be more opportunities for him. He didn't want to leave our son with me in St. John's so I was forced to go along. He found work almost immediately in a print shop. I did another small project for the Winnipeg publisher and a few minor contracts for various ad agencies. But I didn't like Montreal and really missed St. John's and this incredible Newfoundlander I had met.

"Maybe my marriage failed because we immigrated, the stress of getting settled in and starting over, figuring out which directions our lives would be going in. Perhaps I would still be married if we hadn't left. That's a question I'll never know the answer to."

The marriage over, Tomova and her son returned to St. John's eight months later. There she teamed up with her friend and colleague, Vessela Brakalova, to take advantage of a government start-up program for emerging small businesses. In 1993 they launched Vis-A-Vis Graphics "with no investments because we had no money to invest." Tomova recalls the challenges of their first precarious year. "We just started by declaring ourselves open for business. We had no money for advertising so we put together a portfolio and went around to potential clients. We didn't have a computer, which was fine because we wouldn't have known how to use it anyway."

From those dubious beginnings has emerged an innovative company that has earned a reputation for quality work. "Now we can create both traditionally produced work and computer-generated designs, which has helped to give us an edge over our competition."

In 1996 Tomova and her partner, Bill Barry purchased their home on historic Battery Road, just up from and overlooking the harbour. "For the first time in my life I had my own work space. If I made a mess, it was the luxury of my own mess."

In recent years Vis-A-Vis Graphics has been kept busy with the design and development of a series of educational products created by Barry. Known as *The Real Game*, the series has been widely successful in North America and is now being readied for the international market. "The project draws on all of our skills and gives us the satisfaction of seeing our work in thousands of schools all over the world. It keeps us very busy and has grown enormously." Grown, in fact, to the extent that the house on Battery Road has become the workplace and a new family home has been purchased on the outskirts of town.

On the anniversary of her first decade in Canada, Tomova momentarily allows herself to wax reflective on her long journey to freedom and fulfilment. "My dreams are all coming true. I live in beautiful, peaceful surroundings and do the work I love. There are so many opportunities here. Besides illustration and design, I've done print making and have had several successful local shows. I've exhibited my work in Toronto and I've been a jury member for the Governor General's Award for illustration in children's books. Right now I'm in the final stages of illustrating another children's book, this time for Toronto's Kids Can Press.

"I rest easy knowing my son has a good life ahead of him now. He's settled in well here and travelled back to Bulgaria a few times to see his grandparents and cousins. It's a priority of mine that he maintains a strong bond with his family there."

As for the collection of work that Tomova shipped to Cuba in 1990, it became a casualty of her pilgrimage to freedom. But she takes its loss in stride. "I was well aware when I was working on the prints that once they were sent I would never see them again. I have no idea where they are now. The same with everything I had to leave behind in Sofia, including all my art supplies. But that's not important anymore, just part of the price I had to pay. I have no regrets."

Canada wasn't a choice at all; it was my only chance.

I've never second-guessed my decision to leave Bulgaria for Canada, and if I had, my trip back to Sofia in 1995 would have cured any residual doubt once and for all. Although it was nice to visit my family, especially since I had left not knowing if I'd ever see them again, it was like travelling to a foreign country. I was reading a Bulgarian paper on the last leg of the flight to Sofia, and I thought, I'm crazy to be coming back. The paper was filled with crime reports, rape, robbery and more. I was going especially to visit my elderly grandparents and even in their village, the peaceful village where I had grown up on a farm, everyone was carrying a gun now.

My father picked me up from the airport and he was telling me about all the drunkenness and lawlessness, and was debating buying a gun himself. My brother had his brand new van stolen from a parking spot in front of the courthouse. When he reported it to the police, their response was, "A new van? Of course it's going to be stolen. What do you expect?" As if to say: How could you be so stupid. The reality of Bulgaria is that if you have money for a new car, you'd better have the money for bodyguards.

The country is filled with chaos and turmoil. No wonder. Consider the number of hidden agendas and self-interests, with several dozen political parties elbowing each other within one small country. Well, that's Bulgaria.

We arrived as refugees in Gander late on September 9, 1990. We flew on a Cuban airline and throughout the journey my mind was blank, unfocused. My only thought was, would we be allowed in. I couldn't imagine what would happen if we were refused.

The next morning we went for a walk in Gander. I couldn't believe a place could be this clean, this beautiful. It was an unexpected pleasure to inhale deeply; the air felt so pure in my lungs. You don't breathe deeply in Europe, especially Bulgaria where there is much heavy industry. And I couldn't believe how friendly people were. We were walking along a street and a woman came along and said hello. I thought, she must be nuts to risk her safety and talk to strangers.

I came to Canada because of Gander. Canada wasn't a choice; it was my only chance. I didn't know a thing about this country. But from the moment I set foot on the ground in Gander, I never doubted my decision to give up my previous life for a new start here. Not once. I focused on our future, the impetus for our coming. I was never homesick. In fact, the stress of those early months was due to the possibility of being sent back to Bulgaria. Until that was decided, our destiny was completely beyond our control, which I found disconcerting. Only when they officially welcomed us to Canada did I start worrying about how I was going to make a living.

Even before I could speak English, I was made to feel welcome. It's amazing how people can communicate their desire to reach out and be friendly without the benefit of language. I've never been treated badly. Actually, the only people who didn't treat me well were the Bulgarian embassy officials in Ottawa. They didn't want us getting our Canadian visas and passports. But we are Canadian now and they can't touch us.

I didn't care for Montreal. That was the one time I felt like an immigrant, like someone looked down upon. I sensed it every day, while shopping for groceries and going about my routine. And it wasn't because I was awfully sensitive; it was definitely there, in a covert way. However, I knew I wasn't going to be in Montreal for long so I didn't let it get to me.

In Newfoundland I've never experienced any discrimination, not in my personal life nor in my business. I've never felt like an outsider here. I love Newfoundland, the ocean, landscape and people. It's peaceful, quiet and not crowded, a wonderful place to work and live. And that's all I ever set out to attain: a healthy peaceful environment in which to raise my son and do my work.

Here I've found time to garden and go for a walk, luxuries I never had time for in Bulgaria. There, simply getting through the day was a struggle, and you never knew what the next day would bring. Bill wonders why I never use recipes when I cook. Recipes were useless in Bulgaria; there are so many ingredients you can't get. You couldn't plan ahead. You bought what was available that day, and improvised.

When I returned from my trip to Bulgaria in 1995, Bill picked me up at the airport and I found myself thinking how nice it was to be home. This is my home. This is where I belong. I guess I've made the transition in a short period of time.

I was among the last of 3000 Bulgarians who defected at Gander in 1990. Most of them have gone on to other parts of Canada; there are only about 30 of us in St. John's. Everyone is very busy with their work and so we don't engage in many activities as a cultural group. Once in a while we do get together and celebrate with our music and food. But it's not like I'm glued to that group. I also get together with people who've lived here all their lives and it's just as much fun, just as special.

If I'm different in any way, it's in knowing that my career would have gotten off the ground much sooner had I been born here. I had to invest time and energy into planning my run to freedom, and then adjusting and getting re-established. So I've lost several years of career development. Mostly it doesn't bother me but sometimes, when I'm feeling pissed off over something, I get down on myself for not having made the move to emigrate sooner, when I was much younger.

Perhaps another thing that sets me apart is my constant awareness of the incredible personal freedom we have in Canada. This freedom I will always cherish and never take for granted. I know what it's like to live an oppressed life.

On a trip back to Bulgaria in 1997 I noticed more chaos than ever. The currency is worth only twenty-five percent of what it was worth a few years ago. Here in Newfoundland you can count on things moving in a certain direction; there you never know what's happening from year to year. When I first defected I was struck by the difference between Sofia, which I had just left, and Gander, to which I had come. Well, shortly after returning from that trip I drove through Gander and was again struck by the polarities of these two places, the one old, tired and complicated, the other young, fresh and unpretentious. Sophia may be more 'sophisticated' but Gander is the better place to live.

Bill and I went again in 1998, primarily for him to meet my family. My relatives were delighted to meet him and he enjoyed his stay as well. But, it was just a visit, no more.

I'm thankful fate has brought me here. We've bought a house and established a home base. Life is good. I no longer need to limit my shopping to the Salvation Army store, which I had to do for several years. On the other hand, I don't think I'll ever be careless with money. That's just not the way I was brought up.

When we came here we left everything behind, and although my parents tried sending some of my stuff, the only thing that made it through was my winter coat. But it was just too fancy to wear and so I never did. I still have it though—maybe I'm saving it as a souvenir, maybe it'll end up with my future daughter-in law.

My son is a good student—in 1999 he won the provincial school mathematics competition—and he has many friends. He's getting many opportunities I didn't have as a child, like travelling and being exposed to plenty of experiences. He feels at home here and when he travels to Bulgaria to visit his grandparents, he settles in there too. He's fine travelling alone and I'm not worried about his safety. The airlines take good care of him, and he's in good hands with my parents.

One dream I have is to bring my parents here for a visit eventually. I want them to experience a taste of life here, because they don't believe me when I describe what it's like. They think they're okay there, but I want them to see what life *could* be like. They wonder how it is that I've become so serene and content. They need to see this part of the world. They can't imagine how well we live here.

Reverend Louis Vermeersch

OUDENBURG, BELGIUM—SAINT JOHN, NEW BRUNSWICK

Proficient in six languages, servant of the people, teacher, life-long scholar—Reverend Father Louis Vermeersch nonetheless shies at the suggestion that he's cherished by those he served until his retirement in 1989. And yet, the evidence is there, in their accolades and tributes and in the conferring of an Honorary Doctorate by the University of New Brunswick in 1996.

It's a flawless summer morning in Saint John; already a shimmering haze presides over the waters of Grand Bay, liquefies the point where earth meets sky. A grosbeak and an American goldfinch amuse themselves in the birdbath just under the window. A young squirrel scampers repeatedly up a nearby pole, looking for the bird feeder that was there only yesterday.

"Canada has meant freedom," says the amiable Vermeersch who remains much admired for his compassion and social conscience. "Incredible freedom for those of us who came from small European countries where there was barely room to stand anymore."

Even before Louis Vermeersch had fully decided to become a priest, he knew one thing for certain: he wasn't becoming a parish priest because that role seemed too prosaic and without any real challenge. No, if he was going to devote his life to the church, it would be as an unconditional servant of the people.

Born to Flemish parents in Oudenburg, Belgium, in 1920, Vermeersch had every expectation that he would carry on the family's long-standing tradition of mixed farming. "We lived near the sea and much of our land was used to produce crops for seed. I was the oldest of six and when I turned fourteen, I was happy to leave school and return full-time to the farm. It was during the depression so my parents, too, were pleased to have me home."

A reluctant scholar, Vermeersch nonetheless applied himself to

regular evening courses in agronomy over the next six years. So firmly entrenched in agriculture was he that his family began to consider the purchase of an additional property, which would eventually become his to farm. Then, at age 20, his life's journey was abruptly altered. At a spiritual retreat for Catholic youth the question of a religious vocation was first put to him. "My immediate reaction was, no, I wasn't going back to school again. But I couldn't stop thinking about it; my heart was troubled. Each time I sought counsel, I ended up more upset than before. I'd never had a particular leaning in this direction, and now it was as if I'd been hit over the head with a hammer.

"My father and I were in the barn cleaning out the horses when I told him I felt I should go and study for the priesthood. And he began to cry, saying only, 'If it is God's will.' I had never seen him cry before."

In 1940 Vermeersch left his home to study with the Salesians of St. John Bosco, an order of priests known for their work as teachers and missionaries who emphasized service to youth, specifically the poor and forgotten. "I didn't know much about the Salesians at that time but they had a program of study for older students, 'late vocations' they called it, which appealed to me. Now in my early twenties, I really didn't want to go back into class with the 14-year-olds."

However, mere days after he left for the Salesian Seminary in Kortrijk, the Second World War broke out and Belgium was invaded. "So I found myself home again. I figured my vocation was not meant to be and quite happily settled back into farming. But a few weeks later I received a letter from the Salesians saying things had stabilized and classes would proceed as planned. And so I re-packed my bags and left once more."

Vermeersch spent the next eight years studying and completing a novitiate, during which time he became proficient in Latin and Greek. Then, true to his conviction that his life would be one of service, he requested a transfer to missionary territory. He chose China; his superiors decided on Japan. Because Japan was under American military government at the time, he would sail first to America, then travel across the continent to San Francisco, from where he would board a passenger liner on route to Yokohama.

In April 1948, he bade his parents farewell at the port of

Zeebrugge, boarded an empty American cargo carrier, and briefly faltered in his convictions. "It was the only time I ever doubted what I was doing. My parents thought they'd never see me again. Could it be, I thought as I saw my mother leaning on my father in her grief, that our understanding of the scriptural verse—*Whosoever does not leave his mother or father for Me is not fit to enter the gates of heaven*—might be inaccurate? Was God really commanding that we shun our own families in our search of and service to Him? We interpreted everything so literally back then. My heart was heavy as we set out on the Atlantic."

Vermeersch arrived in Japan in the following month. For the next 11 years it would be his home. In 1953 he obtained a degree in philosophy and sociology, and in May of that year he was ordained to the priesthood in Tokyo. By now proficient in English and Italian as well as Japanese, he was appointed to oversee the Salesian's Tokyo-based publishing company, publisher of religious books and magazines. Save for a few exceptions including a French-Japanese dictionary, all releases were in Japanese.

All the while he also worked quietly among the people, counselling, supporting, listening, usually on a one-to-one basis. And he welcomed the teachings they offered in return and relished the opportunity to have his own horizons broadened. "For the first time I realized that Europeans are all young, newcomers really. What do we have as history? A thousand years? Twelve hundred? Well, they can add a few thousand to that, and they actively celebrate their impressive history of language, culture and poetry."

Much as Vermeersch loved the Japanese people and culture, the tropical climate slowly whittled away at his fluctuating health. Reluctantly he returned to Belgium in 1959 for a period of convalescence. "But after a few months I'd had enough of sitting around, and applied to go back to mission territory. I thought I was headed for South Africa but at the last minute my superior told me, 'No, you'll be going to America.' "

And so Vermeersch found himself on a boat to Montreal from where he proceeded by train to New Rochelle, New York. "I spent the summer travelling from one parish to another, preaching. It was always the same sermon, pretty easy work. Then in September I got a phone call from my superior asking me to meet with him in New Rochelle.

"When I arrived there he told me that since I spoke French he was sending me to a small missionary outpost in the northern part of New Brunswick, a place called Jacquet River, where the Salesians operated a residential school for boys in grades six to nine. 'But I don't speak French,' I protested. 'Sure you do, all Belgians speak French,' he said. 'No,' I countered, 'more than half of them speak Flemish.' But he wasn't listening to me, just insisting it would work out, promising it would only be for a year, and reminding me I had taken a vow of obedience. So I agreed; I didn't have much choice. I wasn't even sure exactly where New Brunswick was at that point.

"I arrived at Don Bosco College in Jacquet River on September 22, 1960. The next day I found myself standing in front of 16 French-speaking students. I was to teach them French grammar. Well, I was candid with them. I told them we'd be learning together, starting with our first lesson the following day. Then I dismissed them and went to my own room to prepare my material.

"At the end of the year," Vermeersch recalls wryly, "we all passed the course together."

Although he vowed to make the most of his posting, Vermeersch found the loneliness and isolation almost unbearable. "In Japan I'd had a car, pocket money, intellectual stimulation. Shortly after I arrived in Jacquet River the bay froze over on one side and the woods on the other, and there was only one street light in the entire village. I had not a cent in my pocket, no radio, no newspaper. I couldn't go anywhere. It was a very strict set-up and I told another priest there, 'It's just as if they've condemned me to Siberia.' "

June finally came and Vermeersch packed his bags and left for New York. Again he spent the summer travelling and preaching. Again he was summoned to a meeting in New Rochelle, and again he learned he would be going to Jacquet River. "It would only be until Christmas, my superior assured me. He hadn't found anyone to replace me. Well, three months is not the end of the world, I thought. So I went back. Back to Jacquet River. Back to the same class. Back to more French."

In October the school's director became ill and had to leave. Vermeersch received orders to replace him until Christmas. With a staff of eight and a student body of about 70, he found himself suddenly with the reins in hand.

"Christmas came and I said to the guys, 'Why don't you go home and visit your families. It will do you good.' This had always been forbidden before, so they were pretty happy with their unexpected holiday. While they were gone I phoned New Rochelle and asked about my impending replacement. And my Superior said he wanted to come and discuss this with me in person, at Easter. Canada was too cold for him to come now, he said. I was to stay as director until Easter.

"I told him that was my limit, and he laughed on the phone.

"The guys all figured that since they now had a Belgian director they'd be able to have a beer with their meals on occasion. I said okay, and went to the village liquor store to buy a few cases. I wore my cassock; we were still in cassock then. When the fellow at the store recovered from his surprise on seeing me, he suggested that priests don't buy beer. 'Well I do,' I said, and I did.

"A few hours later the parish priest came by for a visit; I guess the news of my expedition had gotten around. 'We don't buy liquor, Father,' he told me. 'We send our housekeepers to the next town to buy it for us.' It was my first experience with local clerical protocol."

Easter came, and so did Vermeersch's superior from New Rochelle. But instead of bringing the long-promised replacement, he assigned Vermeersch to another three years as school director. "'I don't accept that,' I told him bluntly, 'I've had enough.' 'Well,' he said, 'you've made a vow of obedience and under that vow you are obliged to accept.'

"I guess I still had enough faith in the system because I obliged, but it was very hard. Really, they were using me. And he had a big laugh over it because he'd gotten what he wanted, someone to stay in that … hole. All the other Salesians considered this the place where they dumped people. As I was signing I said, 'Remember, that's the last time the Salesians give me an order.' And he laughed again."

Although Vermeersch could have easily despaired over how he would survive the next three years, he characteristically chose to set his personal anguish aside and focus instead on the mandate at hand. In some ways the school itself was an anomaly, set as it was on the outskirts of the province, an imposing brick structure among the smattering of small, village homes a stone's throw from the changeable Bay of Chaleur. Its Francophone speaking student body, imported from other parts of the province, rarely crossed paths with the villagers who, although predominantly of Acadian descent, spoke mostly English. Vermeersch recognized that the school might not be relevant much longer unless some basic changes to its operations were to be initiated.

As director, his first decision was to discontinue taking sixth graders, thereby allowing the school to dispense greater attention on both the students and the curriculum of grades seven, eight and nine. Up until now New Brunswick's Francophone students had had to contend with English textbooks and curriculums, a situation that prompted Vermeersch's second decision: to adopt the curriculum and textbooks of neighbouring Quebec. In so doing, Don Bosco College became the first school in New Brunswick to offer a truly Francophone education. Two years later Liberal premier Louis Robichaud introduced the province's first French curriculum under the newly minted Equal Opportunity program.

In the next three years Vermeersch strove to make the school more financially self-sufficient, increasing student enrollment by fifty percent. But at the same time he re-assessed his own life's journey and concluded that he was being called to other challenges on a different path. Quietly he began shifting into gear the process for disengagement from the Salesians. When his three-year commitment had been fulfilled, he carried through his resolve to leave the order and reported for duty to the bishop of the local diocese.

"The bishop made me Chaplain of the Hotel Dieu Hospital in the city of Campbellton, about 40 kilometres away. I was given a place to stay, my meals, and a monthly salary of $80. A few months later the bishop informed me that I was also to begin teaching courses in medical ethics, philosophy and religion to the hospital's nursing students. I told him I'd never taught nurses before. He suggested I start studying how to.

"All the chaplains before me had taught Catholicism. But these were young women with their high school diplomas, not kids anymore. And so I told them, 'My course will be about the great religions of the world.

That way, if you have patients who are not Roman Catholic, you'll understand something of their spirituality.' I taught that particular course for almost 18 years in nursing schools in Campbellton, Bathurst, Tracadie and Chatham, all in the northern half of the province."

After five years in Campbellton, Vermeersch was transferred to first one and then another bilingual parish in Bathurst, where he spent the next decade. Although his work at the nursing schools kept him stimulated, he increasingly began to question his relevance as a parish priest. "I kept thinking, I've become a pastor, the role I conscientiously rejected when I first committed myself to the priesthood back in Belgium. Now, more than ever, I wanted to be able to apply my languages and knowledge in a way that would truly be of service. I wanted to be a priest, not a secretary. I was doing 100 marriages and funerals a year, 120 baptisms, and, in between, concentrating on balancing the books. I was 60 years old and needed something more."

His search culminated in a chaplaincy for the thriving, year-round Port of Saint John in southern New Brunswick. It wasn't long before he felt revitalized in his new role. Now the world came to his doorstep and he could minister in a way that drew on his strengths and his own previously broadened horizons. Vermeersch recalls one of the job's more colourful moments: "Come Christmas, we collected parcels from all the churches and distributed them to the sailors. The first ship we boarded was Japanese and when the sailors realized I spoke Japanese they were all eager to speak with me. The second ship was from Korea and all of the officers spoke Japanese, so we experienced the same thing. The third ship we boarded was from Formosa, Taiwan, and again I was able to converse in Japanese. At that point the Anglican chaplain who was with me turned to me and asked, 'How many languages *do* you speak?' Of course he hadn't noticed it was Japanese each time!"

A few months after his arrival, Vermeersch was asked by the bishop of the Saint John diocese to lend support to a local group of Francophones who were hungry for spiritual leadership in their own language. What began as a one-day-a-week commitment gradually grew to the point where Vermeersch found himself pastor of the city's French community. "We were 400 people or more, with no real place to worship together. We started out in the basement of a local hall and then migrated to a neighbouring church where we scheduled our celebration between two English services."

Recognizing an urgent need for Francophones in a predominantly Anglophone region of the province, Vermeersch and a committee of interested stakeholders began negotiating with both federal and provincial governments to establish a French school and cultural centre in Saint John. "We got (then premier) Richard Hatfield and Prime Minister Trudeau working together and they eventually awarded $12.5 million for the construction of a new complex, to be named the Centre Scolaire-Communautaire Samuel-de-Champlain. We worked out an agreement whereby we would be able to celebrate our Masses in the centre's auditorium. When Mr. Hatfield signed over the land, I asked to have a small portion of it set aside for a future parish church. The premier complied and signed five acres over to the bishop of Saint John for a dollar. That was a first for this province, and a Baptist premier made it possible."

Though Vermeersch's parish duties continued to increase as his congregation grew, the disquietude he had previously experienced as a parish priest was now notably absent. This, in a sense, was pioneering work, helping a people to solidify their culture and spirituality. This was where he could draw on his considerable personal resources and make a difference. Coincidentally his work with the port was declining at around the same time, the result of its steady evolution toward automation.

In 1989 Vermeersch received a call from his brother in Australia. "He wanted me to come and bless his son's marriage. Who wouldn't go? I'd never been to Australia before. My brothers in Belgium and their wives were going, and I met up with them in Vancouver. Although they chose to stay a bit longer, I came back right after the wedding because of celebrations scheduled at my parish."

After 44 hours in transit Vermeersch returned home, completely exhausted. In the early hours of the following morning, he was stricken with what he assumed was likely a combination of jet lag and possible food poisoning. The hospital's diagnosis, however, was much more ominous: Vermeersch had suffered a serious heart attack. The day was May 14, 1989, coincidentally the 36th anniversary of his ordination to the priesthood.

"The following March I had a quadruple bypass and then handed in my resignation. I was 70 years old. Nobody should be working past 70, not even the Pope, but that's another issue."

After a lifetime of selfless service and constant deference to the schedules of others, Vermeersch has spent the last several years content in retirement. In good health, he has rediscovered his propensity for growing things and tends lovingly to the gardens and fruit trees he's established on the grounds of his home on Grand Bay. Now eighty years of age, he still readily fills in when local priests are sick or away. The people of Saint John are not apt to forget him anytime soon, and they've shown their gratitude in part by lending his name to the auditorium of Centre Scolaire-Communautaire Samuel-de-Champlain.

As for the five acres of land Vermeersch was able to acquire from Richard Hatfield almost two decades ago, it has become the site of the thoroughly modern Saint-Francois-de-Sales church, completed in the summer of 1998. In some tangible and deeply satisfying way it serves to mark the completion of one man's remarkably eclectic career in the ministry.

"Definitely we accomplished a lot," says Vermeersch by way of downplaying his own pivotal role. "We were a good crew. I wasn't the wheel, just part of the wheel."

I'm not a fanatic about anything except freedom.

I suppose I've always been fairly adaptable, taking a situation that's been thrust upon me and wanting to make the most of it. But I took my exile to Jacquet River very hard. I remember the first winter storm. I was sitting in my room on the second floor of the building and could hear the wind howling. I could see nothing but snow and it reminded me of the stories I'd read as a kid—of North America and snow storms and wolves, of Indians attacking the farms and endless cold and isolation.

My time there made me think considerably about the vocation I had chosen and the path I now found myself on. And although I had embraced a vow of obedience, I came to realize there's a limit to how much one can be manipulated in the name of vows taken. When the Salesians finally realized I was serious about leaving them, they tried to change my mind by offering me a plum position in the United States. I didn't have to think much about it before declining. I'd moved from Belgium to Japan. I'd started to set down roots in the United States before being abruptly transplanted to Canada. No, I'd had enough of moving around. This little corner of Canada had become my home.

Japan had been difficult to leave. I loved the ordinary people, their unencumbered lifestyle. Although their spirituality is mostly limited to weddings and funerals at the Buddhist or Shinto temples, they are warm, friendly, open and filled with ideas. They also value their rich heritage and traditions. Had it not been for the excessive heat and humidity, who knows how long I might have stayed.

I had one more encounter with a tropical climate, years later when, as Port Chaplain, I attended a conference in Mombasa, Kenya. A non-Catholic friend who had resided for a time in Nairobi asked me, "Father, you're going to Mombasa? That's the closest you'll ever come to hell." True to his word, the weather was much like I'd experienced in Japan, a suffocating 35–40 humid degrees. From Mombasa I sent him a post card saying he'd been right in his comparison.

I was 39 when I came to Canada. When you leave one world and enter another there's always the temptation to compare. But comparisons usually yield negatives and often prompt an invitation to dwell on those negatives. I admit that I initially came to Canada against my will and saw only the dark side. My first, slanted impression of Jacquet River was of a region in poverty, only a few people employed, inadequate housing against the fury of winter, terrible climate, and haunting desolation.

But after only two years I began to see a completely different side. I saw freedom—personal freedom and the freedom to seize opportunities. Incredible freedom for those of us who came from small European countries where there was barely room to stand anymore. Here, if you worked hard and had a bit of resolve, you could carve out a future for yourself and your children. And there were possibilities for me too. With fewer priests here than in Belgium, I felt more needed. And there were opportunities for continued learning. When I became a teacher at the nursing school in Campbellton, I didn't know a thing about medical ethics. But I took courses and read books, and felt I had been given a renewed opportunity to enrich myself. Knowing I was doing so to help others, that's when I started living again.

I also tried learning Mi'kmaq, the language of the area's native people. However, I never became proficient enough to preach in Mi'kmaq, although I did learn a few swear words ...

On my first Sunday as hospital chaplain in Campbellton, I preached to a congregation of about 400 assembled in the hospital chapel. I spoke to them in French, which I was speaking quite well by then, although the odd grammatical slip-up was not uncommon. I told them I was happy to be among them because they were all good people—*des bonnes gens* is the proper expression. However, what I inadvertently said was *des gens bons*, pronounced like *jambon*, meaning 'ham.' It might have gone over unnoticed had it not been for an old priest within earshot who chortled spontaneously and loudly suggested they'd all just been compared to a pig's hind end. I became instantly known throughout the diocese!

Many priests at that time were still preaching the old sermons, filled with admonitions and often tied to the perils of breaking the sixth commandment. The focus was usually on the sinfulness of evil thoughts and actions and so on. It was rarely about loving and helping your neighbour. My focus was more on the inherent good in each one of us. Gradually more and more people started coming to Mass at the chapel.

When you've been abroad and had the opportunity to see and absorb different outlooks on life and spirituality, you come to realize that Christianity too can be viewed in many different ways. When you are limited by language as I was during my early years in Japan, you look to your own heart for solutions. You develop self-reliance, self-confidence and perhaps a tendency to think a bit deeper. To see past the official and the obvious, past the letter of the law, that does require both self-confidence and knowledge.

Some preachers, I think, have never thought too deeply about the teachings. And indeed, sometimes it is easier to say: You are a sinner, You are going to be punished, You need to do penance, You have to suffer. But the real thrust of Christianity is that God loves us even if we're not good. The biggest commandment is to love God, but we've also been instructed in scripture to reconcile our disputes and differences with others before presenting ourselves to God.

This type of teaching was, I felt, timely and important. And because of it I became known as a very liberal preacher. Because I chose to dwell on the goodness of the people rather than on our flaws. The church used to be in such a hurry to baptize babies, as if they could be anything less than innocent.

I've had hundreds of Japanese friends who have never heard of Christ. Are they damned to hell? And the hundreds of millions of Chinese and Hindus? Not likely. I've lived in community with so many non-Christians, good people. Perhaps they are better than we are.

I've never been in conflict with the church, although I believe the church has not always taken into account nor capitalized on the potential of its people. It has not always shown a good understanding of reality, which is imperfection, and because of that has not always been merciful. At times I have felt compelled to stand up and speak my heart. I'm not a fanatic about anything except freedom. Personal freedom is sacred and should only be removed when it poses a threat to others. There are complex issues still to be grappled with—abortion, birth control, the freedom for clergy to marry. It's always so easy to jump in and make decisions for others.

Even though my initial years in Canada were a challenge, my life here has been good. Canada is my home. When you come to this country and immerse yourself in ways Canadian, when you offer your talents, when you present yourself as a Canadian and not as a Belgian or Dutchman or whatever, then you put your fellow countrymen at ease in your presence. And then you will be accepted.

CONCLUSION

When I think of the nature of immigration, I'm reminded of a dance that often takes place at wedding celebrations. The music swells. The hands of one dancer find their way to another's shoulders and a rhythmic shuffle begins. A third and fourth join up, and soon a small queue begins to wend its way around the room. Before long it has increased in both numbers and energy, as people—perfect strangers included—unabashedly cut in here and there. Now the queue gyrates around the tables, picking up the stragglers who need a little extra coaxing, cheering them on as they begin to rise from their chairs. Everyone, regardless of age, gender and costume, contributes to the dance. The longer the queue, the more splendid the dance.

It's easy to get bogged down in the underpinnings of Canadian immigration policy; indeed, there are times when the policy itself seems hopelessly entangled in inadequacy. One day we hear that the rising unemployment rate is being driven by the arrival of too many immigrants. A week later we're told that Canada desperately needs newcomers to bolster the country's declining birthrate and to offset losses incurred by our significant 'brain drain'. All the while we wonder what constitutes genuine refugee status, question the bureaucracy and length of time involved in the processing of immigration paperwork, and bristle at the thought that some would-be-newcomers have no qualms about breaking the rules to get here ahead of those who wait their legitimate turn.

The flaws of the system aside (and it's easy to sit in judgement on the Canadian side of the fence), we do well to temper our sentiments with a basic truth kept always in mind: that we, except for Canada's Native population, are newcomers as well. We are, to use a definition noted by Cassandra Bruyns in *The Toronto Star* in 1982, 'immigrants with seniority'.

Whereas Canada's newcomers once came largely from western Europe, they now hail from all parts of the planet. And as the demographics of immigration have shifted, so too have we evolved in our attitudes towards who and what constitute a genuinely meaningful community. There's no denying that our dance has become stronger, more vibrant, and infinitely more interesting in the course of the last one hundred years. With the musical mix of Canadian history and cultural diversity, we have danced into the cities and onto the prairies; we have brought vision and opportunity to the corners of the country and expanded our horizons to the ends of the globe. No doubt we've added complexities to our society, but we've also created innovative strategies and solutions to address our changing needs and issues. We have danced our way through Canada's adolescence and, as others with their accents and brightly coloured costumes joined in, examined our own sense of belonging, of being Canadian.

The women and men introduced in the preceding pages constitute ample proof that Canada has reaped immeasurable benefits from the works, talents and gifts offered by its newer citizens. Furthermore, the people in this book are but a sampling of the hundreds of thousands of newcomers who, along with those of us whom fate has given some degree of seniority, work diligently, quietly, and with pride to make Canada a satisfying community for all.

The music is strong. Shall we dance?

INDEX